An Introduction to
Game-Theoretic
Modelling

Michael Mesterton-Gibbons

Department of Mathematics
Florida State University

Addison-Wesley Publishing Company, Inc.
The Advanced Book Program
Redwood City, California • Menlo Park , California
Reading, Massachusetts • New York • Don Mills, Ontario
Wokingham, United Kingdom • Amsterdam • Bonn
Sydney • Singapore • Tokyo • Madrid • San Juan

Publisher: *Allan M. Wylde*
Mathematics Editor: *Barbara Holland*
Marketing Manager: *Laura Likely*
Production Manager: *Pam Suwinsky*

Library of Congress Cataloging-in-Publication Data

Mesterton-Gibbons, Michael.
     An introduction to game-theoretic modelling / Michael Mesterton-Gibbons.
        p.   cm.
     Includes bibliographical references.
     ISBN 0-201-55439-9 (hb.). -- ISBN 0-201-55448-8 (pbk)
     1. Game theory. 2. Mathematical models. I. Title.
QA269.M464   1991   91-23057
519.3--dc20

Production services by Black Hole Publishing.
Typesetting by Superscript Typography, using the TEX typesetting language.

1 2 3 4 5 6 7 8 9 10-MA-95 94 93 92 91

To Karen

for understanding so patiently,
that one cannot promise not to write another book
after it already exists in one's imagination.

Contents

Preface

This is a short introduction to game theory and applications from the perspective of a mathematical modeller, and includes several original pedagogical games. It covers a range of concepts that have proven useful, or are likely to prove useful, for quantitative modelling in the social, life and management sciences. Its approach is heuristic, but quite systematic, and deals in a unified manner with the central concepts of both classical and evolutionary game theory. In many ways it is a sequel to my earlier work, *A Concrete Approach to Mathematical Modelling,* in which games were not discussed. The mathematical prerequisites are correspondingly modest: calculus, a rudimentary knowledge of matrix algebra and probability, a passing acquaintance with differential equations and that intangible quantity, a degree of mathematical maturity. Naturally, the greater one's maturity, the more contemptuous one can be of formal prerequisites, and the more one is able to proceed ad hoc when the need arises.

There exist several excellent texts on game theory, but their excellence is largely for the mathematical purist. Practices that are de rigueur to the purist are often merely distracting to the modeller—for example, lingering over the elegant theory of zero-sum games (nonzero-sum conflicts are much more common in practice), or proving the existence of a Nash equilibrium in bimatrix games (for which the problem in practice is usually to distinguish among a superabundance of such equilibria); or, more fundamentally, beginning with the most general possible formulation of a game and only later proceeding to specific examples (the essence of modelling is rather the opposite). Such practices are therefore honored in the breach. Instead—and as described more fully in the agenda that follows—the emphasis is on concrete examples, and the direction of pedagogy throughout the book is from specific to general. However bright or well motivated, students usually have limited appetites for rigor and generality, yet have much still to gain from the mathematical experience of capturing ideas and giving them substance—the experience, that is, of modelling. So I hope that this book helps not only to make game theory accessible, but also to convey both its power and scope in divers applications.

Michael Mesterton-Gibbons
Tallahassee, Florida
1991

Acknowledgements

I am very grateful to Lou Gross and Bill Derrick for their perceptive reviews and valuable suggestions; to David Pearce and three anonymous reviewers for other helpful comments and criticism; to Karen Mesterton-Gibbons for moral support and for carefully proofing the manuscript; to Addison-Wesley Publishing Company for their skill and cooperation in turning the manuscript into a book; and to Oxford University's Zoology Department for their hospitality during the sabbatical in which this book was completed.

Agenda

This is a book about mathematical modelling of strategic behavior, which arises whenever the outcome of an individual's actions depends on actions to be taken by other individuals. The individuals may be either human or non-human beings, the actions either premeditated or instinctive. Thus models of strategic behavior are applicable in both the social and the natural sciences.

Examples of humans interacting strategically include store managers fixing prices—the number of customers who buy at one store's price will depend on the price at other stores in the neighborhood; and drivers negotiating a 4-way junction—whether it is advantageous for a driver to assume right of way depends on whether the other drivers concede right of way. Examples of non-humans interacting strategically include birds or spiders disputing a territory—the risk of injury to one animal from being an aggressor will depend on whether the other animal is prepared to fight; and insects foraging for oviposition sites —the number of one insect's eggs that mature into adults at a particular site (where food for growth is limited) will depend on the number of eggs laid there by other insects. These and other strategic interactions will be modelled in detail, beginning in Chapter 1.

To fix ideas, however, it will be helpful first to consider an example that— if somewhat fanciful—will serve to delineate the important distinction between strategic and non-strategic decision making. Let us therefore suppose that the enrollment for some mathematics course is a mere six humans, and that grades for this course are based exclusively on answers to ten questions. Answers are judged to be either satisfactory or unsatisfactory, and the number of satisfactory solutions determines the final letter grade for the course—*A*, *B*, *C*, *D* or *F*. In the usual way, *A* corresponds to 4 units of merit; and *B*, *C*, *D* and *F* correspond to 3, 2, 1 and 0 units of merit, respectively. The students vary in intellectual ability, and all are capable of working either very hard, or only quite hard, or hardly at all; but there is nothing random about student achievement as a function of effort, which is precisely defined as in Table A.1. Thus, for example, Student 5

TABLE A.1   Student achievement (number of satisfactory solutions) in mathematics as a function of effort.

	Very hard ($E = 5$)	Quite hard ($E = 3$)	Hardly at all ($E = 1$)
Student 1	10	8	6
Student 2	8	7	5
Student 3	7	5	3
Student 4	7	4	3
Student 5	5	4	2
Student 6	4	2	1

will produce five satisfactory solutions if she works very hard, but only four if she works quite hard; whereas Student 4 will produce seven satisfactory solutions if he works very hard, but only three if he works hardly at all. The students have complete control over how much effort they apply, and so we refer to effort as a decision variable. Furthermore, for the sake of definiteness, we assume that working very hard corresponds to 5 units of effort, quite hard to 3, and hardly at all to 1. Thus, if we denote effort by E and merit by M, then working very hard corresponds to $E = 5$; obtaining the letter grade A corresponds to $M = 4$; and similarly for the other values of E and M.

Let us now suppose that academic standards are absolute, i.e., the number of satisfactory solutions required for each letter grade is prescribed in advance. Then no strategic behavior is possible. This doesn't eliminate scope for decision making—quite the contrary. If, for example, 9 or 10 satisfactory solutions were required for an A, 7 or 8 for a B, 5 or 6 for a C and 3 or 4 for a D, then Student 3 would earn 3 units of merit for $E = 5$, 2 for $E = 3$, and only 1 for $E = 1$; and if she wished to maximize merit per unit of effort, or M/E, then she would still have to solve a simple optimization problem, namely, to determine the maximum of $3 \div 5 = 0.6, 2 \div 3 = 0.67$ and $1 \div 1 = 1$. The answer, of course, is 1, corresponding to $E = 1$: to maximize M/E, Student 3 should hardly work at all. Nevertheless, such a decision would not be strategic, because its outcome would depend solely on the individual concerned; it would not depend in any way on the behavior of other students.

The story is very different, however, if academic standards are relative, i.e., if letter grades depend on collective student achievement. To illustrate, let s denote number of satisfactory solutions; let b denote the number of satisfactory solutions obtained by the best student, and w the number obtained by the worst; and let grades be assigned according to the following scheme, which awards A to any student in the top fifth of the range, B to any student in the next fifth of the range, and so on:

$$A: \quad \frac{1}{5}(4b + w) \le s \le b$$

$$B: \quad \frac{1}{5}(3b + 2w) \le s < \frac{1}{5}(4b + w)$$

$$C: \quad \frac{1}{5}(2b + 3w) \le s < \frac{1}{5}(3b + 2w)$$

$$D: \quad \frac{1}{5}(b + 4w) \le s < \frac{1}{5}(2b + 3w)$$

$$E: \quad w \le s < \frac{1}{5}(b + 4w).$$

Thus if all students chose $E = 5$, then Student 1 would get A, Student 2 would get B, Students 3 and 4 would get C, and Students 5 and 6 would both fail; whereas if all students chose $E = 1$, then Students 1 and 2 would get A, Students 3 and 4 would get C, Student 5 would get D, and only Student 6 would fail.

Students who wish to maximize M or M/E must now anticipate (and perhaps seek to influence) how hard the others will work, and choose E accordingly. In other words, students who wish to attain their goals must behave strategically. For example, Student 1 is now guaranteed an A if she works at least quite hard; and $E = 3$ yields a higher value of M/E than $E = 5$. But $4/3 = 1.33$ is not the highest value of M/E that Student 1 can obtain. If she knew that Student 2 would work at most quite hard, and if she also knew that either Student 6 would choose $E \le 3$ or Student 5 would choose $E = 1$, then the grading scheme would award her an A no matter how hard she worked—in particular, if she chose $E = 1$. But Students 5 and 6 can avoid failing only if they obtain at least 4 satisfactory solutions and either Student 3 or Student 4 chooses $E = 1$; in which case, $E = 1$ and its six satisfactory solutions would earn Student 1 only B (although it would still maximize M/E). And so on. We have made our point: changing from absolute to relative standards brings ample scope for strategic behavior to an interaction among individuals that otherwise has none.

If an interaction among individuals gives rise to strategic behavior, and if the interaction can be described mathematically, then we will refer to this description as a *game,* and to each individual in the game as a *player.* In other words, game means a mathematical model of conflict or bargaining. Correspondingly, *game theory* is an assemblage of ideas and theorems that attempts to provide a rational basis for resolving conflicts, with or without cooperation. You won't find game so defined in a dictionary—not even in Webster's, where the word has thirteen definitions, or in the Oxford English Dictionary, where over two pages are devoted to the word. But new meanings take time to diffuse into dictionaries; and besides, the study of decision-laden interactions among individuals should perhaps be called something other than game theory. On the other hand, there are at least as many similarities between games in the mathematical modeller's sense, and games in the everyday sense, as there are between—say—the gadget I use to control my computer and a mouse. In any event, game is the word and game theory the phrase we shall use.

As an acknowledged field of study in its own right, game theory began with the publication in 1944 of a treatise on games and economic behavior by John Von Neumann and Oskar Morgenstern.[1] Nevertheless, some game-theoretic concepts have been traced to earlier work by Cournot (1838), Edgeworth (1881), Böhm-Bawerk (1889), Borel (1924) and Zeuthen (1930) in the context of economics, and to Fisher (1930) in the context of evolutionary biology. Given the way things are in the world, it is probably only a matter of time before somebody finds that the first book on game theory was written by Aristotle.

Because—as we saw in the opening paragraphs—conflict can arise among so many different kinds of players, and in such a wide variety of circumstances, we should never expect game-theoretic ideas that are fruitful in one context to be relevant in another (although we should always entertain the possibility that they might be). Nevertheless, many once promising solution concepts—i.e., concepts of what is the best strategy or compromise—have ultimately failed to be satisfactory even in the circumstances for which they were designed, and so we do not discuss them.[2] We concentrate instead on introducing and applying ideas that still hold promise, in particular, Nash equilibrium (Chapter 1), evolutionarily stable strategy (Chapter 2), Pareto-optimality (Chapter 3), core, nucleolus, Shapley value (Chapter 4) and cooperation via reciprocity (Chapter 5).

By tradition, games are classified as either cooperative or noncooperative, although this dichotomy is universally acknowledged to be imperfect: almost every conflict has an element of cooperation, and almost all cooperation has an element of conflict. In this regard we abide, more or less, by tradition: Chapters 1 and 2 are about noncooperative solution concepts, whereas Chapters 3 and 4 are about cooperative ones. But the distinction is blurred in Chapter 5, where we study cooperation within the context of a noncooperative game. Games are also classified as having either strategic form or characteristic function form.[3] For present purposes, it will suffice to say that a game is in characteristic function form if the conflict is analogous to sharing a pie among players who would each like all of it, and who collectively can obtain all of it, but who as individuals cannot obtain any of it; and that otherwise a game is in strategic form. Games

---

[1]   It is customary nowadays to consult either the third edition (Von Neumann and Oskar Morgenstern, 1953) or the second (1947).

[2]   In particular, there is no discussion of the stable set, Von Neumann and Morgenstern's solution concept for characteristic function games.

[3]   Game theorists further distinguish between strategic games in extensive form and strategic games in normal form, but we have no use for this distinction. See, for example, Owen (1982, pp. 1–5).

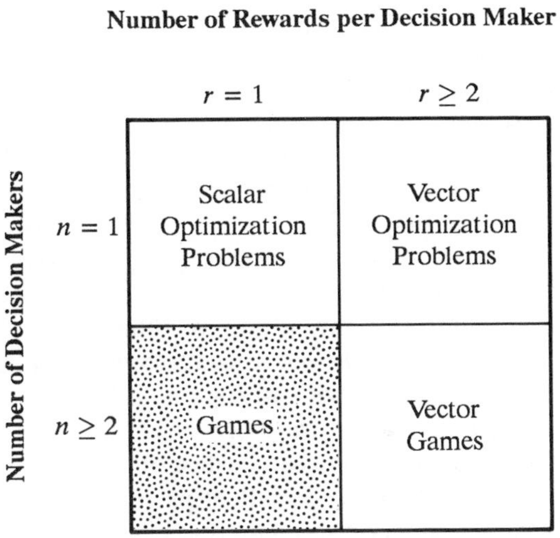

Number of Rewards per Decision Maker

	$r = 1$	$r \geq 2$
$n = 1$	Scalar Optimization Problems	Vector Optimization Problems
$n \geq 2$	Games	Vector Games

Figure A.1   Games in the context of optimization theory.

are studied in characteristic function form in Chapter 4, where we discuss, for example, how to split the costs of a car pool fairly. Games are studied in strategic form in Chapters 1, 2, 3 and 5, where we study, among other things, the behavior of motorists at a 4-way junction, price setting by store managers, and territorial conflict among insects and spiders.

To interpret games in the wider context of optimization theory, it will be helpful now to return for a while to our six mathematics students. Let us suppose that Student 2 will work quite hard ($E = 3$), whereas Students 3 to 6 will work very hard ($E = 5$); and that Student 1 already knows this. If Student 1 is rewarded *either* by high achievement *or* by high achievement per unit effort, then she has a single reward—either M or M/E—and a single decision variable, E, with which to maximize it. If, on the other hand, Student 1 is rewarded *both* by high achievement *and* by high achievement per unit effort, then she has two rewards—M and M/E—but still only a single decision variable, E, with which to maximize them. In the first case, with a single reward, we say that Student 1 faces a *scalar* optimization problem (whose solution is clearly $E = 5$ or $E = 3$ if rewarded by M, but $E = 1$ if rewarded by M/E). In the second case, with two rewards, we say that Student 1 faces a *vector* optimization problem (whose solution is far from clear, because the value of E that maximizes M fails also to maximize M/E, and vice versa). More generally, an optimization problem requires a single decision maker to select a single decision variable (over which this decision maker has complete control) to optimize r rewards; and if $r = 1$

then the problem is a scalar optimization problem, whereas if $r \geq 2$ then the problem is a vector optimization problem.[4,5]

By contrast, the strategic games that we are about to study require each of n decision makers, called players, to a select a single decision variable—called a *strategy*—to optimize a single reward. But each player's reward depends on the other players' strategies; i.e., it depends on decision variables that are completely controlled by the other players. That players lack control over all decision variables affecting their rewards is what makes a game a game, and what distinguishes it from an optimization problem. In this book, we do not discuss optimization problems in their own right, nor do we allow players to have more than one reward—in other words, we do not consider "vector games." Thus our agenda for games falls in the shaded region of Figure A.1.

Now, a strategic interaction can be very complicated, and a game in our sense does not exist unless the interaction can be described mathematically. But this step is often exceedingly difficult, especially if players are many; and especially if we insist—and as modellers we should—that players' rewards be explicitly defined. Therefore, we confine our agenda to strategic interactions that lend themselves readily to a concrete mathematical description—and hence, for the most part, to games with few players. Indeed six is many in this regard: Students 1 to 6, having served us so well, must now depart the scene.

Throughout the book we introduce concepts by means of specific models, later indicating how to generalize them; however, we avoid rigorous statements and proofs of theorems, referring instead to the standard texts. Our approach to games is thus largely the opposite of the classical approach, but has the clear advantage in an introductory text that it fosters substantial progress. We can downplay the issue of what—in most general terms—constitutes a decision maker's reward, because the reward is self-evident in the particular examples we choose.[6] We can demonstrate the usefulness and richness of games while avoiding unnecessary abstractions; even 2-player games in strategic form have enormous potential, which has scarcely begun to be realized. Moreover, we can rely on intuitions about everyday conflicts to strengthen our grasp of game theory's key ideas, and

---

[4]   As we shall see in due course, a decision variable can itself be a vector. What distinguishes a scalar from a vector optimization problem (or a game from a vector game), however, is the number of rewards per decision maker.

[5]   For further examples of optimization problems, see Mesterton-Gibbons (1989): Chapters 3, 7 and Sections 12.1–12.4 for scalar problems, and Sections 12.5–12.6 for vector problems.

[6]   Books that discuss this issue thoroughly include von Neumann and Morgenstern (1953), Luce and Raiffa (1957) and Shubik (1982, 1984). The first of these books defines, of course, the classical approach to the theory of games. The second is an excellent later text covering the same ground and more, but with much less technical mathematical detail. The third is perhaps the most comprehensive book on game theory ever published.

we can be flexible and creative in applying those ideas.

Our agenda is thus defined. We carry out this agenda in Chapters 1–5, giving summaries and suggestions for further reading in commentaries at the ends of the chapters; and in Chapter 6 we critique our accomplishments. There follow solutions—or at least strong hints—for most of the exercises, and so it is assumed of the reader that he or she is sufficiently mature not to consult a solution until a problem has at least been seriously attempted. Which reminds me: We assume throughout that a protagonist is female in odd-numbered chapters and male in even-numbered chapters. This convention is simply the reverse of that which I adopted in *A Concrete Approach to Mathematical Modelling*, and it renders unnecessary the continual use of "his or her" and "he or she" in place of epicene pronouns.

1

Nash Equilibrium & Other Solution Concepts for Noncooperative Games

Motoring behavior provides our first example of a game, which will pave the way for several solution concepts, both in this chapter and later in Chapters 2 and 3. Here the example will introduce what is probably game theory's most enduring concept, Nash's concept of noncooperative equilibrium.

1.1 CROSSROADS: A GAME-THEORETIC ANALYSIS OF A MOTORIST'S DILEMMA

Consider a pair of motorists who are driving in opposite directions along a 2-lane road when they arrive simultaneously at a 4-way junction, where each would like to cross the path of the other. For the sake of definiteness, let us suppose, as in Figure 1.1, that the first motorist, say Nan, is travelling north but would like to go west; whereas the second motorist, say San, is travelling south but would like to go east. Nan and San cannot proceed simultaneously; one must proceed before

1

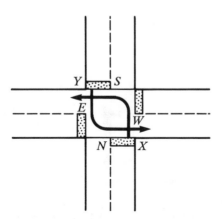

Figure 1.1   The scene of
the action: a crossroad.

the other. Then who should it be? How should the motorists behave? Here's
potential for conflict that's fit for a game. We shall call the game Crossroads.

To keep matters simple, let's suppose that a motorist has but two choices:
she can either wait for the other motorist to turn first, in which case we shall
say that she selects pure strategy W; or she can proceed to turn and hope that
the other motorist will refrain from doing so, in which case we shall say that she
selects pure strategy G.[1] We use the word strategy because we wish to think of
Nan as the first "player" or decision maker, and of San as the second player, in
a 2-person game; and we call G and W pure strategies to distinguish them from
mixed strategies, which we shall introduce in Section 1.3. If Nan selects pure
strategy X, and if San selects pure strategy Y, then we shall say that the players
have jointly selected the pure strategy combination XY. Thus our game has
precisely four pure strategy combinations, namely, GG, GW, WG and WW.

In the case where each player decides to defer to the other (WW), let ϵ denote the time they spend dithering and frantically waving to each other, before
one of them eventually moves. Likewise, in the case where each decides not
to defer (GG), let δ denote the time they spend intimidating each other in the
middle of the junction, until one of them eventually backs down. It seems reasonable to suppose that the time they waste if both are selfish (GG) exceeds that
which they waste if both are altruistic (WW), even if not by much; and we shall
therefore assume throughout the text that

$$0 < \epsilon < \delta < \infty, \tag{1.1}$$

---

[1]   Recall from the agenda that, in place of epicene pronouns, female pronouns will
be used in Chapter 1, male pronouns in Chapter 2, and so on.

even if ϵ/δ is close to 1. Let τ_1 denote the time it takes Nan to negotiate the turn without interruption, i.e., the time that elapses (if San lets her go) between her front bumper crossing the line NX in Figure 1.1 and her back bumper crossing the line EY; and let τ_2 denote the corresponding time for San. We are now in a position to analyze the confrontation from Nan's point of view.

Suppose, first, that pure strategy combination GW is selected—Nan decides to go, San decides to wait. Then Nan suffers a delay of zero. Now suppose that WG is selected—San decides to go, Nan decides to wait. Then Nan suffers a delay of τ_2, the time it takes San to negotiate the junction. Suppose, next, that WW is selected—both decide to wait. Then there follows a bout of rapid gesticulation, after which it is still the case that either Nan or San is first to proceed; they can't just sit there all day. Quite how it is decided who—given WW—should go first is, in a sense, a game within the game of Crossroads, but we shall not attempt to model it explicitly; rather, we shall simply assume that the two motorists are then equally likely to be first to turn. Accordingly, let F denote the motorist who (given WW) turns first. Then F is a random variable, whose sample space is {Nan, San}, and

$$\text{Prob}(F = \text{Nan}) = \frac{1}{2}, \qquad \text{Prob}(F = \text{San}) = \frac{1}{2}. \tag{1.2}$$

We note in passing that F could easily be converted to an integer-valued random variable by labelling Nan as 1 and San as 2, but it is more convenient not to do so.

If Nan turns first ($F = \text{Nan}$), then she suffers a delay of only ϵ; whereas if San turns first ($F = \text{San}$), then Nan—from whose viewpoint we are analyzing the confrontation—suffers a delay of $\epsilon + \tau_2$. Thus the expected value of Nan's delay (given WW) is

$$\epsilon \cdot \text{Prob}(F = \text{Nan}) + (\epsilon + \tau_2) \cdot \text{Prob}(F = \text{San}) = \epsilon + \frac{\tau_2}{2}. \tag{1.3}$$

Suppose, finally, that GG is selected—both decide to go. Then there follows a minor skirmish, of duration δ, which one of the players must eventually win. Let random variable V, with sample space {Nan, San}, denote the victor (given GG); and suppose that if Player k is the victor, then the time she takes to negotiate the junction (given GG) is simply δ greater than she would have taken anyway, i.e., $\delta + \tau_k$. If neither Nan nor San is especially aggressive, then it seems reasonable to suppose that each is as likely as the other to find her path cleared; in which case, (1.2) holds with F replaced by V. If, given GG, Nan is the victor ($V = \text{Nan}$), then she suffers a delay of only δ; whereas if San is the victor ($V = \text{San}$), then Nan suffers a delay of $\delta + \tau_2$. Thus the expected value of Nan's delay (given GG) is

$$\delta \cdot \text{Prob}(V = \text{Nan}) + (\delta + \tau_2) \cdot \text{Prob}(V = \text{San}) = \delta + \frac{\tau_2}{2}. \tag{1.4}$$

We are tacitly assuming that δ and ϵ are both independent of τ_1 and τ_2. You

TABLE 1.1   Nan's payoff matrix.

		San	
		G	W
Nan	G	$-\delta - \tau_2/2$	0
	W	$-\tau_2$	$-\epsilon - \tau_2/2$

TABLE 1.2   San's payoff matrix.

		San	
		G	W
Nan	G	$-\delta - \tau_1/2$	$-\tau_1$
	W	0	$-\epsilon - \tau_1/2$

may be tempted to criticize this assumption—but tread daintily if you do so. In the real world, it is more than likely that δ and ϵ would depend upon various aspects of the personalities of the drivers in conflict. But our model ignores these aspects! It differentiates between Nan and San solely by virtue of their transit times, τ_1 and τ_2; and any dependence of δ and ϵ on these may well be weak.

Because everyone likes delays to be as short as possible, and because making the delay small is the same thing as making the negative of the delay large, we can think of the negative of the delay as the payoff to Nan. Thus the payoffs to Nan associated with the pure strategy combinations GG, GW, WG and WW are, respectively, $-\delta - \tau_2/2, 0, -\tau_2$ and $-\epsilon - \tau_2/2$. It is customary to store these payoffs in a matrix, as in Table 1.1, where the rows correspond to strategies of Player 1 and the columns correspond to strategies of Player 2.

Now, in any particular confrontation, the actual payoff to Nan from pure strategy combination GG or WW is a random variable. If the game is played repeatedly, however, then Nan's average payoff from GG or WW over an extended period should be well approximated by the random variable's expected value; and this is how we justify using expected values as payoffs. Furthermore, for the game to be played repeatedly, it is not necessary that the person Nan confronts, when she finds herself at a 4-way junction in the circumstances described above, be the same individual every time. Rather, San is a generic name for all individuals whose behavior is the same for the purposes of our model (though for other purposes it might be very different); if you like, San is any individual who exhibits San-like simultaneous-left-turning-at-a-4-way-junction behavior. Likewise, for the game to be played repeatedly, the 4-way junction at which Nan confronts a San need not be the same junction every time—a similar junction will suffice.

Nevertheless, some qualifying remarks are in order. Sans that are identical for the purposes of our model must, in theory, all take time τ_2 to negotiate a junction unimpeded—or, which is more to the point, Nan must think that they will all take time τ_2. In practice, however, Nan has limited ability to size up the driver who confronts her momentarily across the junction. Perhaps the best she can do is to place her opponent in one of a finite number of classes. She may, for example, classify her opponents as fast, intermediate or slow; in which case, as Nan flits from junction to junction, not one game but three games are played repeatedly, a game for slow Sans, a game for intermediate Sans and a game for fast Sans. (More generally, some finite number of games would be played repeatedly.) On the other hand, we should not imagine that it is totally unrealistic to suppose that Nan's opponent is the same San every time—perhaps they meet at the same time, and at the same place, as they travel to work in the morning in opposite directions.

To obtain the matrix in Table 1.1, we analyzed the game from Nan's point of view. A similar analysis, from San's viewpoint, yields the payoff matrix in Table 1.2. Indeed it is hardly necessary to repeat the analysis, because the only difference between Nan and San that is incorporated into our model of their conflict—or, as game theorists prefer to say, the only asymmetry between the players—is that Nan's transit time may be different from San's ($\tau_1 \neq \tau_2$). Thus San's payoff matrix is the transpose of Nan's with suffix 2 replaced by suffix 1. Transposition is necessary because rows correspond to strategies of Player 1, and columns to those of Player 2, in both tables.

In terms of game theory, the payoff matrices in Tables 1.1 and 1.2 define a 2-player game in which each player has two pure strategies, G and W. If we assume that Nan and San act out of rational self-interest, *and that they cannot communicate prior to the game,* then the game becomes a noncooperative one. (As we shall discover in Chapter 3, what really distinguishes a noncooperative game from a cooperative game is the inability to make binding commitments; but the players cannot possibly make binding commitments if they cannot even communicate prior to the game.) Not being especially selfish is not necessarily a violation of rational self-interest on the part of Nan or San; and waving at one another does not constitute prior communication. It is therefore legitimate to regard Tables 1.1 and 1.2 as the payoff matrices for a noncooperative, 2-player game.

More generally, a noncooperative, 2-player game in which Player 1 has $s_1 + 1$ pure strategies and Player 2 has $s_2 + 1$ pure strategies is defined by a pair of $(s_1 + 1) \times (s_2 + 1)$ matrices, A, B, in which a_{ij} denotes the payoff to player 1, and b_{ij} the payoff to player 2, from the strategy combination (i, j). If $s_1 = s_2$ and

$$b_{ij} = a_{ji}, \quad 0 \leq i - 1, j - 1 \leq s_1, \tag{1.5}$$

i.e., if B is the transpose of A, then the game is *symmetric*. If

$$a_{ij} + b_{ij} = c, \quad 0 \leq i - 1 \leq s_1, \quad 0 \leq j - 1 \leq s_2, \tag{1.6}$$

where c is a constant, then the game is *constant-sum*; and if, in addition, $c = 0$ then the game is *zero-sum*. Thus Crossroads is symmetric (with $s_1 = 1 = s_2$) if, and only if, $\tau_1 = \tau_2$. Even if $\tau_1 = \tau_2$, however, the game is not constant-sum, because $\delta > \epsilon > 0$.

Crossroads is an example of what game theorists call a bimatrix game in

TABLE 1.3 I's payoff matrix.

		II	
		H	D
I	H	$\frac{1}{2}(\rho - C)$	ρ
	D	0	$\rho/2$

TABLE 1.4 II's payoff matrix.

		II	
		H	D
I	H	$\frac{1}{2}(\rho - C)$	0
	D	ρ	$\rho/2$

strategic form. The additional terminology may appear gratuitous now, but it will be useful later when we study games that are either not bimatrix or not in strategic form. In Section 1.3, we shall attempt to "solve" Crossroads by saying which strategies the players should adopt. Meanwhile, however, we digress to describe a second example of a noncooperative, 2-player game, which arises in evolutionary biology. The example is taken from Maynard Smith (1982).

1.2 THE HAWK-DOVE GAME

Suppose that two animals, I and II, are in conflict over a territory. They have two pure strategies, which—to follow tradition—we will label "Hawk" and "Dove" (but the animals belong to the same species). To play Hawk, or H, one must "escalate"—i.e, act fierce; and if that doesn't scare away the opponent, then one must fight until injury determines a victor. To play Dove, or D, one must first "display"—i.e., merely look fierce, and hope that the opponent is scared away; but if she starts to act fierce, then one must retreat and search for real estate elsewhere. As in Crossroads, there are four pure strategy combinations, namely, HH, HD, DH and DD.

Let ρ be the reproductive value of the territory to I, and let C be the reproductive cost of being injured in a fight. By reproductive value we mean the incremental number of offspring—as opposed to the absolute number—that the territory would yield to the animal (or rather, since the increment is a random variable, its expected value). Thus, if an animal who averages five little ones per breeding season (from the kind of territory that nobody scraps over) can raise this number to eight by acquiring the territory that is in dispute, then $\rho = 8 - 5 = 3$. Similarly, by C we mean the amount by which I's expected offspring would be reduced by virtue of injury.

Let us analyze this territorial conflict from I's point of view. Suppose, first, that strategy combination DH is selected by the players—I plays Dove, II plays Hawk. Then I retreats as soon as II acts fierce, and the payoff in terms of reproductive value is zero. Now suppose that HD is selected—I plays Hawk, II plays Dove. Then II retreats as soon as I acts fierce, and the payoff to I is ρ. Suppose, next, that DD is selected—both I and II play Dove. Then there follows a staring match, during which both animals look fierce but refrain from acting fierce. Let F denote the animal who (given DD) first gets tired of staring and retreats; then F is a random variable, whose sample space is $\{I, II\}$. If neither animal is especially nervous, then it seems reasonable to suppose that each is as likely as the other to be first to retreat, so that $\text{Prob}(F = I) = 1/2 = \text{Prob}(F = II)$. If I retreats first ($F = I$), then its payoff is zero; whereas if II retreats first ($F = II$), then the payoff to I is ρ. Thus the expected value of I's payoff (given DD) is[2]

$$0 \cdot \text{Prob}(F = I) + \rho \cdot \text{Prob}(F = II) = \frac{\rho}{2}. \tag{1.7}$$

Suppose, finally, that HH is selected—both animals play Hawk. Then there follows a major skirmish, which one of the animals must eventually win. Let random variable W, with sample space $\{I, II\}$, denote the winner (given HH); and suppose that neither I nor II is an especially good fighter. Then it seems reasonable to suppose that each is as likely as the other to win; in which case, $\text{Prob}(W = I) = 1/2 = \text{Prob}(W = II)$. If I wins, then her payoff is ρ; but if II wins, then the payoff to I is $-C$. Thus the expected value of I's payoff (given HH) is

$$\rho \cdot \text{Prob}(W = I) + (-C) \cdot \text{Prob}(W = II) = \frac{\rho - C}{2}. \tag{1.8}$$

It follows that I's payoff matrix is as shown in Table 1.3. Moreover, if we assume that the territory's reproductive value and the cost of injury are the same for II as they are for I—i.e., if no asymmetry between the animals appears in our model of their conflict—then it follows immediately that II's payoff matrix is the transpose of I's, or Table 1.4.

We will return to our animals again later, when we shall refer to their game as the Hawk–Dove game (because that is what biologists call it). Meanwhile, however, we return to Nan and San.

1.3   MIXED STRATEGIES, RATIONAL REACTION SETS AND NASH EQUILIBRIUM

To determine which strategy Nan should adopt in Crossroads, let's begin by supposing that San is so slow that

$$\tau_2 > 2\delta > 2\epsilon. \tag{1.9}$$

Then

$$-\delta - \tau_2/2 > -\tau_2, \tag{1.10}$$

and it follows immediately from Table 1.1 that Nan's best strategy is to hit the gas, because every element in the first row of Nan's payoff matrix is greater than

---

[2]   Maynard Smith (1982) associates payoff $\rho/2$ with strategy combination DD by supposing that the resource is shared equally by the two contestants.

the corresponding element in the second row of her matrix. We say that strategy G *dominates* strategy W for Nan, and that G is a *dominant strategy* for Nan; whether San chooses W or G is quite irrelevant. More generally, pure strategy i dominates pure strategy k for Player 1 if $a_{ij} > a_{kj}$ for all $j = 1, \ldots, s_2 + 1$, where A is Player 1's payoff matrix (defined at the end of Section 1.1); and if i dominates k for all $k = 1, \ldots, s_1 + 1, k \neq i$, then i is a dominant strategy. Similarly, pure strategy i dominates pure strategy k for Player 2 if $b_{ji} > b_{jk}$ for all $j = 1, \ldots, s_1 + 1$, where B is Player 2's payoff matrix; and if i dominates k for all $k = 1, \ldots, s_2 + 1, k \neq i$, then i is again a dominant strategy—a dominant strategy, rather than *the* dominant strategy, because both players may have one.

In practice, if (1.9) is used to define a slow San, then we could interpret our model as yielding the following advice: "If you think the driver across the road is a slowpoke, then put down your foot and go." Furthermore, if (1.9) is used to define a slow San, then it might well be appropriate to define an intermediate San by

$$2\delta > \tau_2 > 2\epsilon \qquad (1.11)$$

and a fast San by

$$2\delta > 2\epsilon > \tau_2. \qquad (1.12)$$

If so, then we would certainly also define a slow Nan by $\tau_1 > 2\delta > 2\epsilon$, an intermediate Nan by $2\delta > \tau_1 > 2\epsilon$ and a fast Nan by $2\delta > 2\epsilon > \tau_1$. Note that G is a dominant strategy for San if Nan is slow ($\tau_1 > 2\delta$).[3]

Suppose, now, that either (1.11) or (1.12) is satisfied. Then (1.10) is false; and what's best for Nan is no longer independent of what San chooses, because the second element in row 1 of Nan's payoff matrix is still greater than the second element in row 2, whereas the first element in row 1 is now smaller than the first element in row 2. No pure strategy is obviously better for Nan. Then what should Nan choose?

If sometimes G is better and sometimes W is better (depending on what San chooses), then shouldn't Nan's choice be in some sense a mixture of strategies G and W? One way to mix strategies would be to play G with probability u, and hence W with probability $1 - u$. Accordingly, let N denote Nan's choice of pure strategy. Then N is a random variable, with sample space $\{G, W\}$; and Prob$(N = G) = u$, Prob$(N = W) = 1 - u$. If Nan plays G with probability u, hence W with probability $1 - u$, then we will say that Nan selects *mixed strategy u*, where $0 \leq u \leq 1$.

Similarly, if San plays G with probability v, and hence W with probability $1 - v$, then we shall say that San selects *mixed strategy v*, where $0 \leq v \leq 1$. Thus if S, with sample space $\{G, W\}$, is the random variable that denotes San's pure

---

[3]   We shall ignore as fanciful the possibility that, say, $\tau_2/2$ and δ might actually be equal; in general, only *in*equalities between parameters that aggregate behavior can ever be meaningful.

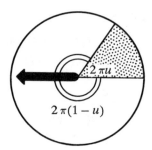

Figure 1.2   Nan's spinning arrow and disk.

strategy, then Prob$(S = G) = v$, and Prob$(S = W) = 1 - v$. If Nan selects mixed strategy u, and if San selects mixed strategy v, then we shall refer to the row vector (u, v) as their *mixed strategy combination*. Thus GG is the same as $(1, 1)$, GW is the same as $(1, 0)$, WG is the same as $(0, 1)$ and WW is the same as $(0, 0)$. Mixed strategy combinations can be represented as points in the unit square of the Cartesian coordinate plane, i.e., the set $\{(u, v) | 0 \le u, v \le 1\}$.[4]

But how could Nan and San arrange all this? Let's suppose that the spinning arrow depicted in Figure 1.2 is mounted on Nan's dashboard. When confronted by San, Nan gives the arrow a quick twirl. If it comes to rest in the shaded sector of the disk, then she plays G; if it comes to rest in the unshaded sector, then she plays W. Thus selecting strategy u means having a disk with a shaded sectoral angle $2\pi u$; and changing one's strategy means changing the disk. What about the time required to spin the arrow—does it matter? Not if San also has a spinning arrow mounted on her dashboard and takes about as long to twirl it (of course, the shaded sector on San's disk would subtend angle $2\pi v$ at the center). And if you think it's a bit far-fetched that motorists would drive around with spinning arrows on their dashboards, then you can think of Nan's spinning arrow as merely the analogue of a mental process through which she decides whether to go or wait at random—but in such a way that she goes, on average, fraction u of the time. Similarly for San. Note, incidentally, the important point that strategies are selected *prior* to interaction—the players arrive at the junction with their disks already shaded.

Let F_1 denote the payoff to Nan. Then F_1 is a random variable with sample space

$$\left\{-\delta - \tau_2/2, \quad 0, \quad -\tau_2, \quad -\epsilon - \tau_2/2\right\}; \tag{1.13}$$

---

[4]   The vertical bar means "such that." In general, $\{x|P\}$ denotes the set of all x such that P is satisfied.

and if Nan and San choose their strategies independently, then

$$\text{Prob}(F_1 = -\delta - \tau_2/2) = \text{Prob}(N = G \text{ and } S = G)$$
$$= \text{Prob}(N = G) \cdot \text{Prob}(S = G) \qquad (1.14)$$
$$= u\,v.$$

Similarly,

$$\text{Prob}(F_1 = 0) = u(1 - v)$$
$$\text{Prob}(F_1 = -\tau_2) = (1 - u)v \qquad (1.15)$$
$$\text{Prob}(F_1 = -\epsilon - \tau_2/2) = (1 - u)(1 - v).$$

Thus, if f_1 denotes the expected value of Nan's payoff from the mixed strategy combination (u, v), then

$$f_1(u, v) = E[F_1]$$
$$= -(\delta + \tau_2/2) \cdot \text{Prob}(F_1 = -\delta - \tau_2/2) + 0 \cdot \text{Prob}(F_1 = 0)$$
$$- \tau_2 \cdot \text{Prob}(F_1 = -\tau_2) - (\epsilon + \tau_2/2) \cdot \text{Prob}(F_1 = -\epsilon - \tau_2/2)$$
$$= \left(\epsilon + \frac{\tau_2}{2} - (\delta + \epsilon)v\right)u + \left(\epsilon - \frac{\tau_2}{2}\right)v - \epsilon - \frac{\tau_2}{2},$$
$$(1.16)$$

after simplification. Similarly, if f_2 denotes the expected value of San's payoff from the strategy combination (u, v), then

$$f_2(u, v) = \left(\epsilon + \frac{\tau_1}{2} - (\delta + \epsilon)u\right)v + \left(\epsilon - \frac{\tau_1}{2}\right)u - \epsilon - \frac{\tau_1}{2}. \qquad (1.17)$$

We will refer to the expected value of a payoff as a *reward*. Thus $f_1(u, v)$ is Nan's reward from the strategy combination (u, v), whereas $f_2(u, v)$ is San's reward from the same combination.

More generally, let Player 1 have $s_1 + 1$ pure strategies with payoff matrix A, and let Player 2 have $s_2 + 1$ pure strategies with payoff matrix B, where both A and B are $(s_1 + 1) \times (s_2 + 1)$ matrices. Let Player 1 select pure strategy i with probability u_i, $1 \le i \le s_1$, and let Player 2 select pure strategy j with probability v_j, $1 \le j \le s_2$. Then the probability with which Player 1 selects strategy $s_1 + 1$, denoted by u_{s_1+1}, and the probability with which Player 2 selects strategy $s_2 + 1$, denoted by v_{s_2+1}, are both determined by the requirement that the probability of choosing one strategy or another is 1:

$$u_{s_1+1} = 1 - \sum_{i=1}^{s_1} u_i, \qquad v_{s_2+1} = 1 - \sum_{j=1}^{s_2} v_j. \qquad (1.18a)$$

Thus Player 1 has only s_1 decision variables, and Player 2 has only s_2 decision variables. Accordingly, let the s_1-dimensional row vector

$$u = \left(u_1, u_2, \ldots, u_{s_1}\right) \qquad (1.18b)$$

be called Player 1's strategy, let the s_2-dimensional row vector

$$v = \left(v_1, v_2, \ldots, v_{s_2}\right) \qquad (1.18c)$$

be called Player 2's strategy, and let the $(s_1 + s_2)$-dimensional row vector (u, v) be the players' joint strategy combination. Then the players' rewards from the strategy combination (u, v) are

$$f_1(u, v) = (u, u_{s_1+1})A(v, v_{s_2+1})^T, \quad f_2(u, v) = (u, u_{s_1+1})B(v, v_{s_2+1})^T, \quad (1.18d)$$

where superscript T denotes transpose.

   Both Nan and San would like their reward to be as large as possible. Unfortunately, Nan does not know what San will do (and San does not know what Nan will do), because this is a noncooperative game. Therefore, Nan should reason as follows: "I do not know which v San will pick—but for every v, I will pick the u that makes $f_1(u, v)$ as large as possible." In this way, Nan obtains a set of points in the unit square. Each of these points corresponds to a strategy combination (u, v) that is rational for Nan, in the sense that for each v (over which Nan has no control) a corresponding u is a strategy that makes Nan's reward as large as possible. We will refer to this set of strategy combinations as Nan's *rational reaction set*, and denote it by R_1. In mathematical terms, we have

$$R_1 = \left\{(u, v) \,|\, 0 \le u \le 1, 0 \le v \le 1, \quad f_1(u, v) = \max_{0 \le \bar{u} \le 1} f_1(\bar{u}, v)\right\}; \qquad (1.19)$$

for each (u, v) in R_1, if Player 2 selects v then a best reply for Player 1 is to select u (*a* best reply rather than *the* best reply because there may be more than one). Note that R_1 is obtained in practice by maximizing f_1 as a function of the single variable u; the maximum, of course, will depend on v.[5]

   Likewise, San should reason as follows: "I do not know which u Nan will pick—but for every u, I will pick the v that makes $f_2(u, v)$ as large as possible." In this way, San obtains a set of points in the unit square. Each of these points corresponds to a strategy combination that is rational for San, in the sense that for each u (over which San has no control) a corresponding v is a strategy that makes San's reward as large as possible. We will refer to this set of strategy combinations as San's rational reaction set, and denote it by R_2. In mathematical terms, we have

$$R_2 = \left\{(u, v) \,|\, 0 \le u \le 1, 0 \le v \le 1, \quad f_2(u, v) = \max_{0 \le \bar{v} \le 1} f_2(u, \bar{v})\right\}; \qquad (1.20)$$

for each (u, v) in R_2, if Player 1 selects u then a best reply for Player 2 is to select v. Note that R_2 is obtained in practice by maximizing f_2 as a function of

---

   [5]   It would perhaps be more accurate to describe R_1 as Player 1's *individually* rational reaction set; nevertheless, we shall abide by tradition. The distinction between individual and group rationality will emerge in Chapter 3.

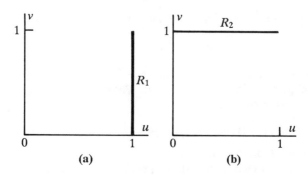

Figure 1.3   Rational reaction sets when $\tau_1 > 2\delta$, $\tau_2 > 2\delta$.

the single variable v; the maximum, of course, will depend on u. Note also the important point that each player can determine her rational reaction set without any knowledge of the other player's reward.

Suppose, for example, that $\tau_2 > 2\delta$, $\tau_1 > 2\delta$ (both drivers are slow). Then because $0 \le v \le 1$ implies that the coefficient of $\bar{u}$ in

$$f_1(\bar{u}, v) = \left(\epsilon(1-v) + \frac{\tau_2}{2} - \delta v\right)\bar{u} + \left(\epsilon - \frac{\tau_2}{2}\right)v - \epsilon - \frac{\tau_2}{2} \tag{1.21}$$

is always positive, $f_1(\bar{u}, v)$ is maximized, for $0 \le \bar{u} \le 1$, by choosing $\bar{u} = 1$. Therefore Nan's rational reaction set is

$$R_1 = \{(u, v) \,|\, u = 1, 0 \le v \le 1\}, \tag{1.22}$$

the edge of the unit square that runs between $(1, 0)$ and $(1, 1)$; see Figure 1.3(a), where R_1 is represented by a thick solid line. Similarly, because $0 \le u \le 1$ implies that the coefficient of $\bar{v}$ in

$$f_2(u, \bar{v}) = \left(\epsilon(1-u) + \frac{\tau_1}{2} - \delta u\right)\bar{v} + \left(\epsilon - \frac{\tau_1}{2}\right)u - \epsilon - \frac{\tau_1}{2} \tag{1.23}$$

is always positive, $f_2(u, \bar{v})$ is maximized, for $0 \le \bar{v} \le 1$, by choosing $\bar{v} = 1$. Therefore San's rational reaction set is

$$R_2 = \{(u, v) \,|\, 0 \le u \le 1, v = 1\}, \tag{1.24}$$

the edge of the unit square that runs between $(0, 1)$ and $(1, 1)$; see Figure 1.3(b), where R_2 is represented by a thin solid line. Of course, all that Figure 1.3 tells us is that the best strategy against a slow driver is G, which we knew long before we began to talk about mixed strategies. But have patience! Something new will shortly emerge.

Notice that the rational reaction sets R_1 and R_2 have a non-empty intersection

$$R_1 \cap R_2 = \{(1, 1)\}. \tag{1.25}$$

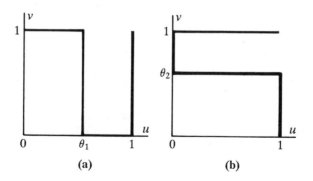

Figure 1.4   Rational reaction sets R_1(▬) and R_2(—) when (a) $\tau_1 < 2\delta < \tau_2$, (b) $\tau_2 < 2\delta < \tau_1$.

The strategy combination $(1, 1)$ which lies in both sets has the following property: if either player selects strategy 1, then the other cannot obtain a greater reward by selecting a strategy other than 1. In other words, no player can increase her reward by a *unilateral* departure from the strategy combination $(1, 1)$. By virtue of having this property, $(1, 1)$ is said to be a *Nash-equilibrium strategy combination*. More generally, (u^*, v^*) is a Nash-equilibrium strategy combination (or simply *Nash equilibrium*) of a noncooperative, 2-player game when, if one player sticks rigidly to her Nash-equilibrium strategy (u^* in the case of Player 1, v^* in the case of Player 2), then the other player cannot increase her reward by selecting a strategy other than her Nash-equilibrium strategy. Alternatively, (u^*, v^*) is a Nash equilibrium if u^* is a best reply to v^* *and* v^* is a best reply to u^*. We note in passing that a pair of dominant strategies—such as $(1, 1)$ in (1.25)—is always a Nash equilibrium; see Exercise 1.3. A still more general definition of Nash equilibrium, for games among arbitrary numbers of players, will be given in Section 1.6.

Now, if we were interested solely in finding the best pair of strategies for two slow drivers ($\tau_1, \tau_2 > 2\delta$), then introducing the concept of Nash equilibrium would be like using a sledgehammer to burst a soap bubble. It is obvious from Figure 1.3 that $(1, 1)$ is the *only* pair of strategies that two rational players would select, for (u, v) will be selected only if u lies in R_1 and v in R_2. Things get a little bit more complicated, however, if either driver is either fast or intermediate.

To determine R_1 and R_2 in these circumstances, it will be convenient first to define parameters θ_1 and θ_2 by

$$(\delta + \epsilon)\,\theta_k = \epsilon + \frac{\tau_k}{2}, \quad k = 1, 2. \tag{1.26}$$

Then, from (1.16)–(1.17),

$$f_1(\bar{u}, v) = (\delta + \epsilon)(\theta_2 - v)\bar{u} + \left(\epsilon - \frac{\tau_2}{2}\right)v - \epsilon - \frac{\tau_2}{2}, \qquad (1.27a)$$

$$f_2(u, \bar{v}) = (\delta + \epsilon)(\theta_1 - u)\bar{v} + \left(\epsilon - \frac{\tau_1}{2}\right)u - \epsilon - \frac{\tau_1}{2}. \qquad (1.27b)$$

If $\tau_1 < 2\delta < \tau_2$ (slow San, fast or intermediate Nan) then $\theta_1 < 1, \theta_2 > 1$, whence the $\bar{u}$ that maximizes $f_1(\bar{u}, v)$, for $0 \le \bar{u} \le 1$, is still $\bar{u} = 1$; whereas the $\bar{v}$ that maximizes $f_2(u, \bar{v})$ is given by[6]

$$\bar{v} = \begin{array}{ll} 1 & \text{if} \quad 0 \le u < \theta_1 \\ \text{any } \bar{v} \text{ such that } 0 \le \bar{v} \le 1 & \text{if} \quad u = \theta_1 \\ 0 & \text{if} \quad \theta_1 < u \le 1. \end{array} \qquad (1.28)$$

Thus R_1 is the same as before; whereas R_2 consists of three straight-line segments, as shown in Figure 1.4(a). We see that, if San has no knowledge of Nan's reward function f_1, then any v such that $0 \le v \le 1$ could be rational for San; because, for all she knows, Nan could select the strategy $u = \theta_1$, to which any v in $0 \le v \le 1$ is a best reply. If, on the other hand, San knows Nan's reward function, then the only rational choice for San is $v = 0$, because only $v = 0$ is a best reply to $u = 1$. Of course, $u = 1$ is also a best reply to $v = 0$, because it's the best reply to anything. Thus $(1, 0)$, the only point in the intersection of R_1 and R_2, is a Nash equilibrium. In terms of pure strategies, the Nash equilibrium is GW; G is a best reply to W (regardless), and W is a slow driver's best reply to an intermediate or fast driver's G.

Similarly, if $\tau_2 < 2\delta < \tau_1$ (slow Nan, fast or intermediate San) then, either from symmetry or from an expression similar to (1.28), R_1 and R_2 are as shown in Figure 1.4(b). If Nan has no knowledge of San's reward function f_2, then any u such that $0 \le u \le 1$ could be rational for Nan; because, for all she knows, San could select the strategy $v = \theta_2$, to which any u in $0 \le u \le 1$ is a best reply. If, on the other hand, Nan knows San's reward function, then the only rational choice for Nan is $u = 0$, because only $u = 0$ is a best reply to $v = 1$. Because $v = 1$ is also a best reply to $u = 0$, $(0, 1)$, the only point in the intersection of R_1 and R_2, is a Nash equilibrium. In terms of pure strategies, this time the Nash equilibrium is WG, but the interpretation is the same: G is a best reply to W, and W is a slow driver's best reply to an intermediate or fast driver's G. We see that our concept of Nash equilibrium depends crucially on each player knowing the other player's reward function (whereas the concept of rational reaction set does not). If such is the case, then it is customary to say that the players have *complete information*.

---

[6] Note that $\bar{v}$ defined by (1.28) is strictly not a function of u, because $\bar{v}$ takes more than one value where $u = \theta_1$; or, if you prefer, $\bar{v}$ is a multi-valued function of u.

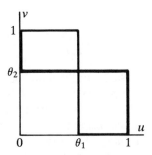

Figure 1.5   Rational reaction sets R_1(━━)
and R_2(———) when $\tau_1 < 2\delta$, $\tau_2 < 2\delta$.

TABLE 1.5   Nash-equilibrium rewards in Crossroads.

(u,v)	$f_1(u,v)$	$f_2(u,v)$
$(1,0)$	0	$-\tau_1$
(θ_1,θ_2)	$-\left(\delta + \dfrac{\tau_2}{2}\right)\theta_2$	$-\left(\delta + \dfrac{\tau_1}{2}\right)\theta_1$
$(0,1)$	$-\tau_2$	0

There is no denying that the concept of Nash equilibrium has desirable properties. Provided each player has knowledge of the other's reward, there's a certain sense in which the solution is self-enforcing, even though there is no explicit cooperation between the players. Consider, however, the case in which neither driver is slow, so that $\tau_1 < 2\delta$, $\tau_2 < 2\delta$ or $\theta_1 < 1$, $\theta_2 < 1$. It is readily shown that the $\bar{u}$ that now maximizes $f_1(\bar{u},v)$, for $0 \le \bar{u} \le 1$, is given by

$$\bar{u} = \begin{array}{ll} 1 & \text{if } 0 \le v < \theta_2 \\ \text{any } \bar{u} \text{ such that } 0 \le \bar{u} \le 1 & \text{if } v = \theta_2 \\ 0 & \text{if } \theta_2 < v \le 1; \end{array} \qquad (1.29)$$

whereas the $\bar{v}$ that now maximizes $f_2(u,\bar{v})$ is still given by (1.28). Thus R_1 and R_2 are as shown in Figure 1.5. We observe at once that

$$R_1 \cap R_2 = \{(1,0), (\theta_1,\theta_2), (0,1)\}. \qquad (1.30)$$

There are therefore three Nash equilibria. Then which do we regard as the solution?

The rewards associated with the three Nash equilibria are given in Table 1.5.

You can readily show that

$$-\left(\delta + \frac{\tau_k}{2}\right)\theta_k - (-\tau_k) = \frac{(2\delta - \tau_k)(\tau_k - 2\epsilon)}{4(\delta + \epsilon)}, \qquad k = 1, 2. \qquad (1.31)$$

Thus $(1, 0)$ is always the best Nash equilibrium for Nan; and (θ_1, θ_2) is second or third best, according to whether $2\delta > \tau_2 > 2\epsilon$ (intermediate San) or $2\delta > 2\epsilon > \tau_2$ (fast San). Again, $(0, 1)$ is always the best Nash equilibrium for San; and (θ_1, θ_2) is second or third best according to whether $2\delta > \tau_1 > 2\epsilon$ (intermediate Nan) or $2\delta > 2\epsilon > \tau_1$ (fast Nan). Even though θ_1 is a best reply to θ_2, and θ_2 is a best reply to θ_1, there is no reason to expect the players to select these strategies, because for each player there is another strategy combination with the best-reply property that yields a higher reward. But if Nan selects her best Nash-equilibrium strategy, namely, $u = 1$, and if San selects her best Nash-equilibrium strategy, namely, $v = 1$, then the resulting strategy combination, namely, $(1, 1)$ does not even belong to a rational reaction set! Then which—if any—of the Nash equilibria should we regard as the solution of the game? Perhaps you would like to give this matter some thought. We will return to it in Chapter 2.

1.4 FOUR WAYS: A GAME-THEORETIC ANALYSIS OF A MOTORIST'S TRILEMMA

Nan and San's dilemma becomes even more intriguing if we allow a third strategy, denoted by C, in which each player's action is contingent upon that of the other. A player who adopts C will select G if the other player selects W, but she will select W if the other player selects G. Let us suppose that, if Nan is a C-strategist, then the first thing she does when she arrives at the junction is to wave San on; but if San replies by waving Nan on, then immediately Nan puts down her foot and drives away. If, on the other hand, San replies by hitting the gas, then Nan waits until San has traversed the junction. But what happens if San is also a C-strategist? As soon as they reach the junction, Nan and San both wave at one another. Nan interprets San's wave to mean that San wants to wait, so Nan drives forward; San interprets Nan's wave to mean that Nan wants to wait, so San also drives forward; and the result is the same as if both had selected strategy G. Thus if a G-strategist can be described as selfish and a W-strategist as an altruist, then a C-strategist could perhaps be described as an impatient altruist.

For the sake of simplicity, let us assume that the game is symmetric, i.e., $\tau_1 = \tau_2$, and denote the common value of these two parameters by τ. Then Nan's payoff matrix, A, is that shown in Table 1.6; and San's payoff matrix, B, is that shown in Table 1.7. As always, the rows correspond to strategies of Player 1 (Nan), and the columns correspond to strategies of Player 2 (San); thus the entry in row i and column j is the payoff, to the player whose payoffs are stored in the

TABLE 1.6   Nan's payoff matrix in Four Ways.

	G	W	C
G	$-\delta - \tau/2$	0	0
W	$-\tau$	$-\epsilon - \tau/2$	$-\tau$
C	$-\tau$	0	$-\delta - \tau/2$

TABLE 1.7   San's payoff matrix in Four Ways.

	G	W	C
G	$-\delta - \tau/2$	$-\tau$	$-\tau$
W	0	$-\epsilon - \tau/2$	0
C	0	$-\tau$	$-\delta - \tau/2$

matrix, if Player 1 selects strategy i and Player 2 selects strategy j. Of course, because the game is symmetric, B is just the transpose of A. To distinguish this game from Crossroads, we will refer to it as Four Ways.

If the drivers are so slow that $\tau > 2\delta$, then it is clear at once that their best strategy is to hit the gas; for every element in the first row of Nan's matrix is at least as great as the corresponding element in the second or third row, and every element in the first column of San's matrix is at least as great as the corresponding element in the second or third column. Thus, if $\tau > 2\delta$, then G is a dominant strategy for both players, and we do not hesitate to regard strategy combination GG as the solution of the game; if there is only one Nash equilibrium, then there is no indeterminacy to resolve.[7] The game becomes interesting, however, when $\tau < 2\delta$, which is the case we shall now analyze. It will be convenient first to define a dimensionless parameter, σ, by

$$\sigma = \frac{\tau}{2\delta}, \tag{1.32}$$

so that $\sigma < 1$. As in Crossroads, no pure strategy is now dominant. We therefore consider mixed strategies .

---

[7]   Even if there were more than one Nash equilibrium, there would be no indeterminacy if all combinations of Nash-equilibrium strategies yielded the same payoffs. This is true in general only for zero sum games; see, for example, Owen (1982) or Wang (1988).

probability u_2, then we shall say that Nan selects strategy u, where $u = (u_1, u_2)$ is a 2-dimensional row vector. Then Nan selects pure strategy C with probability $1 - u_1 - u_2$, whence

$$0 \leq u_1 \leq 1, \qquad 0 \leq u_2 \leq 1, \qquad 0 \leq u_1 + u_2 \leq 1. \qquad (1.33a)$$

Thus Nan's mixed strategies correspond to the points of a closed triangle in 2-dimensional space. Similarly, if San selects G with probability v_1 and W with probability v_2, then we shall say that San selects strategy v, where $v = (v_1, v_2)$ is also a 2-dimensional vector; and because San selects C with probability $1 - v_1 - v_2$, we have

$$0 \leq v_1 \leq 1, \qquad 0 \leq v_2 \leq 1, \qquad 0 \leq v_1 + v_2 \leq 1; \qquad (1.33b)$$

i.e., San's mixed strategies correspond to the same closed triangle in 2-dimensional space. If Nan selects u and San selects v, then we shall say that they jointly select strategy combination (u, v), where $(u, v) = (u_1, u_2, v_1, v_2)$ is a 4-dimensional vector.

The sample space of N, Nan's choice of pure strategy, is now $\{G, W, C\}$ instead of $\{G, W\}$, with $\mathrm{Prob}(N = G) = u_1$, $\mathrm{Prob}(N = W) = u_2$ and $\mathrm{Prob}(N = C) = 1 - u_1 - u_2$. S, San's choice of pure strategy, has the same sample space, but with $\mathrm{Prob}(S = G) = v_1$, $\mathrm{Prob}(S = W) = v_2$ and $\mathrm{Prob}(S = C) = 1 - v_1 - v_2$. The payoff to Nan, F_1, has sample space

$$\left\{-\delta - \tau/2, 0, -\tau, -\epsilon - \tau/2\right\}, \qquad (1.34)$$

the symmetric version of (1.13); and if Nan and San still choose their strategies independently, then

$$
\begin{aligned}
\mathrm{Prob}(F_1 = -\delta - \tau/2) &= \mathrm{Prob}(N = G \text{ and } S = G \text{ or } N = C \text{ and } S = C) \\
&= \mathrm{Prob}(N = G \text{ and } S = G) + \mathrm{Prob}(N = C \text{ and } S = C) \\
&= \mathrm{Prob}(N = G) \cdot \mathrm{Prob}(S = G) \\
&\quad + \mathrm{Prob}(N = C) \cdot \mathrm{Prob}(S = C) \\
&= u_1 v_1 + (1 - u_1 - u_2)(1 - v_1 - v_2).
\end{aligned}
$$
$$(1.35)$$

Similarly,

$$
\begin{aligned}
\mathrm{Prob}(F_1 = 0) &= u_1 v_2 + u_1(1 - v_1 - v_2) + (1 - u_1 - u_2)v_2 \\
\mathrm{Prob}(F_1 = -\tau) &= u_2 v_1 + u_2(1 - v_1 - v_2) + (1 - u_1 - u_2)v_1 \qquad (1.36) \\
\mathrm{Prob}(F_1 = -\epsilon - \tau/2) &= u_2 v_2.
\end{aligned}
$$

Thus Nan's reward, f_1, from the mixed strategy combination (u, v) is

$$
\begin{aligned}
f_1(u, v) &= E[F_1] \\
&= -(\delta + \tau/2) \cdot \text{Prob}(F_1 = -\delta - \tau/2) + 0 \cdot \text{Prob}(F_1 = 0) \\
&\quad - \tau \cdot \text{Prob}(F_1 = -\tau) - (\epsilon + \tau/2) \cdot \text{Prob}(F_1 = -\epsilon - \tau/2) \\
&= -\big(2\delta v_1 + (\delta + \tau/2)(v_2 - 1)\big)u_1 - \big((\delta - \tau/2)(v_1 - 1) + (\delta + \epsilon)v_2\big)u_2 \\
&\quad + (\delta - \tau/2)v_1 + (\delta + \tau/2)(v_2 - 1),
\end{aligned}
$$

$$(1.37)$$

after simplification. Similarly, San's reward, f_2, from the strategy combination (u, v) is

$$
\begin{aligned}
f_2(u, v) &= -\big(2\delta u_1 + (\delta + \tau/2)(u_2 - 1)\big)v_1 - \big((\delta - \tau/2)(u_1 - 1) + (\delta + \epsilon)u_2\big)v_2 \\
&\quad + (\delta - \tau/2)u_1 + (\delta + \tau/2)(u_2 - 1).
\end{aligned}
$$

$$(1.38)$$

Note that, by virtue of symmetry,

$$f_2(u, v) = f_1(v, u), \tag{1.39}$$

for all u and v satisfying (1.33). Note also (Exercise 1.4) that (1.37) and (1.38) are merely special cases of (1.18d).

Let Δ denote the closed triangle in 2-dimensional space that is defined by (1.33). (Note that, because this triangle exists independently of whether we use u or v to label a point in it, Δ is *either* the set of all points in 2-dimensional space that satisfy (1.33a) *or* the set of all points that satisfy (1.33b); the sets are identical.) Although u and v are now vectors, as opposed to scalars, everything we have said about rational reaction sets and Nash equilibria with respect to Crossroads remains true for Four Ways, provided only that we replace $0 \leq u \leq 1$ by $u \in \Delta$ and $0 \leq v \leq 1$ by $v \in \Delta$ (and therefore also $0 \leq \bar{u} \leq 1$ by $\bar{u} \in \Delta$ and $0 \leq \bar{v} \leq 1$ by $\bar{v} \in \Delta$). Thus the players' rational reaction sets in Four Ways are defined by

$$
\begin{aligned}
R_1 &= \Big\{ (u, v) \,|\, u \in \Delta, v \in \Delta, f_1(u, v) = \max_{\bar{u}} f_1(\bar{u}, v) \Big\} \\
R_2 &= \Big\{ (u, v) \,|\, u \in \Delta, v \in \Delta, f_2(u, v) = \max_{\bar{v}} f_2(u, \bar{v}) \Big\}
\end{aligned}
$$

$$(1.40)$$

and the set of all Nash equilibria is $R_1 \cap R_2$. On the other hand, because the rational reaction sets now lie in a 4-dimensional space, as opposed to a 2-dimensional space, we cannot locate the Nash equilibria by drawing diagrams equivalent to Figures 1.3–1.5. We proceed, instead, as follows.

We first define dimensionless parameters γ, α, β and θ by

$$
\gamma = \frac{\epsilon}{\delta}, \qquad \alpha = \frac{(\sigma + \gamma)(\sigma + 1)}{1 + 2\gamma + \sigma^2}, \qquad \beta = \frac{(1 - \sigma)^2}{1 + 2\gamma + \sigma^2} \tag{1.41}
$$

and

$$\theta = \frac{2\epsilon + \tau}{2\epsilon + 2\delta} = \frac{\sigma + \gamma}{1 + \gamma}, \tag{1.42}$$

where σ is defined by (1.32). In view of (1.1), $\alpha, \beta, \gamma, \sigma$ and θ all lie between 0 and 1. If the coefficients of u_1 and u_2 in (1.37) are both negative, then clearly $f_1(u, v)$ is maximized by selecting $u_1 = 0$ and $u_2 = 0$, or $u = (0, 0)$; moreover, $(0, 0)$ is the only maximizing strategy for Player 1. If these coefficients are merely nonpositive, then there will be more than one maximizing strategy; nevertheless, $u = (0, 0)$ will still be one of them. But the coefficient of u_1 in (1.37) is nonpositive when the point (v_1, v_2) lies on or above the line in 2-dimensional space that joins the point $((1 + \sigma)/2, 0)$ to the point $(0, 1)$; whereas the coefficient of u_2 in (1.37) is nonpositive when the point (v_1, v_2) lies on or above the line that joins the point $(1, 0)$ to the point $(0, 1 - \theta)$. Thus the coefficients of u_1 and u_2 in (1.37) are both nonpositive when the point (v_1, v_2) lies in that part of Δ which corresponds to (the interior or boundary of) the triangle marked C in Figure 1.6. Let us denote by $v^C = (v_1^C, v_2^C)$ any strategy for San that corresponds to a point in C. Then what we have shown is that all 4-dimensional vectors of the form

$$(0, 0, v_1^C, v_2^C) \tag{1.43}$$

must lie in R_1.

Extending our notation in an obvious way, let us denote by $v^A = (v_1^A, v_2^A)$ any strategy for San that corresponds to a point in A, by $v^{AC} = (v_1^{AC}, v_2^{AC})$ any strategy for San that corresponds to a point that lies in both A and C, and so on. Then, by considering the various cases in which the coefficient of u_1 or the coefficient of u_2 or both in (1.37) are nonpositive, nonnegative or zero, it is readily shown that all strategy combinations in Table 1.8 must lie in Nan's rational reaction set, R_1; see Exercise 1.5. Furthermore, if we repeat the analysis for f_2 and San (as opposed to f_1 and Nan), and if we denote by $u^A = (u_1^A, u_2^A)$ any strategy for Nan that corresponds to a point in A, by $u^{AC} = (u_1^{AC}, u_2^{AC})$ any strategy for Nan that corresponds to a point in both A and C, and so on, then we readily find that all strategy combinations in Table 1.9 must lie in San's rational reaction set, R_2. Indeed, in view of the symmetry condition (1.39), it is hardly necessary to repeat the analysis.

A strategy combination is a Nash equilibrium if, and only if, it appears both in Table 1.8 and in Table 1.9. Therefore, to find all Nash equilibria, we must match strategy combinations from Table 1.8 with strategy combinations from Table 1.9 in every possible way. For example, consider the first row of Table 1.8. It does not match the first, fourth or sixth row of Table 1.9 because $(1, 0)$ does not lie in A. It does not match the last row of Table 1.9, even for $(v_1, v_2) \in A$, because $\alpha < 1$ (or because $\beta > 0$). Because $(1, 0)$ lies in B and $(0, 1)$ lies in A, however, we can match the first row of Table 1.8 with the second row of Table 1.9; whence $(1, 0, 0, 1)$ is a Nash equilibrium. Likewise, because $(1, 0)$ lies in C and $(0, 0)$ in A, we can match the first row of Table 1.8 with the third row of Table 1.9;

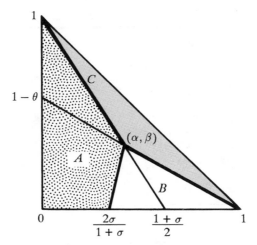

Figure 1.6   The region Δ.

TABLE 1.8 R_1 for Four Ways.

1	0	v_1^A	v_2^A	
0	1	v_1^B	v_2^B	
0	0	v_1^C	v_2^C	
u_1	0	v_1^{AC}	v_2^{AC}	$0 \leq u_1 \leq 1$
0	u_2	v_1^{BC}	v_2^{BC}	$0 \leq u_2 \leq 1$
u_1	u_2	v_1^{AB}	v_2^{AB}	$u \in \Delta, u_1 + u_2 = 1$
u_1	u_2	α	β	$u \in \Delta$

therefore $(1, 0, 0, 0)$ is a Nash equilibrium. Finally, we can match the first row of Table 1.8 with the fifth row of Table 1.9 to deduce that $(1, 0, 0, v_2)$ is a Nash-equilibrium strategy combination when $0 \leq v_2 \leq 1$, because then $(0, v_2)$ lies in A. The Nash equilibria we have found in this way are recorded in rows 1, 3 and 5 of Table 1.10.

Repeating the analysis for the remaining six rows of Table 1.8, we obtain (Exercise 1.6) an exhaustive list of Nash-equilibrium strategy combinations. They are recorded in Table 1.10. The first four rows of this table correspond to equilibria in pure strategies: rows 1 and 2 to equilibria in which one player selects G

TABLE 1.9 R_2 for Four Ways.

u_1^A	u_2^A	1	0	
u_1^B	u_2^B	0	1	
u_1^C	u_2^C	0	0	
u_1^{AC}	u_2^{AC}	v_1	0	$0 \le v_1 \le 1$
u_1^{BC}	u_2^{BC}	0	v_2	$0 \le v_2 \le 1$
u_1^{AB}	u_2^{AB}	v_1	v_2	$v \in \Delta, v_1 + v_2 = 1$
α	β	v_1	v_2	$v \in \Delta$

TABLE 1.10   Nash equilibria for Four Ways.

1	0	0	1	
0	1	1	0	
1	0	0	0	
0	0	1	0	
1	0	0	v_2	$0 \le v_2 \le 1$
0	u_2	1	0	$0 \le u_2 \le 1$
0	1	v_1	0	$2\sigma/(1 + \sigma) \le v_1 \le 1$
u_1	0	0	1	$2\sigma/(1 + \sigma) \le u_1 \le 1$
α	β	α	β	

and the other W, rows 3 and 4 to equilibria in which one player selects G and the other C. The remaining five rows correspond to equilibria in mixed strategies. We see that, although rows 1–4 and 9 of the table correspond to isolated equilibria, there are infinitely many equilibria of the other types. If you thought that having three equilibria to choose from in Crossroads was bad enough, then I wonder what are you thinking now. Which, if any, of all these infinitely many equilibria do we regard as the solution of Four Ways?

Good question! Perhaps you would like to mull it over, at least until Chapter 2. Meanwhile, do Exercise 1.29.

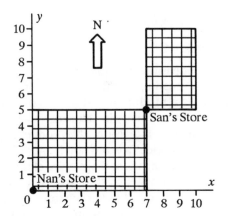

Figure 1.7   Battleground for Store Wars.

1.5   STORE WARS: A CONTINUOUS GAME OF PRICES

Although it is always reasonable to suppose that decision makers have only a finite number of pure strategies, when the number is large it is often convenient to imagine instead that the strategies form a continuum. Suppose, for example, that the price of some item could reasonably lie anywhere between five and ten dollars. Then if a cent is the smallest unit of currency, and if selecting a strategy corresponds to setting the price of the item, then the decision maker has a finite total of 501 pure strategies. Because this number is large, however, it may be preferable to suppose that the price in dollars can take any value between 5 and 10 (and round the optimal strategy to two decimal places). Then rewards are calculated directly, i.e., without the intermediate step of calculating payoff matrices; and the game is said to be *continuous,* to distinguish it from matrix games like Crossroads, Four Ways and the Hawk–Dove game. The definition of Nash equilibrium is not in the least affected; but whereas matrix games are guaranteed to have at least one Nash equilibrium, continuous games may have none at all. These ideas are illustrated by the following example.[8]

A subdivision of area 50 square miles consists of two rectangles of land, as shaded in Figure 1.7; the smaller rectangle measures 15 square miles, the larger rectangle 35. If we take the southwest corner of the subdivision to be the origin of a Cartesian coordinate system Oxy, with x increasing to the east and y to the

---

[8]   For a proof that matrix games have at least one Nash equilibrium, see, for example, Wang (1988). The example Store Wars was suggested by the Hotelling model described in Phlips (1988, 42–45). Phlips assumes that prospective customers are uniformly distributed along a line; whereas Store Wars assumes—in effect—that they are *nonuniformly* distributed along a line.

north, then the subdivision occupies the region

$$\{(x,y) \mid 0 \leq x \leq 7, 0 \leq y \leq 5\} \cup \{(x,y) \mid 7 \leq x \leq 10, 5 \leq y \leq 10\}. \quad (1.44)$$

All roads through the subdivision run either from east to west or from north to south, as indicated by the shading in the diagram. At $(0,0)$ and $(7,5)$ are two stores, each of which sells a product for which the daily demand is uniformly distributed over the 50 square miles, in the sense that customers are equally likely to live anywhere in the subdivision; the product might, for example, be large bags of ice. If buyers select a store solely by weighing the price of the product against the cost of getting there (bags of ice at the first store are identical to those at the second, say), and if each store wishes to maximize revenue from the product in question, then how should the stores set their prices? Because the best price for the first store depends upon the second store's price, and vice versa, the stores' decisions are interdependent; and if we assume that the stores do not communicate with one another, then we have all the necessary ingredients for a noncooperative game. We will call this game Store Wars.

Let Player 1 be Nan, who is manager of the store at $(0,0)$; and let Player 2 be San, who is manager of the store at $(7,5)$.[9] Let p_1 be Nan's price for the product, let p_2 be San's price, and let c be the cost per mile of travel to the store, assumed the same for all customers. Thus the round-trip cost of travel from Nan's store to San's store would be $24c$— no matter how you went, because all roads through the subdivision run from east to west or from north to south. Clearly, if Nan's price were to exceed this round-trip travel cost *plus* San's price for the item in question, then Nan could never expect anyone to buy from her. Accordingly, we can safely assume that

$$p_1 \leq p_2 + 24c. \quad (1.45a)$$

Similarly, because nobody in the larger rectangle can be expected to buy from San if her price exceeds Nan's by the round-trip travel cost between the stores, and assuming that San would like to attract at least some customers from the larger rectangle, we have

$$p_2 \leq p_1 + 24c. \quad (1.45b)$$

Furthermore, there are upper and lower limits to the price that a store can charge for a product; thus we have

$$p_1 \leq \alpha c, \qquad p_2 \leq \alpha c \quad (1.45c)$$

$$p_1 \geq \beta c, \qquad p_2 \geq \beta c \quad (1.45d)$$

where α and β are dimensionless parameters. Except in Exercise 1.13, however, we shall assume throughout that $\beta = 0$; provided that β is sufficiently small, this

---

[9] If Nan were to live near San's store and San were to live near Nan's store, then we could easily explain why they keep meeting each other in Crossroads!

assumption will not affect the principal results of our analysis.[10]

Now, let (X, Y) be the residential coordinates of the next customer for the product in question. Because all roads run either north and south or east and west, her distance from Nan's store is $|X| + |Y|$; whereas her distance from San's store is $|7 - X| + |5 - Y|$. Thus, assuming that she selects a store *solely* by weighing the price of the product against the cost of travel from her residence (she doesn't, for example, buy the product on her way home from work), this customer will buy from Nan if

$$p_1 + 2c(|X| + |Y|) < p_2 + 2c(|7 - X| + |5 - Y|); \qquad (1.46a)$$

whereas she will buy from San if

$$p_1 + 2c(|X| + |Y|) > p_2 + 2c(|7 - X| + |5 - Y|). \qquad (1.46b)$$

But $X \geq 0, Y \geq 0$; thus $|X| + |Y|$ is the same as $X + Y$. Furthermore, the shape of the subdivision precludes either $X > 7, Y < 5$ or $X < 7, Y > 5$; therefore $|7 - X| + |5 - Y|$ is the same thing as $|12 - X - Y|$. But if we had $X + Y > 12$ in (1.46a), then it would now reduce to $p_1 + 24c < p_2$, which violates (1.45b). Accordingly, we can assume that $X + Y \leq 12$ in (1.46a) and rewrite it as $p_1 + 2c(X + Y) < p_2 + 2c(12 - X - Y)$; whence the next customer will buy from Nan if

$$X + Y < \frac{p_2 - p_1}{4c} + 6. \qquad (1.47a)$$

Similarly, if $X + Y \leq 12$, then the next customer will buy from San if

$$X + Y > \frac{p_2 - p_1}{4c} + 6. \qquad (1.47b)$$

If, on the other hand, $X + Y > 12$, then (1.46b) reduces to $p_1 + 24c > p_2$, and the customer will certainly buy from San (because we tacitly assume that if $p_1 + 24c = p_2$, i.e., if the total cost of obtaining the product is the same from either store, then customers will buy from the nearer store). Thus the next customer will buy from San if either $X + Y > 12$ or $X + Y \leq 12$ and (1.47b) is satisfied. But $X + Y > 12$ implies (1.47b) because the right-hand side of (1.47b) is less than or equal to 12 (by virtue of (1.45b)). Thus, in any event, the next customer will buy from San if (1.47b) is satisfied. Of course, San's monopoly over the smaller rectangle was built into the model when we assumed (1.45b).

Because the next customer could live anywhere in the subdivision, X and Y are (continuous) random variables; hence so is $X + Y$. Let G denote its cumu-

---

[10] In terms of the economist's inverse demand curve, with quantity measured along the horizontal axis and price along the vertical axis, αc is the price at which the demand curve meets the vertical axis, whereas βc is simply the cost price of the item. Strictly, however, we ignore questions of supply and demand; or, if you prefer, we assume that demand is infinitely elastic at αc but infinitely inelastic at greater or lower prices.

lative distribution function, i.e., define

$$G(s) = \text{Prob}(X + Y \leq s), \quad 0 \leq s \leq 20; \tag{1.48}$$

and let F_1 denote Nan's payoff from the next customer. Then F_1 is also a random variable, which in view of (1.47) is defined by

$$F_1 = \begin{cases} p_1 & \text{if } X + Y < \dfrac{p_2 - p_1}{4c} + 6 \\ 0 & \text{if } X + Y > \dfrac{p_2 - p_1}{4c} + 6. \end{cases} \tag{1.49}$$

Because F_1 is a random variable, it cannot itself be maximized; but instead we can maximize its expected value, which we shall denote by f_1 and define to be Nan's reward.

It will be convenient to make prices dimensionless, by scaling them with respect to $4c$.[11] Let us therefore define

$$u = \frac{p_1}{4c}, \qquad v = \frac{p_2}{4c}, \tag{1.50}$$

where u is Nan's strategy and v is San's. Then, from (1.48)–(1.50), we have

$$\begin{aligned} f_1(u,v) = E[F_1] &= p_1 \cdot \text{Prob}(X + Y < v - u + 6) + \\ &\quad 0 \cdot \text{Prob}(X + Y > v - u + 6) \\ &= 4cuG(v - u + 6); \end{aligned} \tag{1.51}$$

of course, $\text{Prob}(X + Y = v - u + 6) = 0$, because $X + Y$ is a continuous random variable.[12] Similarly, San's payoff is the random variable

$$F_2 = \begin{cases} 0 & \text{if } X + Y < v - u + 6 \\ 4cv & \text{if } X + Y > v - u + 6 \end{cases} \tag{1.52}$$

and her reward is

$$\begin{aligned} f_2(u,v) = E[F_2] &= 4cv \cdot \text{Prob}(X + Y > v - u + 6) \\ &= 4cv\big(1 - G(v - u + 6)\big). \end{aligned} \tag{1.53}$$

Note that, in view of (1.50), (1.45a) requires $u \leq v + 6$, whereas (1.45b) requires $v \leq u + 6$. Then, in view of (1.45c), the set of all feasible strategy combinations, which we shall denote by D, is

$$D = \{(u,v) \mid 0 \leq u \leq \alpha/4, \quad 0 \leq v \leq \alpha/4, \ |u - v| \leq 6\}. \tag{1.54}$$

---

[11]   The cost of driving round a square-mile block. Because c is a cost per unit length, we must multiply by a distance (here 4) to obtain a quantity with the dimensions of price.
[12]   See, for example, Mesterton-Gibbons (1989, pp. 523–524).

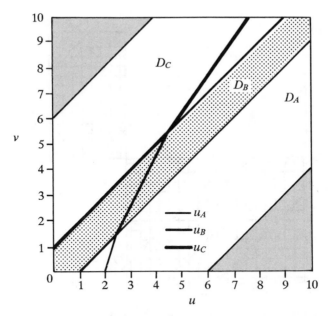

Figure 1.8   The decision set D when $\alpha = 40$. The speckled region is D_B; the dark region lies outside D.

We shall call D the *decision set*. It will be convenient to define three subsets of D by

$$D_A = \{(u,v)\,|\,u \le \alpha/4, \quad v \ge 0, \quad 1 \le u - v \le 6\} \tag{1.55a}$$

$$D_B = \{(u,v)\,|\,0 \le u \le \alpha/4, \quad 0 \le v \le \alpha/4, \quad |u - v| \le 1\} \tag{1.55b}$$

$$D_C = \{(u,v)\,|\,u \ge 0, \quad v \le \alpha/4, \quad 1 \le v - u \le 6\}; \tag{1.55c}$$

then $D = D_A \cup D_B \cup D_C$. For $\alpha = 40$, D is depicted in Figure 1.8. The speckled region is D_B; the dark region lies outside D.

If we assume that customers are uniformly distributed throughout the subdivision, then the cumulative distribution function G is readily calculated with the help of Figure 1.9, because $\text{Prob}(X + Y \le s)$ is just the fraction of the total area of the subdivision that lies below the line $x + y = s$. Suppose, for example, that $0 \le s \le 5$. Then the area below the lowest of the thick solid lines in Figure 1.9 is $s^2/2$; whence the fraction of total area below the line is $s^2/100$ (because the populated area is 50 square miles). Or suppose that $5 \le s \le 7$. Then, similarly, the fraction of total area below the second lowest of the solid lines in Figure 1.9 is $(2s - 5)/20$. Continuing in this manner, and noting that the four remaining thick solid lines in the diagram (on which the coordinates of some key points are marked) pertain to $7 \le s \le 12$, $12 \le s \le 15$, $15 \le s \le 17$ and $17 \le s \le 20$,

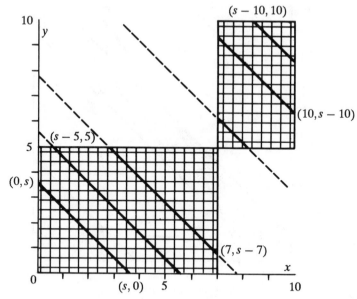

Figure 1.9   Calculation of G defined by (1.48). See text for discussion.

respectively, we find (Exercise 1.7) that $G(s) =$

$$
\begin{cases}
\dfrac{s^2}{100} & \text{if } 0 \le s \le 5 \\[2ex]
\dfrac{2s - 5}{20} & \text{if } 5 \le s \le 7 \\[2ex]
\dfrac{7}{10} - \dfrac{(12 - s)^2}{100} & \text{if } 7 \le s \le 12 \\[2ex]
\dfrac{7}{10} + \dfrac{(s - 12)^2}{100} & \text{if } 12 \le s \le 15 \\[2ex]
\dfrac{6s - 11}{100} & \text{if } 15 \le s \le 17 \\[2ex]
1 - \left(\dfrac{20 - s}{10}\right)^2 & \text{if } 17 \le s \le 20.
\end{cases}
\tag{1.56}
$$

Note that $0 \le s \le 5$ corresponds to D_A in (1.55), $5 \le s \le 7$ to D_B and $7 \le s \le 12$ to D_C. Note also that, because San has a monopoly over the upper rectangle in Figure 1.9, $G(s)$ for $s \ge 12$ is not needed (but is included in (1.56) for the sake of completeness).

We are now in a position to obtain the rational reaction sets (which are defined by (1.40) with $(u, v) \in D$ in place of $u \in \Delta$, $v \in \Delta$). We begin with R_1.

From (1.51), (1.53) and (1.56), f_1 and f_2 are defined throughout D by $f_1(u, v) =$

$$f_1^A(u, v) = \frac{cu(v - u + 6)^2}{25} \qquad \text{if} \quad (u, v) \in D_A$$

$$f_1^B(u, v) = \frac{cu(2v - 2u + 7)}{5} \qquad \text{if} \quad (u, v) \in D_B \qquad (1.57a)$$

$$f_1^C(u, v) = \frac{cu(70 - (u - v + 6)^2)}{25} \qquad \text{if} \quad (u, v) \in D_C$$

and $f_2(u, v) =$

$$f_2^A(u, v) = \frac{cv(u - v + 4)(v - u + 16)}{25} \qquad \text{if} \quad (u, v) \in D_A$$

$$f_2^B(u, v) = \frac{cv(2u - 2v + 13)}{5} \qquad \text{if} \quad (u, v) \in D_B \qquad (1.57b)$$

$$f_2^C(u, v) = \frac{cv(30 + (u - v + 6)^2)}{25} \qquad \text{if} \quad (u, v) \in D_C.$$

From (1.57), if $(u, v) \in D_A$, so that $v + 1 \leq u \leq v + 6$, then

$$\frac{\partial f_1}{\partial u} = \frac{c}{25} (v - u + 6)(v - 3u + 6), \qquad (1.58)$$

which is positive for $u < (v + 6)/3$ and negative for $(v + 6)/3 < u < v + 6$. Thus f_1 has its maximum for $u \leq v + 6$ where $u = (v + 6)/3$. If $(v + 6)/3 \leq v + 1$, however, then the maximum for $v + 1 \leq u \leq v + 6$ will occur where $u = v + 1$. In other words, if the maximum of f_1 over the region D_A occurs at $u = u_A(v)$, then

$$u_A(v) \quad = \quad \begin{cases} \dfrac{1}{3}v + 2 & \text{if} \quad 0 \leq v \leq 3/2 \\[2mm] v + 1 & \text{if} \quad 3/2 \leq v \leq \alpha/4. \end{cases} \qquad (1.59a)$$

The curve $u = u_A$ is represented in Figure 1.8 by a thin solid line. If $(u, v) \in D_B$, so that $v - 1 \leq u \leq v + 1$, then $\partial f_1 / \partial u$ is positive for $u < (2v + 7)/4$ and negative for $u > (2v + 7)/4$; thus if the maximum of f_1 over the region D_B occurs at $u = u_B(v)$, then $u_B(v) =$

$$\begin{cases} v + 1 & \text{if} \quad 0 \leq v \leq 3/2 \\[2mm] \dfrac{1}{2}v + \dfrac{7}{4} & \text{if} \quad 3/2 \leq v \leq 11/2 \\[2mm] v - 1 & \text{if} \quad 11/2 \leq v \leq \alpha/4. \end{cases} \qquad (1.59b)$$

Similarly (Exercise 1.8), if the maximum of f_1 over the region D_C occurs where

$u = u_C(v)$, then $u_C(v) =$

$$\frac{1}{3}\left(2(v-6) + \sqrt{(v-6)^2 + 210}\right) \quad \begin{array}{ll} v-1 & \text{if} \quad 1 \le v \le 11/2 \\[2mm] & \text{if} \quad 11/2 \le v \le \alpha/4. \end{array} \qquad (1.59c)$$

The curves $u = u_C$ and $u = u_B$ are represented in Figure 1.8 by, respectively, a thick solid line and a line of medium thickness; $u = u_C$ appears to consist of straight line segments, but for $v \ge 11/2$ it has a slight downward curvature. If we use Figure 1.8 to locate the peak of $f_1(u,v)$ as a function of u for each $v \in D$, then R_1 is just the locus of the peaks; that is,

$$\max_{u} f_1(\bar{u}, v) = \max\left[f_1(u_A(v), v), f_1(u_B(v), v), f_1(u_C(v), v)\right], \qquad (1.60)$$

and Nan's rational reaction set is

$$R_1 = \{(u_A(v), v) \mid 0 \le v \le 3/2\}$$
$$\cup \{(u_B(v), v) \mid 3/2 \le v \le 11/2\}$$
$$\cup \{(u_C(v), v) \mid 11/2 \le v \le \alpha/4\}. \qquad (1.61)$$

To verify (1.61), suppose, for example, that $0 \le v \le 3/2$. Then f_1 is larger along $u = u_A(v)$ than elsewhere in D_A, including the boundary with D_B; but because this boundary is where f_1 is maximized on D_B (for $0 \le v \le 3/2$), f_1 must be larger along $u = u_A(v)$ than elsewhere in both D_A and D_B, including its boundary with D_C (when $1 \le v \le 3/2$); but because this boundary is where f_1 is maximized on D_C (for $1 \le v \le 3/2$), f_1 must be larger along $u = u_A(v)$ than anywhere else in D (for $0 \le v \le 3/2$). Similarly for $3/2 \le v \le \alpha/4$. The set R_1 is sketched in Figure 1.11 for $\alpha = 40$. Note in particular that Nan's rational reaction to $v = 0$ would be $u = 2$. Thus, even if San were to give away the product ($p_2 = 0$), Nan should still charge $p_1 = 8c$ for it, because she would still attract customers who reside south or west of the line $x + y = 4$.

Although R_1 is clearly *connected*—it's all in one piece—connectedness is not a general property of rational reaction sets. To see this, note that if $\alpha = 40$, and if the maxima of f_2 over the regions D_A, D_B and D_C occur where $v = v_A(u)$, $v = v_B(u)$ and $v = v_C(u)$, respectively, then from Exercise 1.9 $v_A(u) =$

$$\frac{1}{3}\left(2(u-6) + \sqrt{(u-6)^2 + 300}\right) \quad \begin{array}{ll} u-1 & \text{if} \quad 1 \le u \le 17/2 \\[2mm] & \text{if} \quad 17/2 \le u \le 10, \end{array} \qquad (1.62a)$$

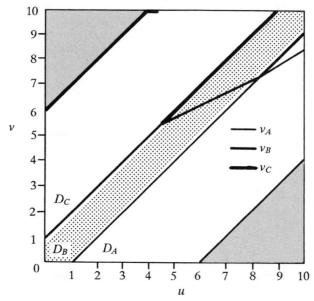

Figure 1.10   A set of points that contains R_2 when $\alpha = 40$.
The speckled region is D_B; the dark region lies outside D.

because $\max(0, u - 6) \leq v \leq u - 1$ for (u, v) in D_A; $v_B(u) =$

$$
\begin{cases}
u + 1 & \text{if} \quad 0 \leq u \leq 9/2 \\
\dfrac{1}{2}u + \dfrac{13}{4} & \text{if} \quad 9/2 \leq u \leq 17/2 \\
u - 1 & \text{if} \quad 17/2 \leq u \leq 10,
\end{cases}
\tag{1.62b}
$$

because $\max(0, u - 1) \leq v \leq u + 1$ for (u, v) in D_B; and $v_C(u) =$

$$
\begin{cases}
u + 6 & \text{if} \quad 0 \leq u \leq 4 \\
10 & \text{if} \quad 4 \leq u \leq 9/2, \\
u + 1 & \text{if} \quad 9/2 \leq u \leq 9,
\end{cases}
\tag{1.62c}
$$

because $u + 1 \leq v \leq u + 6$ for (u, v) in D_C. Note that $v = v_C(u)$ is not strictly a function but rather a multi-valued function; it is double-valued at $u = 9/2$, because $v = 11/2$ and $v = 10$ both maximize $f_2(9/2, v)$. The graphs of $v = v_A(u)$, $v = v_B(u)$ and $v = v_C(u)$ are depicted in Figure 1.10. It now follows from

$$
\max_{\bar{v}} f_2(u, \bar{v}) = \max[f_2(u, v_A(u)), \, f_2(u, v_B(u)), \quad f_2(u, v_C(u))]
\tag{1.63}
$$

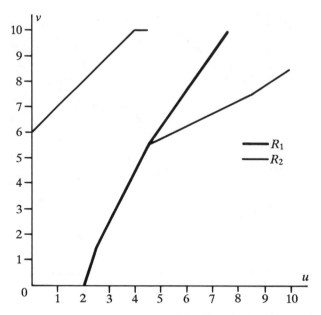

Figure 1.11   Rational reaction sets R_1 and R_2 for Store Wars when $\alpha = 40$.

and Figure 1.10 that San's rational reaction set is

$$R_2 = \{(u, v_C(u)) \mid 0 \le u \le 9/2\}$$

$$\cup \{(u, v_B(u)) \mid 9/2 \le u \le 17/2\}$$

$$\cup \{(u, v_A(u)) \mid 17/2 \le u \le 10\}. \qquad (1.64)$$

The set R_2 is sketched in Figure 1.11. Notice that because the maximum, $121c/10$, of

$$f_2(9/2, v) = \frac{c}{25}\left(30 + \left(v - \frac{21}{2}\right)^2\right) \qquad (1.65)$$

on $11/2 \le v \le 10$ occurs at both ends of the interval, and because $f_2(9/2, v)$ is less than $121c/10$ at every intermediate point, the rational reaction set is disconnected along $u = 9/2$; it contains both $(9/2, 11/2)$ and $(9/2, 10)$, but no points that lie between. Nevertheless, the two rational reaction sets still intersect one another at the (only) Nash equilibrium

$$(u^*, v^*) = \left(\frac{9}{2}, \frac{11}{2}\right). \qquad (1.66)$$

If this equilibrium is accepted as the solution of the noncooperative game then,

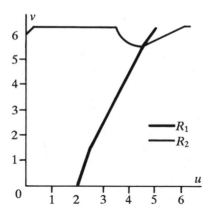

Figure 1.12   Rational reaction sets R_1 and R_2 for Store Wars when $\alpha = 8\sqrt{10}$.

from (1.50), Nan's price should be $p_1 = 18c$, and San's should be $22c$.

The result obtained in (1.66) is, of course, strongly dependent on the value we have chosen for α. Indeed $\alpha = 40$ has a critical property: it is the largest value of α for which a Nash equilibrium exists. As α increases beyond 40, the left endpoint of the right-hand segment of R_2 moves away from $D_B \cap D_C$ into the interior of D_B, so that $R_1 \cap R_2 = \varnothing$, the empty set. As α moves below 40, on the other hand, the same endpoint moves into the interior of D_C, and there is a second critical value, namely, $\alpha = 8\sqrt{10}$, at which R_2 becomes connected; for this value of α, R_1 and R_2 are sketched in Figure 1.12. These results are best left to the exercises, however; see Exercises 1.10–1.12. Then try Exercise 1.26.

1.6   STORE WARS II: A 3-PERSON, NONCOOPERATIVE GAME

We could easily turn Store Wars into a 3-player game by placing a third store, say Zan's, somewhere else in the subdivision, perhaps at the northeast corner; but it would significantly complicate the mathematics. Therefore, we shall devise an example of a 3-player game—Store Wars II—by supposing instead that the interior of some circular island is uninhabitable, so that all prospective customers for a certain product must reside on the island's circumference. To be specific, let us suppose that Nan's store is at the most northerly point of the island, and that Van's store is east of Nan's and one third of the way from Nan's store to the most southerly point of the island—which is also the location of the third store, Zan's; Nan is Player 1, Van Player 2 and Zan Player 3. Let a miles be the radius of this island, and let $a\theta$ denote distance along the circumference measured clockwise from the most northerly point. Then $0 \leq \theta < 2\pi$, and the location of a cus-

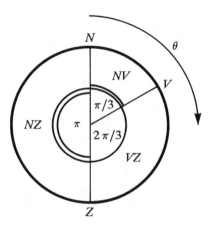

Figure 1.13   Map of battleground
for Store Wars II.

tomer's residence is determined by her θ-coordinate, with Nan's store at $\theta = 0$, Van's at $\theta = \pi/3$, and Zan's at $\theta = \pi$. The island is sketched in Figure 1.13.

We will suppose that customers are uniformly distributed along the circumference. Thus if random variable Θ denotes the θ-coordinate of a randomly chosen customer, and if G is Θ's cumulative distribution function, then

$$\text{Prob}(0 \leq \theta_1 < \Theta < \theta_2 < 2\pi) = \frac{(\theta_2 - \theta_1)}{2\pi}. \tag{1.67}$$

For example, if NV denotes the event that Θ lies between 0 and $\pi/3$, VZ the event that Θ lies between $\pi/3$ and π, and NZ the event that Θ lies between π and 2π (see Figure 1.13), then from (1.67) we have

$$\text{Prob}(NV) = \frac{1}{6}, \qquad \text{Prob}(VZ) = \frac{1}{3}, \qquad \text{Prob}(NZ) = \frac{1}{2}. \tag{1.68}$$

Let p_i denote Player i's price for the product in question, $i = 1, 2, 3$. Then we shall assume, as in Section 1.5, that the difference in prices between adjacent stores does not exceed the round-trip cost of travel between them. Thus if travel costs c dollars per mile, then

$$|p_1 - p_2| \leq 2a\pi c/3, \qquad |p_2 - p_3| \leq 4a\pi c/3, \qquad |p_1 - p_3| \leq 2a\pi c. \tag{1.69}$$

As in Section 1.5, there are lower and upper bounds on the prices:

$$\beta c \leq p_i \leq \alpha c, \qquad i = 1, 2, 3; \tag{1.70}$$

but again as in Section 1.5, we shall assume throughout that $\beta = 0$.

Now, let Θ the residential coordinate of the next customer (hence $0 \leq \Theta \leq 2\pi$); and suppose, as in Section 1.5, that this customer selects a store solely by weighing the price of the product against the cost of travel from her residence. Then, in view of (1.69), she will always buy from one of the two stores between which she lives. The customer will buy from Nan either if $p_1 + 2ac\Theta < p_2 + 2ac(\pi/3 - \Theta)$, in which case (1.69) implies $0 \leq \Theta < \pi/3$; or if $p_1 + 2ac(2\pi - \Theta) < p_3 + 2ac(\Theta - \pi)$, in which case (1.69) implies $\pi < \Theta < 2\pi$. In the first case, the customer resides in the sector denoted by NV in Figure 1.13, but the total cost of buying from Nan is less than the total cost of buying from Van; whereas in the second case, the customer resides in the sector denoted by NZ in Figure 1.13, but the total cost of buying from Nan is less than the total cost of buying from Zan. As usual, we need not worry about the event that, for example, $p_1 + 2ac\Theta$ equals $p_2 + 2ac(\pi/3 - \Theta)$ precisely, because the event is associated with probability zero. Thus the next customer will buy from Nan if

$$0 \leq \Theta \leq \frac{\pi}{6} + \frac{p_2 - p_1}{4ac} \quad \text{or} \quad \frac{3\pi}{2} + \frac{p_1 - p_3}{4ac} < \Theta < 2\pi. \tag{1.71}$$

From (1.67), the probability of this event is

$$\frac{1}{2\pi}\left(\frac{\pi}{6} + \frac{p_2 - p_1}{4ac}\right) + \frac{1}{2\pi}\left(2\pi - \left(\frac{3\pi}{2} + \frac{p_1 - p_3}{4ac}\right)\right) = \frac{1}{3} + \frac{p_2 - 2p_1 + p_3}{8ac\pi}. \tag{1.72a}$$

Similarly, the customer will buy from Van either if $p_2 + 2ac(\pi/3 - \Theta) < p_1 + 2ac\Theta$, in which case (1.69) implies $0 \leq \Theta < \pi/3$; or if $p_2 + 2ac(\Theta - \pi/3) < p_3 + 2ac(\pi - \Theta)$, in which case (1.69) implies $\pi/3 < \Theta < \pi$. The customer will therefore buy from Van if $\Theta > \pi/6 + (p_2 - p_1)/4ac$ in sector NV or $\Theta < 2\pi/3 + (p_3 - p_2)/4ac$ in sector VZ; i.e, if

$$\frac{\pi}{6} + \frac{p_2 - p_1}{4ac} < \Theta < \frac{2\pi}{3} + \frac{p_3 - p_2}{4ac};$$

and from (1.67), the probability of this event is

$$\frac{1}{4} + \frac{p_1 - 2p_2 + p_3}{8ac\pi}. \tag{1.72b}$$

A similar calculation (Exercise 1.14) shows that the next customer will buy from Zan if $2\pi/3 + (p_3 - p_2)/4ac < \Theta < 3\pi/2 + (p_1 - p_3)/4ac$, and that the probability of this event is

$$\frac{5}{12} + \frac{p_1 - 2p_3 + p_2}{8ac\pi}. \tag{1.72c}$$

Of course, the three probabilities in (1.72) must sum to 1.

For $i = 1, 2, 3$, let the random variable F_i denote Player i's payoff from the next customer; its expected value, $f_i = E[F_i]$, is Player i's reward. By analogy with (1.49), F_1 is p_1 if (1.71) is satisfied and zero otherwise, so that Nan's reward is simply p_1 times (1.72a). Likewise, Van's reward is simply p_2 times (1.72b), and Zan's reward is p_3 times (1.72c). It will be convenient, however, to make prices dimensionless by scaling them with respect to $8\pi ac$. Accordingly, we define strategies u, v and z for Nan, Van and Zan by

$$u = \frac{p_1}{8\pi ac}, \qquad v = \frac{p_2}{8\pi ac}, \qquad z = \frac{p_2}{8\pi ac}. \tag{1.73}$$

Then the players' rewards are

$$f_1(u,v,z) = 8ac\pi u \left(\frac{1}{3} + v - 2u + z\right), \tag{1.74a}$$

$$f_2(u,v,z) = 8ac\pi v \left(\frac{1}{4} + u - 2v + z\right), \tag{1.74b}$$

$$f_3(u,v,z) = 8ac\pi z \left(\frac{5}{12} + u - 2z + v\right); \tag{1.74c}$$

and from (1.69) and (1.70) with $\beta = 0$, the players' decision set is

$$D = \left\{(u,v,z) \mid 0 \le u,v,z \le \alpha/8a\pi, \ |u-v| \le \frac{1}{12}, |v-z| \le \frac{1}{6}, |u-z| \le \frac{1}{4}\right\}. \tag{1.75}$$

Extending (1.19) in an obvious way, rational reaction sets R_1, R_2 and R_3 for a 3-player, noncooperative game are defined by

$$R_1 = \left\{(u,v,z) \in D \mid f_1(u,v,z) = \max_{\bar{u}} f_1(\bar{u},v,z)\right\}, \tag{1.76a}$$

$$R_2 = \left\{(u,v,z) \in D \mid f_2(u,v,z) = \max_{\bar{v}} f_2(u,\bar{v},z)\right\}, \tag{1.76b}$$

$$R_3 = \left\{(u,v,z) \in D \mid f_3(u,v,z) = \max_{\bar{z}} f_3(u,v,\bar{z})\right\}. \tag{1.76c}$$

Furthermore, the strategy combination (u^*,v^*,z^*) is a Nash equilibrium if u^* is a best reply to (v^*,z^*), v^* a best reply to (u^*,z^*) and z^* a best reply to (u^*,v^*); i.e., if Player 1 has nothing to gain by selecting $u \ne u^*$ when Players 2 and 3 have already selected (v^*,z^*), Player 2 has nothing to gain by selecting $v \ne v^*$ when Players 1 and 3 have already selected (u^*,z^*) and Player 3 has nothing to gain by selecting $z \ne z^*$ when Players 1 and 2 have already selected (u^*,v^*). Thus (u^*,v^*,z^*) is a Nash equilibrium if $f_1(u^*,v^*,z^*) \ge f_1(u,v^*,z^*)$ for all $(u,v^*,z^*) \in D$, $f_2(u^*,v^*,z^*) \ge f_2(u^*,v,z^*)$ for all $(u^*,v,z^*) \in D$ and $f_3(u^*,v^*,z^*) \ge f_3(u^*,v^*,z)$ for all $(u^*,v^*,z) \in D$; or, which is the same thing, if

$$(u^*,v^*,z^*) \in R_1 \cap R_2 \cap R_3. \tag{1.77}$$

To obtain R_1, we must maximize f_1 as a function of u for all v and z, subject to the constraint that $(u,v,z) \in D$; to obtain R_2, we must maximize f_2 as a function of v for all u and z, subject to the same constraint; and similarly, to obtain R_3 we must maximize f_3 as a function of z for all u and v. In general, the rational reaction sets of a 3-player game are more difficult to calculate and visualize than those of a 2-player game, because they are sets of points in a 3-dimensional space. Fortunately, however, it is not always necessary to characterize them completely in order to find the points they have in common (the Nash equilibria). In the case of Store Wars II, it is straightforward to show that that if α in (1.70) is sufficiently large (which we assume), then the maximum of (1.74a) as a function of u occurs where

$$u = \frac{1}{4}\left(\frac{1}{3} + v + z\right), \tag{1.78a}$$

provided $(u,v,z) \in D$; that the maximum of (1.74b) as a function of v occurs where

$$v = \frac{1}{4}\left(\frac{1}{4} + u + z\right); \tag{1.78b}$$

and that the maximum of (1.74c) as a function of z occurs where

$$z = \frac{1}{4}\left(\frac{5}{12} + u + v\right), \tag{1.78c}$$

provided in each case that $(u,v,z) \in D$. Now, if (u^*,v^*,z^*) is a Nash equilibrium strategy combination, then (u^*,v^*,z^*) must belong to $R_1 \cap R_2 \cap R_3$. But if we regard (1.78) as a set of simultaneous linear equations, then it is easily shown (Exercise 1.15) that its unique solution is

$$(u^*,v^*,z^*) = \left(\frac{1}{6}, \frac{3}{20}, \frac{11}{60}\right); \tag{1.79}$$

and, furthermore, that this point belongs to D. Therefore $(u^*,v^*,z^*) \in R_1 \cap R_2 \cap R_3$, and (u^*,v^*,z^*) is the only point in $R_1 \cap R_2 \cap R_3$—provided, of course, that α is sufficiently large. We might therefore regard (1.79) as the solution of Store Wars II; in which case, Nan should charge $4ac\pi/3$ dollars, Van $6ac\pi/5$ dollars, and Zan $22ac\pi/15$ dollars for the product in question.

The concepts of rational reaction set and Nash equilibrium generalize in the obvious way to n-player noncooperative games. Let the players correspond to the integers between 1 and n, and let N be the set of players; i.e., $N = \{1,2,\ldots,n\}$. Let Player k's strategy be denoted by w^k, for all $k \in N$; thus, for example, in Store Wars II we have $w^1 = u$, $w^2 = v$ and $w^3 = z$. Possibly w^k is a vector; for example, in Four Ways we have $w^1 = (u_1,u_2)$ and $w^2 = (v_1,v_2)$. Let the vector

$$w = (w^1, w^2, \ldots, w^n) \tag{1.80}$$

be called the players' joint strategy combination. Note that w is a "vector of vectors"; if Player k controls s_k variables, so that w^k is an s_k-dimensional vector, then the dimension of w is $s_1 + s_2 + \cdots + s_n$. The players' rewards can now be written succinctly as $f_1(w), f_2(w), \ldots, f_n(w)$. Let $w\|\overline{w}^k$ denote the joint strategy combination that is identical to w except for Player k's strategy, which is $\overline{w}^k$; i.e., define

$$w\|\overline{w}^k = (w^1, \ldots, w^{k-1}, \overline{w}^k, w^{k+1}, \ldots, w^n); \tag{1.81}$$

thus, in particular, $w\|w^k = w$. Let the set of all feasible w—the decision set—be denoted by D. Then, for $k \in N$, Player k's rational reaction set is defined by

$$R_k = \left\{ w \in D \,|\, f_k(w) = \max_{\overline{w}^k} f_k(w\|\overline{w}^k) \right\} \tag{1.82}$$

of which (1.76) is a special case. Moreover, if we define $w\backslash w^k$ to be that part of the joint strategy combination which is not under the control of Player k, i.e., if we define

$$w\backslash w^k = (w^1, , \ldots, w^{k-1}, w^{k+1}, \ldots, w^n), \tag{1.83}$$

then

$$w^* \equiv \left((w^*)^1, (w^*)^2, \ldots, (w^*)^n \right) \in D \tag{1.84}$$

is a Nash equilibrium if, for all $k \in N$, Player k's $(w^*)^k$ is a best reply to the other players' $w^*\backslash(w^*)^k$; no player has an incentive to deviate from her Nash-equilibrium strategy if all the other players adhere to theirs. It now follows at once that w^* is a Nash equilibrium strategy combination if for any $\overline{w}$

$$f_k(w^*) \geq f_k(w^*\|\overline{w}^k), \qquad k \in N; \tag{1.85}$$

or, which is the same thing, if

$$w^* \in R_1 \cap R_2 \cap \cdots \cap R_n. \tag{1.86}$$

Furthermore, if (1.85) is satisfied with strict inequality (for $\overline{w}^k \neq (w^*)^k$), then we say that w^* is a *strong* Nash-equilibrium strategy combination; see, for example, Exercises 1.24, 1.27 and 1.30.

For games with more than three players, it is usually a difficult problem to calculate Nash equilibria and rational reaction sets (and even for 2- and 3- player games the problem need not be trivial). We will therefore not dwell on such cases. There do exist theorems on necessary conditions for Nash equilibria, however; see, for example, Vincent and Grantham (1981). These theorems enable one to eliminate points in D that are not equilibria; and remaining candidates can be tested for the Nash equilibrium property by applying definition (1.85), as in Exercise 1.16.

1.7   MAX-MIN STRATEGIES

Our studies of bimatrix games have revealed a difficulty with Nash equilibrium as a solution concept for noncooperative games: a game may have more than one equilibrium. In our studies of continous games, however, we have seen that a Nash equilibrium *can* be unique; in which case, is it not reasonable to regard it as the game's solution? Not necessarily. A further difficulty with our concept of Nash equilibrium is that we have had to assume complete information: every player must know every other player's reward function. But suppose that each player knows only her own reward function—what is then her best strategy? A possible answer involves the concept of max-min strategy, which we describe in this section.

Let us first define the players' *minimizing functions*, $m_1, m_2, \ldots, m_n$ by

$$m_k(w^k) = \min_{w \backslash w^k} f_k(w), \qquad k \in N. \tag{1.87}$$

For each value of w^k, Player k's minimizing function tells her the minimum value of her reward with respect to $w \backslash w^k$, i.e., the variables controlled by the other players. In particular, for a 2-player game we have

$$m_1(u) = \min_v f_1(u, v), \qquad m_2(v) = \min_u f_2(u, v). \tag{1.88}$$

Suppose, for example, that San is an intermediate or slow driver in Crossroads, for which Nan's reward function is

$$f_1(u, v) = \left(\epsilon + \frac{\tau_2}{2} - (\delta + \epsilon)v \right) u + \left(\epsilon - \frac{\tau_2}{2} \right) v - \epsilon - \frac{\tau_2}{2}, \tag{1.89}$$

from (1.16). Then because $\epsilon < \tau_2/2$, the coefficient of v in f_1, namely, $\epsilon - \tau_2/2 - (\delta + \epsilon)u$, is always negative, and so f_1 is minimized with respect to v by $v = 1$. Thus, from (1.88), Nan's minimizing function is given by

$$m_1(u) = f_1(u, 1) = (\tau_2/2 - \delta)u - \tau_2, \qquad \epsilon < \tau_2/2. \tag{1.90}$$

For $k \in N$, we now define a *max-min* strategy for Player k to be a w^k that maximizes $m_k(w^k)$; we denote this max-min strategy by $\tilde{w}^k$, and we refer to $\tilde{w}$ as a joint max-min strategy combination. In Crossroads with $\epsilon < \tau_2/2$, for example, it is clear from (1.90) that $\bar{u} = 0$ (always wait) is the unique max-min strategy for Nan if $\tau_2/2 < \delta$, whereas $\bar{u} = 1$ (always go) is the unique max-min strategy for Nan if $\tau_2/2 > \delta$. Thus (provided $\tau_2/2 \neq \delta$) Nan's max-min strategy when San is intermediate or slow is always a pure strategy: W if San is intermediate, G if San is slow. But a max-min strategy for a matrix game need not be a pure strategy. For example, in Crossroads with $\epsilon > \tau_2/2$ (whence $\delta > \tau_2/2$), it follows from (1.88)–(1.89) that

$$m_1(u) = \begin{cases} (\epsilon + \tau_2/2)(u - 1) & \text{if } (\delta + \epsilon)u \leq \epsilon - \tau_2/2 \\ (\tau_2/2 - \delta)u - \tau_2 & \text{if } (\delta + \epsilon)u > \epsilon - \tau_2/2, \end{cases} \tag{1.91}$$

so that Nan's unique max-min strategy when San is fast is the mixed strategy $\bar{u} = (\epsilon - \tau_2/2)/(\delta + \epsilon)$. A max-min strategy need not be unique, however; note that any strategy would be a max-min strategy for Nan if $\epsilon < \tau_2/2$, $\delta = \tau_2/2$, because m_1 would then be independent of u, from (1.90).

The concept of max-min strategy rests on the idea that, no matter which w^k is chosen, the other players will do their worst by making the reward f_k as small as possible—in fact equal to $m_k(w^k)$; and it responds by selecting the best of these worst rewards, namely, $m_k\left((\widetilde{w})^k\right)$. A max-min strategy is a fail-safe strategy. It is absolutely fail-safe when it is a pure strategy (see Exercise 1.17); and it is fail-safe on the average when it is a mixed strategy in a bimatrix game, or when the rewards in a continous game are expected values. But a max-min strategy is also in general a very pessimistic strategy, because if the other players do not know Player k's reward function, then how could they minimize it—except, perhaps, by chance? Not surprisingly, $\widetilde{w}$ rarely belongs to every player's rational reaction set and frequently belongs to no player's rational reaction set; see Exercise 1.19. But there is one important exception: if a 2-player game is zero-sum, ie., if

$$f_1(u,v) + f_2(u,v) = 0, \qquad \text{for all } (u,v) \in D, \tag{1.92}$$

then $\widetilde{w} \in R_1 \cap R_2$; see Exercise 1.18. In this very special case, there is no need to argue over the merits of max-min strategies versus Nash-equilibrium strategies because the two coincide. Such happy circumstances are rare, however, in game-theoretic modelling.

1.8   COMMENTARY

In Chapter 1 we have introduced the concepts of pure strategy, payoff matrix (Section 1.1), mixed strategy, rational reaction set and Nash equilibrium (Sections 1.3, 1.6). We have used them to analyze bimatrix games with two (Sections 1.1–1.3) or three (Section 1.4) pure strategies, as well as 2-person (Section 1.5) and 3-person (Section 1.6) continuous games. We have discovered that neither existence nor uniqueness of Nash equilibrium is assured in general; however, existence is assured for bimatrix games (if we allow mixed strategies). A proof that every bimatrix game has at least one Nash equilibrium strategy combination, based on Nash's (1951) application of the Brouwer fixed-point theorem to n-person games, appears in Owen (1982, pp. 127–128). Existence theorems do not tell us how to compute Nash equililbria, however, and we have seen that this task can be far from trivial—even for 2-player games.

Our treatment of Nash equilibrium, the central concept in noncooperative game theory, has been predicated on complete information; but the concept extends to games of *incomplete* information, in which players do not know their opponents' rewards but are able to quantify their feelings about them. Indeed there now exists a large body of work, which derives from Harsanyi (1967, 1968a, 1968b), on so-called Bayesian Nash equilibrium; see, for example, Rasmusen (1989) and references therein. But this literature is largely against the spirit and beyond the scope of our agenda, and so we have confined our treatment of incomplete information to the concept of max-min strategy (Section 1.7).

EXERCISES   1

1.1 Obtain the reward functions f_1, f_2 for the animals engaged in the Hawk-Dove contest of Section 1.2. Sketch the rational reaction sets (i) when ρ (reproductive value of territory) $> C$ (reproductive cost of injury) and (ii) when $\rho < C$. Find all Nash equilibria. How is this game related to Crossroads mathematically?

Hint: You can add or subtract the same number from every entry in the payoff matrices without altering the nature of the game.

1.2 Suppose that Crossroads is symmetric, with $\tau_1 = \tau = \tau_2$; and suppose, further, that both drivers are neither especially fast nor especially slow, i.e., $2\delta > \tau > 2\epsilon$. Show directly from the payoff matrices in Tables 1.1 and 1.2 that the pure strategy combinations GG and WW cannot be Nash equilibria. Thus WW cannot be chosen by two rational players, because if either selected W then the other would have an incentive to deviate from W; and similarly for GG.

1.3 Show that a pair of dominant strategies in a 2-player, noncooperative game is always the unique Nash-equilibrium strategy combination.

1.4 Show that (1.37) and (1.38) are special cases of (1.18).

1.5 Verify Tables 1.8 and 1.9.

Hint: The line joining $\big((2\sigma/(1 + \sigma), 0\big)$ to (α, β) in Figure 1.6 corresponds to equal coefficients; the point (α, β) corresponds to vanishing coefficients.

1.6 Verify Table 1.10.

1.7 Obtain (1.56). Deduce the probability density function g of the random variable $X + Y$ and verify that g is continuous.

1.8 Obtain (1.57) and (1.59).

1.9 Obtain (1.62).

1.10 Show that Store Wars has no Nash equilibrium point when $\alpha = 44$.

1.11 Find R_2 for Store Wars when $\alpha = 8\sqrt{10}$.

1.12 According to Figure 1.11, when $\alpha = 40$, there is a value of p_1 for which San's rational reaction to an increase in p_1 should be to lower her price. Does this make sense? Interpret.

1.13 How would the rational reaction sets sketched in Figures 1.11 and 1.12 differ if β were greater than zero in (1.45)?

1.14 Verify (1.72).

1.15 Verify that (1.79) is the solution of (1.78). Show that this point belongs to D defined by (1.75).

1.16 Verify by applying (1.85) that (1.79) is a Nash equilibrium for Store Wars II. Why is the price ceiling αc important in Store Wars, but unimportant in Store Wars II; or, if you prefer, why would letting $\alpha \to \infty$ in (1.70) have no effect?

1.17 Show that if Player 1 and Player 2 are rational, then their rewards from a bimatrix game can never be less than

$$\max_i \left\{ \min_j a_{ij} \right\}, \quad \max_j \left\{ \min_i b_{ij} \right\},$$

respectively, where A is Player 1's $(s_1 + 1) \times (s_2 + 1)$ payoff matrix, B is Player 2's payoff matrix and $0 \le i - 1 \le s_1, 0 \le j - 1 \le s_2$.

1.18 Show that for a 2-person, noncooperative, zero-sum game, a max-min strategy is always a Nash-equilibrium strategy, and vice versa.

1.19 Use Crossroads to establish that

   (i)   A 2-player game need not be zero-sum for a joint max-min strategy combination to be a Nash equilibrium.

   (ii)   A joint max-min strategy combination may lie in no player's rational reaction set.

   (iii)   Even if a joint max-min strategy combination lies in no player's rational reaction set, the combination may be equivalent to a Nash equilibrium in terms of the associated rewards.

1.20 Find all max-min strategies for Store Wars II, as described in Section 1.6.

1.21 Find all Nash equilibria of Store Wars II in the case where Zan's store is located at $\theta = 3\pi/2$ (as opposed to $\theta = \pi$).

1.22 Find all max-min strategies for Four Ways.

1.23 Find all max-min strategies for Store Wars in Section 1.5.

1.24 **(i)**   To allow for asymmetry between owner and intruder in a territorial contest, Maynard Smith (1982, p. 22) adds a third strategy, Bourgeois, to the Hawk-Dove game in Section 1.2. A Bourgeois plays Hawk if an owner but Dove if an intruder; thus Bourgeois, denoted by B, is a conditional strategy (like C in Four Ways). If, in a contest chosen at random, two contestants are equally likely to be owner or intruder, write down the payoff matrices for the resulting H–D–B game and show that BB is a strong Nash-equilibrium strategy combination if $\rho < C$.

   (ii)   How realistically is the asymmetry modelled if the game is still symmetric?

Hint for (i): You can show that B is a strong Nash-equilibrium strategy without computing f_1 or f_2.

1.25 The symmetric 2-player bimatrix game with payoff matrices

$$A = \begin{bmatrix} R & S \\ T & P \end{bmatrix}, \qquad B = \begin{bmatrix} R & T \\ S & P \end{bmatrix},$$

where

$$T > R > P > S, \qquad 2R > S + T,$$

is known in the literature of the social and biological sciences as the "prisoner's dilemma." Sketch the players' rational reactions sets and find all Nash equilibria.

1.26 Store Wars III is a noncooperative game of prices between two stores, whose potential customers are uniformly distributed along the line segment $0 \leq x \leq L$. The
first store is at $x = a$ and the second at $x = b$, where $0 \leq a < b \leq L$. Assuming
that the price difference does not exceed the cost of travel between the stores, i.e,
$|p_1 - p_2| \leq 2c(b - a)$, where p_i is Player i's price and c the unit cost of travel, sketch
the players' rational reaction sets and find all Nash equilibria (if any).

1.27 (i) Greater sophistication is added to the Hawk-Dove game of Section 1.2 by
defining a third strategy, R, for Retaliator (Maynard Smith, 1982, pp. 17–18).
A Retaliator always begins by displaying, but then escalates and prepares for
battle if her opponent escalates; thus R, like C in Four Ways or Bourgeois
in Exercise 1.24, is a conditional strategy. In confrontations between D and
R, the Retaliator will sometimes intuit that her opponent is a really a Dove
and exploit her by escalating. The probability that a Retaliator will secure a
disputed territory in such a confrontation is therefore of the form $(1 + \lambda)/2$,
where $\lambda > 0$ is small (and hence the probability that the Dove will secure it is
$(1 - \lambda)/2$, as opposed to 1/2 in Section 1.2). Write down the payoff matrices
for the resulting H–D–R game and show that RR is a strong Nash-equilibrium
strategy combination.

(ii) Is R the only Nash-equilibrium strategy?

1.28 A noncooperative, bimatrix game with three pure strategies has payoff matrices

$$A = \begin{bmatrix} -\lambda & \rho & -\rho \\ -\rho & -\lambda & \rho \\ \rho & -\rho & -\lambda \end{bmatrix}, \quad B = A^T,$$

where $|\lambda|$ is much smaller than ρ. What could this game model? Find all Nash-
equilibrium strategies (i) when $\lambda > 0$ and (ii) when $\lambda < 0$.

1.29 In Section 1.4 we assumed that the payoff associated with the strategy combination
$(0, 0, 0, 0)$, or CC, was identical to the payoff associated with the strategy combination $(1, 0, 1, 0)$, or GG; in both cases, the payoff was $-(\delta + \tau/2)$. In practice,
however, if Nan and San both selected pure strategy $C = (0, 0)$, then the time they
spent negotiating or intimidating each other might not be quite the same as if they
had both selected $G = (1, 0)$. Accordingly, let us denote the time by μ (instead
of δ); we would still expect it to exceed the dithering time associated with strategy
combination $(0, 1, 0, 1)$, or WW, and so (1.1) is replaced by

$$0 < \epsilon < \delta < \infty, \qquad 0 < \epsilon < \mu < \infty.$$

To distinguish this new set of circumstances from Four Ways (where $\mu = \delta$), we shall
refer to the game in which $\mu \neq \delta$ (but $\mu, \delta > \epsilon$) as Carrefour. Thus, because the
payoff associated with CC is now $-(\mu + \tau/2)$, the payoff matrices for Carrefour are

$$A = \begin{bmatrix} -\delta - \tau/2 & 0 & 0 \\ -\tau & -\epsilon - \tau/2 & -\tau \\ -\tau & 0 & -\mu - \tau/2 \end{bmatrix}, \quad B = A^T.$$

Find all Nash-equilibrium strategy combinations for Carrefour when

(i) $\delta = 3$, $\epsilon = 2$, $\mu = 4$, $\tau = 2$

(ii) $\delta = 4$, $\epsilon = 2$, $\mu = 3$, $\tau = 2$.

1.30   Show that $(1, 0)$ and $(0, 1)$ are both strong Nash-equilibrium strategy combinations in Crossroads.

1.31   How does relaxing the assumption $|p_1 - p_2| \leq 2c(b - a)$ in Store Wars III (Exercise 1.26) affect the existence of a unique Nash equilibrium?

2

Evolutionary Stability
& Other Criteria
for Equilibrium Selection

We discovered in Chapter 1 that a noncooperative game can have several Nash equilibria. If one of these equilibria is to be regarded as the solution of the game, then we must introduce criteria for distinguishing it from all the others. Three such criteria are compared in this chapter.

2.1 HARSANYI AND SELTEN'S CRITERION

A general theory of equilibrium selection has been developed by Harsanyi and Selten (1988). It is based on what its authors call the tracing procedure. The theory is elaborate, and to discuss it in depth would divert us too far from our goal; nevertheless, we shall at least suggest the thinking that underlies the theory. Some further details of the tracing procedure are given in an appendix to this chapter.

45

Accordingly, consider once more the game of Crossroads. For the sake of definiteness, let us suppose that

$$1 > \theta_1 > \theta_2 > \frac{1}{2}; \tag{2.1a}$$

or, which in view of (1.26) is exactly the same thing, that

$$2\delta > \tau_1 > \tau_2 > \delta - \epsilon. \tag{2.1b}$$

You will recall that τ_1 is the time it takes our northbound driver, called Ned in this chapter, to traverse the junction unimpeded; and that τ_2 is the corresponding transit time for our southbound driver, called Sed in this chapter. Because $\tau_1/2 < \delta$ and $\tau_2/2 < \delta$ from (2.1), neither driver is slow. Let us also suppose that both players know there are three Nash equilibria; and that both are attempting, *without communicating with one another,* to choose a strategy that will make their joint selection a Nash equilibrium.

The two players might achieve their goal by means of the following thought experiment. Let each player guess what is best for the other; specifically, let Ned guess that Sed should select $v = q$, and let Sed guess that Ned should select $u = p$. Then, because Ned is trying to think like a Sed when he selects q for him, and because Sed is trying to think like a Ned when he selects p for him, it is not unreasonable to regard the strategy combination (p, q) as a first *tentative* solution of the game (even if it lies in neither player's rational reaction set). Furthermore, let Ned be aware (for whatever reason) that $u = p$ is the choice that Sed would (tentatively) consider best for him, and let Sed be aware that $v = q$ is the choice that Ned would consider best for him; thus it is common knowledge that (p, q) is the tentative solution. It would be quite unreasonable to regard (p, q) as the firm solution, however, because the u that Sed picks for Ned cannot possibly be as good as the u that Ned would pick for himself; and similarly for Sed. The tentative solution must therefore be revised. How should Ned and Sed revise it?

For the sake of definiteness, let us suppose that

$$1 > \theta_1 > p > 0, \qquad 1 > \theta_2 > q > 0; \tag{2.2}$$

thus, from Figure 1.5, (p, q) is below, and to the left of, both R_1 and R_2. Because $(1, q)$ is in R_1, Ned's best reply to Sed's tentative selection, $v = q$, is $u = 1$; likewise, because $(p, 1)$ is in R_2, Sed's best reply to Ned's tentative selection, $u = p$, is $v = 1$. Does this mean that the players should switch from (p, q) to $(1, 1)$? No, this would be too drastic a correction, because it would thrust each player from a strategy combination that lies below his rational reaction set to a strategy combination that lies above it. On the other hand, it does entice us to believe that Ned should edge toward R_1, and that Sed should edge toward R_2, in the direction of $(1, 1)$. Let us therefore suppose that, without communicating (purely by virtue of a mutual thought experiment), Ned and Sed revise their tentative solution by displacing (u, v) along the straight line that joins (p, q) to $(1, 1)$.

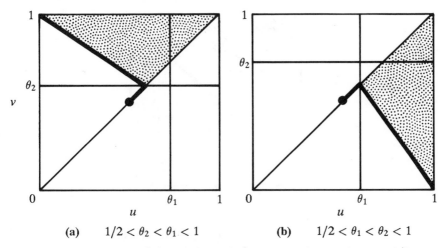

(a) $1/2 < \theta_2 < \theta_1 < 1$ **(b)** $1/2 < \theta_1 < \theta_2 < 1$

Figure 2.1.   The result of the players' thought experiment when $p = 1/2 = q$.

Let us suppose that Ned and Sed perturb their tentative solution a fraction t of the distance between (p,q) and $(1,1)$, so that their new tentative solution is at the point $\big(p + t(1-p), q + t(1-q)\big)$. A repetition of their thought experiment will now convince them that they should continue to move along the line joining (p,q) to $(1,1)$ if t is sufficiently small; or, in view of (2.2), if

$$t < \min(t_1, t_2), \tag{2.3}$$

where we define

$$t_1 = \frac{\theta_2 - q}{1 - q}, \qquad t_2 = \frac{\theta_1 - p}{1 - p}. \tag{2.4}$$

Let Ned and Sed perform further repetitions of their fictitious experiment, increasing the value of t continuously. Provided that (2.3) is satisfied, they will continue to perturb in the direction of $(1,1)$. At $t = \min(t_1, t_2)$, however, the tentative solution will reach either R_1 or R_2, according to whether $t_1 < t_2$ or $t_1 > t_2$. Then the player whose rational reaction set has been reached no longer has a single best reply to the other player's (revised) tentative solution; rather, any of his strategies is a best reply. This multiplicity of best replies does not persist, however; t need be increased only infinitesimally beyond $\min(t_1, t_2)$ for the player in question once more to have a single best reply (but 0 instead of 1).

To make things a little clearer, let us suppose that

$$p = \frac{1}{2} = q. \tag{2.5}$$

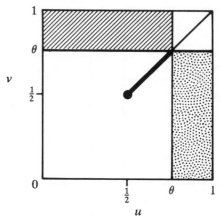

Figure 2.2   The result of the players' thought
experiment when $p = 1/2 = q$, $\theta_1 = \theta = \theta_2$.

Thus the tentative initial guess is at the point (1/2, 1/2), and each player believes
that the other is equally likely to use either of his two pure strategies. In view of
(2.1a), we have $t_1 < t_2$, or $\min(t_1, t_2) = t_1$, so that Ned's rational reaction set is
first to be reached, at the point (θ_2, θ_2); see Figure 2.1(a), where the path traced
out by the thought experiment is denoted by a solid black line. At (θ_2, θ_2), $v = 1$
is still Sed's unique best reply; but any u such that $0 \leq u \leq 1$ is a best reply for
Ned. Thus, if the players continue their train of thought, any $(u, 1)$ could replace
$(1, 1)$ as their target point, as indicated by the shaded triangle in Figure 2.1(a).
As soon as the tentative solution shifts into this triangle, however, Ned has again
a unique best reply, namely, $u = 0$; whereas Sed's best reply remains $v = 1$. Thus
the players would move toward $(0, 1)$. This point lies in both R_1 and R_2, and is
therefore a Nash equilibrium. The fictitious experiment has selected $(0, 1)$ as
the solution of Crossroads—assuming, of course, that $\theta_1 > \theta_2$.

The briefest of glances at Figure 2.1(b) shows that if the order of the sub-
scripts 1 and 2 in (2.1) were reversed, then the thought process would select (1, 0)
as the solution of the game instead. Thus, according to the theory of Harsanyi
and Selten, if there is no reason to suppose that either driver should prefer one
pure strategy to the other at the outset ($p = 1/2 = q$), then the solution of
Crossroads is that the slower driver should defer to the faster driver.[1]

At first sight, this solution appears eminently reasonable; and there is certainly nothing wrong with (2.5). Nevertheless, neither player may have reason
to suppose that his opponent is either faster or slower than he himself; in which

---

[1]   We have not, however, obtained this solution quite by the method that Harsanyi and
Selten advocate; for details of their tracing procedure, see the appendix to this chapter.

case, he should probably assume that $\tau_1 = \tau_2 = \tau$, say. Then the game is symmetric; and, by analogy with (1.42), it is convenient to define

$$\theta = \frac{2\epsilon + \tau}{2\epsilon + 2\delta} \tag{2.6}$$

(which is less than 1 because $\tau/2 < \delta$). Now $\theta_1 = \theta_2 = \theta$; and a glance at Figure 2.2 shows that the fictitious experiment would bring the players to the mixed-strategy Nash equilibrium at (θ, θ).

Unfortunately, we shall see in the next section that this equilibrium has an undesirable property.

2.2 KALAI AND SAMET'S CRITERION

Recall that (u^*, v^*) is a Nash equilibrium when, if Player 1 adheres to u^*, then Player 2 cannot increase his reward by selecting a strategy other than v^*; and, if Player 2 adheres to v^*, then Player 1 cannot increase his reward by selecting a strategy other than u^*. Thus (θ, θ) is a Nash equilibrium of the symmetric version of Crossroads because Ned has no better choice than θ if Sed selects θ, and vice versa. Now, let us concede that it is somehow possible to select a mixed strategy; and let us suppose that Sed really wants to select θ, but because of human frailty instead selects $\theta + z$, where $|z|$ is exceedingly small—as small as you please—but not actually zero. In other words, the shaded sector of the disk beneath the spinning arrow in Figure 1.2 is marginally bigger or smaller than he intended it to be. Then $u = \theta$ is no longer a best reply for Ned; rather, $u = 1$ is his best reply if $z < 0$, whereas $u = 0$ is his best reply if $z > 0$. Similar considerations apply, of course, to Sed.

Let the set of all points to which an equilibrium strategy combination, say (u^*, v^*), is a best reply be known as that equilibrium's *domain of stability;* and denote this domain of stability by $S((u^*, v^*))$. To be quite precise: (u, v) belongs to $S((u^*, v^*))$ if, and only if, for *all* (u, v) in $S((u^*, v^*))$,

$$f_1(u^*, v^*) \geq f_1(u, v^*) \tag{2.7a}$$

and

$$f_2(u^*, v^*) \geq f_2(u^*, v); \tag{2.7b}$$

where, on using (1.27) with $\tau_1 = \tau_2 = \tau$ and $\theta_1 = \theta_2 = \theta$, f_1 is defined by

$$f_1(u, v) = (\delta + \epsilon)\{(\theta - v)u - \theta(1 + v)\} + 2\epsilon v \tag{2.8a}$$

and, by virtue of symmetry, f_2 is defined by

$$f_2(u, v) = f_1(v, u) = (\delta + \epsilon)\{(\theta - u)v - \theta(1 + u)\} + 2\epsilon u, \tag{2.8b}$$

for $0 \leq u, v \leq 1$. Then the trouble with the equilibrium (θ, θ) is that its domain of stability consists purely of itself; i.e.,

$$S((\theta, \theta)) = \{(\theta, \theta)\}. \tag{2.9}$$

On the other hand, the domain of stability of the equilibrium $(1, 0)$ is the whole of the speckled rectangle in Figure 2.2 (including its boundary); i.e.,

$$S((1, 0)) = \{(u, v) \mid \theta \leq u \leq 1, \quad 0 \leq v \leq \theta\}. \tag{2.10}$$

Similarly, the domain of stability of the equilibrium $(0, 1)$ is the whole of the striped rectangle in Figure 2.2 (again including its boundary); i.e.,

$$S((0, 1)) = \{(u, v) \mid 0 \leq u \leq \theta, \quad \theta \leq v \leq 1\}. \tag{2.11}$$

Thus the equilibria at $(1, 0)$ and $(0, 1)$ do not have the awkward property that if a player makes a small mistake in calculating his Nash-equilibrium strategy, but the other player does not, then the latter's strategy is no longer a best reply to the former's.

More formally, following Kalai and Samet (1984), we say that a Nash equilibrium is *persistent* if its domain of stability contains a neighbourhood of the equilibrium—if we can draw a circle of radius z, center the equilibrium, such that the intersection of the circle's interior with the square $\{(u, v) \mid 0 \leq u, v \leq 1\}$ lies completely inside the equilibrium's domain of stability. It does not matter how small the circle is, just so long as its radius is bigger than zero. Thus $(1, 0)$ and $(0, 1)$ are both persistent equilibria; indeed, in either case, the radius z of the circle in question can be as large as θ. But (θ, θ) is not a persistent equilibrium, because no such z exists.

Kalai and Samet suggest that we might distinguish among Nash equilibria by eliminating those that are not persistent. This alternative theory of equilibrium selection would therefore suggest that, in the symmetric version of Crossroads, $(1, 0)$ and $(0, 1)$ are both acceptable as equilibria, whereas (θ, θ) is not.

To recapitulate: If we apply the theory of Harsanyi and Selten to the symmetric version of Crossroads, then we select an equilibrium that is not persistent. If, on the other hand, we apply the theory of Kalai and Samet, then we do not know whether $(1, 0)$ or $(0, 1)$ should be the solution of the game. We must therefore decide whether persistence is a desirable property; and if so, then we must somehow break the tie between $(1, 0)$ and $(0, 1)$. Any suggestions?

2.3   MAYNARD SMITH'S CRITERION

While you are still pondering this dilemma, we shall make matters even more intriguing by introducing yet another criterion for equilibrium selection, our third. As in Section 2.2, we will discuss the criterion for the symmetric version of Crossroads.

Suppose that the following thoughts occur to Ned, who has three Nash-equilibrium strategies, namely, $u^* = 0$, $u^* = \theta$ and $u^* = 1$. From Table 1.5, $u = 1$ is best for Ned if—and only if—Sed selects Nash-equilibrium strategy $v^* = 0$. But why should Sed select $v = 0$? No reason at all. On the other hand, if Sed is to select from only three Nash-equilibrium strategies, namely, $v^* = 0$, $v^* = \theta$ and $v^* = 1$, and if Ned doesn't know which strategy Sed will pick, then Ned might as well hope that Sed will choose $v^* = 0$. So let Ned select $u^* = 1$.

Now suppose that Ned's thoughts have also occurred to Sed, who is also rational. Then, clearly, Sed will select strategy $v^* = 1$, which is his best strategy if—and only if—Ned selects $u^* = 0$. But, of course, Ned does not select $u^* = 0$, and Sed does not select $v^* = 0$; rather, they select in this way the strategy combination $(1, 1)$. The associated reward is

$$f_1(1, 1) = -\tau/2 - \delta = f_2(1, 1). \tag{2.12}$$

We don't have only one Ned, however, nor only one Sed; rather, we have a huge population of Neds and Seds, all confronting one another across 4-way junctions, all day long, day in, day out, all over the land. All of these Neds and Seds are rational. So why shouldn't the thoughts that have just occurred to our Ned and Sed occur to all of them? No reason at all. So before very long we have a huge population of Neds and Seds, all of whom are playing strategy 1. Indeed there is no longer any reason to distinguish between players by calling one Ned and the other Sed, and so we shall refer to them all as Ed.

Then suddenly, one day, it occurs to an Ed that, if everyone but he is playing strategy 1, then there is no longer any uncertainty about the strategy his opponent will choose. Because nobody but this particular Ed has had this brainwave, the next Ed he meets is bound to select $v^* = 1$. Now, the trouble with Nash equilibrium arises because players in a noncooperative game do not know for sure which Nash-equilibrium strategy their opponent will select. All of a sudden, however, the requisite information is available to an Ed; because, on the day when he has his brainwave, his reward function reduces to

$$f_1(u, v) = f_1(u, 1) = (\tau/2 - \delta)u - \tau. \tag{2.13}$$

Because $\tau < 2\delta$, $f_1(u, 1)$ is maximized by selecting $u = 0$. Does this mean that the Ed should begin to play $u = 0$? After all, isn't $(0, 1)$ a Nash equilibrium?

It is true that $(0, 1)$ is a Nash equilibrium; but playing $u = 0$ is a rational long-term strategy only if Ed is sure that his next opponent will adhere to $v = 1$. But if one Ed has had this brainwave (and there are so many Eds on the road that, sooner or later, one of them is bound to have the brainwave), do you think he can keep it to himself? Not likely. You know how word gets around. Before very long, all the Eds in the world will have figured out that if everyone else is selecting strategy 1, then they would do better to select strategy 0; 0 is a better reply than 1 to strategy 1 because (from a Ned's point of view)

$$f_1(0,1) - f_1(1,1) = \delta - \tau/2 > 0, \tag{2.14a}$$

or, which is exactly the same thing (but from a Sed's point of view),

$$f_2(1,0) - f_2(1,1) = \delta - \tau/2 > 0. \tag{2.14b}$$

But then everyone will be playing strategy 0. Thus the next strategy combination selected will be, not (0, 1), but rather (0, 0); and the associated reward will be

$$f_1(0,0) = -\tau/2 - \epsilon = f_2(0,0). \tag{2.15}$$

Because $\epsilon < \delta$, we have to admit that the reward associated with (0, 0) is greater than that associated with (1, 1). But the strategy combination (1, 1) did not persist, because an Ed had a brainwave, word got around, and before very long the whole world had evolved to (0, 0). Of course, we should never have expected the world to remain at (1, 1), because (1, 1) is not a Nash equilibrium; indeed it doesn't lie in either player's rational reaction set. Likewise, (0, 0) lies in neither player's rational reaction set, and so we don't expect the world to remain at (0, 0); it is just as inevitable that some Ed somewhere will try something else as it was when the world stood at (1, 1). This Ed already knows, however, that neither $u^* = 1$ nor $u^* = 0$ is a decent long-term strategy. But $u^* = 0$, $u^* = \theta$ and $u^* = 1$ are his *only* Nash-equilibrium strategies. Therefore, out of sheer desperation, Ed will select $u^* = \theta$.

Because everyone else is playing $u^* = 0$, our Ed's reward will be

$$f_1(\theta,0) = -(1 - \theta)(\epsilon + \tau/2). \tag{2.16}$$

In the usual way, because

$$f_1(\theta,0) - f_1(0,0) = \theta(\epsilon + \tau/2) > 0, \tag{2.17}$$

it won't be long before word gets around that θ is a better reply to 0 than 0 is, and it won't be much longer before all the Eds in the world are playing it. The world is now at (θ, θ). Thus every Ed in the world who is contemplating strategy u can safely assume that his opponent will select strategy θ; in which case, his reward function reduces to

$$f_1(u,\theta) = -(\delta + \tau/2)\theta = f_2(\theta,u), \tag{2.18}$$

which is independent of u; i.e.,

$$f_1(u,\theta) = f_1(\theta,\theta) = f_2(\theta,\theta) = f_2(\theta,u) \tag{2.19}$$

for all values of u, $0 \le u \le 1$. No strategy can yield a higher reward against an opponent who selects θ than $u = \theta$ itself yields.

Suppose, however, that an Ed decides, in the usual way, to start playing a different Nash-equilibrium strategy from θ, say $u^* = 1$. Because $f_1(1,\theta) = f_1(\theta,\theta)$, this Ed does no better against an opponent who selects θ than by selecting θ himself. On the other hand, this Ed does no worse; and he may therefore be tempted to continue selecting $u^* = 1$. What happens now? Will 1 become fashionable? Not likely! If 1 begins to catch on, then sooner or later this Ed will meet another Ed who is using strategy 1, and Ed's reward from this encounter will be $f_1(1, 1)$. If Ed had stuck to using θ then his reward would have been $f_1(\theta, 1)$. But

$$f_1(\theta, 1) - f_1(1, 1) = (1 - \theta)(\delta - \tau/2), \qquad (2.20)$$

which is positive, because $\theta < 1$, $\tau < 2\delta$. Thus, although a player who switches from θ to 1 will do precisely as well against an opponent who still uses θ, he will fare worse against an opponent who also has switched from θ to 1; therefore, switching from θ to 1 is a bad idea. Similarly, because of (2.17), it is a bad idea to switch from θ to the other Nash-equilibrium strategy, namely, 0. More generally, because

$$f_1(\theta, u) - f_1(u, u) = (\delta + \epsilon)(\theta - u)^2 > 0 \qquad (2.21)$$

unless $u = \theta$, it would be irrational for an individual to switch from θ to any other strategy. In other words, once the world has arrived at the strategy combination (θ, θ), the world will stay at (θ, θ). It thus appears that the Nash equilibrium (θ, θ) has a measure of long-term stability, which the other two Nash equilibria do not possess. We shall refer to a strategy that is stable in this sense as *uninvadable*. Thus θ is an uninvadable strategy for Crossroads, whereas 0 and 1 are invadable.

The concept of uninvadability yields a further criterion for distinguishing between Nash equilibria: eliminate strategies that are invadable. In the game we have just considered, however, there is complete symmetry between any two players. The model cannot distinguish between them; or, if you prefer, there are no grounds whatsoever for calling one player Ned and the other one Sed. Therefore, any Nash equilibrium (u^*, v^*) that the whole world adopts must show symmetry also between strategies; i.e., $u^* = v^*$. Thus our latest criterion would eliminate the Nash equilibria $(0, 1)$ and $(1, 0)$ purely on the grounds that symmetry between players requires symmetry between strategies, because a strategy cannot be uninvadable unless first of all it is universally adoptable. But this symmetry argument provides only a necessary condition for uninvadability; a sufficient condition is provided by (2.21).

To define the concept of uninvadability more formally, first note that, because of the symmetry, i.e., because $f_2(u, v) = f_1(v, u)$, the reward to a player who selects u against a player who selects v is always

$$f(u, v) = (\delta + \epsilon)\{(\theta - v)u - \theta(1 + v)\} + 2\epsilon v, \qquad (2.22)$$

from (2.8); there is no need for a suffix 1 or 2, and so we drop it.[2] Then strategy u^* is uninvadable if, in a large population of players who almost all select it, u^*

---

[2]   This symmetry between the players' rewards does not, of course, imply $f(u, v) = f(v, u)$. Indeed it is clear from (2.22) that $f(u, v) - f(v, u) = (u - v)\tau \neq 0$ for $u \neq v$.

yields a greater reward than any "deviant" strategy, say v, that might instead be selected by the diminutive remainder of the population. One discerns an echo of Kant's categorical imperative to behave in such a way that, if everyone did so, then each would benefit; because it is broadly true that the player who selects an uninvadable strategy behaves in such a way that, if virtually everyone did so, then anyone who failed to do so would fail to benefit.

It is only broadly true, however; and it cannot be too strongly emphasized that uninvadability can crucially depend on the assumption that a deviant strategy is uniformly adopted by the diminutive remainder in the previous paragraph—or, which amounts to the same thing, that if there are several deviant strategies then they are adopted at different times (as in the narration above). To see this, and at the same time make our definition more precise, let us temporarily assume that there are m deviant strategies, say $v_1, v_2, \ldots, v_m$; subsequently we shall assume that $m = 1$. Let $1 - p$ be the proportion of the population that selects the uninvadable strategy u^*, let p_k be the proportion that selects deviant strategy v_k and let V be the strategy selected by a player's next opponent. Then V is a random variable, with sample space $\{v | 0 \leq v \leq 1\}$; and, in the absence of any further information, a player's probability distribution over his next opponent is given by

$$\text{Prob}(V = u^*) = 1 - p, \tag{2.23a}$$

$$\text{Prob}(V = v_k) = p_k, \quad k = 1, 2, \ldots, m, \quad \sum_{k=1}^{m} p_k = p, \tag{2.23b}$$

where p is a very small positive number (whence so are $p_1, p_2, \ldots, p_m$).

If V is a random variable, then so is $f(u^*, V)$. Thus $f(u^*, V)$ is a payoff, not a reward; but we can convert it into a reward, which we shall denote by R, if we calculate its expected value over the distribution of V. Accordingly, the reward of a player who selects u^* is

$$\begin{aligned}
R(u^*) = E[f(u^*, V)] &= f(u^*, u^*) \cdot \text{Prob}(V = u^*) \\
&\quad + \sum_{k=1}^{m} f(u^*, v_k) \cdot \text{Prob}(V = v_k) \\
&= (1 - p)f(u^*, u^*) + \sum_{k=1}^{m} p_k f(u^*, v_k);
\end{aligned} \tag{2.24a}$$

whereas the reward of a player who selects deviant strategy v_j is

$$R(v_j) = E[f(v_j, V)] = f(v_j, u^*) \cdot \text{Prob}(V = u^*) + \sum_{k=1}^{m} f(v_j, v_k) \cdot \text{Prob}(V = v_k)$$

$$= (1 - p)f(v_j, u^*) + \sum_{k=1}^{m} p_k f(v_j, v_k).$$

$$(2.24b)$$

Thus

$$R(u^*) - R(v_j) = (1 - p)\{f(u^*, u^*) - f(v_j, u^*)\} + \sum_{k=1}^{m} p_k\left(f(u^*, v_k) - f(v_j, v_k)\right),$$

$$j = 1, 2, \ldots, m. \qquad (2.25)$$

But p is much less than 1, and so are $p_1, p_2, \ldots, p_m$. Thus u^* is an uninvadable strategy if

$$f(u^*, u^*) > f(v_j, u^*), \qquad j = 1, 2, \ldots, m, \qquad (2.26a)$$

because the first term in (2.25) then dominates the sum of the last m terms. If there exists j such that

$$f(v_j, u^*) = f(u^*, u^*), \qquad (2.26b)$$

however, so that the first term in (2.25) is identically zero, then u^* is an uninvadable strategy if

$$f(u^*, v_k) > f(v_j, v_k), \qquad k = 1, 2, \ldots, m, \qquad (2.26c)$$

for all such j. On the other hand, u^* is clearly not an uninvadable strategy if

$$f(u^*, u^*) < f(v_j, u^*) \qquad (2.27)$$

for any $j = 1, 2, \ldots, m$. Of particular interest is the case where $m = 1$ (and hence $p_1 = p$), so that the deviant strategy is uniformly adopted by a diminutive fraction p of the population; then we prefer to denote the single deviant strategy by v, rather than v_1, and sufficient conditions (2.26) for an uninvadable strategy become

$$\text{EITHER} \quad f(u^*, u^*) > f(v, u^*) \qquad (2.28a)$$
$$\text{OR} \quad f(u^*, u^*) = f(v, u^*) \quad \text{AND} \quad f(u^*, v) > f(v, v) \quad (2.28b)$$

for all $v \neq u^*$. Crudely speaking, (2.28a) says that v-strategists cannot even enter a population of u^*-strategists; whereas (2.28b) says that v-strategists can enter, but they cannot proliferate. An equivalent statement of these conditions is

$$f(u^*, u^*) \geq f(v, u^*) \quad \text{for all } v \neq u^* \qquad (2.29a)$$
$$\text{AND EITHER} \quad f(u^*, u^*) > f(v, u^*) \qquad (2.29b)$$
$$\text{OR} \quad f(u^*, v) > f(v, v) \quad \text{for all } v \neq u^*, \qquad (2.29c)$$

from which it is clear that an uninvadable strategy is of necessity a Nash-equilibrium strategy (Exercise 2.2). We stress that replacing (2.26) by (2.28) or (2.29) does not necessarily limit the number of deviant strategies to one; but it does require that alternative deviant strategies be adopted sequentially. For an illustration of how to analyze simultaneously adopted deviant strategies, see Section 2.5.

We should also stress that the principal difference between $m = 1$ (uniform deviation) and $m > 1$ (multiple deviation) is the difference between (2.29c) and (2.26c). If (2.28a) is satisfied for all $v \neq u^*$ (including in particular $v_1, \ldots, v_m$), then (2.26a) is also satisfied; however, (2.29c) does not imply (2.26c), as the following paragraph will illustrate. If, for all $v \neq u^*$, (2.28a)—and hence (2.26a)—is satisfied, then u^* possesses a stronger measure of uninvadability than if only (2.28b) were satisfied, because u^* is then resistant to multiple deviation (provided of course that the total probability of deviation, namely, $p = p_1 + \cdots + p_m$ is still small). Accordingly, if (2.28a) is satisfied for all $v \neq u^*$, then we say that u^* is *strongly* uninvadable. It is also useful to be able to distinguish between uninvadable strategies and those that merely satisfy (2.29a); and we will follow Axelrod (1984) by saying that if (2.29a) is satisfied, then u^* is *collectively stable*. To say that u^* is collectively stable is really to say neither more nor less than that u^* is a symmetric Nash-equilibrium strategy; nevertheless, the terminology is useful, because it signifies at once that the game is played between an individual and the rest of a population (as opposed to between specific individuals). Likewise, to say that u^* is strongly uninvadable is merely to say that (u^*, u^*) is a strong Nash-equilibrium strategy combination (Exercise 2.2); but the new terminology is again more evocative of the game's inherent symmetry. Obviously, every strongly uninvadable strategy is also uninvadable, and every uninvadable strategy is also collectively stable.

To illustrate the effects of multiple deviation versus uniform deviation on a strategy that is uninvadable, but not strongly uninvadable, let us now apply (2.26)–(2.28) to Crossroads in the case where $\theta < 1$ (for $\theta > 1$, see Exercise 2.1). From (2.22), $\theta < 1$ implies both $f(1, 1) < f(0, 1)$ and $f(0, 0) < f(1, 0)$; whence (2.27) implies that neither $u^* = 1$ nor $u^* = 0$ is an uninvadable strategy. We are not surprised: neither $(0, 0)$ nor $(1, 1)$ is a Nash equilibrium. Thus the only candidate for uninvadable strategy is the remaining Nash-equilibrium strategy, namely, $u^* = \theta$. The two deviant strategies are, say, $v_1 = 0$ and $v_2 = 1$; whence (2.22) implies that (2.26b) is satisfied for both $j = 1$ and $j = 2$. Thus (2.26c) would require both

$$f(\theta, 0) > f(0, 0), \qquad f(\theta, 1) > f(0, 1) \qquad\qquad (2.30a)$$

(for $j = 1$) and

$$f(\theta, 0) > f(1, 0), \qquad f(\theta, 1) > f(1, 1) \qquad\qquad (2.30b)$$

(for $j = 2$). Although $f(\theta, 0) > f(0, 0)$ and $f(\theta, 1) > f(1, 1)$ from (2.21), it is clear from (2.22) that $f(\theta, 1) < f(0, 1)$ and $f(\theta, 0) < f(1, 0)$; thus (2.30a) and (2.30b) are false. Indeed (2.25) implies

$$
\begin{aligned}
R(\theta) - R(0) &= p_1\big(f(\theta, 0) - f(0, 0)\big) + p_2\big(f(\theta, 1) - f(0, 1)\big) \\
&= \theta(\delta + \epsilon)\,(\theta p_1 - (1 - \theta)p_2), \\
R(\theta) - R(1) &= p_1\big(f(\theta, 0) - f(1, 0)\big) + p_2\big(f(\theta, 1) - f(1, 1)\big) \\
&= (1 - \theta)(\delta + \epsilon)\,(-\theta p_1 + (1 - \theta)p_2),
\end{aligned}
\tag{2.31}
$$

so that

$$
R(\theta) = (1 - \theta)\,R(0) + \theta\,R(1)
\tag{2.32}
$$

must lie between $R(0)$ and $R(1)$, and hence cannot exceed both of them. On the other hand, sufficient conditions (2.28) are clearly satisfied by $u^* = \theta$, for any $0 \le \nu \le 1$.

Is it reasonable to assume that at most one deviant strategy is adopted at any given time? Unfortunately, the answer to this question depends explicitly upon the dynamics of interaction between the players, which our model fails to capture explicitly (in its current state of development). The requisite dynamics is at least quite plausible, however: a lone player selects a deviant strategy, discovers that it rewards him less than the orthodox strategy and reverts to orthodoxy before another player has a chance to deviate. Moreover, the lower the frequency of deviation, the more reasonable the assumption.

The frequency of deviation is widely thought to be sufficiently low when conflict arises in the context of evolutionary biology, because strategies can be identified with inherited behavior and deviations with mutations. Thus the dynamic of gossip and rumor—or whatever it was that made word get around in Crossroads—is replaced by the dynamic of genetic transmission. In repeated plays of Crossroads, the composition of the population (in terms of strategies) changes because successful strategists are imitated by other drivers; whereas, in the course of biological evolution, the composition of a population (again in terms of strategies) changes because successful strategists leave more offspring (who are assumed to inherit genes for the successful strategy). In either case, however, the frequency of a successful strategy increases because "success breeds success"—whether metaphorically, as in the case of Crossroads, or literally, as in the context of evolution—and so the difference between the two dynamics, in terms of their effects on the composition of a population, is largely a matter of time scales. Indeed the concept of uninvadable strategy was first defined in connection with the Hawk-Dove game of Section 1.2 by Maynard Smith and Price (1973); who, because of the context, named the concept *evolutionarily stable strategy*—or ESS. It has since been developed extensively by Maynard Smith (1982) and others.[3] Henceforward, we will find it a convenient abuse

---

[3]   See Section 2.9 for more recent references.

of language to refer to uninvadable strategies as evolutionarily stable strategies (or ESSs), and to strongly uninvadable strategies as strong ESSs—regardless of whether the context is biological or sociological.

With the Hawk-Dove game still in mind, let us redefine θ according to

$$\theta = \frac{\rho}{C}, \tag{2.33}$$

where ρ is the reproductive value of the territory in dispute and C the (reproductive) cost of injury. Then, from Exercise 1.1, the reward to an animal that selects u (for its probability of playing Hawk, or H) against an animal that selects v is

$$f(u, v) = \frac{1}{2}\left(\rho(1 - v) + (\rho - Cv)u\right) = \frac{1}{2}\left(\rho(1 - v) + C(\theta - v)u\right). \tag{2.34}$$

If $\rho > C(\theta > 1)$, then there is a unique Nash-equilibrium strategy, $u^* = 1$, because H is then a dominant pure strategy; (2.28a) or (2.29b) is satisfied with $u^* = 1$ for all $0 \leq v < 1$, so that $u^* = 1$ is an ESS. If $\rho < C(\theta < 1)$, on the other hand, then there are three Nash-equilibrium strategies, namely, $u^* = 0$, $u^* = \theta$ and $u^* = 1$; and (Exercise 2.3) it is readily deduced from (2.28) or (2.29) that $u^* = \theta$ is an ESS, whereas $u^* = 0$ and $u^* = 1$ are not.[4] Note that θ is small when C is large. Thus a possible explanation for the rarity in nature of protracted fights is that the cost of injury is much too high.

We conclude this section by returning briefly to Four Ways. Despite the profusion of Nash equilibria in Table 1.10, it is clear at once that only one of them is symmetric between strategies, i.e, satisfies $u = v$. You will recall that $u = (u_1, u_2)$ and $v = (v_1, v_2)$ are vectors in Four Ways, so that symmetry between strategies requires $u_1 = v_1$ and $u_2 = v_2$. Thus the lone candidate is the last row of Table 1.10, i.e., $(u, v) = (\alpha, \beta, \alpha, \beta)$. Let us define the vector ζ by

$$\zeta = (\alpha, \beta). \tag{2.35}$$

Then $u^* = \zeta$ is the only candidate for uninvadability.

Now, from (1.37), the reward to a player who selects $u = (u_1, u_2)$ against an opponent who selects $v = (v_1, v_2)$ is

$$f(u, v) = -\left(2\delta v_1 + (\delta + \tau/2)(v_2 - 1)\right)u_1 - \left((\delta - \tau/2)(v_1 - 1) + (\delta + \epsilon)v_2\right)u_2$$
$$+ (\delta - \tau/2)v_1 + (\delta + \tau/2)(v_2 - 1). \tag{2.36}$$

We readily find (Exercise 2.4) that

$$f(\zeta, \zeta) = f(v, \zeta) \tag{2.37a}$$

---

[4]   The rational reaction sets are the same as in the symmetric version of Figure 1.5 if $\theta < 1$; whereas if $\theta > 1$, then they are the same as in Figure 1.3.

and that

$$f(\zeta, v) - f(v, v) = \delta(v_1 + v_2 - \alpha - \beta)^2 + \delta(v_1 - \alpha)^2 + \epsilon(v_2 - \beta)^2, \quad (2.37b)$$

which is greater than zero for all $v \neq \zeta$. This establishes that $u^* = \zeta$ is an uninvadable strategy.

For further analysis of Four Ways, see Exercise 2.5.

2.4 SEX ALLOCATION: A CONTINUOUS GAME WITH AN ESS

The concept of evolutionarily stable strategy is by no means limited in application to bimatrix games like Crossroads. Nevertheless, the concept is designed for games between members of a large population, as opposed to games between specific individuals. If, therefore, we wish to demonstrate that a continuous game can have an ESS, then we cannot use Store Wars as an example. We present instead a simple model of sex allocation in animals, which derives from Fisher (1930, pp. 142–143) but is here adapted from Charnov (1982) and Maynard Smith (1982).

Suppose that an animal can determine the sex of its offspring. Then what proportion of its offspring should be male, and what proportion female? In answering this question, we will make matters simple by supposing that the animal is the female of her species, that after mating she always produces C children, and that sons and daughters are equally costly to raise. According to Darwin, the animal will behave so as to transmit as many of her genes as possible to posterity. We can capture this idea most simply by supposing that the animal will maximize the number of genes she transmits to the second generation, i.e., to her grandchildren. Sex ratio clearly cannot affect the size of the first generation—for if the animal's objective were simply to maximize number of children, then what would it matter if they were male or female?

Let u be the proportion of offspring that is male; we will refer to u as the animal's strategy. Then the animal always has uC sons and $(1 - u)C$ daughters after mating, and the number of genes she transmits to the first generation is proportional to C. We will imagine that our animal plays a game against every other female in her population, and that all such females adopt strategy v; that is, they have vC sons and $(1 - v)C$ daughters after mating. Thus the decision set $D = \{(u, v) | 0 \leq u, v \leq 1\}$ is the same as in Crossroads; however, whereas Crossroads is a bimatrix game, the sex allocation game is continuous. We therefore assume that our animal is the kind that lays thousands of eggs—a fish, perhaps. Otherwise, it would not be legitimate to assume that strategies are continuous variables.

Let σ_m denote the proportion of sons who survive to maturity, and σ_f the proportion of daughters. Then, if the population is so large that our animal's choice of strategy will have negligible effect on the number of sons, s, and number of daughters, d, in the next generation, then

$$\frac{d}{s} = \frac{\sigma_f(1 - v)}{\sigma_m v}.$$

(2.38)

Let us now assume that females always find a mate, because some males will mate more than once if $d > s$; and that males are equally likely to find a mate if $d < s$, equally likely to find a second mate if $s < d < 2s$, and so on. Thus, if M denotes the number of times that a son mates, then M is a random variable with expected value $E[M] = d/s$.[5]

Now, the number of genes that our animal transmits to the second generation is proportional to

$$F = \sigma_f(1 - u)C \cdot C + \sigma_m uC \cdot CM,$$

(2.39)

because $\sigma_f(1 - u)C$ of her daughters and $\sigma_m uC$ of her sons survive to maturity; and a daughter always produces C offspring, whereas a son produces C offspring per mating. (It does not matter whether sons and daughters mate; the daughter's genes would be counted by the first term in (2.39), and the son's genes by the second.) We will say that F is the animal's payoff. But F is a random variable, whose expected value is

$$f = E[F] = \sigma_f(1 - u)C^2 + \sigma_m uC^2 E[M] = C^2(\sigma_f(1 - u) + \sigma_m ud/s).$$

(2.40)

Thus, on using (2.38), the animal's reward—the expected value of F—is defined by

$$f(u, v) = C^2 \sigma_f \left\{ 1 + u \left(\frac{1 - 2v}{v} \right) \right\}.$$

(2.41)

The reward of her opponent, i.e., the reward of the population, is $f(v, u)$; or, if you prefer, $f_1(u, v) = f(u, v)$ and $f_2(u, v) = f(v, u)$.

It is now straightforward (Exercise 2.10) to calculate the rational reaction sets. The picture that emerges is the special case of Figure 1.5 for which $\theta_1 = 1/2 = \theta_2$. The only symmetric Nash equilibrium is $(u^*, v^*) = (1/2, 1/2)$, and it is readily verified that $u^* = 1/2$ is an ESS. Thus, in the highly idealized circumstances described, our animal's population should evolve to produce equal numbers of sons and daughters—irrespective of the proportions of sons and daughters that survive to maturity.

---

[5]   There are two ways to derive this result. The first is simply to observe that it is obvious. The second is to suppose that $(k - 1)s \leq d < ks$, where $k \geq 1$ is an integer, and observe that $M = k - 1$ if a son fails to mate a k-th time but $M = k$ if the son does mate a k-th time; then, because the probability of a k-th mating is, by assumption, $(d - (k - 1)s)/s$, and the probability of no k-th mating therefore $(ks - d)/s$, we have $E[M] = (k - 1) \cdot (ks - d)/s + k \cdot (d - (k - 1)s)/s = d/s$.

2.5   AN EXAMPLE OF POPULATION DYNAMICS

We have already seen in Section 2.3 that the strategy $u^* = \theta$ is not uninvadable for fast driving in Crossroads if the deviant strategies $v_1 = 0$ and $v_2 = 1$ occur simultaneously. What happens in these circumstances depends explicitly upon the dynamics of interaction among all the players in the population of drivers. A simple model of those dynamics is now presented.[6]

Let us assume that, at time $t \geq 0$, the fraction of drivers playing deviant strategy 0 is $p_1(t)$, whereas the fraction of drivers playing deviant strategy 1 is $p_2(t)$; we will assume that p_1 and p_2 are both differentiable functions. Then the fraction of drivers playing strategy θ is $1 - p(t)$, where $p(t) = p_1(t) + p_2(t)$; and the average reward of the population at time t is

$$\overline{R} = (1 - p)R(\theta) + p_1 R(0) + p_2 R(1), \tag{2.42}$$

where $R(0)$, $R(\theta)$ and $R(1)$ are defined by (2.24). Note that $R(0)$, $R(\theta)$ and $R(1)$ now all depend upon t, because p_1 and p_2 depend upon t. Note also that, for all $t \geq 0$, the point $\big(p_1(t), p_2(t)\big)$ must belong to the triangle

$$\Delta = \big\{ (p_1, p_2) \,|\, p_1 \geq 0, p_2 \geq 0, p_1 + p_2 \leq 1 \big\}. \tag{2.43}$$

Furthermore, both $p_1(0) > 0$ and $p_2(0) > 0$; otherwise there is no danger that strategy θ might be invaded. The triangle Δ is sketched in Figure 2.3.

It seems reasonable to assume that the fraction of drivers using a deviant strategy would increase if the reward from that strategy were greater than average. Thus $dp_1/dt > 0$ if $R(0) > \overline{R}$, and $dp_2/dt > 0$ if $R(1) > \overline{R}$. Dynamics consistent with these assumptions are defined by the pair of differential equations

$$\frac{1}{p_1} \frac{dp_1}{dt} = k(R(0) - \overline{R}), \qquad \frac{1}{p_2} \frac{dp_2}{dt} = k(R(1) - \overline{R}), \tag{2.44}$$

where $k > 0$ is a constant of proportionality. From (2.32) and (2.42) we have

$$
\begin{aligned}
R(0) - \overline{R} &= \big(p_2 + \theta(1 - p)\big) \big(R(0) - R(1)\big), \\
R(1) - \overline{R} &= \big(1 - p_2 - \theta(1 - p)\big) \big(R(1) - R(0)\big),
\end{aligned}
\tag{2.45a}
$$

whereas from (2.31) we have

$$R(0) - R(1) = (\delta + \epsilon)\big(-\theta p_1 + (1 - \theta)p_2\big). \tag{2.45b}$$

---

[6]   It requires some familiarity with phase-plane analysis; see, for example, Mesterton-Gibbons (1989, pp. 46–52).

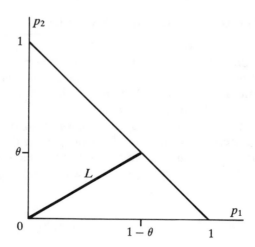

Figure 2.3   Triangle in $p_1 - p_2$ plane
that contains $\big(p_1(t), p_2(t)\big)$ for all $t \geq 0$.

Thus, on substituting (2.45) into (2.44), we obtain the following pair of nonlinear ordinary differential equations for the evolution of the point $(p_1(t), p_2(t))$:

$$\frac{dp_1}{dt} = k(\delta + \epsilon)p_1 \left\{ \theta(1 - p_1) + (1 - \theta)p_2 \right\} \left\{ -\theta p_1 + (1 - \theta)p_2 \right\}$$
$$\frac{dp_2}{dt} = k(\delta + \epsilon)p_2 \left\{ \theta p_1 + (1 - \theta)(1 - p_2) \right\} \left\{ \theta p_1 - (1 - \theta)p_2 \right\}. \tag{2.46}$$

From these equations we can deduce the values of $p_1(\infty)$ and $p_2(\infty)$. Then the long-term fraction of drivers adopting strategy θ is $1 - p_1(\infty) - p_2(\infty)$.

It is clear from inspection of (2.46) that, above the line segment

$$L = \left\{ (p_1, p_2) \in \Delta | \theta p_1 - (1 - \theta)p_2 = 0 \right\} \tag{2.47}$$

in Figure 2.3, dp_1/dt is positive and dp_2/dt negative; whereas below L, dp_1/dt is negative and dp_2/dt positive. Therefore, any trajectory that begins in the interior of Δ must end on L as $t \to \infty$ (and every point on L is an equilibrium of dynamical system (2.46)). To check that the trajectory cannot leave Δ across the boundary where $p_1 + p_2 = 1$, we need only observe that along that boundary we have

$$\frac{dp_2}{dp_1} = \frac{dp_2/dt}{dp_1/dt} = -\frac{p_2\{\theta p_1 + (1 - \theta)(1 - p_2)\}}{p_1\{\theta(1 - p_1) + (1 - \theta)p_2\}} = -1. \tag{2.48}$$

Thus trajectories that begin where $p_1 + p_2 = 1$ must end precisely at $(1 - \theta, \theta)$ as $t \to \infty$; and trajectories that begin in the interior must remain in the interior, because trajectories cannot cross.

The long-term fraction of drivers using strategy θ, $p(\infty)$, is indeterminate; it depends upon $p_1(0)$ and $p_2(0)$. Nevertheless, drivers not using θ must use strategies 0 and 1 in the ratio

$$\frac{p_1(\infty)}{p_2(\infty)} = \frac{1 - \theta}{\theta}. \tag{2.49}$$

Without the ability to recognize individual drivers, the sub-population in which fraction θ always plays pure strategy G and fraction $1 - \theta$ always plays pure strategy W is indistinguishable from the sub-population in which every driver plays mixed strategy θ (G with probability θ, W with probability $1 - \theta$). Thus, although in theory strategy θ is susceptible to simultaneous invasions by deviant strategies 0 and 1, whether in practice θ is invadable is, at the very least, a moot point. Note, however, that this conclusion is strongly dependent upon equations (2.46), which yield no more than a phenomenological description of the dynamics of interaction.

Now try Exercise 2.11.

2.6   GAMES RESTRICTED TO PURE STRATEGIES.
MULTIPLE EVOLUTIONARILY STABLE STRATEGIES

The games we analyzed in Sections 2.3 and 2.4 have unique evolutionarily stable strategies. It is possible, however, for a game to have more than one ESS. Then which ESS will the population adopt? To answer this question we must again model dynamics explicitly, and to this end we adapt the model of Section 2.5.

Let us first observe, however, that we are not obliged to allow mixed strategies, and for certain purposes it is preferable to dispense with them. For games so restricted to pure strategies, it is convenient to frame a new definition of ESS in terms of the payoff matrix—which contains all possible payoffs, because only pure strategies are allowed. Accordingly, let A be the payoff matrix for a symmetric game restricted to m pure strategies; that is, let a_{ij} be the payoff to strategy i against strategy j, for $1 \le i, j \le m$. Then the analogue of (2.29) is that for $1 \le k \le m$, strategy k is evolutionarily stable if

$$a_{kk} \ge a_{jk} \quad \text{for all } j = 1, \ldots, m \tag{2.50a}$$

$$\text{AND EITHER} \quad a_{kk} > a_{jk} \tag{2.50b}$$

$$\text{OR} \quad a_{kj} > a_{jj} \quad \text{for all } j = 1, \ldots, m \text{ such that } j \ne k. \tag{2.50c}$$

If (2.50b) is satisfied for all $j = 1, \ldots, m$ such that $j \ne k$, then strategy k is a strong ESS. If (2.50a) is satisfied, but for some $j \ne k$ neither (2.50b) nor (2.50c) is satisfied, then strategy k is merely collectively stable.

Having made this definition, let us now set $m = 2$ and consider the special case of a game restricted to two pure strategies with payoffs satisfying

$$a_{22} > a_{12} > a_{11} > a_{21}; \tag{2.51}$$

an example of this game will appear in (5.21). Because $k = 1$ and $k = 2$ both satisfy (2.50b), both strategies are strong ESSs.[7] Then which will emerge as the winning strategy in a large population of players, some of whom adopt strategy 1, the remainder of whom adopt strategy 2? The answer depends on initial conditions.

By analogy with the previous section, let us suppose that the specific growth rate of the fraction of population adopting strategy k is proportional to the difference between the reward to strategy k, denoted by W_k, and the average reward to the entire population, denoted by $\overline{W}$. Let $x_1 = x_1(t)$ and $x_2 = x_2(t)$ be the proportions adopting strategy 1 and 2, respectively, at time t. If the integer-valued random variable $J(t)$ denotes the strategy adopted by a player's opponent at time t, and if the population interacts at random, then with negligible error we have

$$\text{Prob}(J = j) = x_j, \qquad j = 1, 2; \tag{2.52}$$

whence the expected value of the payoff to strategy k is

$$W_k = \sum_{j=1}^{2} a_{kj} \cdot \text{Prob}(J = j) = a_{k1}x_1 + a_{k2}x_2, \qquad k = 1, 2. \tag{2.53}$$

Similarly, the average reward to the population is

$$\overline{W} = x_1 W_1 + x_2 W_2 = a_{11}x_1^2 + (a_{12} + a_{21})x_1 x_2 + a_{22}x_2^2; \tag{2.54}$$

and so

$$\frac{1}{x_1}\frac{dx_1}{dt} = \kappa(W_1 - \overline{W}), \qquad \frac{1}{x_2}\frac{dx_2}{dt} = \kappa(W_2 - \overline{W}), \tag{2.55}$$

where κ is a constant of proportionality. On using $x_1 + x_2 = 1$, either of these equations reduces to

$$\begin{aligned}
\frac{dx_2}{dt} &= \kappa x_2(1 - x_2)(W_2 - W_1) \\
&= \kappa x_2(1 - x_2)\{(a_{22} - a_{12} + a_{11} - a_{21})x_2 - (a_{11} - a_{21})\};
\end{aligned} \tag{2.56}$$

see Exercise 2.13. Thus dx_2/dt is positive or negative according to whether $x_2 > \gamma$ or $x_2 < \gamma$, where

$$\gamma = \frac{a_{11} - a_{21}}{a_{22} - a_{12} + a_{11} - a_{21}}. \tag{2.57}$$

If $x_2(0) < \gamma$, then (2.56) implies that $x_2(t) \to 0$ as $t \to \infty$, so that strategy 1 wins over the population; whereas if $x_2(0) > \gamma$, then (2.56) implies that $x_2(t) \to 1$ as $t \to \infty$, so that strategy 2 wins instead.

---

[7] As it happens, the two pure strategies are the only evolutionarily stable strategies—pure or mixed—of this game; see Exercise 2.12. Thus, with regard to population dynamics, no generality whatsoever is lost by restricting this game to pure strategies.

More generally, in a game restricted to m pure strategies, let $x_k = x_k(t)$ be the proportion adopting strategy k at time t, let

$$W_k = \sum_{j=1}^{m} a_{kj}x_j \tag{2.58}$$

be the reward to strategy k, and let

$$\overline{W} = \sum_{k=1}^{m} x_k W_k \tag{2.59}$$

be the average reward to the entire population. Then the long-term dynamics can be described by the differential equations

$$\frac{1}{x_k}\frac{dx_k}{dt} = \kappa(W_k - \overline{W}), \qquad k = 1,\ldots,m. \tag{2.60}$$

These dynamics are usually referred to as Taylor-Jonker dynamics, after Taylor and Jonker (1978). Note that if

$$x_1(0) + x_2(0) + \cdots + x_m(0) = 1 \tag{2.61}$$

—which must, of course, hold—then (2.60) implies

$$x_1(t) + x_2(t) + \cdots + x_m(t) = 1, \qquad 0 \leq t < \infty; \tag{2.62}$$

see Exercise 2.14.

In biological evolution, where success breeds success in the sense that individuals with genes for a successful strategy leave behind more offspring (with the same genes) than players without those genes, the generation in which success is bred is physically distinct from the generation in which, as it were, success originated; and it may be more appropriate to describe game dynamics, not by differential equations, but rather by difference equations—especially if successive generations do not overlap (as with many insect populations). Furthermore, even if successful strategies are passed on by imitation (as opposed to genetic transmission), it may be legitimate to think of the population as composed of discrete generations of players—even though the individuals in the population are the same from one "generation" to the next. In repeated plays of Crossroads, for example, success breeds success in the sense that today's successful strategy will be copied tomorrow by drivers who used a different strategy today; moreover, those who used it successfully today will continue to use it tomorrow. Thus the successful strategy will appear with greater frequency in tomorrow's population, and we can think of today's and tomorrow's populations as discrete generations of drivers—if you like, less savvy drivers and more savvy drivers—even though the two populations are composed of the same individuals.

Accordingly, let us now adapt Taylor-Jonker dynamics from differential equations to difference equations. For $n = 0, 1, 2, \ldots$, let $\overline{W}(n)$ denote the average expected payoff to the population in the n-th generation; and, for $k = 1, 2, \ldots, m$, let $W_k(n)$ and $x_k(n)$ denote the values of x_k and W_k in the n-th generation. Then, by analogy with (2.58) and (2.59), we have

$$W_k(n) = \sum_{j=1}^{m} a_{kj} x_j(n), \qquad k = 1, 2, \ldots, m, \tag{2.63}$$

and

$$\overline{W}(n) = \sum_{k=1}^{m} x_k(n) W_k(n). \tag{2.64}$$

We will assume that if $W_k(n) > \overline{W}(n)$ then strategy k appears with greater frequency in generation $n + 1$, and that if $W_k(n) < \overline{W}(n)$ then strategy k appears with lesser frequency in generation $n + 1$, in such a way that the proportions playing strategy k at iterations $n + 1$ and n are in the ratio $W_k(n)/\overline{W}(n)$. Thus, because this ratio of proportions equals $x_k(n + 1)/x_k(n)$, the population evolves according to

$$x_k(n + 1) = \frac{x_k(n) W_k(n)}{\overline{W}(n)}, \qquad 1 \le k \le m, \qquad 0 \le n < \infty, \tag{2.65a}$$

which in view of Exercise 2.14 can also be written as

$$\frac{x_k(n + 1) - x_k(n)}{x_k(n)} = \sum_{\substack{j=1 \\ j \ne k}}^{m} \frac{(W_k(n) - W_j(n)) x_j(n)}{\overline{W}(n)}, \qquad 1 \le k \le m. \tag{2.65b}$$

We will use (2.65) to describe dynamics both in Exercise 2.22 and in Chapter 5.

In the context of games restricted to pure strategies, we shall find it convenient to say that strategy i *infiltrates* strategy k if $x_i(0)$ is a very small positive number but $x_k(0)$ is close to 1. Clearly, up to $m - 1$ strategies can infiltrate strategy k, because the sum of $m - 1$ very small positive numbers is still a very small positive number; and so we will distinguish two cases by saying that strategy k is subject to *pure* infiltration by strategy i if strategy i is the only infiltrator (i.e., $x_j(0) = 0$ if $j \ne k$ and $j \ne i$), but that strategy k is subject to *mixed* infiltration if there is more than one infiltrator. Now, regardless of whether we use (2.60) or (2.65) to describe the subsequent dynamics, the vector $x(\infty) = (x_1(\infty), x_2(\infty), \ldots, x_m(\infty))$ yields the ultimate composition of the population; in other words, the population evolves to $x(\infty)$. If $x_i(\infty) > x_i(0)$, so that $x_k(\infty) < 1$, then we shall say that strategy i *invades* strategy k; if also $x_i(\infty) = 1$ (hence $x_k(\infty) = 0$), then we shall say that strategy i *eliminates* strategy k. (If, on the other hand, $x_k(\infty) = 1$, then we shall say that strategy k eliminates the infiltra-tors.) But note that strategy i can invade strategy k without eliminating it. We will find this terminology especially useful in Chapter 5.

Now, by analogy with Section 2.3, if strategy k is an ESS then it is stable against pure infiltration; i.e., if strategy i is the only infiltrator, then strategy k will always eliminate it (see Exercise 2.21). Furthermore, if strategy k is a strong ESS then it is stable against mixed infiltration; i.e., strategy k will eliminate ev-ery infiltrator (again, see Exercise 2.21). But if strategy k is not a strong ESS, or if strategy k is only collectively stable, then —as we shall illustrate both in Exercise 2.22 and in Section 5.5—the outcome of mixed infiltration will depend on specific details of the dynamics, whether (2.60) or (2.65). An important pos-sibility is that $x(\infty) = \xi$, where at least two components of the vector ξ are nonzero. In that case, if $x(0) \approx \xi$ implies $x(\infty) = \xi$, then we shall refer to ξ as an *evolutionarily stable state* (comprising a mixture of strategies). If, however, $x(0) \approx \xi$ implies only that $x(\infty)$ is close to ξ, then ξ is merely *metastable*; and, as we shall illustrate below and in Section 5.5, one or more of the strategies in such a metastable mixture may ultimately be eliminated through persistent infiltration by other strategies.

Before proceeding to the following section, we digress to remark that equa-tions (2.65a) are a special case of first order, nonlinear difference equations of the form

$$x_j(n + 1) = G_j\big(x_1(n),,\ldots,x_m(n)\big), \qquad j = 1,\ldots,m, \qquad (2.66a)$$

where $G_1,\ldots,G_m$ are nonlinear functions of $x_1,\ldots,x_m$. They can be written more succinctly in vector form as

$$x(n + 1) = G\big(x(n)\big), \qquad (2.66b)$$

where the vector x and the vector-valued function G are defined by

$$x(n) = \big(x_1(n),x_2(n),\ldots,x_m(n)\big)$$
$$G = (G_1,\ldots,G_m). \qquad (2.67)$$

In the particular examples that appear in this book, the dynamics of (2.66) will turn out to be rather simple: as n increases, the vector $x(n)$ will progress toward an equilibrium vector $x(\infty) = x^*$, where x^* satisfies $x^* = G(x^*)$. Furthermore, for given $x(0)$, it will be easy to generate the sequence $x(1)$, $x(2)$, $x(3),\ldots$, by computer, recursively from (2.66). Nevertheless, the dynamics of equations of type (2.66) are potentially very complicated, and a considerable variety of pe-riodic and even chaotic behavior is possible; see, for example, Devaney (1989, 1990), Devaney and Keen (1989), or Wiggins (1990).

2.7   OWNERS AND INTRUDERS. A CONDITIONAL ESS IN A GAME RESTRICTED TO PURE STRATEGIES

We have yet to consider the possibility that an individual's role during a conflict may vary, and that strategies may therefore be role-dependent. For example, in conflicts over a lady's heart among knights of The Middle Ages, a much recommended strategy was to be as gentle as a lamb in the role of courtier, but as fierce as a lion in the role of warrior. Insofar as rewards must take account of all possible changes of role throughout a conflict, game-theoretic modelling is more difficult when strategies are role-dependent. Nevertheless, if the strategy set is the same for the entire population, then it may still be possible to describe the conflict as a symmetric game, and to apply the concept of evolutionary stability. We illustrate this possibility by modelling a territorial conflict among animals, who may encounter one another in the role of either owner or intruder.

The existence of two roles—here owner and intruder—introduces an obvious asymmetry among players at any particular encounter. But the conflict consists of all encounters, and a strategy must be selected before the start of the conflict. Thus if all players initially face the same probabilities of being owner or intruder at any particular encounter, for any given strategy combination, then the game is still truly symmetric.

Before proceeding, we note that a role-dependent strategy is merely one example of a strategy in which the action taken on some move depends upon the value then realized by some random variable. The nature of this dependence is fully known at the start of the game—otherwise the rule for action couldn't be a strategy—but the precise action taken is conditional upon the value realized by the random variable. We will refer to such strategies as conditional strategies. Thus a role-dependent strategy is a conditional strategy. But the random variable in question need not be a player's role: it could instead, for example, be a physiological state variable, as we shall briefly discuss at the end of Section 2.9; or the action taken by an opponent on a previous encounter, as we shall see in Chapter 5.

Having negotiated these preliminaries, let us now imagine that a violent hurricane has wracked the homes of some population of animals, of whom there are, say, N. But the hurricane has also created some new habitat, in which there are M suitable sites for a home; and naturally, our animals come scurrying in to find one. We will assume (except in Exercise 2.23) that there are more than enough sites for all, i.e., $N < M$; or $\sigma < 1$, where

$$\sigma = \frac{N}{M}. \tag{2.68}$$

The sites—which we assume to be equally valuable to all animals —are randomly distributed across the habitat, however; and in each unit of time there is only probability ϵ that an animal will find a site. Furthermore, there is no guarantee that the site so found isn't already occupied by another animal; in which case, we shall refer to the occupier as the owner, and to the other animal as the intruder. The intruder can either attack the owner—in the hope of obtaining a site without further search—or surrender the site to its owner and look for another one. Likewise, if the intruder attacks, then the owner can either also attack, or else surrender the site to the intruder—who then becomes the owner—and search for another. What should an animal do in these circumstances—attack, surrender, or a bit of both?

To obtain an answer to this question—more precisely, to determine an evolutionarily stable strategy for the population—we will now make some rather bold assumptions. If two animals actually engage in a fight, then they are equally likely to win, and the loser is always injured before surrendering; but there is probability λ that the victor is also injured. Injured animals do not recover (within the time scale of the conflict), and are unable to fight or search for a site; and sites are worthless to an injured animal. Thus fights should not be lightly undertaken. Finally, we will assume that the animals cannot wait forever for a site—rather, to achieve their long-term objective of reproduction, they must secure a site within K units of time. We could imagine, perhaps, that the unit of time is an hour, that the new habitat becomes available at dawn, and that a site is required by dusk; in which case, a reasonable value for K might be 15, and we shall use this later for illustration. But the precise value of K will turn out to be unimportant, provided only that K is neither too large nor too small; see Exercises 2.15 and 2.16.

To help us keep track of the population, let us now define four possible states that an animal can occupy, namely:

$$\begin{array}{l}
\text{1. Uninjured owner} \\
\text{2. Injured owner} \\
\text{3. Uninjured non-owner} \\
\text{4. Injured non-owner.}
\end{array} \qquad (2.69)$$

Thus if t denotes time, then an animal's objective is to be in state 1 when $t = K$. We will analyze the conflict over territories as a game restricted to the following four pure strategies for uninjured animals:

$$\begin{array}{ll}
HH: \text{Attack if owner, attack if intruder} \\
HD: \text{Attack if owner, surrender if intruder} \\
DH: \text{Surrender if owner, attack if intruder} \\
DD: \text{Surrender if owner, surrender if intruder}
\end{array} \qquad (2.70)$$

where H stands for Hawk and D stands for Dove, as in Section 1.2; HH and DD are unconditional strategies, whereas HD and DH are conditional strategies. Because we have assumed that injured animals are unable to search or fight, the question of strategy for an injured animal does not arise. If the injury is sustained in losing, then the animal remains in state 4 until $t = K$; whereas if the injury is sustained in winning, then the animal remains on its site until it is attacked by an (uninjured) intruder, in which case it surrenders the territory immediately (or it remains on its site until $t = K$ if no one attacks). We will call this game Owners and Intruders.

Although Owners and Intruders is a game restricted to pure strategies, it will facilitate analysis if we first define appropriate mixed strategies (and later concentrate on the special case of interest). Accordingly, let u_1 be the (conditional) probability that an animal attacks if he is an owner, and u_2 the probability that an animal attacks if he is an intruder. Then an animal's strategy can be represented by the vector $u = (u_1, u_2)$, with

$$HH = (1, 1), \quad HD = (1, 0), \quad DH = (0, 1), \quad DD = (0, 0). \qquad (2.71)$$

It is important to note that the strategy $u = (u_1, u_2)$ differs from the mixed strategy we defined in Section 1.4, because the (conditional) probabilities u_1 and u_2 are completely independent, and so both can take any value between 0 and 1. In other words, we allow (u_1, u_2) to be any point in the square $0 \le u_1, u_2 \le 1$; whereas, in Section 1.4, (u_1, u_2) was confined to the triangle (1.33).

As usual, to determine whether u is an ESS, we must obtain an expression for the reward $f(u, v)$ to a representative u-strategist in a population of v-strategists. Several steps are required to derive this expression (so let us be patient). To begin with, let the random variable $X_u(t)$ denote a u-strategist's state at time t, so that X_u has sample space $\{1, 2, 3, 4\}$. We will suppose that animals can change their state only at discrete instants of time, say $t = k$, where k is a positive integer; and we will denote the probability that a u-strategist is in state j at time k (i.e., immediately after time k) by $x_j(k)$. Thus, for $j = 1, \ldots, 4$,

$$x_j(k) = \text{Prob}(X_u(k) = j). \qquad (2.72\,a)$$

Strictly, because x_j depends on u, we should use the notation $x_j(k, u)$—but that would be unnecessarily cumbersome. Instead, therefore, we shall use $x_j(k)$ for the probability that a u-strategist is in state j at time k, and

$$y_j(k) = \text{Prob}(X_v(k) = j) \qquad (2.72\,b)$$

(rather than $x_j(k, v)$) for the probability that a v-strategist is in state j at time k. Then, because any animal, whether u-strategist or v-strategist, must be in one of the four states defined by (2.69) at time k, we have

$$
\begin{aligned}
x_1(k) + x_2(k) + x_3(k) + x_4(k) = 1, 0 \le k \le K \\
y_1(k) + y_2(k) + y_3(k) + y_4(k) = 1, 0 \le k \le K.
\end{aligned}
\qquad (2.73)
$$

Furthermore, if animals are injured only by fighting (animals injured by the hurricane fail to reach the new habitat), then all animals must be in state 3 initially;

and so if $x(k)$ denotes the vector $(x_1(k), x_2(k), x_3(k), x_4(k))$, and $y(k)$ the vector $(y_1(k), y_2(k), y_3(k), y_4(k))$, for any $k \geq 0$, then

$$x(0) = (0, 0, 1, 0) = y(0). \tag{2.74}$$

For $1 \leq i, j \leq 4$, let $\phi_{ij}(k, u, v)$ be the conditional probability that a u-strategist in a population of v-strategists is in state j at time $k + 1$, given that he is in state i at time k; that is, define

$$\phi_{ij}(k, u, v) = \text{Prob}(X_u(k + 1) = j \,|\, X_u(k) = i), \qquad 1 \leq i, j \leq 4, \tag{2.75}$$

where $\text{Prob}(Y \,|\, Z)$ is standard notation for the conditional probability of Y, given Z. This time, it really is necessary to use more explicit notation, because we have to distinguish between, on the one hand, the probability that a u-strategist goes from state i to state j, which is $\phi_{ij}(k, u, v)$; and, on the other hand, the probability that a v-strategist goes from state i to state j, which is

$$\text{Prob}(X_v(k + 1) = j \,|\, X_v(k) = i) = \phi_{ij}(k, v, v), \qquad 1 \leq i, j \leq 4. \tag{2.76}$$

We make at this point an additional assumption, namely, N is so large that every v-strategist is effectively playing only against v-strategists; although the population contains a single u-strategist, if N is very large then the probability that a v-strategist will meet that u-strategist is negligible. For $j = 1, \ldots, 4$ and $0 \leq k \leq K - 1$, we now have

$$x_j(k + 1) = \sum_{i=1}^{4} \text{Prob}(X_u(k + 1) = j \,|\, X_u(k) = i) \cdot \text{Prob}(X_u(k) = i)$$
$$= \sum_{i=1}^{4} x_i(k) \phi_{ij}(k, u, v) \tag{2.77a}$$

and

$$y_j(k + 1) = \sum_{i=1}^{4} \text{Prob}(X_v(k + 1) = j \,|\, X_v(k) = i) \cdot \text{Prob}(X_v(k) = i)$$
$$= \sum_{i=1}^{4} y_i(k) \phi_{ij}(k, v, v). \tag{2.77b}$$

Note that

$$\sum_{j=1}^{4} \phi_{ij}(k, u, v) = 1, \qquad 1 \leq i \leq 4, \quad 0 \leq u, v \leq 1, \tag{2.78}$$

because if a u-strategist is in state i at time k, then at time $k + 1$ it must either remain in state i or enter one of the other states.

An animal's objective is to end the conflict as uninjured owner of a site, and so it is reasonable to regard

$$F(u,v) = \begin{cases} 1 & \text{if } X_u(K) = 1 \\ 0 & \text{if } X_u(K) \geq 2 \end{cases} \tag{2.79}$$

as the payoff to a u-strategist against a v-strategist. But F, so defined, is a random variable, which cannot itself be maximized; therefore, in the usual way, we assume instead that the reward to a u-strategist against a v-strategist is

$$f(u,v) = E[F(u,v)] = 1 \cdot \text{Prob}(X_u(K) = 1) + 0 \cdot \text{Prob}(X_u(K) \geq 2) = x_1(K), \tag{2.80}$$

where E denotes expected value. Here, we have again taken liberties with notation, because the dependence of $f(u,v)$ on K is suppressed on the left-hand side of (2.80); whereas the dependence of $x_1(K)$ on u and v is suppressed on the right-hand side. But any other notation would be unnecessarily cumbersome.

We can deduce $x_1(K)$ from (2.74) and (2.77) if we first obtain an explicit expression for the 4×4 matrix $\phi(k,u,v)$, defined by (2.75). The key assumptions we make in this regard are that searching animals are equally likely to find any site; that at most one animal intrudes upon a site per unit of time; and that animals and sites are both so numerous that $N \rightarrow \infty$ and $M \rightarrow \infty$, but in such a way that σ defined by (2.68) is finite. The first assumption may be questionable, but it greatly simplifies analysis. On the other hand, the second assumption has been forced upon us by our earlier assumption that an animal can change state only at $t = k$, where k is an integer; if we allowed multiple intrusions during the same unit of time, then we would also have to allow multiple changes of state. Similarly, the third assumption has been forced on us by the assumption we made to arrive at (2.77). How unreasonable in practice are these assumptions? See Exercise 2.17.

Granted these assumptions, let us first suppose that the u-strategist is in state 1 (uninjured owner) at time k. Then it can move into state 4 (injured non-owner) only if it is intruded upon, is attacked, attacks back, and then loses; whereas it can move into state 3 (uninjured non-owner) only if it is intruded upon, is attacked, and promptly surrenders; and it can move into state 2 (injured owner) only if it is intruded upon, is attacked, attacks back, and then wins, but sustains an injury. At time k, the expected number of uninjured non-owners is $Ny_3(k)$, because all of them are v-strategists; and each finds a site during the interval $k < t < k + 1$ with probability ϵ. Because, as we have just assumed, they are all equally likely to find any site, the probability that one of them finds the particular site now occupied by our u-strategist is ϵ/M. The probability that one of them does not find the u-strategist is therefore $1 - \epsilon/M$, the probability that none of them finds the u-strategist is that number raised to the power of $Ny_3(k)$, and so the probability that at least one of them intrudes is

$$1 - \left(1 - \frac{\epsilon}{M}\right)^{Ny_3(k)} \equiv 1 - \left(1 - \frac{\epsilon}{M}\right)^{M\sigma y_3(k)}. \tag{2.81}$$

Thus, in the limit as $M \to \infty$, the probability that at least one uninjured non-owner locates the u-strategist is $q(y_3(k))$, where we define

$$q(y_3) = 1 - e^{-\epsilon\sigma y_3} \tag{2.82}$$

(and e denotes the exponential function). In view of our second assumption above, we intepret $q(y_3(k))$ as the probability that an uninjured non-owner intrudes during the interval $k < t < k + 1$. (In the event that more than one animal locates the site, we must simply assume that the u-strategist interacts with the first, and that later arrivals ignore them both.) Then, because another animal attacks as intruder with probability v_2, and because the u-strategist attacks as owner with probability u_1, and loses with probability 1/2 (conditional upon attacking), the probability that a non-owner intrudes *and* attacks, *and* that the u-strategist attacks *and* loses, is $q(y_3(k))$ times v_2 times u_1 times 1/2; all conditional, of course, on the u-strategist being in state 1, and assuming that the intruder's attack probability is independent of the u-strategist's surrender probability. We have thus established that

$$\phi_{14}(k,u,v) = \frac{1}{2}u_1v_2q(y_3(k)). \tag{2.83a}$$

Similarly, because the u-strategist surrenders as owner with probability $1 - u_1$, we have

$$\phi_{13}(k,u,v) = (1 - u_1)v_2q(y_3(k)); \tag{2.83b}$$

and, because the u-strategist wins with probability 1/2 but (conditional upon winning) sustains an injury with probability λ, we have

$$\phi_{12}(k,u,v) = \frac{1}{2}\lambda u_1v_2q(y_3(k)). \tag{2.83c}$$

The probability that the u-strategist remains in state 1 is now readily deduced from (2.78) with $i = 1$:

$$\phi_{11}(k,u,v) = 1 - \left(1 - \frac{1}{2}(1 - \lambda)u_1\right)v_2q(y_3(k)). \tag{2.83d}$$

Let us next suppose that the u-strategist is in state 2 (injured owner). Then the u-strategist is injured and does not recover, whence

$$\phi_{21}(k,u,v) = 0 = \phi_{23}(k,u,v); \tag{2.84a}$$

the u-strategist either remains an injured owner or becomes an injured non-owner. Given that it is already injured, it surrenders its site if it is intruded upon, which happens with probability $q(y_3(k))$; and attacked, which happens with probability v_2. Thus, on using (2.78) with $i = 2$, we have

$$\phi_{22}(k) = 1 - v_2 q(y_3(k)), \qquad \phi_{24}(k) = v_2 q(y_3(k)). \tag{2.84b}$$

Third, let us suppose that the u-strategist is in state 3 (uninjured non-owner). Then it will descend into state 4 (injured non-owner) only if it intrudes upon an uninjured owner, attacks, is attacked back, and then loses. At time k, the expected number of uninjured owners is $Ny_1(k)$, because every one of them is a v-strategist; whence, if the u-strategist finds a site, then the probability that it is occupied by an uninjured owner is $Ny_1(k)/M = \sigma y_1(k)$. The u-strategist finds a site during the interval $k < t < k + 1$ with probability ϵ; and if it is occupied, then the u-strategist attacks as intruder with probability u_2, is attacked back by the owner with probability v_1, and subsequently loses with probability 1/2. Thus, multiplying all the conditional probabilities together, we have

$$\phi_{34}(k,u,v) = \frac{1}{2}\sigma \epsilon u_2 v_1 y_1(k). \tag{2.85a}$$

Similarly, because (conditional upon an intrusion and engagement) the u-strategist wins and is injured with probability $\lambda/2$, we have

$$\phi_{32}(k,u,v) = \frac{1}{2}\lambda \sigma \epsilon u_2 v_1 y_1(k). \tag{2.85b}$$

Just as the conditional probability that a site is occupied by an uninjured owner is $\sigma y_1(k)$, so the probability that a site is occupied by an injured owner is $\sigma y_2(k)$. Thus the probability that the u-strategist finds a site, whose occupier is either injured or uninjured, *and* does not attack is ϵ times $\sigma(y_1(k) + y_2(k))$ times $1 - u_2$. The probability that the u-strategist does not find a site is $1 - \epsilon$. In either case, it remains in state 3. Thus

$$\phi_{33}(k,u,v) = 1 - \epsilon + \epsilon \sigma(1 - u_2)(y_1(k) + y_2(k)); \tag{2.85c}$$

and (2.78) with $i = 3$ implies

$$\phi_{31}(k,u,v) = \epsilon \left(1 - \sigma(1 - u_2)\{y_1(k) + y_2(k)\} - \frac{1}{2}\sigma(1 + \lambda)u_2 v_1 y_1(k) \right). \tag{2.85d}$$

Finally, because an injured animal is unable to search, even for unoccupied sites, we have

$$\phi_{41}(k) = 0, \quad \phi_{42}(k) = 0, \quad \phi_{43}(k) = 0, \quad \phi_{44}(k) = 1. \tag{2.86}$$

The matrix $\phi(k)$ has now been defined.

Substitution of (2.83)–(2.86) into (2.77) leads to a set of eight first-order,

TABLE 2.1   The sequences $x(1),\ldots,x(15)$ and $y(1),\ldots,x(15)$ for $x(0)$ and $y(0)$ defined by (2.74), ϵ, λ and σ defined by (2.90), and (u,v) defined by (2.91).

K	$x_1(K)$	$x_2(K)$	$x_3(K)$	$x_4(K)$	$y_1(K)$	$y_2(K)$	$y_3(K)$	$y_4(K)$
1	0.3000	0.0000	0.7000	0.0000	0.3000	0.0000	0.7000	0.0000
2	0.4689	0.0047	0.5147	0.0117	0.4627	0.0041	0.5230	0.0102
3	0.5757	0.0099	0.3891	0.0253	0.5645	0.0087	0.4046	0.0223
4	0.6477	0.0145	0.2995	0.0382	0.6335	0.0129	0.3198	0.0338
5	0.6984	0.0185	0.2337	0.0494	0.6828	0.0166	0.2565	0.0442
6	0.7350	0.0218	0.1841	0.0591	0.7192	0.0197	0.2079	0.0532
7	0.7621	0.0245	0.1462	0.0672	0.7468	0.0224	0.1698	0.0610
8	0.7824	0.0268	0.1169	0.0739	0.7683	0.0246	0.1395	0.0677
9	0.7979	0.0286	0.0940	0.0795	0.7851	0.0264	0.1151	0.0733
10	0.8098	0.0301	0.0760	0.0842	0.7985	0.0280	0.0954	0.0781
11	0.8190	0.0313	0.0616	0.0881	0.8093	0.0293	0.0792	0.0821
12	0.8262	0.0323	0.0502	0.0913	0.8181	0.0304	0.0660	0.0856
13	0.8319	0.0331	0.0410	0.0940	0.8252	0.0313	0.0550	0.0884
14	0.8365	0.0338	0.0336	0.0962	0.8311	0.0321	0.0460	0.0909
15	0.8401	0.0343	0.0276	0.0980	0.8359	0.0327	0.0385	0.0929

nonlinear difference equations of the form

$$x_j(k + 1) = H_j(x_1(k),\ldots,x_4(k), y_1(k),\ldots,y_4(k)), \qquad j = 1,\ldots,4$$
$$y_j(k + 1) = H_{j+4}(x_1(k),\ldots,x_4(k), y_1(k),\ldots,y_4(k)), \qquad j = 1,\ldots,4 \tag{2.87a}$$

where $H_1,\ldots,H_8$ are nonlinear functions of $x_1,\ldots,x_4,y_1,\ldots,y_4$ (whose dependence on u and v has been suppressed by the notation); see Exercise 2.18. If we relabel y_1 as x_5, y_2 as x_6, y_3 as x_7 and y_4 as x_8, then (2.87) has the form of (2.66) with $m = 8$ and $G = H$:

$$x(k + 1) = H(x(k)), \qquad 0 \le k \le K - 1. \tag{2.87b}$$

Note that although (2.87) describes short-term dynamics, and (2.65) describes long-term dynamics, the two dynamics have a common mathematical structure. For any strategy combination (u,v), and for any value of K, the vectors $x(K)$ and $y(K)$ are now readily calculated from K successive iterations of (2.87). From (2.74) and (2.77) with $k = 0$ we have

$$x(1) = (\epsilon, 0, 1 - \epsilon, 0) = y(1), \tag{2.88}$$

whence from (2.77) with $k = 1$:

$$x_1(2) = \epsilon(2 - \epsilon) - \sigma\epsilon^2(1 - \epsilon)\left\{1 - u_2 + \frac{1}{2}(1 + \lambda)u_2 v_1\right\}$$
$$- \epsilon\left(1 - e^{-\sigma\epsilon(1-\epsilon)}\right)\left(1 - \frac{1}{2}(1 - \lambda)u_1\right)v_2. \tag{2.89}$$

TABLE 2.2 Payoff matrix in Owners and Intruders for various values of λ, when $K = 15$, $\epsilon = 0.1$, $\sigma = 0.7$ and $x(0)$ and $y(0)$ are defined by (2.74).

0.621	0.704	0.685	0.794	0.592	0.686	0.665	0.794	0.504	0.623	0.602	0.794
0.594	0.671	0.575	0.671	0.579	0.671	0.557	0.671	0.531	0.671	0.502	0.671
0.603	0.704	0.673	0.794	0.589	0.686	0.673	0.794	0.544	0.623	0.673	0.794
0.571	0.671	0.543	0.671	0.571	0.671	0.543	0.671	0.571	0.671	0.543	0.671
$\lambda = 0$				$\lambda = 0.2$				$\lambda = 0.9$			

From (2.80), if $K = 2$ then (2.89) is an expression for $f(u, v)$. For larger values of K, however, the calculation of f is clearly a task for the computer. Suppose, for example, that

$$\epsilon = 0.3, \qquad \lambda = 0.4, \qquad \sigma = 0.7 \tag{2.90}$$

and

$$(u, v) = (0.3,\ 0.7,\ 0.6,\ 0.4), \tag{2.91}$$

so that the u-strategist attacks with probabililty 0.3 as owner and 0.7 as intruder, whereas the rest of the population attack with probability 0.6 as owner and 0.4 as intruder. Then you can readily verify, by using a computer to solve (2.87) recursively, that the vectors $x(K)$ and $y(K)$ have the values given in Table 2.1, for various values of K. If $K = 15$, for example, then $f(u, v) = 0.8401$.

Having demonstrated how to calculate $f(u, v)$ for arbitrary (u, v), let us now return to Owners and Intruders. According to Section 2.6, we relabel HH as strategy 1, HD as strategy 2, DH as strategy 3 and DD as strategy 4; and, for $1 \leq i, j \leq 4$, we denote the payoff to strategy i against a population using strategy j by a_{ij}. Then, from (2.71), the payoff matrix is

$$A = \begin{bmatrix} f(1,1,1,1) & f(1,1,1,0) & f(1,1,0,1) & f(1,1,0,0) \\ f(1,0,1,1) & f(1,0,1,0) & f(1,0,0,1) & f(1,0,0,0) \\ f(0,1,1,1) & f(0,1,1,0) & f(0,1,0,1) & f(0,1,0,0) \\ f(0,0,1,1) & f(0,0,1,0) & f(0,0,0,1) & f(0,0,0,0) \end{bmatrix} \tag{2.92}$$

and is readily found by computer—provided, of course, we have first agreed on the value of K. Note that A's dependence on K is suppressed by the notation.

Suppose, for illustration, that $K = 15$, $\epsilon = 0.1$ and $\sigma = 0.7$. Then for various values of λ, the payoff matrix is recorded in Table 2.2. By direct application of (2.50), we see that HH is the only ESS when $\lambda = 0$. Thus, when the price of victory is zero, a population of inveterate Hawks is uninvadable. When $\lambda = 0.2$, on the other hand, the price of victory—a 20% risk of being unable to profit from the victory through injury—is sufficiently high that the game has two evolutionarily stable strategies, namely, HH and DH. A population of inveterate Hawks is still uninvadable, but a population of animals who surrender as owners but attack as intruders is also uninvadable. Which of these strategies is ultimately adopted by the population must be determined by *long-term* dynamics, corresponding to those of (2.65), and will depend on the proportions using different strategies initially (and, of course, has nothing to do with $x(0)$ and $y(0)$, which merely define the state in which a particular game begins). Finally, when $\lambda = 0.9$, the price of victory is so high that the only ESS is *DH*, and a population of inveterate fighters is readily invaded. If *DD* were absent from the population, then *HD* would also be evolutionarily stable (delete the last row and column from the third matrix in Table 2.2). But *HD* is only collectively stable in the presence of *DD*, which means that *DD* cannot be prevented from drifting into an *HD* population and changing its composition to a mixture of *HD* and *DD*; see Exercise 2.22. If this mixed population is now infiltrated by *HH* or *DH*, however, then (see Exercise 2.22) the proportion of *HD* will decrease and the proportion of *DD* will increase, because *DD* does better than *HD* against either *HH* or *DH*; in terms of Section 2.6, the mixed population is metastable. If either *HH* or *DH* were to infiltrate repeatedly, then the proportion of *DD* could become quite large (with a corresponding reduction in the proportion of *HD*). But *DD* is not even collectively stable, and is readily invaded by either *HH* or *DH*. Thus, as illustrated in Exercise 2.22, the population would eventually evolve from the metastable mixture of *HD* and *DD* to the sole ESS, namely, *DH*.[8]

Two points are illustrated by the above analysis. First, the evolutionary stability of a particular strategy can depend on one of the game's parameters, e.g., λ in Table 2.2. A further example of this possibility arises in Section 5.9. Second, and more importantly, whether a strategy is an ESS is always a function of the other strategies present (more fundamentally, a model's prediction's are always a function of the assumptions on which it is based). When $\lambda = 0.9$ in Owners and Intruders, for example, the presence or absence of inveterate doves (*DD*) is critical to the evolutionary stability of *HD*. The relevance of this second point will emerge again in Section 5.5.

How do ϵ and σ affect evolutionarily stability? See Exercise 2.19. For fixed ϵ, σ and λ, how sensitive are our results to the value of K? See Exercise 2.15. More generally, how good are the assumptions on which our model is based? See Exercise 2.17.

---

[8]   If the frequency of one of the strategies in a metastable mixture decreases over time without interference by strategies other than those already represented in the mixture, then the reduction can be said to be caused by *random drift;* whereas, if the frequency of a metastable strategy decreases because it does less well against an infiltrator than other strategies in the mixture, then the reduction can be said to be caused by *selection pressure.*

2.8 SPIDERS IN A SPIN—AN ESS?

It may seem surprising that a population would always be meek in the role of occupier but aggressive in the role of intruder, despite this rule's advantage— when universally obeyed—that nobody would ever fight. After all, if someone knocked on your door tonight and demanded your property, would you turn it over and run off to attack the neighbor? Your property is more valuable to you than your neighbor's property, of course; and we made the assumption in Section 2.7 that sites were equally valuable to all animals. But even in cases where this assumption is reasonable, it is perhaps surprising that strategy DH would ever prevail in nature. Indeed it is far commoner for territorial conflicts to be settled by behavior that approximates the strategy HD—see Maynard Smith (1982, p. 97). An example of behavior that resembles DH is therefore of interest.

According to Burgess (1976), the behavior of the Mexican spider, *Oecobius civitas*, features a curious combination of tolerance and avoidance. Burgess provides the following description:

> On the underside of the rock that shelters the spiders each individual weaves a small open-ended tube of silk that is its hiding place; around this retreat the spider constructs a thin, encircling alarm-system net close to the surface of the rock. The pair of structures makes up the spider's web, which is generally found in a hollow or a crevice of the rock. If a spider is disturbed and driven out of its retreat, it darts across the rock and, in the absence of a vacant crevice to hide in, may seek refuge in the hiding place of another spider of the same species. If the other spider is in residence when the intruder enters, it does not attack but darts out and seeks a new refuge of its own. Thus once the first spider is disturbed the process of sequential displacement from web to web may continue for several seconds, often causing a majority of the spiders in the aggregation to shift from their home refuge to an alien one. ... Moreover, within the local population the shift to another spider's shelter may be a semipermanent move. The reason is that when the spiders are undisturbed, they occupy a fixed web position for long periods.

Could this be an example of strategy DH at work in nature? It appears from Burgess's account that virtually all spiders are uninjured homeowners when a disturbance occurs; and so if Owners and Intruders is to provide even an approximate description of what happens subsequently, then we should at least start the game with virtually all players in state 1, and just a few in state 3. If, for example, 1% of owners are disturbed initially, then we should replace (2.74) by

$$x(0) = (0.99,\ 0,\ 0.01,\ 0) = y(0). \tag{2.93}$$

But the payoff matrix (2.92) is still readily computed from successive iterations of the difference equation (2.87), and our conclusions are essentially the same. When $K = 15$, $\epsilon = 0.1$ and $\sigma = 0.7$, for example, the payoff matrices for $\lambda = 0$ and $\lambda = 0.9$ are as shown in Table 2.3. We see that HH is still the unique ESS when $\lambda = 0$, and that DH is still the unique ESS when $\lambda = 0.9$.

The values we have chosen for ϵ, λ, σ and K are totally arbitrary. But whether

TABLE 2.3   Payoff matrix in Owners and Intruders for $\lambda = 0$ and $\lambda = 0.9$, when $K = 15, \epsilon = 0.1, \sigma = 0.7$ and $x(0)$ and $y(0)$ are defined by (2.93).

0.9924	0.9952	0.9937	0.9979	0.9875	0.9927	0.9899	0.9979
0.9910	0.9937	0.9895	0.9937	0.9885	0.9937	0.9857	0.9937
0.9917	0.9952	0.9937	0.9979	0.9883	0.9927	0.9937	0.9979
0.9895	0.9937	0.9870	0.9937	0.9895	0.9937	0.9870	0.9937
	$\lambda = 0$				$\lambda = 0.9$		

a strategy is evolutionarily stable is essentially unaffected by K; and its dependence on ϵ, λ and σ is quite robust, depending only on whether these parameters are small or large—see Exercises 2.15 and 2.19. We can therefore hazard a cautious guess as to why *O. civitas* behaves as it does. Let us posit that the supply of sites is adequate $(1 - \sigma$ sufficiently large); and that one spider's web is as good as another's in terms of snaring prey, so that sites are all equally valuable to all animals. Then our model suggests that the spider *O. civitas* may have evolved to *DH* because *DD*—inveterate Dove—cannot be prevented from drifting into an *HD* population; and because the probability of winning a fight without injury, i.e., $1 - \lambda$, is too low for *HH* to be evolutionarily stable. Of course, this is mere speculation—but we cannot explain observed behavior unless first of all we speculate about it!

On the other hand, even speculative models should at least be self-consistent, and in Exercise 2.17 you were asked to criticize some assumptions we made in Section 2.7. You must have wondered what kind of animal could be so mobile as to be equally likely to reach all sites in a unit of time, in the limit as $M \to \infty$. We can rescue this assumption to some extent by supposing that the habitat is small—and Burgess (1976) does say that *O. civitas* lives under crowded conditions. But if the habitat is so small, can we really assume that at most one animal intrudes on a site per unit of time? We can also rescue this assumption by supposing that the unit of time is small—and Burgess's spiders exchange their homes on a time scale of several seconds (if only realtors were so efficient). Because K has essentially no effect on the ESS, decreasing the time unit (which, for a contest of given duration, is equivalent to increasing K) should leave our conclusions more or less intact. In practice, however, we would achieve the same end by choosing some common time unit—a second, say—and simply supposing that ϵ is small. Then $q(y_3)$ in (2.82) can be approximated by $\epsilon \sigma y_3$; see Exercise 2.20.

2.9   COMMENTARY

In Chapter 2 we have introduced three criteria for distinguishing among Nash equilibria, due to Harsanyi and Selten (Section 2.1), Kalai and Samet (Section 2.2) and Maynard Smith (Section 2.3). Theirs are by no means the only criteria, but were chosen to illustrate both a diversity of ideas and a variety of predictions; and, in the case of Maynard Smith's criterion, because the concept of evolutionary stability is central to Sections 2.4–2.8 and Chapter 5. Alternative criteria—all amply expounded in the monograph by van Damme (1987)—include Selten's (1975) concept of perfectness (insensitivity to arbitrary small random errors in playing a pure strategy) and Myerson's (1978) concept of properness (modified perfectness that assigns lower probability to a more costly error than to a less costly error). In the symmetric version of Crossroads, both perfectness and properness select the same equilibrium as evolutionary stability selects (hence, for the sake of variety, our choice of persistence). Indeed there is at least some truth to the notion that perfectness and properness belong to the same conceptual flock as evolutionary stability; whereas the tracing procedure—described in the appendix to this chapter—is arguably a bird of a different feather. Furthermore, Harsanyi and Selten's criterion, augmented where necessary by their "logarithmic tracing procedure" (which we do not, however, discuss in the appendix), is the only criterion that guarantees uniqueness.

In Section 2.4, we applied the concept of evolutionary stability to predict sex ratio. In Sections 2.5 and 2.6, we discussed population dynamics in terms of strategy composition, and we adapted our definition of evolutionary stability to games restricted to pure strategies. In Sections 2.7 and 2.8, we further applied the concept of evolutionary stability, this time to a territorial conflict in which players can change their roles.

There now exists a substantial theoretical literature on the concept of ESS (although it appears that no one has yet provided an *a priori* reason for the constants of proportionality in (2.60) to be the same in all m equations); see, for example, Hines (1987), Hofbauer and Sigmund (1988), and Vincent and Brown (1988). Later contributions include Vickers and Cannings (1988), Cannings and Vickers (1988), Cressman (1990), Lessard (1990), and references therein. Much of this literature deals with bimatrix games, although (as we have seen in Sections 2.4 and 2.7) the scope of Maynard Smith's solution concept is far more general. Most of this literature assumes that the population is infinite. Nevertheless, recent work includes finite-population analyses by Maynard Smith (1988), Schaffer (1988) and Crawford (1990). Infinite- versus finite-population effects are also studied in Sections 5.6–5.8, in the context of a game restricted to pure strategies.

How much is lost in such a restriction to pure strategies? If one takes the view that mixed strategies are merely proxies for unmodelled aspects of a conflict, then the answer in theory is nothing. An example will help to illustrate. Recall once more the game of Four Ways, and suppose that drivers do not have spinning arrows on their dashboards; rather, they select pure strategy C when their hearts are racing, pure strategy G when both their hearts are racing *and* they have sweaty palms, and otherwise strategy W. Nevertheless, the probabilities of being in these various states of agitation correspond to the probabilities of selecting G, W or C in the ESS of Section 2.3. Thus, when behavior is averaged over time, drivers appear to adopt a mixed strategy; yet in fact they adopt a conditional pure strategy that is state-dependent (just as strategies in Owners and Intruders were role-dependent). A conditional pure strategy can also be time-dependent; perhaps, for example, drivers select C when their palms are sweaty on Mondays, Wednesdays and Thursdays, but G if their palms are sweaty on Tuesdays and Fridays. More generally, a player's state can be defined to incorporate almost any physiological or environmental variable; and if decisions can depend on both state and time in a sufficiently general way, then it is arguable that mixed strategies are quite unnecessary. (In practice, of course, it may not be so easy to ensure that all relevant physiological or environmental variables are adequately represented.)

Here two remarks are in order. First, although the decision rule in such games is deterministic—in the sense that the functional relationship between state, time and action taken is deterministic—the state remains a random variable; thus the "internal" uncertainty that mixed strategies bring to a player's decisions is replaced by the "external" uncertainty of a player's state. Second, we must ultimately allow for mistakes by the players. But this uncertainty can also be externalized by considering purely deterministic (but conditional) decision rules of the form, "If you think that the state variable is that, then do this" (and then computing rewards by taking expectations over an appropriate probability distribution).

All things considered, dynamic games with conditional pure strategies are much more appealing as behavioral models than static games with mixed strategies, and state-dependent, dynamic games have begun to appear quite frequently in the recent literature; see, for example, McNamara and Houston (1987, 1988), Houston and McNamara (1988), Mangel and Clark (1988, pp. 261–279), Kaitala *et al.* (1989), Clark and Ydenberg (1990) and Mangel (1990a). The analysis of such games is often extremely difficult, however; and so even if in theory one regards mixed strategies as merely a stopgap, one is often in practice still grateful to have them.

EXERCISES 2

2.1 Show that $u = 1$ is an uninvadable strategy of the symmetric version of Crossroads when $\theta > 1$. (Show that $f(1, 1) > f(v, 1)$ for all v such that $0 \leq v < 1$.) This appears to say that if both drivers are slow then both drivers should select G. Do you think it would be better to replace "both drivers are slow" by "the junction is fast?" Comment.

2.2 (i)   Show that an uninvadable strategy is always a Nash-equilibrium strategy.

(ii) Show that if u^* is a strongly uninvadable strategy, then (u^*, u^*) must be a strong Nash-equilibrium strategy combination.

(iii) If (u^*, v^*) is a strong Nash-equilibrium strategy combination, are u^* and v^* strongly uninvadable?

2.3 Using (2.27) and (2.28), show that $u^* = \theta$ is an ESS for the Hawk-Dove game when $\theta < 1$, whereas $u^* = 0$ and $u^* = 1$ are not; here θ is defined by (2.33).

2.4 Verify (2.37).

2.5 Show that if $\delta > \tau/2$ in Four Ways, then the uninvadable strategy mixes all three pure strategies with positive probability, but that C should not be selected with greater probability than 1/3.

2.6 Show that Bourgeois is an evolutionarily stable strategy in the Hawk-Dove-Bourgeois game defined in Exercise 1.24.

2.7 Find all evolutionarily stable strategies in the game of the prisoner's dilemma, defined by Exercise 1.25.

2.8 Show that $R = (0, 0)$ and $(1/2, 1/2)$, i.e., an equal mixture of H and D, are both evolutionarily stable strategies in the Hawk-Dove-Retaliator game defined by Exercise 1.27.

2.9 Show that $(1/3, 1/3)$, in which each pure strategy is played with the same probability, is an ESS of the game defined by Exercise 1.28 if $\lambda > 0$, but that there is no ESS if $\lambda < 0$.

2.10 Find the rational reaction sets for the sex allocation game of Section 2.4. Verify that $u^* = 1/2$ is an ESS.

2.11 In Section 2.3 we showed that strategy θ in Crossroads could not be invaded by strategy 0 or strategy 1 in isolation. Reconcile this conclusion with dynamical model (2.46) in Section 2.5.

2.12 Show that if (2.51) is satisfied, then the only evolutionarily stable strategies—pure or mixed—of the symmetric game with payoff matrix

$$A = \begin{bmatrix} a_{11} & a_{12} \\ a_{21} & a_{22} \end{bmatrix}$$

are the two pure strategies.

2.13 Verify (2.56).

2.14 (i) Establish (2.62).

(ii) Show that (2.61) and (2.65) imply

$$x_1(n) + x_2(n) + \cdots + x_m(n) = 1, \qquad 0 \le n < \infty.$$

2.15 Demonstrate by computer that the precise value of K in Owners and Intruders is unimportant, provided it is neither too large nor too small.

2.16 Suppose that K in Owners and Intruders is a random variable whose distribution is known. How must the analysis be modified? How are the conclusions affected?

2.17 How consistent are our assumptions in Section 2.7 that searching animals are equally likely to find any site, that at most one animal intrudes upon a site per unit of time, and that animals and sites are infinitely numerous, but in such a way that σ defined by (2.68) is finite?

2.18 Obtain $H_1, \ldots, H_8$ in equation (2.87) as functions of $x_1, \ldots, x_4, y_1, \ldots, y_4$.

2.19 How does the ESS in Owners and Intruders depend upon ϵ and σ?

2.20 Use Taylor expansion of (2.82) to show that if ϵ is small, then $q(y_3)$ in Owners and Intruders can be replaced by $\epsilon \sigma y_3$. How good is this approximation in practice?

2.21 In the context of symmetric games restricted to pure strategies (Section 2.6):

   (i)   show that any ESS is stable against pure infiltration

   (ii)   show that a strong ESS is stable against mixed infiltration

   (iii)   show that a dominant strategy is also a strong ESS.

2.22 In this exercise, you will use a calculator or computer to solve (2.65) with Table 2.2's payoff matrix for $\lambda = 0.9$.

   (i)   Take
$$x(0) = (\delta_1, \alpha, \delta_2, \delta_3),$$
   where δ_1, δ_2 and δ_3 are small positive numbers and $\alpha = 1 - \delta_1 - \delta_2 - \delta_3$, and solve (2.65) for various values of α close to 1 (e.g., in the range $0.9 < \alpha < 1$). Show that $x(n) \rightarrow (0, c, 0, 1 - c)$ as $n \rightarrow \infty$, where c is close to 1 but $c < \alpha$.

   (ii)   For each value of c in (i), solve (2.65) for various values of
$$x(0) = (\delta_1, c - \delta_1, \delta_2, 1 - c - \delta_2),$$
   where δ_1 and δ_2 are small positive numbers. Show that $x(n) \rightarrow (0, c_1, 0, 1 - c_1)$ as $n \rightarrow \infty$, where c_1 is close to c but $c_1 < c$. Together, (i) and (ii) illustrate how infiltration by HH or DH can steadily reduce the proportion of HD and increase the proportion of DD.

   (iii)   Now solve (2.65) with
$$x(0) = \frac{1}{3}(1 - \alpha, 3\alpha, 1 - \alpha, 1 - \alpha)$$
   for various values of $\alpha \in (0, 1)$. Show that there is a critical value of α, say α_c, such that if $\alpha > \alpha_c$ then $x(n) \rightarrow (0, c, 0, 1 - c)$ as $n \rightarrow \infty$, where $c < \alpha$; but if $\alpha < \alpha_c$, then $x(n) \rightarrow (0, 0, 1, 0)$ as $n \rightarrow \infty$. These dynamics illustrate that repeated infiltration by HH and DH will ultimately cause the population to evolve to DH, as described in Section 2.7. What is the value of α_c?

   Note: $x(0)$ in this exercise is the initial composition of the population in Section 2.6; it has nothing to do with the initial distribution of states for a play of Owners and Intruders.

   (iv)   Criticize the use of (2.65) with (2.63) and (2.92) for the long-term dynamics of Owners and Intruders.

2.23 Analyze the game of Owners and Intruders for $\sigma > 1$, where σ is defined by (2.68).

   Hint: How must (2.85) be modified?

APPENDIX TO CHAPTER 2: THE TRACING PROCEDURE

The tracing procedure of Harsanyi (1975) is a method for associating a unique Nash equilibrium with all tentative solutions of a noncooperative, n-person

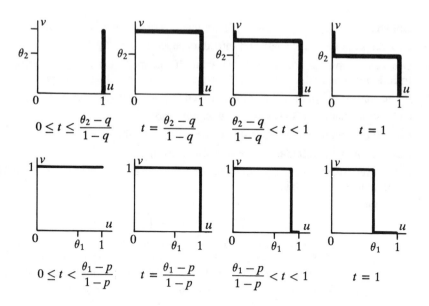

Figure 2A.1 $R_1(t)$ and $R_2(t)$ for $0 \leq t \leq 1$, $\theta_1 > p$, $\theta_2 > q$. The upper four diagrams show $R_1(t)$, the lower four diagrams $R_2(t)$.

game. We will describe the method only as it applies to a 2-person, noncooperative game, and in particular to Crossroads. Further details are given by Harsanyi and Selten (1988), who denote by priors what we have called tentative solutions (because their method is closely related to Bayesian methods in decision theory. Thus (p, q) is the prior for Crossroads, and the Nash equilibrium that the tracing procedure selects is a function of p and q. More generally, the Nash equilibrium selected by Harsanyi and Selten's theory is always dependent on the prior.)

The tracing procedure obtains the solutions depicted in Figure 2.1 by considering the infinite sequence of games defined for $0 \leq t \leq 1$ by reward functions H_1 and H_2, where

$$H_1(u,v) = (1 - t)f_1(u,q) + tf_1(u,v), \qquad 0 \leq t \leq 1 \qquad (2A.1a)$$
$$H_2(u,v) = (1 - t)f_2(p,v) + tf_2(u,v), \qquad 0 \leq t \leq 1. \qquad (2A.1b)$$

Thus Player k's reward, $H_k(u,v)$, is a convex linear combination of his actual reward, $f_k(u,v)$, and the reward associated with naively assuming that the other player will select his prior strategy—which is $f_1(u,q)$ in the case of Player 1 (Ned), and $f_2(p,v)$ in the case of Player 2 (Sed). As t increases from 0 to 1, the weight shifts continously from the reward associated with assuming that the other player selects his prior to the actual reward of the game. For Crossroads, it is readily shown that

$$H_1(u,v) = (\delta + \epsilon)(\theta_2 - (1 - t)q - tv)u + (\epsilon - \tau_2/2)(tv + (1 - t)q)$$
$$- \epsilon - \tau_2/2 \qquad (2A.2a)$$

$$H_2(u,v) = (\delta + \epsilon)(\theta_1 - (1 - t)p - tu)v + (\epsilon - \tau_1/2)(tu + (1 - t)p)$$
$$- \epsilon - \tau_1/2. \qquad (2A.2b)$$

Because the rewards H_1 and H_2 depend upon t, the rational reaction sets R_1 and R_2 will also depend upon t; we therefore denote them by $R_1(t)$ and $R_2(t)$. Assuming, as in (2.2), that $\theta_2 > q$, $R_1(t)$ is depicted in the upper four diagrams of Figure 2A.1, for $0 \leq t \leq 1$. You can see that R_1 changes at $t = t_1$ (defined by (2.4)) from a vertical line to an inverted L; thereafter, there is a horizontal segment at

$$v = \frac{\theta_2 - (1 - t)q}{t}, \qquad (2A.3)$$

which moves downward from $v = 1$ to $v = \theta_2$ as t increases from t_1 to 1. Similarly, assuming that $\theta_1 > p$, $R_2(t)$ is depicted for $0 \leq t \leq 1$ in the lower four diagrams of Figure 2A.1. It changes at $t = t_2$ (defined by (2.4)) from a horizontal line to an inverted L; thereafter, there is a vertical segment at

$$u = \frac{\theta_1 - (1 - t)p}{t}, \qquad (2A.4)$$

which moves leftward from $u = 1$ to $u = \theta_1$ as t increases from t_2 to 1.

Let us now assume that (2.5) holds, i.e., $p = 1/2 = q$. Then it is clear from Figure 2A.1 that $R_1(t) \cap R_2(t)$, the set of all Nash equilibria, evolves with t according to Figure 2A.2 when $\theta_1 > \theta_2$. For $t < t_1$ there is a unique equilibrium at $(1, 1)$; at $t = t_1$ there is a line segment of equilibria stretching from $(1, 1)$ to $(0, 1)$; for $t_1 < t < t_2$ there is a unique equilibrium at $(0, 1)$; at $t = t_2$ there is an additional line segment of equilibria stretching from $(1, (\theta_1 + \theta_2 - 1)/(2\theta_1 - 1))$ to $(1, 0)$; and thereafter there are three equilibria, one at $(1, 0)$, one at $(0, 1)$ and one at

$$\left(\frac{1}{2}, \frac{1}{2}\right) + \frac{1}{t}\left(\theta_1 - \frac{1}{2}, \theta_2 - \frac{1}{2}\right), \qquad (2A.5)$$

which, as indicated by the arrow in Figure 2A.2, migrates from $\left(1, (\theta_1 + \theta_2 - 1)/(2\theta_1 - 1)\right)$ to (θ_1, θ_2) as t increases from t_2 to 1. Likewise, when $\theta_2 > \theta_1$, $R_1(t) \cap R_2(t)$ evolves with t according to Figure 2A.3. For $t < t_2$ there is a unique equilibrium at $(1, 1)$; at $t = t_2$ there is a line segment of equilibria stretching from $(1, 1)$ to $(1, 0)$; for $t_2 < t < t_1$ there is a unique equilibrium at $(1, 0)$; at $t = t_1$ there is an additional line segment of equilibria stretching from $\left((\theta_1 + \theta_2 - 1)/(2\theta_2 - 1), 1\right)$ to $(0, 1)$; and thereafter there are three equilibria, one at $(1, 0)$, one at $(0, 1)$ and one at the point defined by (2A.5), which migrates from $\left((\theta_1 + \theta_2 - 1)/(2\theta_2 - 1), 1\right)$ to (θ_1, θ_2) as t increases from t_1 to 1.

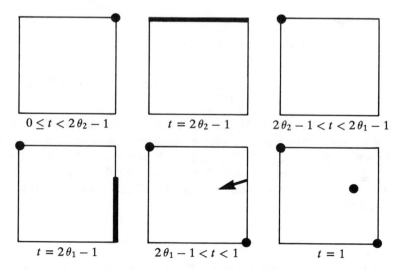

Figure 2A.2 Evolution $R_1(t) \cap R_2(t)$
for $p = 1/2 = q, \theta_1 > \theta_2$.

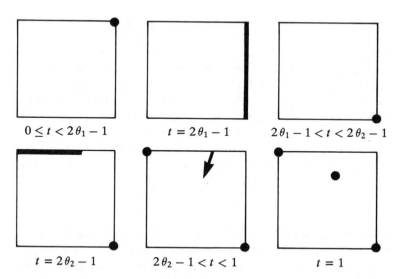

Figure 2A.3 Evolution $R_1(t) \cap R_2(t)$
for $p = 1/2 = q, \theta_1 < \theta_2$.

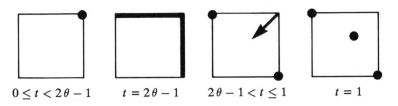

$$0 \le t < 2\theta - 1 \qquad t = 2\theta - 1 \qquad 2\theta - 1 < t \le 1 \qquad t = 1$$

Figure 2A.4   Evolution $R_1(t) \cap R_2(t)$
for $p = 1/2 = q, \theta_1 = \theta_2 = \theta$.

Now imagine that t is plotted on a third axis, perpendicular to the page. Then, as t increases from 0 to 1, $R_1(t) \cap R_2(t)$ will trace out a set of curves in space. Only one of the three Nash equilibria at $t = 1$ has the distinguishing property that it can be reached from the single Nash equilbrium $(1, 1)$ at $t = 0$ by moving continuously along one of the curves, as you can readily verify from Figures 2A.2–2A.3. This distinguished equilibrium is Harsanyi's solution (which agrees with Figure 2.1).

If $\theta_1 = \theta_2$, however, then Figure 2A.4 shows that all three equilibria at $t = 1$ can be reached from $(1, 1)$ at $t = 0$ by moving continuously along the curves. For such contingencies, Harsanyi and Selten have proposed a modification of the tracing procedure, which they call the logarithmic tracing procedure. Broadly speaking, it resolves the indeterminacy by selecting the Nash equilibrium that is nearest to the center of the strategy set; whence, in particular, its prediction for the symmetric version of Crossroads agrees with Figure 2.2. If you are interested in the details, then you should consult Harsanyi and Selten (1988, p. 165).

The general theory of Harsanyi and Selten does not consist solely of the tracing procedures; rather, it includes a rational for selecting the prior. Again, if you are interested in the details, you should consult Harsanyi and Selten (1988, Chapter 5).

3

Cooperative Games in Strategic Form

Consider a game between two players, and let each choose a single variable—u for the first player, v for the second. Then to every feasible strategy combination (u, v), i.e., to every (u, v) in the decision set D, there corresponds a vector of rewards (f_1, f_2); and the equations $f_1 = f_1(u, v), f_2 = f_2(u, v)$ define a vector-valued function, f, from the decision set D, which is a subset of the u-v plane, into the f_1-f_2 plane. In Crossroads, for example, f_1 and f_2 are defined by (1.16)–(1.17). The range of the function f, i.e., the region of the f_1-f_2 plane onto which f maps D, is known as the *reward set*; it contains all reward vectors that are achievable by some combination of strategies in D. We denote the reward set by $\overline{F}$. Note that f is not in general invertible; i.e., the equations $f_1 = f_1(u, v), f_2 = f_2(u, v)$ do not define a (single-valued) function from $\overline{F}$ onto D. (We saw in Exercise 1.19, for example, that when both drivers in Crossroads are fast, the joint max-min strategy combination $(\bar{u}, \bar{v})$ and the Nash-equilibrium strategy combination (θ_1, θ_2) are mapped to the same point in $\overline{F}$ by f; however, $(\bar{u}, \bar{v}) \neq (\theta_1, \theta_2)$.)

The concept of reward set is readily generalized to games among n players, the k-th of whom selects an s_k-dimensional strategy vector; f is then a vector-valued function from a space of dimension $s_1 + s_2 + \cdots + s_k$ into a space of dimension n. But the concept is most useful for $n = 2$. For $n = 3$ the reward set is difficult to sketch, and for $n > 3$ it is difficult even to visualize.

For games between specific individuals who are able to make binding agreements with one another if it benefits them to do so, Nash's concept of noncooperative equilibrium loses its appeal to various cooperative solution concepts (the most enduring of which is still due to Nash); and in understanding why, we will find that a picture of the reward set is worth several thousand words. Accordingly, an analysis of the reward set for the game of Crossroads will serve as our springboard to cooperative games. In this chapter, we shall refer to such games as cooperative games in strategic form—merely to distinguish them from cooperative games in characteristic-function form, which are the subject of Chapter 4.

We begin, as promised, by returning to Chapter 1's game of Crossroads. For the sake of simplicity, we shall assume throughout that Nan and San are both fast drivers. Therefore

$$2\delta > 2\epsilon > \tau_1, \tau_2. \tag{3.1}$$

3.1   PARETO-OPTIMALITY: THE RATIONALITY BEHIND COOPERATION

For the game of Crossroads, the reward vector f is defined by (1.16)–(1.17), i.e.,

$$f_1(u,v) = \left(\epsilon + \frac{\tau_2}{2} - (\delta + \epsilon)v\right)u + \left(\epsilon - \frac{\tau_2}{2}\right)v - \epsilon - \frac{\tau_2}{2}, \tag{3.2a}$$

$$f_2(u,v) = \left(\epsilon + \frac{\tau_1}{2} - (\delta + \epsilon)u\right)v + \left(\epsilon - \frac{\tau_1}{2}\right)u - \epsilon - \frac{\tau_1}{2}. \tag{3.2b}$$

Suppose, for example, that game is symmetric ($\tau_1 = \tau_2$) with

$$\delta = 3, \qquad \epsilon = 2, \qquad \tau_1 = 2 = \tau_2. \tag{3.3}$$

Then

$$f_1 = 3(u - 1) + (1 - 5u)v, \qquad f_2 = u - 3 + (3 - 5u)v. \tag{3.4}$$

The reward set $\overline{F}$ is the image of the decision set

$$D = \{(u,v) \mid 0 \leq u, v \leq 1\}$$

under the mapping defined by (3.4). To obtain $\overline{F}$, imagine that D is covered by an infinity of line segments parallel to the v-axis. On each of these line segments u is constant, but v increases from 0 to 1. Let us first obtain the image under (3.4)

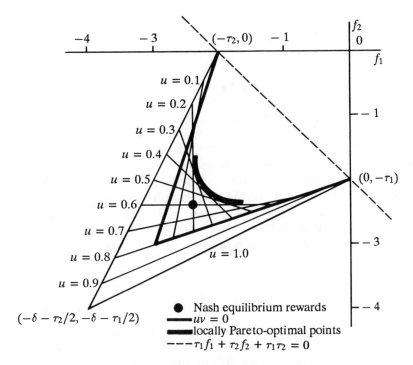

Figure 3.1 The reward set for Crossroads, where $(0, -\tau_1)$ and $(-\tau_2, 0)$ are globally Pareto-optimal.

of one of these line segments, then allow u to vary between 0 and 1. The images of all the line segments together (with some duplication) will constitute $\bar{F}$.

Consider, therefore, the line segment $L(c)$ defined by

$$L(c) = \{(c, v) \mid 0 \le v \le 1\}, \tag{3.5}$$

on which $u = c = $ constant (and $0 \le c \le 1$). The image of $L(c)$ under the mapping f is

$$f(L(c)) = \{(f_1, f_2) \mid f_1 = 3(c-1) + (1-5c)v, f_2 = c - 3 + (3-5c)v \text{ for } v \in [0, 1]\}, \tag{3.6}$$

from (3.4). Eliminating v, we see that $f(L(c))$ is part of the line in the f_1-f_2 plane with equation

$$(3 - 5c)f_1 + (5c - 1)f_2 + 10c^2 - 8c + 6 = 0; \tag{3.7}$$

see Exercise 3.1. But $f(L(c))$ is not the whole of this line, because $0 \le v \le 1$; rather, it is that part which extends in the f_1-f_2 plane from the point $(3c-3, c-3)$, corresponding to $v = 0$, to the point $(-2-2c, -4c)$, corresponding to $v = 1$. The line segment $f(L(c))$ is sketched in Figure 3.1 for values of c at increments of 0.1 between 0 and 1. For example, $f(L(0))$, which is the image of side $u = 0$ of the unit square, is that part of the line $3f_1 - f_2 + 6 = 0$ which stretches from $(-3, -3)$ to $(-2, 0)$. It is marked in Figure 3.1 as the upper prong of a V-shape, the lower prong of which is the image of side $v = 0$ of the unit square and satisfies $f_1 - 3f_2 - 6 = 0$. Again, $f(L(1))$, which is the image of side $u = 1$ of the unit square, is that part of the line $f_1 - 2f_2 - 4 = 0$ which stretches from $(-4, -4)$ to $(0, -2)$. In Figure 3.1 it is the lower prong of the larger V-shape, the upper prong of which is the image of side $v = 1$ of the unit square and satisfies $2f_1 - f_2 + 4 = 0$ (Exercise 3.1).

A glance at Figure 3.1 now reveals that the reward set is a curvilinear triangle, which is reminiscent of the the open mouth of a fledgling (and the picture is similar for all other values of δ, ϵ, τ_1 and τ_2 such that (3.1) is satisfied). The straight edges of the triangle have equations $2f_1 - f_2 + 4 = 0, f_1 - 2f_2 - 4 = 0$. The curved edge of the triangle is the curve to which every line segment in the family

$$\left\{ f(L(c)) \mid 0 \le c \le \frac{4}{5} \right\} \tag{3.8}$$

is a tangent; we call this curve the *envelope* of the family. This envelope has two straight segments. The first runs between $(-11/5, -3/5)$ and $(-2, 0)$; it corresponds to limiting member $L(0)$ of family (3.8), and hence has equation $3f_1 - f_2 + 6 = 0$. The second straight segment of the envelope runs between $(-3/5, -11/5)$ and $(0, -2)$; it corresponds to limiting member $L(4/5)$ of family (3.8), and so has equation $f_1 - 3f_2 - 6 = 0$. To find the equation of the curved part of the envelope between $(-11/5, -3/5)$ and $(-3/5, -11/5)$: suppose that the line segment $f(L(c))$ has equation

$$\psi(f_1, f_2, c) = 0, \tag{3.9}$$

so that ψ is defined by the left-hand side of (3.7); and that it touches the envelope at the point with coordinates $(F_1(c), F_2(c))$, so that the parametric equation of the envelope is

$$f_1 = F_1(c), \quad f_2 = F_2(c), \qquad 0 \le c \le 4/5. \tag{3.10}$$

Then, from (3.9), the vector normal to $f(L(c))$ has direction $(\partial\psi_1/\partial f_1, \partial\psi_2/\partial f_2)$; and, from (3.10), the tangent vector to the envelope has direction $(F_1'(c), (F_2'(c))$, where a prime denotes differentiation. Because these two vectors must be perpendicular at the point $(F_1(c), F_2(c))$, we have $(\partial\psi_1/\partial f_1)F_1'(c) + (\partial\psi_2/\partial f_2) F_2'(c) = 0$. But $(F_1(c), F_2(c))$ must lie on $f(L(c))$, whence $\psi(F_1(c), F_2(c), c) = 0$. If we differentiate this last equation with respect to c, then we obtain $\partial\psi_1/\partial f_1 F_1'(c) +]\partial\psi_2/\partial f_2 F_2'(c) + \partial\psi_1/\partial c = 0$; therefore, $\partial\psi_1/\partial c = 0$ at $(F_1(c), F_2(c))$.

Thus $\psi = 0$ and $\partial \psi_1 / \partial c = 0$ are two equations that must be satisfied by all points (f_1, f_2) on the envelope. By eliminating c between these equations, we obtain the envelope's equation (Exercise 3.2):

$$25(f_1 - f_2)^2 - 40(f_1 + f_2) - 176 = 0. \tag{3.11}$$

Thus the curved edge of $\overline{F}$ has equation

$$3f_1 - f_2 + 6 = 0 \quad \text{if} \quad -\frac{3}{5} \leq f_2 \leq 0 \tag{3.12a}$$

$$25(f_1 - f_2)^2 - 40(f_1 + f_2) - 176 = 0 \quad \text{if} \quad f_1 \leq -\frac{3}{5}, \quad f_2 \leq -\frac{3}{5} \tag{3.12b}$$

$$f_1 - 3f_2 - 6 = 0 \quad \text{if} \quad -\frac{3}{5} \leq f_1 \leq 0. \tag{3.12c}$$

We note in passing that

$$\psi(f_1, f_2, c) = 0 = \frac{\partial \psi}{\partial c}(f_1, f_2, c) \tag{3.13}$$

would yield the parametric equations of the envelope of (3.8), even if $\psi = 0$ were not a straight line.

Now, if Nan and San had agreed to cooperate, then which point of $\overline{F}$ would be most agreeable to them? Suppose that they were somehow to pick a tentative point. Then, because Nan wants f_1 to be as large as possible and San wants f_2 to be as large as possible, points just above or to the right of this tentative point would always be at least as agreeable to them, no matter where in the reward set the tentative point lay. Therefore, Nan and San would revise their tentative point. Proceeding in this manner, the two players would quickly eliminate all points either in the interior of the reward set or on the southern or western edge, because all such points could be improved upon by moving infinitesimally upwards or to the right. Thus agreeable points must lie on (3.12).

But even part of this curved edge can be eliminated. Implicit differentiation of (3.11) yields

$$\frac{df_2}{df_1} = \frac{5(f_1 - f_2) - 4}{5(f_1 - f_2) + 4}, \tag{3.14}$$

whence the tangent to the curve (3.12) is parallel to the f_1-axis at $(-8/5, -12/5)$, and to the f_2-axis at $(-12/5, -8/5)$; see Exercise 3.3. Between $(-8/5, -12/5)$ and $(-3/5, -11/5)$, the slope increases from 0 to 1/3; thereafter it is constant. Hence both f_1 and f_2 are greater at every point between $(-8/5, -12/5)$ and $(0, -2)$ than they are at $(-8/5, -12/5)$. All such points, with the exception of $(0, -2)$, are improvable, and so Nan and San would eliminate them. Likewise, f_1 and f_2 are greater at every point between $(-12/5, -8/5)$ and $(-2, 0)$ then they are at $(-12/5, -8/5)$; all such points, with the exception of $(-2, 0)$, are improvable and would be eliminated. Thus the only remaining points on (3.12) are

$(-2,0)$, $(0,-2)$ and points that lie between $(-8/5,-12/5)$ and $(-12/5,-8/5)$. If one of these points has been reached, then it is impossible to move to a *neighboring* point in the reward set—i.e., a point in the reward set that is arbitrarily close but nevertheless distinct—without making at least one player worse off. Such points are therefore said to be *locally unimprovable*, or *locally Pareto-optimal*. But among these points, $(-2,0)$ and $(0,-2)$ possess an even stronger measure of unimprovability: it is impossible to move from either one to *any* point in the reward set without making at least one player worse off. Such points are said to be globally unimprovable, or globally Pareto-optimal; and clearly, global Pareto-optimality implies local Pareto-optimality. Locally Pareto-optimal points of $\overline{F}$ are marked in Figure 3.1 by a solid curve from $(-8/5,-12/5)$ to $(-12/5,-8/5)$; note, however, that the endpoints are excluded.

More formally, the strategy combination (u,v) is locally unimprovable, or locally Pareto-optimal, if there exists no neighboring point $(\overline{u},\overline{v})$ in D such that

$$\text{EITHER}\quad f_1(\overline{u},\overline{v}) > f_1(u,v) \quad \text{AND} \quad f_2(\overline{u},\overline{v}) \geq f_2(u,v)$$
$$\text{OR}\quad f_1(\overline{u},\overline{v}) \geq f_1(u,v) \quad \text{AND} \quad f_2(\overline{u},\overline{v}) > f_2(u,v); \tag{3.15}$$

and (u,v) is globally unimprovable, or globally Pareto-optimal, if there exists *no* point $(\overline{u},\overline{v})$ anywhere in D such that (3.15) is satisfied. Note that if (u,v) and $(\overline{u},\overline{v})$ are neighboring points in D, then $(f_1(u,v),f_2(u,v))$ and $(f_1(\overline{u},\overline{v}),f_2(\overline{u},\overline{v}))$ are neighboring points in $\overline{F}$, because f_1 and f_2 are continuous functions.

These definitions are adequate for our purposes, and would hold even if Player 1 had a vector u of strategies, and Player 2 a vector v of strategies (as in Section 1.4). Nevertheless, we pause to remark that the concept of Pareto-optimality is readily generalized to games among an arbitrary number of players—say n—as follows. Let $N = \{1,2,\ldots,n\}$ denote the set of players, and for each $k \in N$ let Player k have an s_k-dimensional vector of strategies, which we denote by w^k; thus $w^1 = u$, $w^2 = v$ in (3.15). For each $k \in N$, let Player k's reward be $f_k = f_k(w)$, where w denotes the strategy combination $(w^1,w^2,\ldots,w^n)$; and let D be the set of all feasible w, or decision set. Then the strategy combination w is locally Pareto-optimal if there exists *no* other neighboring point $\overline{w} = (\overline{w}^2,\overline{w}^2,\ldots,\overline{w}^n)$ in D such that

$$f_k(\overline{w}) \geq f_k(w) \quad \text{for } all \quad k \in N \quad \text{AND} f_i(\overline{w}) > f_i(w) \quad \text{for } some\ i \in N; \tag{3.16}$$

and w is globally unimprovable, or globally Pareto-optimal, if there exists *no* point $\overline{w}$ anywhere in D such that (3.16) is satisfied.

Clearly, provided the players have agreed to cooperate, any strategy combination that is not locally Pareto-optimal would be irrational, because the players could agree to a neighboring combination that would yield no less a reward for all of them and a somewhat greater reward for at least one of them. It is not so clear that a combination would be irrational if it were not globally Pareto-optimal, however, because the only globally Pareto-optimal points in Figure 3.1 are $(0, -2)$ and $(-2, 0)$; and although these points represent best possible outcomes for Nan or San as individuals, it is difficult to see how both as a group could agree to either. Therefore, we shall proceed on the assumption that the best cooperative strategy combination in a cooperative game must be at least locally Pareto-optimal, but not necessarily globally Pareto-optimal; and if only a single combination were locally Pareto-optimal, then we would not hesitate to regard it as the solution of the game. These special circumstances almost never arise, however; rather, many strategy combinations are locally Pareto-optimal. Accordingly, we denote the set of all locally Pareto-optimal strategy combinations by P, and the set of all globally Pareto-optimal strategy combinations by P_G. Of course, $P \supset P_G$: a strategy cannot be globally Pareto-optimal unless first of all it is locally Pareto-optimal.

To obtain P for the version of Crossroads defined by (3.3), all we need do is to substitute (3.4) into (3.12b); after simplification, we obtain (Exercise 3.3)

$$[10(u + v) - 8]^2 = 0. \tag{3.17}$$

But in Figure 3.1 the thick solid curve corresponds to values of u between 1/5 and 3/5. Thus P consists of the line segment in the u-v plane that joins $(1/5, 3/5)$ to $(3/5, 1/5)$; together, of course, with $(0, 1)$ and $(1, 0)$. In mathematics:

$$P = \{(0,1)\} \cup \left\{(u,v) \mid u + v = \frac{4}{5}, \; \frac{1}{5} < u < \frac{3}{5}\right\} \cup \{(1,0)\}. \tag{3.18a}$$

Also, clearly,

$$P_G = \{(0,1)\} \cup \{(1,0)\}. \tag{3.18b}$$

The set P is sketched in Figure 3.2. Note that P is disconnected—it consists of three separate pieces—and excludes $(1/5, 3/5)$ and $(3/5, 1/5)$, as indicated by the open circles in Figure 3.2. Furthermore, although every locally Pareto-optimal reward vector lies on the boundary of $\overline{F}$, all but two locally Pareto-optimal strategy combinations lie in the interior of D.

If you are familiar with the implicit function theorem, then you will recognize that (3.17) could also have been obtained from the vanishing of the Jacobian of the mapping defined by (3.4), i.e., from

$$\begin{vmatrix} \dfrac{\partial f_1}{\partial u} & \dfrac{\partial f_1}{\partial v} \\[2mm] \dfrac{\partial f_2}{\partial u} & \dfrac{\partial f_2}{\partial v} \end{vmatrix} = 0; \tag{3.19}$$

see Exercise 3.4. This happens because, on the one hand, the mapping f is locally invertible wherever (3.19) does not vanish; and, on the other hand, if you think of the unit square in the u-v plane as a sheet of rubber that must be stretched or shrunk by the mapping f until it corresponds to the reward set, then the envelope lies where the sheet gets folded back on itself by f. The mapping is not

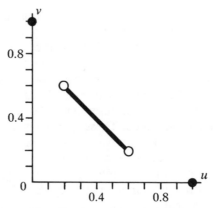

Figure 3.2   The bargaining set for Crossroads
with $\delta = 3, \epsilon = 2, \tau_1 = 2 = \tau_2$.

locally invertible here because, for points in $\overline{F}$ that are arbitrarily close to the
envelope, it is impossible to say whether the inverse image in the unit square
should correspond to the upper of the two folds or to the lower one.

     If P contains more than a single strategy combination, then which element
of P is the solution of the game? We will consider this question in Section 3.3. It
is already clear from Figure 3.1 that the question is worth answering, however,
because both Nan and San prefer *any* strategy combination in P to the Nash
equilibrium (3/5, 3/5), which gives each a reward of only $-12/5$. On the other
hand, P may be too large a set from which to select a solution, and in this regard
it will be convenient to introduce some new terminology. For $k \in N$, let $\tilde{f}_k$
denote Player k's max-min reward; that is, define $\tilde{f}_k = m_k(\tilde{w}^k)$, where m_k is the
minimizing function defined by (1.87) and $\tilde{w}^k$ is a max-min strategy for Player k.
If $f_k(w) \geq \tilde{f}_k$, i.e., if w gives Player k at least her max-min reward, then we say
that w is individually rational for Player k; and we define the *bargaining set* P^* by

$$P^* = \left\{w \in P | f_k(w) \geq \tilde{f}_k \quad \text{for all} \quad k \in N\right\}. \tag{3.20}$$

Thus the bargaining set contains all locally Pareto-optimal strategy combinations
that are individually rational for all players. Now, it would make no sense for
Player k to accept the reward $f_k(w)$ if $f_k(w) < \tilde{f}_k$, because she could obtain at
least $\tilde{f}_k$ without any cooperation at all. Accordingly, in Section 3.3 we will seek
cooperative solutions that are not only locally Pareto-optimal, but also individually rational for all players; in other words, solutions that lie not only in P but also
in P^*. (Note, however, that P^* coincides with P for the game whose reward set is
sketched in Figure 3.1; because, from Exercise 1.19 and (3.3), $\tilde{f}_1 = -12/5 = \tilde{f}_2$.)

3.2 NECESSARY CONDITIONS FOR PARETO-OPTIMALITY

To determine whether a strategy combination $w \in D$ is locally improvable, we compare the rewards at w with those at a neighboring point, say $w + \lambda h$, where the vector h yields the direction of movement from w and λ is a small number; h must not be the zero vector. If there exists $\lambda > 0$, no matter how small, such that $f_k(w + \lambda h) \geq f_k(w)$ for all $k \in N$ and $f_i(w + \lambda h) > f_i(w)$ for some $i \in N$, then w is not (either locally or globally) Pareto-optimal, because $w + \lambda h$ is an improved strategy combination—provided, of course, that $w + \lambda h \in D$. Accordingly, we define h to be an *admissible direction* at w if $w + \lambda h \in D$ for sufficiently small $\lambda > 0$. Clearly, any h is admissible at w in the interior of D; whereas only the zero vector and vectors that point into the interior are admissible at w on the boundary of D. Suppose, for example, that $u = w^1$, $v = w^2$ and that D is the unit square $\{(u, v) | 0 \leq u, v \leq 1\}$. Then $h = (h_1, h_2)$ must satisfy $h_1 \geq 0$ to be admissible on the side $u = 0$; however, h_2 is unrestricted on $u = 0$—except at the points $(0, 0)$, where we require $h_2 \geq 0$, and $(0, 1)$, where we require $h_2 \leq 0$. Similar considerations apply to the other three sides of the square (although any h is admissible in the interior).

Now if, at w, there exists an admissible direction h and a number $\lambda > 0$, no matter how small, such that $f_k(w + \lambda h) - f_k(w) \geq 0$ for all $k \in N$ and $f_i(w + \lambda h) - f_i(w) > 0$ for some $i \in N$, then $w \notin P$ (and hence $w \notin P^*$). In principle, by applying this test to each $w \in D$ in turn, we could systematically eliminate all locally improvable strategy combinations. The test is not practicable, however, because D contains infinitely many points.

To devise a practicable test for Pareto-optimality, it is necessary to make assumptions about the nature of the functions f_k—principally, that f_k is (at least once) differentiable for all $k \in N$. From little more than this assumption, it is possible to derive necessary and sufficient conditions for Pareto-optimality that have considerable generality; see, for example, Vincent and Grantham (1981). To follow this approach in its full generality would greatly distract us from our purpose, however, and so we shall assume instead that each player controls only a single variable. Then Player k's strategy, w^k, is no longer a vector but rather a scalar, which we prefer to denote by w_k; and the joint strategy combination w is an n-dimensional row vector, namely, $w = (w_1, w_2, \ldots, w_n)$. Furthermore, we shall restrict our attention to *necessary conditions* for Pareto-optimality; which, as we shall see, eliminate most—but not all—improvable strategy combinations.

Let us now recall that if f_k is differentiable with respect to w_k for all $k \in N$, then from Taylor's theorem for functions of several variables we have

$$f_k(w + \lambda h) - f_k(w) = \lambda \frac{\partial f_k}{\partial w} h^T + o(\lambda), \tag{3.21}$$

where $\partial f_k / \partial w$ is the gradient vector defined by

$$\frac{\partial f_k}{\partial w} \equiv \left(\frac{\partial f_k}{\partial w_1}, \frac{\partial f_k}{\partial w_2}, \ldots, \frac{\partial f_k}{\partial w_n} \right),$$

h is the row vector defined by $h = (h_1, h_2, \ldots, h_n)$, h^T is the transpose of h, $\lambda > 0$, and $o(\lambda)$ denotes terms so small that you can divide them by λ and the result will still tend to zero as $\lambda \to 0$. The first term on the right-hand side of (3.21) dominates $o(\lambda)$ for sufficiently small λ if $\partial f_k / \partial w \cdot h^T \neq 0$. Therefore, if

$$\frac{\partial f_k}{\partial w} h^T > 0, \qquad k = 1, 2, \ldots, n \quad \text{for } any \text{ admissible direction } h, \qquad (3.22)$$

then w is not (either locally or globally) Pareto-optimal; because then (3.21) and (3.22) imply that

$$f_k(w + \lambda h) - f_k(w) > 0 \qquad (3.23)$$

for all $k \in N$ for sufficiently small $\lambda(> 0)$, so that $w + \lambda h$ is an improved strategy combination. Strategy combinations that do not satisfy (3.22) are *candidates* for Pareto-optimality; however, we cannot be sure that they are Pareto-optimal, even locally. Accordingly, let us denote by P_{nec} the set of all $w \in D$ that do not satisfy (3.22), and by P^*_{nec} the set of all $w \in P_{nec}$ that are individually rational for all players. Then $P_{nec} \supset P$ and $P^*_{nec} \supset P^*$; but $P_{nec} \neq P$ and $P^*_{nec} \neq P^*$, at least in general.

Suppose, for example, that $n = 2$ and set $u = w_1$, $v = w_2$. Then (3.22) requires us to eliminate $(u, v) \in D$ if

$$\frac{\partial f_1}{\partial u} h_1 + \frac{\partial f_1}{\partial v} h_2 > 0 \qquad \text{AND} \qquad \frac{\partial f_2}{\partial u} h_1 + \frac{\partial f_2}{\partial v} h_2 > 0 \qquad (3.24)$$

for any admissible direction $h = (h_1, h_2)$. To be quite specific, let us consider the version of Crossroads defined by (3.3). Then, from (3.4), (u, v) is not Pareto-optimal if

$$(3 - 5v)h_1 + (1 - 5u)h_2 > 0 \qquad \text{AND} \qquad (1 - 5v)h_1 + (3 - 5u)h_2 > 0 \quad (3.25)$$

for any admissible (h_1, h_2). Now, $h = (1, 0)$ is an admissible direction everywhere in the unit square except on the side $u = 1$. Accordingly, from points in the square such that $0 \leq u < 1, 0 \leq v \leq 1$ we must exclude those where $3 - 5v > 0$ *and* $1 - 5v > 0$, i.e., points where $v < 1/5$. Similarly, because $h = (-1, 0)$ is an admissible direction everywhere in the square except on the side $u = 0$, from points in the unit square such that $0 < u \leq 1, 0 \leq v \leq 1$ we must exclude those where $3 - 5v < 0$ *and* $1 - 5v < 0$, i.e., points where $v > 3/5$. Continuing in this manner, we find that choosing $h = (0, 1)$ excludes points where $u < 1/5$ from points such that $0 \leq u \leq 1, 0 \leq v < 1$; and that choosing $h = (0, -1)$ excludes points where $u > 3/5$ from points such that $0 \leq u \leq 1$, $0 < v \leq 1$. Now the only points remaining are $(0, 1)$, $(1, 0)$ and those which

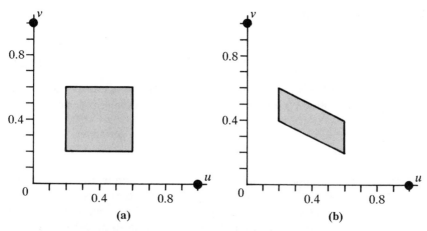

Figure 3.3   Sets that contain the set of Pareto-optimal points.

satisfy $1/5 \leq u, v \leq 3/5$. This set of candidates for Pareto-optimality is sketched in Figure 3.3(a).

We know already from Section 3.1 that $(0, 1)$ and $(1, 0)$ are globally Pareto-optimal. Let us therefore concentrate on the region $\{(u, v) | 1/5 \leq u, v \leq 3/5\}$. Because this square lies totally within the interior of D, any h is admissible. We can choose, for example, $h = (2, 1)$. Then (3.25) requires us to exclude (u, v) such that $5u + 10v < 7$ *and* $5u + 10v < 5$, i.e., points where $u + 2v < 1$. Similarly, choosing $h = (-2, -1)$ requires us to exclude points such that $5u + 10v > 7$ *and* $5u + 10v > 5$, i.e., points where $u + 2v > 7/5$. We have now reduced our set of candidates for Pareto-optimality to the parallelogram sketched in Figure 3.3(b).

We could eliminate improvable points indefinitely in this manner, but let us not prolong our agony. From (3.25), $h = (1, 1)$ rules out points in the shaded region of Figure 3.3(b) where $4 - 5(u + v) > 0$, whereas $h = (-1, -1)$ rules out points in that region where $4 - 5(u + v) < 0$; therefore, all locally Pareto-optimal points must satisfy $u + v = 4/5$. We have therefore shown that

$$P_{\text{nec}} = \{(0, 1)\} \cup \left\{ (u, v) \, | \, u + v = \frac{4}{5}, \quad \frac{1}{5} \leq u \leq \frac{3}{5} \right\} \cup \{(1, 0)\}. \qquad (3.26)$$

Note, however, that (3.25) is unable to eliminate $(1/5, 3/5)$ and $(3/5, 1/5)$ as candidates, although we already know from Section 3.1 that neither point is Pareto-optimal. Thus $P_{\text{nec}} \supset P$ but $P_{\text{nec}} \neq P$—compare (3.26) to (3.18).

The guesswork involved in choosing an admissible direction that yields useful information is clearly unsatisfactory, and we can eliminate much of it by having recourse to the so-called "Theorem of the Alternative." A special case of this theorem, which will suffice for our purposes, is the following: if J is an $n \times n$

matrix and K an $m \times n$ matrix, then *either* there exists a $1 \times n$ (row) vector h such that

$$Jh^T > 0^n, \qquad Kh^T \geq 0^m; \tag{3.27}$$

or there exists a $1 \times n$ vector η with nonnegative components and at least one positive component, and a $1 \times m$ vector μ with nonnegative components, such that

$$\eta J + \mu K = 0_n; \tag{3.28}$$

but *never both.* Here 0^n stands for the $n \times 1$ zero vector, 0_n stands for the $1 \times n$ zero vector, and a vector inequality $w > 0$ (or $w \geq 0$) means that every component of the vector w must be positive (or nonnegative); thus, in the statement of the theorem, $\eta \geq 0_n, \eta \neq 0_n, \mu \geq 0_m$. For a proof of the theorem of the alternative, see Mangasarian (1969).

Now, under our one-strategy-per-player assumption, constraints on the admissibility of h at a given point can always be written in the form $Kh^T \geq 0^m$, for suitable K and m, and the n inequalities (3.22) are equivalent to $Jh^T > 0^n$, where J is the Jacobian matrix

$$J(w) = \begin{bmatrix} \dfrac{\partial f_1}{\partial w_1} & \dfrac{\partial f_1}{\partial w_2} & \cdots & \dfrac{\partial f_1}{\partial w_n} \\[2mm] \dfrac{\partial f_2}{\partial w_1} & \dfrac{\partial f_2}{\partial w_2} & \cdots & \dfrac{\partial f_2}{\partial w_n} \\[2mm] \vdots & \vdots & \vdots\vdots\vdots & \vdots \\[2mm] \dfrac{\partial f_n}{\partial w_1} & \dfrac{\partial f_n}{\partial w_2} & \cdots & \dfrac{\partial f_n}{\partial w_n} \end{bmatrix} \tag{3.29}$$

for the particular w whose Pareto-optimality is being tested. Observe that (3.22) precludes alternative (3.27); therefore, we must have (3.28). In particular, because $K = {}_m0_n$ (the $m \times n$ zero matrix) for points in the interior of D (where any h is admissible), and because η must not be the zero vector, we deduce from (3.28) that $\eta J(w) = 0_n, \eta \neq 0_n$ if w is an interior, Pareto-optimal point. It follows immediately from the theory of linear algebra that if w is an interior, Pareto-optimal point then

$$|J(w)| = 0, \tag{3.30}$$

i.e., the determinant of the Jacobian must vanish at w; (3.19) is a special case of this result. The result does not imply that every interior point w satisfying (3.30) is a candidate for Pareto-optimality, however, because more than just $|J| = 0$ is implied by $\eta J = 0_n, \eta \neq 0_n$. When $n = 2$, for example, $\eta J = 0_n$ becomes

$$\eta_1 \frac{\partial f_1}{\partial u} + \eta_2 \frac{\partial f_2}{\partial u} = 0, \quad \eta_1 \frac{\partial f_1}{\partial v} + \eta_2 \frac{\partial f_2}{\partial v} = 0, \tag{3.31}$$

where $\eta = (\eta_1, \eta_2)$; and $(\eta_1, \eta_2) \neq (0,0)$, $(\eta_1, \eta_2) \geq (0,0)$ allows just three possibilities for η, namely, that $\eta_1 = 0$ and $\eta_2 > 0$, that $\eta_1 > 0$ and $\eta_2 = 0$, or that $\eta_1 > 0$ and $\eta_2 > 0$. From (3.31), the first case requires $\partial f_2/\partial u = 0 = \partial f_2/\partial v$; the second case requires $\partial f_1/\partial u = 0 = \partial f_1/\partial v$; and the third requires $\partial f_1/\partial u \cdot \partial f_2/\partial u < 0$ and $\partial f_1/\partial v \cdot \partial f_2/\partial v < 0$. For the version of Crossroads defined by (3.3), you can easily verify that these restrictions on interior unimprovable points correspond to (3.26).

We can also apply (3.28) to boundary points. Consider, for example, $(1,0)$. The restrictions on h at that point are $h_1 \leq 0, h_2 \geq 0$, whence $m = 2$ and

$$K = \begin{bmatrix} -1 & 0 \\ 0 & 1 \end{bmatrix}. \tag{3.32}$$

Also

$$J = J((1,0)) = \begin{bmatrix} 3 & -4 \\ 1 & -2 \end{bmatrix}. \tag{3.33}$$

Therefore $\eta J + \mu K = 0_n = 0_2$ becomes

$$\begin{bmatrix} \eta_1 & \eta_2 \end{bmatrix} \begin{bmatrix} 3 & -4 \\ 1 & -2 \end{bmatrix} + \begin{bmatrix} \mu_1 & \mu_2 \end{bmatrix} \begin{bmatrix} -1 & 0 \\ 0 & 1 \end{bmatrix} = \begin{bmatrix} 0 & 0 \end{bmatrix} \tag{3.34}$$

or $3\eta_1 + \eta_2 - \mu_1 = 0$, $-4\eta_1 - 2\eta_2 + \mu_2 = 0$; and these equalities are easily satisfied with $\eta \geq 0_2$, $\eta \neq 0_2$, $\mu \geq 0_2$. Therefore $(1,0)$ is a candidate for Pareto-optimality. On the other hand, for the point $(0,0)$, where the restrictions on h are $h \geq 0_2$, so that K is the 2×2 identity matrix, a similar analysis yields the equalities

$$3\eta_1 + \eta_2 + \mu_1 = 0, \qquad \eta_1 + 3\eta_2 + \mu_2 = 0. \tag{3.35}$$

Now $\mu \geq 0_2$ implies $3\eta_1 + \eta_2 \leq 0$, $\eta_1 + 3\eta_2 \leq 0$, which contradicts $\eta \geq 0_2$, $\eta \neq 0_2$. Thus $(0,0)$ is not Pareto-optimal. Again, at points other than $(1,0)$ and $(1,1)$ on the side of D where $u = 1$, the only restriction on h is $h_1 \leq 0$, so that $m = 1$, and $K = \begin{bmatrix} -1 & 0 \end{bmatrix}$. Now $\eta J + \mu K = 0_2$ yields $(3 - 5v)\eta_1 + (1 - 5v)\eta_2 - \mu_1 = 0$, $4\eta_1 + 2\eta_2 = 0$, the second of which contradicts $\eta \geq 0_2$, $\eta \neq 0_2$ regardless of the value of v. Continuing in this manner, the remaining improvable points on the boundary of D are readily eliminated; see Exercise 3.6. Then try Exercise 3.7.

3.3   THE NASH BARGAINING SOLUTION

Despite the theorem of the alternative, eliminating improvable points is rarely a straightforward exercise, even if $n = 2$ (if you don't believe me, please attempt to calculate the bargaining set for Store Wars). On the other hand, bargaining points—i.e., strategy combinations in the bargaining sets—are almost never unique; so that, even after the strenuous labor of calculating P^*, we are still faced with the problem of deciding which w in P^*, say $w = \hat{w}$, should be the solution of the game. If it were somehow possible to determine $\hat{w}$ without first calculating P^*, then clearly we could save ourselves a great deal of trouble. One such approach to determining $\hat{w}$ is provided by Nash's (1950) bargaining solution, which we now describe.

Because Player k benefits from cooperation with the other players only if she obtains a reward in excess of the max-min reward she can guarantee for herself, we will define

$$\bar{x}_k = f_k(w) - \tilde{f}_k \tag{3.36}$$

to be Player k's benefit of cooperation from the joint strategy combination $w \in D$; for $w \in P^*, \bar{x}_k \geq 0$. Because, for each $k \in N$, Player k wants $\bar{x}_k$ to be as large as possible (and certainly nonnegative), an agreeable choice of the vector

$$\bar{x} = (\bar{x}_1, \bar{x}_2, \ldots, \bar{x}_n) \tag{3.37}$$

should lie as far as possible from the origin (and in the nonnegative orthant) of the n-dimensional space of cooperation benefits. But how should one measure distance in this space? Should one use the formula

$$\bar{d} = \bar{x}_1 + \bar{x}_2 + \cdots + \bar{x}_n \quad ? \tag{3.38}$$

Or the formula

$$\bar{d} = \bar{x}_1 \cdot \bar{x}_2 \cdots \bar{x}_n \quad ? \tag{3.39}$$

Or yet another formula with the property that all players prefer a larger value of $\bar{d}$ to a smaller one? Clearly, there is no limit to the number of such formulae!

Now, each player measures her cooperation benefit according to her own scale of merit, i.e., subjectively. Suppose, however, that there exists some "objective" scale of merit, against which a supreme arbitrator could assess all the players' subjective valuations; and let one unit of objective merit equal γ_k units of Player k's subjective merit, for all $k \in N$. Then the objective distances corresponding to (3.38) and (3.39), which the supreme arbitrator could perhaps supply, are

$$\bar{d} = \frac{\bar{x}_1}{\gamma_1} + \frac{\bar{x}_2}{\gamma_2} + \cdots + \frac{\bar{x}_n}{\gamma_n} \tag{3.40}$$

and

$$\bar{d} = \frac{\bar{x}_1}{\gamma_1} \cdot \frac{\bar{x}_2}{\gamma_2} \cdots \frac{\bar{x}_n}{\gamma_n} = \frac{\bar{x}_1 \bar{x}_2 \ldots \bar{x}_n}{\gamma_1 \gamma_2 \cdots \gamma_n}, \tag{3.41}$$

respectively.

But who is this supreme arbitrator? Who is this person who is capable of assigning values to the numbers $\gamma_1, \gamma_2, \ldots, \gamma_n$—or, as game theorists prefer to say, of making *interpersonal comparisons of utility*? Suppose there is no such person. If distance is measured according to (3.38), then this is a most unfortunate circumstance, because we cannot maximize the corresponding objective distance (3.40) until we know the values of $\gamma_1, \gamma_2, \ldots, \gamma_n$. If distance is measured according to (3.39), however, then it matters not a whit—maximizing (3.39) and maximizing (3.41) are one and the same thing, for any values of $\gamma_1, \gamma_2, \ldots, \gamma_n$. Thus formula (3.39) has a very desirable property that (3.38) and other formulae do not possesses. We will say that $\hat{w} \in P^*$ is a *Nash bargaining solution* if $\hat{w}$ maximizes

$$\bar{d}(w) = (f_1(w) - \tilde{f}_1) \cdot (f_2(w) - \tilde{f}_2) \cdots (f_n(w) - \tilde{f}_n) \tag{3.42}$$

over P^*; and if $\hat{w}$ is unique—i.e., if no other $w \in P^*$ satisfies $d(w) = \bar{d}(\hat{w})$—then we shall regard $\hat{w}$ as the solution of our cooperative game in strategic form.

In practice, we can often obtain $\hat{w}$ by maximizing $\bar{d}(w)$, not over P^*, but rather over the whole of D, and then checking that $\hat{w}$ is individually rational for all players; i.e., that $\hat{w} \in D^*$, where we define

$$D^* = \{w \in D \,|\, f_k(w) \geq \tilde{f}_k \quad \text{for all} \quad k \in N\}, \tag{3.43}$$

so that (3.20) implies $P^* = P \cap D^*$. It is clear that $\hat{w}$ so found must be globally (and hence also locally) Pareto-optimal; for if $\hat{w}$ were improvable, then the improved strategy combination would yield a larger value of $\bar{d}$. If, of course, the w that maximizes $\bar{d}(w)$ over D does not belong to D^*, then we must maximize $\bar{d}(w)$ over D^* instead. Either way, we can find $\hat{w}$ that maximizes $\bar{d}(w)$ over P^* without actually calculating P^*. Both cases are illustrated by the following two examples.

First, let us calculate the Nash bargaining solution for Store Wars II from Section 1.6. From Exercise 1.20, the max-min rewards for Nan, Van and Zan are, respectively, $\tilde{f}_1 = ac\pi/9$, $\tilde{f}_2 = ac\pi/16$ and $\tilde{f}_3 = 25ac\pi/144$. Therefore, from (1.74), we have

$$f_1(u, v, z) - \tilde{f}_1 = 8ac\pi \left\{ u \left(\frac{1}{3} + v - 2u + z \right) - \frac{1}{72} \right\}, \tag{3.44a}$$

$$f_2(u, v, z) - \tilde{f}_2 = 8ac\pi \left\{ v \left(\frac{1}{4} + u - 2v + z \right) - \frac{1}{128} \right\}, \tag{3.44b}$$

$$f_3(u, v, z) - \tilde{f}_3 = 8ac\pi \left\{ z \left(\frac{5}{12} + u - 2z + v \right) - \frac{25}{1152} \right\}; \tag{3.44c}$$

whence on using (3.42) with $w = (u, v, z)$,

$$\bar{d} = \frac{(ac\pi)^3}{20736} \{24u(1 + 3v - 6u + 3z) - 1\} \{32v(1 + 4u - 8v + 4z) - 1\} \cdot$$
$$\{96z(5 + 12u - 24z + 12v) - 25\}. \tag{3.45}$$

To obtain $(\hat{u}, \hat{v}, \hat{z})$ we maximize $\bar{d}$ over the decision set D defined by (1.75). For the sake of definiteness, let us suppose that the value of α, which defines the maximum price in (1.70), is $\alpha = 80a\pi$. Then D consists of all (u, v, z) such that

$$0 \leq u, v, z \leq 10, \quad -\frac{1}{12} \leq u - v \leq \frac{1}{12}, \quad -\frac{1}{6} \leq v - z \leq \frac{1}{6}, \quad -\frac{1}{4} \leq u - z \leq \frac{1}{4}.$$
$$(3.46)$$

Note that if u, v and z were not constrained by a price ceiling, i.e., if $\alpha \to \infty$ in (1.70), then $\bar{d}$ would be unbounded on D (because without the constraints $u \leq 10, v \leq 10$ and $z \leq 10, \bar{d}$ would increase without bound as $t \to \infty$ on the line defined by $u = t, v = t$ and $z = t$). Thus collusion among storekeepers is bad for the consumer. It enables one of the players—from Figure 1.13, clearly Zan—to set her price at the ceiling αc, with the others not far behind; whereas competition in Section 1.6 kept prices in rein.

Maximizing (3.45) subject to (3.46) is a problem in constrained nonlinear programming, a discussion of which would take us far beyond our brief.[1] Therefore, we will simply observe that routines for solving such problems—for example, the IMSL routine NCONG—are now widely available on large computers.[2] By using NCONG or a similar routine, we discover that the maximum of (3.45) on D occurs where $u = 9.98, v = 9.95$ and $z = 10$; for all practical purposes, the prices are at their ceiling. The corresponding rewards are $f_1 = 25.8ac\pi > \tilde{f}_1$, $f_2 = 26.3ac\pi > \tilde{f}_2$ and $f_3 = 27.7ac\pi > \tilde{f}_3$, confirming that $(9.98, 9.95, 10)$ $\in D^*$ (which, however, we have not had to calculate). If we compare the Nash-bargaining rewards to the Nash-equilibrium rewards $f_1 = 0.44ac\pi, f_2 = 0.36ac\pi$ and $f_3 = 0.54ac\pi$, obtained in Section 1.6, then we see how much the players benefit by collusion. Note that Van's reward is greater than Nan's under cooperation, whereas Nan's reward is greater than Van's under competition; in both cases, however, Van's price is lower than Nan's.

The $\hat{w}$ that maximizes $\bar{d}$ need not be unique, however, as our second example—Crossroads with fast drivers—illustrates. From Exercise 1.19, when $2\epsilon > \tau_1, \tau_2$ the max-min rewards are $\tilde{f}_1 = m_1(\bar{u}) = -(\delta + \tau_2/2)\theta_2$ and $\tilde{f}_2 = m_2(\bar{v}) = -(\delta + \tau_1/2)\theta_1$, where $\theta_k = (2\epsilon + \tau_k)/(2\epsilon + 2\delta)$ is defined by (1.26) and m_1, m_2 are defined by (1.88). Thus, from (3.2), we have

$$f_1(u, v) - \tilde{f}_1 = ((\epsilon - \tau_2/2) - (\delta + \epsilon)u)(v - \theta_2), \qquad (3.47a)$$

$$f_2(u, v) - \tilde{f}_2 = ((\epsilon - \tau_1/2) - (\delta + \epsilon)v)(u - \theta_1); \qquad (3.47b)$$

---

[1]   For a discussion of constrained nonlinear programming see, for example, Chapters 10, 12 and 13 of Luenberger (1984) or Chapters 9 and 10 of Jeter (1986).

[2]   A calling program for the IMSL routine NCONG appears in the appendix to this chapter. This or a similar routine will enable you to obtain the Nash bargaining solutions for Store Wars and Store Wars II; see Exercise 3.9.

and (3.42) yields

$$\bar{d}(u,v) = (u - \theta_1)\{(\epsilon - \tau_2/2) - (\delta + \epsilon)u\}(v - \theta_2)\{(\epsilon - \tau_1/2) - (\delta + \epsilon)v\}. \quad (3.48)$$

In the special case of (3.3), we have

$$\bar{d}(u,v) = \frac{1}{25}(5u - 3)(1 - 5u)(5v - 3)(1 - 5v). \quad (3.49)$$

The maximum of (3.49) over $D = \{(u,v)|0 \leq u,v \leq 1\}$ occurs at $(u,v) = (1,1)$, but $(1,1) \notin D^*$. Accordingly, we must maximize $\bar{d}$ over D^* instead; and, from Exercise 3.8, we find that the maximum, 24/25, occurs at both $(1,0)$ and $(0,1)$. It appears that there are two Nash bargaining solutions, each of which is the best possible outcome for one of the players; and, as we have remarked already in Section 3.1, it is difficult to see how they could agree to either.

Here two remarks are in order. First, the game of Crossroads defined by (3.3) is symmetric ($\tau_1 = \tau_2$). There is no basis for distinguishing between the players, and so any cooperative solution should also be symmetric, i.e., satisfy $u = v$. But P^* in Figure 3.2 contains only a single symmetric strategy combination, namely, $(u,v) = (2/5, 2/5)$. We therefore propose that the solution of this cooperative game should be neither $(1,0)$ nor $(0,1)$, but rather $(2/5, 2/5)$, the center of the bargaining set in Figure 3.2.[3]

Second, the function $\bar{d}$ defined by (3.49) achieves its maximum twice on D^* only because the game is symmetric. In general, if Crossroads is asymmetric, i.e., if $\tau_1 \neq \tau_2$, then the Nash bargaining solution is again unique. Suppose, for example, that

$$\delta = 5, \quad \epsilon = 3, \quad \tau_1 = 4, \quad \tau_2 = 2. \quad (3.50)$$

Then (Exercise 3.8) the unique Nash bargaining solution is $(\hat{u}, \hat{v}) = (0,1)$, i.e., Nan always waits and San always goes. This solution is intuitively attractive because, although both drivers are fast, San is considerably faster; and so it makes good sense for Nan to let her whip across the junction before she dawdles into gear herself.

More fundamentally, there is no unique Nash bargaining solution for the game defined by (3.3) because $\bar{F}$ is not convex; i.e., it isn't possible to join any two points in $\bar{F}$ by a straight line segment that never leaves $\bar{F}$ (consider, for example, $(1,0)$ and $(0,1)$). If $\bar{F}$ is convex, then Nash's bargaining solution is always unique; see, for example, Exercise 3.11.

---

[3]   This solution corresponds to a local maximum on D^* of the function $\bar{d}$ defined by (3.49).

3.4 INDEPENDENT VERSUS CORRELATED STRATEGIES

The difference between what is rational for an individual and what is rational for a group is exemplified by comparing the noncooperative Nash-equilibrium solution for the game of Crossroads defined by (3.3) with the ad hoc cooperative solution derived at the end of the previous section. Nan and San's Nash bargaining rewards are $-11/5$; whereas their Nash-equilibrium rewards are only $-12/5$. Clearly, each prefers $-11/5$ to $-12/5$, and so it is in their mutual interest to select their cooperative strategies $u = 2/5 = v$ over their Nash-equilibrium strategies $u^* = 3/5 = v^*$; in other words, to be less aggressive and assume right of way less often. If, however, Nan were to select $u = 2/5$ without first reaching an understanding with San, then from Figure 1.5 (with $\theta_1 = 3/5 = \theta_2$) the rational thing for San to do would be to select $v = 1$ (always go), because $(2/5, 1) \in R_2$. It would be irrational for San to select $v = 2/5$, because $(2/5, 2/5) \notin R_2$. Likewise, if Nan knew that San would play $v = 2/5$ then the rational thing for Nan to do, from a selfish point of view, would be to welch on San and play $u = 1$, because $(1, 2/5) \in R_1$. Thus cooperative solutions are rational only if there is a gentlewoman's agreement among the players—however enforced, whether voluntarily or by compulsion—to abide by their bargaining strategies. Indeed in theory, it is merely the existence or absence of such an agreement that determines whether a game is cooperative or noncooperative. In practice, however, what often determines whether a game is cooperative or noncooperative is whether or not the game is among specific individuals who meet repeatedly in similar circumstances, recognize one another, and have the ability to communicate; for rational beings will avail themselves of any device for maximizing rewards—including, if they have the means, cooperation.

Provided the players can trust one another, however, then the potential exists for even greater benefits from cooperation than are possible when strategies are chosen independently. Consider, for example, Crossroads. As in Section 1.3, we can imagine that each driver has a spinning arrow on her dashboard, which determines whether to go or wait in any particular confrontation. Now, it is obvious intuitively that if Nan's arrow always came to rest over the shaded sector of her disk when San's arrow came to rest over the unshaded part of her disk, and vice versa, then the two players would never waste any time wondering who should go after WW or who should back down after GG, because the only pure strategy combinations ever selected would be WG or GW. Of course, WG and GW are not the only pure strategy combinations selected, because the players spin their arrows independently, and all angles of rest between 0 and 2π are equally likely.

If the players have already agreed to cooperate, however, then they can further reduce delays by agreeing to *correlate* strategies, as follows. Naturally, there is potential for such collaboration only when Crossroads is played between two specific individuals—a particular Nan and a particular San.

Let us imagine that, after agreeing to cooperate, this Nan and San discard their individual spinning arrows and replace them by a large arrow and disk at the junction itself (which can be started by remote control). This disk is divided into four sectors, which subtend angles $2\pi\omega_{11}$, $2\pi\omega_{12}$, $2\pi\omega_{21}$ and $2\pi\omega_{22}$, respectively. If the arrow comes to rest in the first sector, then Nan and San will both go (GG); if in the second sector, then Nan will go but San will wait (GW); if in the third sector, then San will go but Nan will wait (WG); and if in the fourth sector, then Nan and San will both wait (WW). The device is equivalent to selecting pure strategy combination (i, j) with probability ω_{ij}, for $i, j = 1, 2$. Thus

$$\omega_{11} + \omega_{12} + \omega_{21} + \omega_{22} = 1; \tag{3.51}$$

and Nan's reward f_1, the expected value of her payoff F_1, is

$$
\begin{aligned}
f_1 &= -(\delta + \tau_2/2) \cdot \text{Prob}(GG) + 0 \cdot \text{Prob}(GW) \\
&\quad - \tau_2 \cdot \text{Prob}(WG) - (\epsilon + \tau_2/2) \cdot \text{Prob}(WW) \\
&= -(\delta + \tau_2/2)\omega_{11} + 0 \cdot \omega_{12} - \tau_2\omega_{21} - (\epsilon + \tau_2/2)\omega_{22} \\
&= -(\delta + \tau_2/2)\omega_{11} - \tau_2\omega_{21} - (\epsilon + \tau_2/2)\omega_{22}
\end{aligned}
\tag{3.52}
$$

from Table 1.1. Similarly, San's reward is

$$f_2 = -(\delta + \tau_1/2)\omega_{11} - \tau_1\omega_{12} - (\epsilon + \tau_1/2)\omega_{22}. \tag{3.53}$$

We will refer to the vector $\omega = (\omega_{11}, \omega_{12}, \omega_{21}, \omega_{22})$ as a *correlated strategy*.

When Nan and San had two separate arrows and chose independent strategies u and v, we had $\omega_{11} = uv$, $\omega_{12} = u(1 - v)$, $\omega_{21} = (1 - u)v$ and $\omega_{22} = (1-u)(1-v)$, from (1.14)–(1.15). Thus maximization of f_1 and f_2 when strategies are selected independently is equivalent to maximization of f_1 and f_2 in (3.52)–(3.53) under the constraints

$$\omega_{11} + \omega_{12} = u, \qquad \omega_{11} + \omega_{21} = v \tag{3.54}$$

and, of course, (3.51); whereas maximization of f_1 and f_2 when strategies are correlated is subject only to (3.51). Because there are (two) fewer constraints, we can expect maximum rewards to be larger.

Now, in designing their disk, Nan and San do not hesitate to set $\omega_{11} = 0 = \omega_{22}$, which increases both f_1 and f_2; as we have remarked already, it is obvious that nothing can be gained under correlated strategies by selecting GG or WW. Therefore, from (3.51)–(3.53), Nan and San reduce their task to selecting ω_{12} and ω_{21} such that $\omega_{12} + \omega_{21} = 1$, with rewards $f_1 = -\tau_2\omega_{21}$ and $f_2 = -\tau_1\omega_{12}$. Thus, regardless of which ω_{12} (and hence ω_{21}) the players choose, the corresponding rewards will satisfy

$$\tau_1 f_1 + \tau_2 f_2 + \tau_1\tau_2 = 0, \qquad f_1 \leq 0, \quad f_2 \leq 0. \tag{3.55}$$

Their reward pair will therefore lie in the the f_1-f_2-plane on the line segment that joins $(-\tau_2, 0)$ and $(0, -\tau_1)$; and every point on this line segment is achievable by some choice of correlated strategies. Furthermore, from Figure 3.1 (or the equivalent diagram for other values of the parameters δ, ϵ, τ_1 and τ_2), this line segment lies on or above the Pareto-optimal boundary of $\overline{F}$ at every point; in particular, in the case where $\delta = 3$, $\epsilon = 2$ and $\tau_1 = 2 = \tau_2$, it lies above the point that corresponds to the ad hoc cooperative solution we found at the end of Section 3.3. It thus appears that if you are going to cooperate, then you might as well correlate.

There is, however, a price to be paid—which reward pair on this line segment yields the solution of the game? Intuition suggests that we should select the "fair" solution

$$f_1 = -\frac{\tau_1 \tau_2}{\tau_1 + \tau_2} = f_2, \qquad (3.56)$$

achieved by the correlated strategy ω for which $\omega_{11} = 0 = \omega_{22}$ and

$$\omega_{12} = \frac{\tau_2}{\tau_1 + \tau_2}, \qquad \omega_{21} = \frac{\tau_1}{\tau_1 + \tau_2}. \qquad (3.57)$$

(but see Exercise 3.11). If we accept this solution, however, then tacitly we have made an interpersonal comparison of utilities: we have assumed that a minute of San's time is worth a minute of Nan's, so that if they can save a minute together, then each should reap 30 seconds of the benefits. But who is to say whether Nan's time and San's time are equally valuable? What if Nan is a brain surgeon and San a cashier—then couldn't one argue that San's time is more valuable than Nan's, if they meet in the morning on their way to work (because if San is five minutes late for work she may lose her job, whereas if Nan is five minutes late for work—well, do you really expect a brain surgeon to be on time?). Nevertheless, there are many circumstances in which interpersonal comparisons of utility are quite acceptable—for example, Nan and San may both be brain surgeons, or both cashiers—and if the price is small then we shall happily pay it.

If we agree to correlate strategies, however, and if we agree to make interpersonal comparisons of utility (my time's worth as much as your time, my dollar's just as good as your dollar, etc.), then solving a game loses much of its strategic interest. It becomes instead a matter of seeking a fair distribution among the players of some benefit of cooperation (e.g., time saved, money saved), of which there exists a definite total amount. Or, if you prefer, there's a finite pie to be distributed among the players, and we need to establish how big a slice is a player's just desert (dessert?). But already we are talking about characteristic function games, and these are the subject of the following chapter.

3.5 COMMENTARY

In Chapter 3 we have introduced the most important concepts of cooperative games in strategic form, namely, Pareto-optimality (Sections 3.1 and 3.2), Nash bargaining solutions (Section 3.3), and independent versus correlated strategies (Section 3.4). In Section 3.3 we introduced the Nash bargaining solution in the context of independent strategies. Usually, however, the solution is applied in the context of correlated strategies. The reward set is then always convex (so that local Pareto-optimality and global Pareto-optimality are equivalent); and, as remarked at the end of Section 3.3, a unique Nash bargaining solution is then guaranteed. For a proof of this fact and further properties of Nash's bargaining solution see, for example, Owen (1982). Note, finally, that although Nash's bargaining solution appears to be the most enduring solution concept for co-operative games in strategic form, it is by no means the only one; others are described by, for example, Shubik (1984, pp. 196–200).

EXERCISES   3

3.1 **(i)**   Verify (3.7).

    (ii)   Show that the image of the line segment $\{(u, 0)|0 \le u \le 1\}$ under the mapping f defined by (3.4) is that part of the line $f_1 - 3f_2 - 6 = 0$ which extends from $(-3, -3)$ to $(0, -2)$. Note that this image is largely coincident with $f(L(4/5))$, but that $f(L(4/5))$ does not extend between $(-3/5, -11/5)$ and $(0, -2)$.

    (iii)   Show that the image of the line segment $\{(u, 1)|0 \le u \le 1\}$ under the mapping f defined by (3.4) is that part of the line $2f_1 - f_2 + 4 = 0$ which extends from $(-4, -4)$ to $(-2, 0)$.

3.2 **(i)**   Show that (3.11) is the envelope of the family of lines $\psi(f_1, f_2, c) = 0$, where

$$\psi(f_1, f_2, c) = (3 - 5c)f_1 + (5c - 1)f_2 + 10c^2 - 8c + 6$$

    is defined by the left hand side of (3.7) and c is any real number (not necessarily satisfying $0 \le c \le 4/5$).

    (ii)   Show that this envelope meets (touches) the line (3.12a) at the point $(-11/5, -3/5)$, and crosses the f_1-axis where $f_1 > -2$; and that it meets the line (3.12c) at the point $(-3/5, -11/5)$, and crosses the f_2-axis where $f_2 > -2$. Why are the two small curvilinear triangles enclosed by the envelope, the lines and the axes not part of the reward set?

3.3 **(i)**   Deduce from (3.14) that the tangent to the curved edge of $\overline{F}$ is parallel to the f_1-axis at $(-8/5, -12/5)$, and to the f_2-axis at $(-12/5, -8/5)$.

    (ii)   Which strategy combinations correspond to these two points?

    (iii)   Verify (3.17)–(3.18).

3.4   Verify that (3.19) vanishes where $u + v = 4/5$.

3.5   Using the method of Section 3.1, find the bargaining set for Crossroads when $\delta = 5$, $\epsilon = 3$, $\tau_1 = 4$, $\tau_2 = 2$. Sketch the reward set, marking in particular all locally or globally Pareto-optimal points.

3.6   Use the theorem of the alternative (Section 3.2) to show that no points other than $(1, 0)$ and $(0, 1)$ on the boundary of the unit square are Pareto-optimal in Crossroads

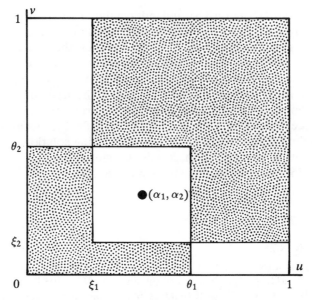

Figure E3.1

when $\delta = 3, \epsilon = 2, \tau_1 = 2 = \tau_2$.

3.7   Use the theorem of the alternative to find P^*_{nec} for Crossroads when $\delta = 5, \epsilon = 3$, $\tau_1 = 4, \tau_2 = 2$. Verify that your results agree with those you obtained in Exercise 3.5.

3.8   (i)   For Chapter 1's original (asymmetric) game of Crossroads between fast drivers, show that D^* is the unshaded region in Figure E3.1, where ξ_1 and ξ_2 are defined by

$$(\delta + \epsilon)\xi_1 = \epsilon - \frac{\tau_2}{2}, \qquad (\delta + \epsilon)\xi_2 = \epsilon - \frac{\tau_1}{2},$$

θ_1 and θ_2 are defined by (1.26), and the point marked by a dot has coordinates

$$[\alpha_1, \alpha_2] = \frac{\epsilon}{\delta + \epsilon}[1, 1] + \frac{(\tau_1 - \tau_2)}{4(\delta + \epsilon)}[1, -1].$$

(ii)   Describe the Nash bargaining solution.

(iii)   With regard to the discussion at the end of Section 3.3, does the Nash bargaining solution invariably lack uniqueness when the game is symmetric?

3.9   If you have access to nonlinear programming routines on your computer, obtain Nash bargaining solutions for:

(i)   the version of Store Wars considered in Section 1.5

(ii)   the version of Store Wars II considered in Exercise 1.21.

3.10   For the game of the prisoner's dilemma defined by Exercise 1.25:

    (i)   Show that $P_G = P$, and find P^*

    (ii)   Find the Nash bargaining solution.

3.11   Find the Nash bargaining solution under correlated strategies of Chapter 1's original (asymmetric) game of Crossroads. Is $f_1 = f_2$ at this solution?

Hint: From (3.52) and (3.53), the vector $f = (f_1, f_2)$ from the origin to the point with coordinates (f_1, f_2) is a "convex linear combination" of the vectors $(-\delta - \tau_2/2, -\delta - \tau_1/2)$, $(0, -\tau_1)$, $(-\tau_2, 0)$ and $(-\epsilon - \tau_2/2, -\epsilon - \tau_1/2)$, i.e., a linear combination with nonnegative coefficients that sum to 1, according to (3.51). The point (f_1, f_2) must therefore lie somewhere in the triangle with vertices $(-\delta - \tau_2/2, -\delta - \tau_1/2)$, $(0, -\tau_1)$ and $(-\tau_2, 0)$. In other words, this triangle is $\overline{F}$ under correlated strategies. Thus finding $\widehat{\omega}$ corresponds to maximizing the area of a rectangle, one corner of which is constrained to lie on the line with equation (3.55).

APPENDIX TO CHAPTER 3. A CALLING PROGRAM FOR THE IMSL ROUTINE NCONG

The IMSL routine NCONG finds the minimum of a function $f = f(x)$ subject to constraints of the form

$$g_j(x) = 0, \qquad \text{for} \quad j = 1, \dots, m_e \qquad (3A.1)$$

$$g_j(x) \geq 0, \qquad \text{for} \quad j = m_e + 1, \dots, m \qquad (3A.2)$$

$$x_\ell \leq x \leq x_u, \qquad (3A.3)$$

where $x = (x_1, x_2, \dots, x_n)$ is an n-dimensional vector and f and g are assumed to be continuously differentiable. Because we wish to *maximize* (3.45) subject to (3.46), rather than minimize it, we have $f = -\overline{d}$; but because a multiplicative constant such as $(ac\pi)^3/20736$ can have no effect on the optimum, we may as well leave it out (the routine may select a different scaling factor). Clearly, constraints (3.46) can all be written in the form of (3A.1)–(3A.3) with $x_1 = u$, $x_2 = v$, $x_3 = z$; for example, $-1/12 \leq u - v$ is incorporated by defining $g_1(x) = x_1 - x_2 + 1/12$. For technical reasons, it is best to incorporate $0 \leq x \leq 10$, not through (3A.3) but rather through (3A.2); thus we take $m_e = 0, m = 12$ (as opposed to $m = 6$) and choose large negative and positive numbers for the components of the arrays XLB and XUB, respectively.

The routine NCONG is described in the IMSL Math/Library manual (IMSL 1987, pp. 903–908). If the function f has several local minima, then all must be found from separate guesses; thereafter, it is trivial to select the global minimum. The following program, in which $u = v = z = 2$ is used as the initial guess, yielded the maximum of (3.45) subject to constraints (3.46) on FSU's Cyber 850 computer; and the program is easily modified for the purposes of Exercise 3.9. For definitions of parameters, consult the IMSL manual.

```
PROGRAM NASH (INPUT,OUTPUT,TAPE5=INPUT,TAPE6=OUTPUT)
PARAMETER (IBTYPE=0, IPRINT=1,M=12,MAXITN=100,ME=0,N=3)
REAL FVALUE, X(N), XGUESS(N), XLB(N), XUB(N)
INTEGER K
EXTERNAL FCN,GRAD, NCONG,WRRRN
DATA XLB/-1.E6,-1.E6,-1.E6/, XUB/1.E6,1.E6,1.E6/, XGUESS/2.E0,2.E0,2.E0/
CALL NCONG(FCN,GRAD,M,ME,N,XGUESS,IBTYPE,XLB,XUB,
&              IPRINT,MAXITN,X,FVALUE0
CALL WRRRN('THE SOLUTION IS ',N,1,X,N,0)
END


SUBROUTINE FCN(M,ME,N,X,ACTIVE,F,G)
INTEGER M,ME,N
REAL X(*), G(*)
REAL A,B,C,U,V,Z
LOGICAL ACTIVE(*)
U = X(1)
V = X(2)
Z = X(3)
A = 24*U*(1+3V-6U+3Z) -1
B = 32*V*(1+4U-8V+4Z) -1
C = 96*Z*(5+12U-24Z+12V) -25
```
C MULTIPLY OBJECTIVE FUNCTION BY -1 TO CONVERT MAXIMIZATION
C PROBLEM TO MINIMIZATION PROBLEM
```
F = -A*B*C
IF(ACTIVE(1)) G(1) = U-V+1/12
IF(ACTIVE(2)) G(2) = V-U+1/12
IF(ACTIVE(3)) G(3) = V-Z+1/6
IF(ACTIVE(4)) G(4) = Z-V+1/6
IF(ACTIVE(5)) G(5) = U-Z+1/4
IF(ACTIVE(6)) G(6) = Z-U+1/4
IF(ACTIVE(7)) G(7) = U
IF(ACTIVE(8)) G(8) = V
IF(ACTIVE(9)) G(9) = Z
IF(ACTIVE(10)) G(10) = 10-U
IF(ACTIVE(11)) G(11) = 10-V
IF(ACTIVE(12)) G(12) = 10-Z
RETURN
END


SUBROUTINE GRAD(M,ME,MMAX,N,X,ACTIVE,F,G,DF,DG)
INTEGER I,M,ME,MMAX,N
REAL X(*), F, G(*), DF(*), DG(MMAX,*)
REAL A,B,C,U,V,Z
LOGICAL ACTIVE(*)
U = X(1)
```

```
    V = X(2)
    Z = X(3)
    A = 24*U*(1+3V−6U+3Z) −1
    B = 32*V*(1+4U−8V+4Z) −1
    C = 96*Z*(5+12U−24Z+12V) −25
C SET GRADIENT OF OBJECTIVE FUNCTION
    DF(1) = 128*A*(9*Z*B+V*C)+24*(1+3*V−12*U+3*Z)*B*C
    DF(2) = 72*B*(16*Z*A+U*C) + 32*(1+4*U−16*V+4*Z)*A*C
    DF(3) = 8*C*(16*V*A+9*U*B) + 96*(5+12*U−48*Z+12*V)*A*B
C MULTIPLY GRADIENT BY −1 TO CONVERT TO MINIMIZATION PROBLEM
    DO 1 I=1,3
  1 DF(I) = −DF(I)
C SET GRADIENTS OF CONSTRAINT FUNCTIONS
    IF (ACTIVE(1)) THEN
      DG(1,1) = 1
      DG(1,2) = −1
      DG(1,3) = 0
    ENDIF
    IF (ACTIVE(2)) THEN
      DG(2,1) = −1
      DG(2,2) = 1
      DG(2,3) = 0
    ENDIF
    IF (ACTIVE(3)) THEN
      DG(3,1) = 0
      DG(3,2) = 1
      DG(3,3) = −1
    ENDIF
    IF (ACTIVE(4)) THEN
      DG(4,1) = 0
      DG(4,2) = −1
      DG(4,3) = 1
    ENDIF
    IF (ACTIVE(5)) THEN
      DG(5,1) = 1
      DG(5,2) = 0
      DG(5,3) = −1
    ENDIF
    IF (ACTIVE(6)) THEN
      DG(6,1) = −1
      DG(6,2) = 0
      DG(6,3) = 1
    ENDIF
```

```
IF (ACTIVE(7)) THEN
  DG(7,1) = 1
  DG(7,2) = 0
  DG(7,3) = 0
ENDIF
IF (ACTIVE(8)) THEN
  DG(8,1) = 0
  DG(8,2) = 1
  DG(8,3) = 0
ENDIF
IF (ACTIVE(9)) THEN
  DG(9,1) = 0
  DG(9,2) = 0
  DG(9,3) = 1
ENDIF
IF (ACTIVE(10)) THEN
  DG(10,1) = −1
  DG(10,2) = 0
  DG(10,3) = 0
ENDIF
IF (ACTIVE(11)) THEN
  DG(11,1) = 0
  DG(11,2) = −1
  DG(11,3) = 0
ENDIF
IF (ACTIVE(12)) THEN
  DG(12,1) = 0
  DG(12,2) = 0
  DG(12,3) = −1
ENDIF
RETURN
END
```

4

Characteristic Function Games: Distributing the Benefits of Cooperation

A characteristic function game is a purely cooperative game among n players who seek a fair distribution for a benefit that is freely transferable. It is assumed that all players would like as much as possible of the benefit, and that one unit of the benefit is worth the same to all players; thus, in terms of Section 3.4, characteristic function games imply interpersonal utility comparisons. Usually, but not necessarily, the benefit to be shared is money. In this chapter, we introduce two solution concepts for characteristic function games, the nucleolus and the Shapley value.

The fairness of a distribution is assumed to depend on the bargaining strengths of the various coalitions that could possibly form among some, but not all, of the players. Nevertheless, and at first sight paradoxically, the fundamental assumption of a characteristic function game is that all players are cooperating. In other words, a *grand coalition* of all n players has formed—perhaps voluntarily, but the grand coalition may also have been enforced by the action of some

115

external agent or circumstance. Thus coalitions of fewer than n players can use as bargaining leverage the strength they *would* have had without the others, *if* the others weren't there; but the grand coalition can never actually dissolve (or the theory dissolves with it).

It will be convenient in this chapter to regard each player as a fictitious coalition of one person; however, characteristic function games are interesting only when there could exist true coalitions of less than all the players. Therefore, we shall assume throughout that $n \geq 3$.[1] It will also be convenient henceforward to refer to characteristic function games as "c-games," the term coined by Shubik (1982, p. 131).

As usual, we introduce solution concepts by means of examples.

4.1   CAR POOLING AS A C-GAME. THE CHARACTERISTIC FUNCTION AND REASONABLE SET

Jed, Ned and Ted are neighbors; their houses are marked J, N and T, respectively, in Figure 4.1. They work in the same office at the same times on the same days, and in order to save money they would like to form a car pool. They must first agree on how to share the costs of this cooperative venture, however; or, which is the view we prefer to adopt, on how to share the car pool's benefits. We explore the matter in this section. Later, in Section 4.3, we shall consider adding a fourth neighbor, Zed, to the car pool.

Let's suppose that Jed, Ned and Ted drive identical cars, and that the cost of driving to work, *including depreciation,* is k dollars per mile (where probably $k < 1$); because depreciation is included, it doesn't matter whose car is used (though in practice they might well take turns). Let the distance to work from point F in the diagram, where the road through their neighborhood crosses a freeway, be d miles. Then Jed lives $4 + d$ miles from work, whereas Ned and Ted are both $3 + d$ miles away. Let Jed be Player 1, Ned Player 2 and Ted Player 3; and let $c(\{i\})$ denote Player i's cost in dollars of driving to work alone. Then, assuming that each player selects the shortest route,

$$c(\{1\}) = (4 + d)k, \quad c(\{2\}) = (3 + d)k, \quad c(\{3\}) = (3 + d)k. \tag{4.1}$$

Round-trip travel costs are just twice these amounts.

Let $c(\{1, 2, 3\})$ denote the cost in dollars if all three players drive to work in a single car, again assuming that the shortest route is always adopted. Then, clearly,

$$c(\{1, 2, 3\}) = (7 + d)k \tag{4.2}$$

(regardless of whose car is used). If Jed and Ned were to form a car pool without

---

[1]   For $n = 2$, both the nucleolus and the Shapley value give the players equal shares of the benefit to be shared; see Exercises 4.7 and 4.17.

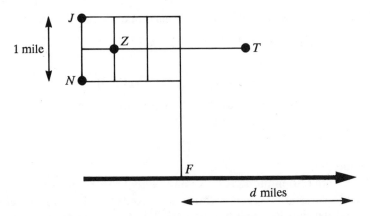

Figure 4.1   Jed, Ned, Ted and Zed's stomping ground.

Ted, then the cost would be

$$c(\{1,2\}) = (4 + d)k \tag{4.3}$$

(again assuming the shortest route—and, of course, that they would use Jed's car). Similarly, the costs of car pools that excluded Ned or Jed would be

$$c(\{1,3\}) = (6 + d)k = c(\{2,3\}); \tag{4.4}$$

it would not matter whose car Ned and Ted used, although Jed and Ted would have to use Jed's. We have now calculated the travel costs associated with each of the seven coalitions that three players could form, namely, $\{1\}$, $\{2\}$, $\{3\}$, $\{1,2\}$, $\{1,3\}$, $\{2,3\}$ and $\{1,2,3\}$. More generally, among n players there could be $2^n - 1$ coalitions.

Let $\overline{v}(S)$ denote the benefit of cooperation associated with the coalition S. Then

$$\overline{v}(S) = \sum_{i \in S} c(\{i\}) - c(S) \tag{4.5}$$

i.e., the difference between the sum of the costs that the individual members of S would have to bear if they did not cooperate and the cost to S when they club together. For example, the benefit associated with the grand coalition $\{1,2,3\}$ among all three players is saving

$$\overline{v}(\{1,2,3\}) = c(\{1\}) + c(\{2\}) + c(\{3\}) - c(\{1,2,3\}) = (3 + 2d)k \tag{4.6}$$

dollars. A car pool without Ted would save Jed and Ned

$$\overline{v}(\{1,2\}) = c(\{1\}) + c(\{2\}) - c(\{1,2\}) = (3 + d)k \tag{4.7}$$

dollars; whereas the benefits of cooperations that excluded Ned or Jed would be

$$\bar{v}(\{1,3\}) = c(\{1\}) + c(\{3\}) - c(\{1,3\}) = (1+d)k \qquad (4.8)$$

and

$$\bar{v}(\{2,3\}) = c(\{2\}) + c(\{3\}) - c(\{2,3\}) = dk, \qquad (4.9)$$

respectively. Of course, the benefit of cooperation associated with not cooperating is precisely zero; that is, from (4.5) with $S = \{i\}$,

$$\bar{v}(\{i\}) = 0 \qquad (4.10)$$

for any value of i.

For the sake of definiteness, let's imagine that the car pool $\{1,2,3\}$ will always use Jed's car, so that it is Jed who actually foots the bills. How much should Ned and Ted pay Jed for each one-way trip? Let us suppose that Jed receives fraction x_1 of the grand car pool's benefit $(7+d)k$, and that Ned and Ted receive fractions x_2 and x_3, respectively; clearly,

$$0 \le x_1 \le 1, \quad 0 \le x_2 \le 1, \quad 0 \le x_3 \le 1, \quad x_1 + x_2 + x_3 = 1. \qquad (4.11)$$

Then Ned or Ted should pay Jed the amount

$$c(\{i\}) - (3 + 2d)kx_i \qquad (4.12)$$

dollars per trip, where $i = 2$ for Ned and $i = 3$ for Ted; and (4.12) with $i = 1$ is the part of the bill that Jed must pay himself. Our task is therefore to determine the fractions x_1, x_2 and x_3.

Now, (4.6)–(4.10) define a function $\bar{v}$ from the set of all coalitions among three players into the real numbers. We call $\bar{v}$ the characteristic function of the c-game. Note that, for set-theoretic purposes, it is convenient to suppose that the set of all coalitions of three players contains, in addition to $\{1\}, \{2\}, \{3\}, \{1,2\}$, $\{1,3\}, \{2,3\}$ and $\{1,2,3\}$, the "empty coalition" $\varnothing$, which, because it contains no players, cannot benefit from cooperation. For completeness, therefore, we append

$$\bar{v}(\varnothing) = 0. \qquad (4.13)$$

Note that (4.13) is not a gratuitous appendage; if in any doubt, compute the right-hand side of (4.20) with $T = \{i\}$.

The number $\bar{v}(S)$, the benefit that the players in S can obtain if they cooperate with each other but not with the players outside S, is a measure of the bargaining strength of the coalition S. It is convenient, however, to express this strength as a fraction of the strength of the grand coalition $\{1,2,3\}$. Accordingly, we define the *normalized characteristic function* v by

$$v(S) = \frac{\bar{v}(S)}{\bar{v}(\{1,2,3\})}, \qquad (4.14)$$

where S is any coalition. Thus

$$\nu(\{i\}) = 0, \qquad i = 1,2,3$$

$$\nu(\{1,2\}) = \frac{3+d}{3+2d}, \qquad \nu(\{1,3\}) = \frac{1+d}{3+2d}, \qquad \nu(\{2,3\}) = \frac{d}{3+2d},$$

$$\nu(\{1,2,3\}) = 1.$$

$$(4.15)$$

More generally, for a c-game among n players, let the set of all players or grand coalition be denoted by N; i.e., $N = \{1,2,\ldots,n\}$. Then the normalized characteristic function, ν, of the game is defined by

$$\nu(S) = \frac{\overline{\nu}(S)}{\overline{\nu}(N)}, \tag{4.16}$$

where S is any of the 2^n coalitions (including $\oslash$); or, which is the same thing, S is any of the 2^n subsets of N. Note that (4.16) does not make sense unless $\overline{\nu}(N) > 0$, that is, unless the benefits of cooperation are positive, and we shall assume throughout that this condition is satisfied. (C-games that satisfy $\overline{\nu}(N) > 0$ are said to be *essential*, whereas c-games such that $\overline{\nu}(N) = 0$ are *inessential*; thus we restrict attention to the essential variety.)[2]

Now, with regard to the car pool, our task is to determine a 3-dimensional vector

$$x = (x_1, x_2, x_3) \tag{4.17}$$

stipulating how the benefits of cooperation are to be distributed among the grand coalition $\{1,2,3\}$; x must satisfy (4.11). We will refer to x as an *imputation*, and to the i-th component of x, namely x_i, as Player i's *allocation* at x. Furthermore, for each coalition S, we will refer to the sum

$$\sum_{i \in S} x_i$$

of allocations of players in S as the coalition's allocation at x (or as the amount that x allocates to S). More generally, an imputation of a c-game among n players is an n-dimensional vector

$$x = (x_1, x_2, \ldots, x_n) \tag{4.18}$$

---

[2]   If benefits are first defined such that $\overline{\nu}(\{i\}) \neq 0$, $i = 1,2,\ldots,n$, as would have happened in the car pool if we had first defined $\overline{\nu} = -c$, then the benefits associated with acting alone must first be subtracted out (as in (4.5)) before the benefits of cooperation are properly defined; in which case, (4.16) must be replaced by

$$\nu(S) = \frac{\overline{\nu}(S) - \sum_{i \in S} \overline{\nu}(\{i\})}{\overline{\nu}(N) - \sum_{i=1}^{n} \overline{\nu}(\{i\})}.$$

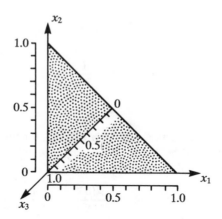

Figure 4.2   The set of imputations for a 3-player c-game.

such that

$$x_i \geq 0, \qquad i = 1, 2, \ldots, n \qquad\qquad (4.19a)$$

and

$$x_1 + x_2 + \cdots + x_n = 1; \qquad\qquad (4.19b)$$

the i-th component of x, namely x_i, is Player i's allocation at x. We will denote the set of all imputations by X. Thus $x \in X$ if and only if (4.19) is satisfied; obviously, if $x_i \geq 0$ for all $i \in N$, then (4.19b) implies $x_i \leq 1$ for all $i \in N$.

If x satisfies (4.19b), then x is said to be either *Pareto-optimal* or *group rational*, because (assuming that the whole of the benefit $\bar{v}(N)$ is allocated to the players) it is impossible to increase one player's allocation without decreasing that of another. If x satisfies (4.19a), then x is said to be *individually rational*, because each player is at least as well off in the grand coalition as he would have been all by himself. Thus imputations are vectors that are both individually and group rational.

For $n = 3$, because $x_3 \geq 0$ implies $0 \leq x_1 + x_2 \leq 1$, X can be represented in two dimensions as a right-angled isosceles triangle. From Figure 4.2, where X is shaded, we see that x_1 increases to the east and x_2 to the north; whereas x_3 increases to the southwest. We should bear in mind, however, that this representation is a distortion, albeit a convenient one, of the true picture, which is that X is a 2-dimensional equilateral triangle imbedded in 3-dimensional space. More generally, for a c-game among n players, X is an $(n - 1)$-dimensional "hypertriangle"—more commonly known as a *simplex*—in n-dimensional space.

Which of the infinitely many imputations in X can be regarded as a fair distribution of the benefits of cooperation? We can attempt to answer this question by considering the order in which the grand coalition might actually form. Suppose, for example, that the c-game has n players, where $n \geq 4$; and that when the grand coalition of all n players forms, Player a is first to join, Player b is second, Player c is third, and Player i fourth, where a, b, c and i are any positive integers between 1 and n. Let $T = \{a, b, c, i\}$. Then, because the players have joined in the given order, it is reasonable to say that Player a has contributed $\nu(\{a\}) - \nu(\varnothing) = 0$ to the grand coalition, that Player b has added $\nu(\{a, b\}) - \nu(\{a\}) = \nu(\{a, b\})$, that Player c has added $\nu(\{a, b, c\}) - \nu\{a, b\})$, and that Player i has added $\nu(T) - \nu(\{a, b, c\})$; in which case, $\nu(T) - \nu(\{a, b, c\})$ is Player i's fair allocation. But we can write $\nu(\{a, b, c\})$ more succinctly as $\nu(T - \{i\})$, where $T - \{i\}$ denotes all the players in T except i; thus $\nu(T) - \nu(T - \{i\})$ is Player i's fair allocation. More generally, if Player i is the j-th player to join, and if $T - \{i\}$ denotes the $j-1$ players who have joined already, then $\nu(T) - \nu(T - \{i\})$ is a fair allocation for i. Unfortunately, we do not know the identity of T; there are 2^{n-1} coalitions containing i (see Exercise 4.16), and T could be any one of them. What we can be sure about, however, is that if we calculate $\nu(T) - \nu(T - \{i\})$ for every coalition containing i, then a fair allocation for Player i should not exceed the maximum of those 2^{n-1} numbers. Accordingly, we shall refer to the set of imputations such that

$$x_i \leq \max_T \left(\nu(T) - \nu(T - \{i\}) \right) \tag{4.20}$$

for all values of $i = 1, 2, \ldots, n$ as the *reasonable set*, where the maximum in (4.20) is taken over all coalitions T that contain $\{i\}$. We note in passing that if A and B are sets then, quite generally, $A - B$ denotes the set of all elements in A but not in B; i.e.,

$$A - B = \{x \mid x \in A, x \notin B\}. \tag{4.21}$$

Returning now to the car pool, let us suppose, for the sake of definiteness, that the office where Jed, Ned and Ted all work is 9 miles from the point marked F in Figure 4.1. Then $d = 9$ in (4.15); and if x belongs to the reasonable set we must, in particular, have

$$x_1 \leq \max \left(\nu(\{1, 2, 3\}) - \nu(\{2, 3\}), \quad \nu(\{1, 2\}) - \nu(\{2\}), \right.$$

$$\left. \nu(\{1, 3\}) - \nu(\{3\}), \quad \nu(\{1\}) - \nu(\varnothing) \right)$$

$$= \max \left(1 - \frac{3}{7}, \quad \frac{4}{7} - 0, \quad \frac{10}{21} - 0, \quad 0 - 0 \right) = \frac{4}{7},$$

on taking $i = 1$ in (4.20). Similarly, on taking $i = 2$ and then $i = 3$ in (4.20), we must also have (Exercise 4.1)

$$x_2 \leq \max \left(\frac{11}{21}, \frac{3}{7}, \frac{4}{7} \right) = \frac{4}{7}, \quad x_3 \leq \max \left(\frac{3}{7}, \frac{10}{21}, \frac{3}{7} \right) = \frac{10}{21}.$$

The reasonable set consists of points that satisfy both these inequalities and

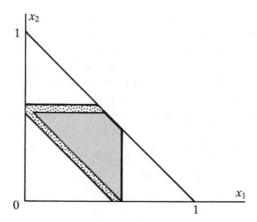

Figure 4.3   The reasonable set (light and dark shading)
and the core (dark shading) for the 3-person car pool with $d = 9$.

(4.11). Because $x_3 = 1 - x_1 - x_2$, the inequality $x_3 \leq 10/21$ is equivalent to $x_1 + x_2 \leq 11/21$; whence the reasonable set is the hexagon depicted by the shaded regions (both light and dark) in Figure 4.3. We see that, although (4.20) excludes imputations near the corners of X—it would not be reasonable to give most of the benefits of car pooling to a single player—the concept of reasonable set provides minimal constraints on what we may consider a fair imputation. Nevertheless, the thinking that led to (4.20), when suitably refined, is capable of yielding an attractive solution concept for c-games, and we shall give it our attention in Section 4.7.

Before proceeding, a word about notation. For most purposes, it is preferable to regard imputations of a 3-player game as vectors in 3-dimensional space; but X is 2-dimensional, and for graphical purposes it is preferable to regard the imputations as points in two dimensions. Thus the corner $(1, 0)$ of the triangle in Figure 4.3 represents the (unreasonable) imputation $(1, 0, 0)$, which would give all the benefits of cooperation to Jed; the corner $(0, 1)$ represents the imputation $(0, 1, 0)$, which would give all the benefits of cooperation to Ned; and the corner $(0, 0)$ represents the imputation $(0, 0, 1)$, which would give all the benefits of cooperation to Ted. More generally, from (4.11), the point (x_1, x_2) of the triangle in Figure 4.3 represents the imputation $(x_1, x_2, 1 - x_1 - x_2)$.

4.2   THE CORE, RATIONAL EPSILON-CORE AND
LEAST RATIONAL CORE

The concept of reasonable set has enabled us to exclude the most unreasonable points from the set of imputations for the car pool. But infinitely many imputations still remain. If we are serious about helping Jed, Ned and Ted reach agreement over the car pool, then we had better find a way to exclude more of X.

A concept that is useful in this regard is that of *excess*. For each imputation $x \in X$ of an n-player c-game, the excess of the coalition S at x, denoted by $e(S,x)$, is the difference between the fraction of the benefits of cooperation that S can obtain for itself, even if it does not cooperate with players outside S, and the fraction of the benefits of cooperation that x allocates to S; that is,

$$e(S,x) = v(S) - \sum_{i \in S} x_i. \qquad (4.22)$$

For example, for the car pool of Section 4.1 with $d = 9$ we have

$$e(\{1,2\},x) = \frac{4}{7} - x_1 - x_2$$

$$e(\{1,3\},x) = \frac{10}{21} - x_1 - x_3 = x_2 - \frac{11}{21} \qquad (4.23)$$

$$e(\{2,3\},x) = \frac{3}{7} - x_2 - x_3 = x_1 - \frac{4}{7}.$$

For any c-game it follows from (4.22) that

$$e(\{i\},x) = -x_i, \qquad i = 1,2,3, \qquad (4.24a)$$

and

$$e(\varnothing,x) = 0 = e(N,x). \qquad (4.24b)$$

If $e(S,x) > 0$, then the players in S will regard the imputation x as unfair, because they would receive greater benefits if they did not have to form the grand coalition. It therefore seems sensible—if possible—to exclude imputations such that $e(S,x) > 0$ for some coalition S (even if only one). The imputations that remain—if any—are said to form the *core* of the c-game. Here, and in the following section, we assume that the core exists; and, for reasons that will soon emerge, we will denote it by $C^+(0)$. Thus, in set-theoretic notation,

$$C^+(0) = \{x \in X \mid e(S,x) \leq 0 \quad \text{for } all \text{ coalitions } S\}. \qquad (4.25)$$

For example, from (4.23), the core of the car-pool game with $d = 9$ is the dark quadrilateral in Figure 4.3.[3] If the core exists, then it must be a subset of the reasonable set (though possibly the whole of it, as in Exercise 4.10). But the game may have no core (or, if you prefer, $C^+(0) = \varnothing$), and we shall consider this possibility in Section 4.4.

---

[3]   The core of a 3-player c-game need not be a quadrilateral; it can be a point, a line segment, a triangle, a pentagon (as in Exercise 4.10) or a hexagon.

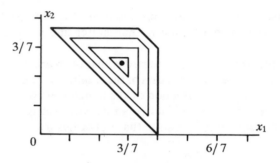

Figure 4.4   Rational ϵ-core boundaries for $\epsilon = 0$ (outer quadrilateral), $\epsilon = -1/21, \epsilon = -2/21, \epsilon = -1/7$ and $\epsilon = -11/63$ (dot) when $d = 9$ in the car-pool game of Section 4.1.

By excluding imputations that lie inside the reasonable set but outside the core (the speckled region in Figure 4.3), we move nearer to a car pool agreement. But infinitely many imputations still remain. Then which of them represents the fairest distribution of the benefits of cooperation?

From Jed's point of view, the best points in the dark quadrilateral of Figure 4.3 lie on the boundary where $x_1 = 4/7$; from Ned's point of view, they lie on the boundary where $x_2 = 11/21$; and from Ted's point of view they lie on the boundary where $x_1 + x_2 = 4/7$. It thus appears that the fairest compromise would be somehow to locate the "center" of the core. But how do we find an imputation that we can reasonably interpret as the center? One approach would be to move the walls of the boundary inward, all at the same speed, until they coalesce in a point. Suppose, for example, that we move the walls inward at the rate of one unit every 21 seconds. Then, after 1/21 seconds, we will have shrunk the boundary to the inner of the two quadrilaterals in Figure 4.4. If we continue at the same rate, then after 2/21 seconds we will have shrunk the boundary to the outer of the two triangles, and after 1/7 seconds to the inner triangle. Ultimately, after 11/63 seconds, the boundary will collapse to the point $(25/63, 22/63)$, which is marked by a dot in Figure 4.4. We might therefore propose that the fair solution of the game is the imputation

$$x^* = \frac{1}{63}(25, 22, 16); \tag{4.26}$$

in which case, it follows from (4.12) that Jed and Ned should each pay $14k/3$ dollars of the cost per trip, whereas Ted should pay $20k/3$ dollars. Ted should pay most because Jed must go out of his way to drive him home.

For arbitrary n-person c-games, we can generalize the ideas that led to (4.26) by defining the *rational ϵ-core*. The rational ϵ-core, denoted by $C^+(\epsilon)$, is the set of all imputations at which no coalition other than $\oslash$ or N has a greater excess than ϵ, where ϵ may be positive, negative or zero; that is,

$$C^+(\epsilon) = \{x \in X \,|\, e(S,x) \leq \epsilon \quad \text{for } \textit{all} \text{ coalitions } S$$
$$\text{such that} \quad S \neq \oslash, \quad S \neq N\}. \tag{4.27}$$

Thus the core (if it exists) is the rational 0-core. By (4.24b), the restrictions $S \neq \oslash, S \neq N$ are unnecessary if $\epsilon \geq 0$; but ϵ may be negative, in which case $C^+(\epsilon)$ is the set to which the core has shrunk after 1 second, when its walls are moved inward at $|\epsilon|$ units per second.

With a view to later developments, it will be convenient to introduce notation for the set of all coalitions that are neither the empty coalition nor the grand coalition; we denote it by Σ^0. Thus $S \in \Sigma^0$ if and only if $N \supset S, S \neq \oslash$ and $S \neq N$. Then we can define the rational ϵ-core more succinctly as

$$C^+(\epsilon) = \{x \in X \,|\, e(S,x) \leq \epsilon \quad \text{for} \quad S \in \Sigma^0\}. \tag{4.28}$$

But at imputation $x, e(S,x) \leq \epsilon$ for all S if and only if the maximum of $e(S,x)$, taken over all coalitions in Σ^0, is less than or equal to ϵ. Accordingly, and again with a view to later developments, let us define a function ϕ from X to the real numbers by

$$\phi(x) = \max_{S \in \Sigma^0} e(S,x). \tag{4.29}$$

Then we can define the rational ϵ-core even more succinctly as

$$C^+(\epsilon) = \{x \in X \,|\, \phi(x) \leq \epsilon\}. \tag{4.30}$$

Reducing ϵ shrinks $C^+(\epsilon)$; but if ϵ is too small, then there are no imputations such that $e(S,x) \leq \epsilon$ for all $S \in \Sigma^0$. Thus there is a least value of ϵ for which $C^+(\epsilon)$ exists. Indeed, if we denote this value by ϵ_1, then it is clear that

$$\epsilon_1 = \min_{x \in X} \phi(x); \tag{4.31}$$

because reducing ϵ causes more and more imputations to violate the condition $\phi(x) \leq \epsilon$, until all that remain finally are the imputations for which ϕ attains its minimum on X. We shall refer to $C^+(\epsilon_1)$, the set over which ϕ attains its minimum, as the *least rational core*. With a view to later developments, however, it will be convenient to have an alternative notation for the least rational core; accordingly, we denote it also by X^1. Thus $C^+(\epsilon_1)$ and X^1 are the same subset of X.

Returning to the car pool for illustration, x belongs to $C^+(\epsilon)$ if, on using (4.23),

$$\frac{4}{7} - x_1 - x_2 \leq \epsilon, \qquad x_2 - \frac{11}{21} \leq \epsilon, \qquad x_1 - \frac{4}{7} \leq \epsilon \tag{4.32a}$$

and, on using (4.24a),

$$-x_1 \leq \epsilon, \qquad -x_2 \leq \epsilon, \qquad -x_3 \leq \epsilon; \qquad (4.32b)$$

or, which is the same thing (verify), if

$$-\epsilon \leq x_1 \leq \frac{4}{7} + \epsilon, \qquad -\epsilon \leq x_2 \leq \frac{11}{21} + \epsilon, \qquad \frac{4}{7} - \epsilon \leq x_1 + x_2 \leq 1 + \epsilon. \quad (4.33)$$

Note that if $\epsilon > 0$ then (4.32b) is superseded by condition (4.19a), that allocations be nonnegative. The boundary of the region corresponding to (4.33) is sketched in Figure 4.4 for $\epsilon = 0$ (outer quadrilateral), $\epsilon = -1/21$ (inner quadrilateral), $\epsilon = -2/21$ (outer triangle) and $\epsilon = -1/7$ (inner triangle); the triangles, and the open curves consisting of the longest three sides of the quadrilaterals, are $\phi = \epsilon$ contours of the function defined by (4.29). The dot corresponds to the least rational core, which is

$$X^1 = \{x^*\} = \{(25/63, \ 22/63, \ 16/63)\}. \qquad (4.34)$$

Note that the value $\epsilon_1 = -11/63$ can be found analytically, but we postpone this matter until Section 4.3.

Now $e(S,x)$ is a measure of coalition S's dissatisfaction with the imputation x. If $e(S,x) > 0$ then S's allocation from x would be less than the benefit it could obtain for itself, and the players in S would rather dissolve the grand coalition than accept x (but they cannot dissolve it, because a fundamental assumption of c-game analysis is that the grand coalition has formed). If $e(S,x) = 0$ then the players in S would be indifferent between maintaining or dissolving the grand coalition. On the other hand, if $e(S,x) < 0$, then the players in S would prefer to remain in the grand coalition (even if it were possible to dissolve it). Regardless of whether $e(S,x)$ is positive or negative, however, the lower the value of $e(S,x)$, the lower the dissatisfaction of the players in S with imputation x (or, if you prefer, the higher their satisfaction). If $x \in C^+(\epsilon)$, then no coalition's dissatisfaction exceeds ϵ (or no coalition's satisfaction is less than $-\epsilon$); and the lower the value of ϵ, the lower the value of the maximum dissatisfaction among all coalitions that could possibly form. Thus if $X^1 = C^+(\epsilon_1)$ contains a single imputation, say x^*, then x^* minimizes maximum dissatisfaction; and to the extent that minimizing maximum dissatisfaction is fair, then x^* is the fair solution of the game. Until Section 4.7, we shall assume henceforward that minimizing maximum dissatisfaction is indeed equivalent to fairness.

Although $X^1 = C^+(\epsilon_1)$ must always exist, it need not contain only one imputation; it may contain infinitely many. Then which imputation should be regarded as the fair solution? We address this matter in Section 4.5. Meanwhile, the least rational core is an adequate solution concept, because in Sections 4.3 and 4.4 we consider only games for which X^1 contains a single imputation, denoted by x^*. Before proceeding, however, we pause to note that—although reducing ϵ always shrinks $C^+(\epsilon)$, until eventually at $\epsilon = \epsilon_1$ it disappears—because

$C^+(\epsilon)$ is a subset of X it is not quite true that increasing ϵ always expands $C^+(\epsilon)$. Rather, there is a maximum value of ϵ, say ϵ_0, beyond which the inequalities $e(S,x) \leq \epsilon$ are all superseded by $x \in X$. Thus if $\epsilon \geq \epsilon_0$ then $C^+(\epsilon) = X$; or, if you prefer, X is the greatest rational core. For example, by moving the walls outward in Figure 4.4 we see that $\epsilon_0 = 3/7$ for the 3-person car pool with $d = 9$.

4.3   A 4-PERSON CAR POOL AS A C-GAME

The purpose of the present section is twofold: to present an example of a 4-player game, and to show how to calculate X^1. Accordingly, let Jed, Ned and Ted have a fourth neighbor, Zed, whose house is marked Z in Figure 4.1. He works in Jed, Ned and Ted's office at the same times and on the same days, owns the same kind of small car, and in order to save money would like to join their car pool. Now, in practice it might happen that the existing car pool would bargain with Zed as a unit, so that the bargaining would reduce to a 2-player game; but we wish to consider a 4-person game. Let us therefore assume, at least until the end of the section, that Zed is a good friend of all the others, and that they work out the costs of the 4-person car pool from scratch. As stated in the previous section, we will also assume that a fair distribution of the benefits of cooperation is one that minimizes maximum dissatisfaction. Thus our task is to calculate the least rational core of a 4-player game.

With $n = 4$, and hence $N = \{1,2,3,4\}$, there are 15 coalitions excluding $\oslash$. Let us assume that Zed is Player 4, and that Jed, Ned and Ted are Players 1, 2 and 3, as before. Now, it is clear from Section 4.1 that the value of k has no effect on the outcome; therefore, we may as well express the costs in units of k dollars. Then from Figure 4.1 we readily find that the costs of the car pools that could possibly form are given by

$$c(\{1\}) = 4 + d, \quad c(\{2\}) = 3 + d, \quad c(\{3\}) = 3 + d, \quad c(\{4\}) = 3 + d$$
$$c(\{1,2\}) = 4 + d, \quad c(\{1,3\}) = 6 + d, \quad c(\{1,4\}) = 4 + d$$
$$c(\{2,3\}) = 6 + d, \quad c(\{2,4\}) = 4 + d, \quad c(\{3,4\}) = 5 + d$$
$$c(\{1,2,3\}) = 7 + d, \quad c(\{1,2,4\}) = 5 + d, \quad c(\{1,3,4\}) = 6 + d$$
$$c(\{2,3,4\}) = 6 + d, \quad c(\{1,2,3,4\}) = 7 + d; \tag{4.35}$$

naturally, costs are predicated on travel by the shortest route. From (4.5), we deduce that the benefits of cooperation associated with the various car pools are given by

$$\bar{v}(\{i\}) = 0, \qquad i = 1,2,3,4,$$
$$\bar{v}(\{1,2\}) = 3 + d, \quad \bar{v}(\{1,3\}) = 1 + d, \quad \bar{v}(\{1,4\}) = 3 + d$$
$$\bar{v}(\{2,3\}) = d, \quad \bar{v}(\{2,4\}) = 2 + d, \quad \bar{v}(\{3,4\}) = 1 + d$$
$$\bar{v}(\{1,2,3\}) = 3 + 2d, \quad \bar{v}(\{1,2,4\}) = 5 + 2d, \quad \bar{v}(\{1,3,4\}) = 4 + 2d$$
$$\bar{v}(\{2,3,4\}) = 3 + 2d, \quad \bar{v}(\{1,2,3,4\}) = 6 + 3d. \tag{4.36}$$

For the sake of definiteness, let us suppose that $d = 2$ (you may consider this value of d to be unrealistic, but higher values are considered in Exercises 4.5 and 4.6). Then, from (4.14), the normalized characteristic function is defined by

$$v(\{i\}) = 0, \qquad i = 1, 2, 3, 4,$$

$$v(\{1,2\}) = \frac{5}{12}, \quad v(\{1,3\}) = \frac{1}{4}, \quad v(\{1,4\}) = \frac{5}{12},$$

$$v(\{2,3\}) = \frac{1}{6}, \quad v(\{2,4\}) = \frac{1}{3}, \quad v(\{3,4\}) = \frac{1}{4},$$

$$v(\{1,2,3\}) = \frac{7}{12}, \quad v(\{1,2,4\}) = \frac{3}{4}, \quad v(\{1,3,4\}) = \frac{2}{3},$$

$$v(\{2,3,4\}) = \frac{7}{12}, \quad v(\{1,2,3,4\}) = 1. \tag{4.37}$$

Thus the rational ϵ-core consists of imputations $x = (x_1, x_2, x_3, x_4)^T$ that satisfy

$$-x_1 \le \epsilon, \quad -x_2 \le \epsilon, \quad -x_3 \le \epsilon, \quad -x_4 \le \epsilon, \tag{4.38a}$$

$$\frac{5}{12} - x_1 - x_2 \le \epsilon, \quad \frac{1}{4} - x_1 - x_3 \le \epsilon, \quad \frac{5}{12} - x_1 - x_4 \le \epsilon,$$

$$\frac{1}{6} - x_2 - x_3 \le \epsilon, \quad \frac{1}{3} - x_2 - x_4 \le \epsilon, \quad \frac{1}{4} - x_3 - x_4 \le \epsilon, \tag{4.38b}$$

$$\frac{7}{12} - x_1 - x_2 - x_3 \le \epsilon, \quad \frac{3}{4} - x_1 - x_2 - x_4 \le \epsilon,$$

$$\frac{2}{3} - x_1 - x_3 - x_4 \le \epsilon, \quad \frac{7}{12} - x_2 - x_3 - x_4 \le \epsilon \tag{4.38c}$$

and

$$x_1 + x_2 + x_3 + x_4 = 1; \tag{4.39}$$

if $\epsilon > 0$, of course, then (4.38a) is superseded by condition (4.19a) that allocations be nonnegative. On using (4.39) to eliminate x_4 from (4.38), we find that $C^+(\epsilon)$ is the 3-dimensional simplex of vectors $x \in X$ such that

$$-\epsilon \le x_1 \le \frac{5}{12} + \epsilon, \qquad -\epsilon \le x_2 \le \frac{1}{3} + \epsilon, \qquad -\epsilon \le x_3 \le \frac{1}{4} + \epsilon, \tag{4.40a}$$

$$\frac{5}{12} - \epsilon \le x_1 + x_2 \le \frac{3}{4} + \epsilon, \qquad \frac{1}{4} - \epsilon \le x_1 + x_3 \le \frac{2}{3} + \epsilon,$$

$$\frac{1}{6} - \epsilon \le x_2 + x_3 \le \frac{7}{12} + \epsilon, \tag{4.40b}$$

$$\frac{7}{12} - \epsilon \le x_1 + x_2 + x_3 \le 1 + \epsilon. \tag{4.40c}$$

You should verify for yourself that (4.38) and (4.40) are equivalent; for example, the second of (4.40a) combines the second of (4.38a) with the third of (4.38c), whereas the third of (4.40b) combines the third and fourth of (4.38b).

We can now determine ϵ_1. From the first of (4.40a) we have $\epsilon \leq 5/12 + \epsilon$, or $\epsilon \geq -5/24$; similarly, from the second and third of (4.40a), we have $\epsilon \geq -1/6$, $\epsilon \geq -1/8$. We derive four similar inequalities from (4.40b) and (4.40c). For example, the second of (4.40b) yields $\epsilon \geq -1/3$; however, none of these inequalities supersedes $\epsilon \geq -1/8$. Therefore, we have so far established only that $\epsilon_1 \geq -1/8$. But adding the first two inequalities of (4.40a) yields

$$-2\epsilon \leq x_1 + x_2 \leq \frac{3}{4} + 2\epsilon, \tag{4.41}$$

which in conjunction with the first of (4.40b) yields

$$\frac{5}{12} - \epsilon \leq \frac{3}{4} + 2\epsilon, \qquad -2\epsilon \leq \frac{3}{4} + \epsilon; \tag{4.42}$$

or $\epsilon \geq -1/9$, $\epsilon \geq -1/4$, the second of which is superseded by the first. Hence $\epsilon_1 \geq -1/9$. Again, adding all three of the inequalities in (4.40a) yields

$$-3\epsilon \leq x_1 + x_2 + x_3 \leq 1 + 3\epsilon, \tag{4.43}$$

which in conjunction with (4.40c) yields

$$\frac{7}{12} - \epsilon \leq 1 + 3\epsilon, \qquad -3\epsilon \leq 1 + \epsilon; \tag{4.44}$$

or $\epsilon \geq -5/48$, $\epsilon \geq -1/4$, the second of which is superseded by the first. Thus $\epsilon_1 \geq -5/48$. Continuing in this manner, we obtain a further four lower bounds on ϵ; but none of them supersedes $\epsilon \geq -5/48$. No further restrictions on ϵ are implied by (4.40); ϵ can be as small as it pleases, as long as it satisfies $\epsilon \geq -5/48$. We conclude that

$$\epsilon_1 = -\frac{5}{48}. \tag{4.45}$$

With $\epsilon = -5/48$, the first inequality of (4.40c) and the second of (4.43) together imply that

$$\frac{11}{16} \leq x_1 + x_2 + x_3 \leq \frac{11}{16}; \tag{4.46}$$

whence, of course, $x_1 + x_2 + x_3 = 11/16$. We can now eliminate x_3 from (4.40); whence, after simplification, the least rational core consists of imputations satisfying

$$\frac{5}{24} \leq x_1 \leq \frac{5}{16}, \qquad \frac{1}{8} \leq x_2 \leq \frac{11}{48}, \qquad \frac{13}{24} \leq x_1 + x_2 \leq \frac{7}{12}. \tag{4.47}$$

Clearly, these inequalities are satisfied only if $x_1 = 5/16$ and $x_2 = 11/48$; whence, from (4.46) and (4.39), the least rational core is

$$X^1 = C^+(-5/48) = \{(5/16, \ 11/48, \ 7/48, \ 5/16)\}. \tag{4.48a}$$

In other words, the fairest distribution of the benefits of cooperation (according to our agreed criterion) is given by the imputation

$$x^* = (5/15, \ 11/48, \ 7/48, \ 5/16). \tag{4.48b}$$

By analogy with (4.12), it is clear from (4.36) that Player i should contribute

$$c(\{i\}) - (6 + 3d)x_i = c(\{i\}) - 12x_i \tag{4.49}$$

to the cost per trip (which, you will recall, is measured in units of k dollars). Thus Jed and Ned should each cover 2.25 units of the total cost of 9 units; whereas Ted should contribute 3.25 units, and Zed only 1.25. Again, Ted is penalized for being the outlier.

Now, it could be argued that this fair solution is more than fair to the newcomer Zed, and hence less than fair to the other three. If Jed, Ned and Ted were to bargain as a unit then we would have, in effect, a 2-player c-game with costs

$$c(\bar{1}) = 9, \qquad c(\bar{2}) = 5, \qquad c(\bar{1}, \bar{2}) = 9 \tag{4.50}$$

and hence benefits

$$\bar{v}(\bar{1}) = 0 = \bar{v}(\bar{2}), \qquad \bar{v}(\bar{1}, \bar{2}) = 5, \tag{4.51}$$

where $\bar{1} = \{1, 2, 3\}$ and $\bar{2} = \{4\}$. From Exercise 4.7 the fair solution of this modified c-game is to share the benefits of cooperation equally between $\bar{1}$ and $\bar{2}$. Thus Zed would have to contribute 2.5 units—twice as much as previously— whereas Jed, Ned and Ted would have reduced their total costs from 7.75 units to 6.5. How would they distribute the extra benefit of 1.25 units among themselves? No two of them could secure part of this benefit by acting without the other; the benefit would accrue only if all three of them agreed to gang up on Zed. Thus Jed, Ned and Ted would be led to a c-game with normalized characteristic function defined by

$$\begin{aligned} v(S) &= 0 \quad \text{if} \quad S \neq \{1, 2, 3\} \\ v(\{1, 2, 3\}) &= 1. \end{aligned} \tag{4.52}$$

Again from Exercise 4.7, the fair solution of this game is to share the extra benefit equally. Thus Jed, Ned and Ted would each reduce their cost per trip by 5/12 of a unit; so that Jed and Ned would cover 11/6 units of the total cost of 9 units, whereas Ted would contribute 17/6 units (and Zed 5/2). Whether this solution or the previous solution was ultimately adopted, however, would depend upon details of how the car pool formed.

We remark, finally, that the method we used to determine $C^+(\epsilon_1)$ for a 4-player game applies even more readily to 3-player games. In particular, it can be used to deduce (4.34) from (4.33); see Exercise 4.2. For further examples, see Exercises 4.3–4.6 and 4.10.

4.4   LOG-HAULING: A CORELESS *C*-GAME

Many years ago when they were young and sprightly, Zan and Zed felled enough trees to make 150 8-foot logs, which they neatly stacked in their yard. They had intended to turn the logs into a cabin; but years went by, and never did they find the time. Now Zan and Zed are too old to lift the logs, and no longer need the cabin. They have therefore decided to sell the logs for a dollar each to the first person or persons who will haul them away, and they have placed an advertisement in the local newspaper.

In response to this advertisement, three people and their pickup trucks arrive simultaneously at Zan and Zed's at the appointed time. These eager beavers, who would all like to haul as many of the bargain logs as possible, are our old friends Jed (Player 1), Ned (Player 2) and Ted (Player 3). Jed's truck can haul 45 logs, Ned's can haul 60 and Ted's can haul 75. If there were 180 logs, then all three could leave with a full load. Unfortunately, however, there are only 150 logs; and because our friends all arrived simultaneously, no one can claim to have arrived first. Moreover, because the logs are too heavy for one person to lift, the players cannot resort to a scramble; they must cooperate. Then how do they divvy up the logs? We must solve another *c*-game.

Let $\bar{\nu}(S)$, the benefit of cooperation that accrues to coalition S, be the number of logs that the players in S can haul without the help of players outside S. Then, clearly:

$$\bar{\nu}(\{i\}) = 0, \qquad i = 1, 2, 3$$
$$\bar{\nu}(\{1,2\}) = 105, \quad \bar{\nu}(\{1,3\}) = 120, \qquad (4.53)$$
$$\bar{\nu}(\{2,3\}) = 135, \quad \bar{\nu}(\{1,2,3\}) = 150.$$

The characteristic function is therefore defined by

$$\nu(\{1,2\}) = \frac{7}{10}, \qquad \nu(\{1,3\}) = \frac{4}{5}, \qquad \nu(\{2,3\}) = \frac{9}{10} \qquad (4.54)$$

and, of course, $\nu(\{i\}) = 0, i = 1, 2, 3, \nu(N) = 1$. It follows readily (Exercise 4.8) that the imputation $x = (x_1, x_2, x_3)$ belongs to $C^+(\epsilon)$ if and only if

$$-\epsilon \le x_1 \le \frac{1}{10} + \epsilon, \quad -\epsilon \le x_2 \le \frac{1}{5} + \epsilon, \quad \frac{7}{10} - \epsilon \le x_1 + x_2 \le 1 + \epsilon; \quad (4.55)$$

and the sum of the second and fourth inequalities is consistent with the fifth if and only if $7/10 - \epsilon \le 3/10 + 2\epsilon$, or $\epsilon \ge 2/15$. Thus $\epsilon_1 = 2/15$. We conclude immediately that the game has no core.

Whenever a game is coreless or, which is the same thing, whenever $\epsilon_1 > 0$ (if $\epsilon_1 = 0$ then the core contains a single imputation), the maximum dissatisfaction must be positive; no matter which imputation is selected, at least one coalition (and in this particular case, every coalition) will have a lower allocation than if the grand coalition did not form. Thus Jed, Ned and Ted all wish that one of the other two had not arrived, or had arrived late; but he did arrive, and the three of them must reach an agreement. C-games assume that the grand coalition has formed, but have nothing to say about how it formed. If the game has a core, then it is probable that the grand coalition formed voluntarily; the more players the merrier (up to a point), because everyone benefits from the cooperation. If, on the other hand, the game has no core, then the players were probably coerced into forming the grand coalition; the fewer players the better (down to a point), but no one can be barred from playing. To put it another way, c-games with cores are about sharing a surplus of benefits, whereas coreless games are about rationing a shortage of benefits; but in either case the existence of the grand coalition is assumed, and the least rational core, if it contains a single imputation, offers a solution that's fair in the sense of minimizing maximum dissatisfaction.

With $\epsilon = 2/15$, it is readily shown that (4.55) can be satisfied only if $x_1 = 7/30$ and $x_2 = 1/3$; see Exercise 4.8. Thus the least rational core is

$$X^1 = C^+(-2/15) = \{(7/30, 1/3, 13/30)\}; \qquad (4.56)$$

whence the fair solution is that Jed should get 35, Ned 50 and Ted 65 of the 150 logs. Our fair solution distributes the 30-log shortage equally among the players. Whether this is the conclusion that Jed, Ned and Ted would actually reach, however, is an open question.[4] Would it be fairer to give each player 50 logs in the first instance, but then transfer 5 of Jed's logs to Ned or Ted because Jed can haul only 45? If so, then how many of the extra 5 logs should Ted get? Well, what do you think?

4.5   THE NUCLEOLUS

The boundary of the core does not always collapse to a single point when we move its walls inward at a uniform rate; that is, the least rational core may contain more than one imputation. Then what is the center of the core in such cases? An answer is provided by the "nucleolus," which we introduce in this section.[5]

---

[4]   There remains the problem of who should put the logs on the trucks (assume that they all have family to help at home). Because it takes two to lift a log, and because the players' allocations are in the ratio 7:10:13, it seems fairest for Jed to lift 70 logs, Ned to lift 100 and Ted 130. For example, Ted could lift all 35 of Jed's logs, 12 with Jed and 23 with Ned; Ned could lift all 50 of his own logs, 20 with Jed and 30 with Ted; and Ted could lift all 65 of his own logs, 27 with Ned and 38 with Jed.

[5]   The concept of nucleolus is due to Schmeidler (1969). Strictly, the concept we

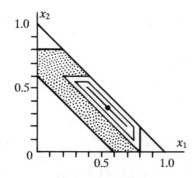

Figure 4.5 Reasonable set (hexagon) and rational ϵ-cores for $\epsilon = 0$ (outer quadrilateral), $\epsilon = -1/20$ and $\epsilon = -1/10$ (line segment) when $d = 1$ in the 3-person car-pool. The quadrilaterals are $\phi = \epsilon$ contours, where ϕ is defined by (4.29). The dot denotes the nucleolus.

Let us begin by returning to the 3-person car pool of Section 4.1. If $d = 1$ then, from (4.15), the characteristic function is defined by

$$\nu(\{1,2\}) = \frac{4}{5}, \qquad \nu(\{1,3\}) = \frac{2}{5}, \qquad \nu(\{2,3\}) = \frac{1}{5} \qquad (4.57)$$

and, of course, $\nu(N) = 1$, $\nu(\{i\}) = 0$, $i = 1, 2, 3$. It is questionable whether a car pool would really form for such a low value of d; but the value is convenient for our present purpose, and higher values of d are considered in the exercises. From Exercise 4.2, the rational ϵ-core is

$$C^+(\epsilon) = \{x \in X \mid -\epsilon \leq x_1 \leq \frac{4}{5}+\epsilon, \quad -\epsilon \leq x_2 \leq \frac{3}{5}+\epsilon, \quad \frac{4}{5}-\epsilon \leq x_1+x_2 \leq 1+\epsilon\},$$
$$(4.58)$$

where X is defined by (4.11); for example, $C^+(0)$ and $C^+(-1/20)$ are the quadrilaterals depicted in Figure 4.5. By the method of Section 4.3, it is readily found that $\epsilon_1 = -1/10$ (because (4.58) implies $4/5 - \epsilon \leq 1 + \epsilon$); whence the least rational core is

$$X^1 = \{x \in X \mid 1/10 \leq x_1 \leq 7/10, \ 1/10 \leq x_2 \leq 1/2, \ x_1 + x_2 = 9/10.\} \quad (4.59)$$

It no longer contains a single imputation; rather, it contains infinitely many imputations, which correspond to points of the line $x_1 + x_2 = 9/10$ between $(x_1, x_2) = (2/5, 1/2)$ and $(x_1, x_2) = (7/10, 1/5)$ in Figure 4.5. Which of all these imputations is the fair solution of the game?

---

introduce is Maschler, Peleg and Shubik's "lexicographic center"; however, the lexicographic center coincides with the nucleolus. See Maschler *et al.* (1979, pp. 331–336).

To answer this question, let us continue to assume that fairness means minimizing maximum dissatisfaction. Now, by construction, for $x \in X^1$ the maximum dissatisfaction of any coalition is $\epsilon_1 = -1/10$; that is, every coalition obtains at least 1/10 more of the benefits of cooperation than it could obtain if the grand coalition had not formed. We can verify this by using (4.22) and (4.57) to compute the excesses at $x \in X^1$:

$$e(\{1,2\},x) = -\frac{1}{10}, \qquad e(\{1,3\},x) = x_2 - \frac{3}{5}, \qquad e(\{2,3\},x) = x_1 - \frac{4}{5},$$

$$e(\{1\},x) = -x_1, \qquad e(\{2\},x) = -x_2, \qquad e(\{3\},x) = -\frac{1}{10}. \qquad (4.60)$$

Because $2/5 \leq x_1 \leq 7/10$ and $1/5 \leq x_2 \leq 1/2$, none of these excesses exceeds $-1/10$. Moreover, for two coalitions, namely, $S = \{1,2\}$ and $S = \{3\}$, the minimum is actually achieved; and because $e(S,x)$ is independent of $x(\in X^1)$ for these two coalitions, we can vary x within X^1 without affecting their excesses. For the other four coalitions, however, $e(S,x)$ remains a function of x; and so by varying x we can find imputations that minimize their maximum excess, i.e., minimize the maximum of $e(\{1,3\},x)$, $e(\{2,3\},x)$, $e(\{1\},x)$ and $e(\{2\},x)$. In other words, coalitions $\{1,2\}$ and $\{3\}$, being indifferent among all imputations in X^1, are already as satisfied as it is possible to make them; so we exclude them from further reckoning and concentrate instead on reducing the dissatisfaction of the remaining coalitions below $-1/10$. (What this means in practice, of course, is that Ted has been allocated a tenth of the benefits; whereas Jed and Ned have together been allocated nine tenths, but it is not yet clear how to divvy it up between them.)

With a view to generalization, let Σ^1 denote the set of coalitions whose excess can be reduced below ϵ_1 by an imputation in X^1; that is, define

$$\Sigma^1 = \{S \in \Sigma^0 \mid \text{ there exists } x \in X^1 \text{ such that } e(S,x) < \epsilon_1\}, \qquad (4.61)$$

so that our 3-person car pool with $d = 1$ has $\Sigma^1 = \{\{1\}\{2\}, \{1,3\}, \{2,3\}\}$. Still with a view to generalization, for $x \in X^1$ let

$$\phi_1(x) = \max_{S \in \Sigma^1} e(S,x) \qquad (4.62)$$

be the maximum excess at imputation x of the remaining coalitions; and let ϵ_2 be its minimum, i.e.,

$$\epsilon_2 = \min_{x \in X^1} \phi_1(x). \qquad (4.63)$$

Furthermore, let X^2 consist of all imputations at which ϕ_1 achieves its minimum, i.e.,

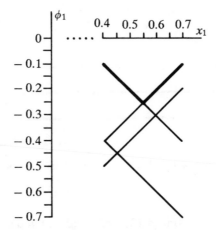

Figure 4.6   Graph of ϕ_1 defined by (4.63).

$$X^2 = \{x \in X^1 \mid \phi_1(x) = \epsilon_2\}. \tag{4.64}$$

Then, in the case of the car pool, because $x_1 + x_2 = 9/10$ for $x \in X^1$, ϕ_1 can be regarded as function of x_1 alone; and, from (4.60) - (4.62), we have

$$\phi_1(x) = \max\left(x_2 - \frac{3}{5}, \quad x_1 - \frac{4}{5}, \quad -x_1, -x_2\right)$$

$$= \max\left(\frac{3}{10} - x_1, \quad x_1 - \frac{4}{5}, \quad -x_1, \quad x_1 - \frac{9}{10}\right), \tag{4.65}$$

for $2/5 \le x_1 \le 7/10$.

The graph of ϕ_1 is sketched in Figure 4.6. You can see at a glance that ϕ_1 takes its minimum $-1/4$ where $x_1 = 11/20$. Thus $\epsilon_2 = -1/4$ and

$$X^2 = \left\{\frac{1}{20}(11, \ 7, \ 2)\right\}; \tag{4.66}$$

X^2 contains just the single imputation

$$x^* = \frac{1}{20}(11, \ 7, \ 2). \tag{4.67}$$

From (4.60), the coalitions for which $-1/4$ is the actual excess at x^* are $\{1,3\}$ and $\{2,3\}$; for $\{1\}$ and $\{2\}$, of course, the excesses at x^* are $-11/20$ and $-7/20$, respectively. Because X^2 contains a single imputation, no further variation of x is possible. We have reduced unfairness as much as possible. Thus x^* is the

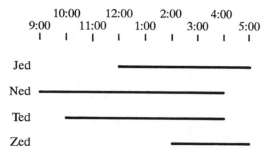

Figure 4.7 Antique dealers' business hours.

solution of the c-game. From (4.12), Jed, Ned and Ted's fair (fare?) shares of the cost per trip are $9k/4$, $9k/4$ and $7k/2$, respectively.

The ideas we have just developed to reach this solution are readily generalized to games with more than three players, for which the least rational core need be neither a point nor a line segment.[6] Consider, for example, the following 4-person variation of Exercise 4.10. Jed, Ned, Ted and Zed (not the same guys who work in the office) are antique dealers, who conduct their businesses in separate but adjoining rooms of a common premises. Their advertised office hours are shown in Figure 4.7; for example, Ted's advertised hours are from 10:00 a.m. until 4:00 p.m. Because the dealers have other jobs and the store is never so busy that one guy couldn't take care of everyone's customers, it is in the dealers' interests to pool their time in minding the store: there is no need for two people between 10:00 a.m. and noon or between 4:00 p.m. and 5:00 p.m, for three people between noon and 2:00 p.m., or for four people between 2:00 p.m. and 4:00 p.m. Cooperation will enable dealers to leave earlier than their advertised closing hours, or arrive later than their advertised opening hours, or both. But how much earlier or later? What is a fair allocation of store-minding duty for each of the dealers?

Let Jed, Ned, Ted and Zed be Players 1, 2, 3 and 4, respectively, and let the benefit of cooperation to coalition S be the number of dealer-hours that S saves by pooling time. Then $\bar{v}(\{i\}) = 0$, $i = 1, 2, 3, 4$, because no time is saved if no one cooperates; $\bar{v}(\{1,2\}) = 4$, because either Jed or Ned can mind the other's business between noon and 4:00; $\bar{v}(N) = 13$, where $N = \{1, 2, 3, 4\}$, because only 8 of the dealer-hours currently advertised are actually necessary; and so on. Thus the normalized characteristic function v is defined (Exercise 4.11) by

---

6   Even if the least rational core is a line segment, X^2 need not be its mid-point. Although the walls of the least rational core are moved inward at the same speed, the components of the velocities of inward movement along the line segment corresponding to the least core need not be equal. For an example, see Exercise 4.12.

$$\nu(\{i\}) = 0, \qquad i = 1, 2, 3, 4,$$

$$\nu(\{1,2\}) = \frac{4}{13}, \quad \nu(\{1,3\}) = \frac{4}{13}, \quad \nu(\{1,4\}) = \frac{3}{13},$$

$$\nu(\{2,3\}) = \frac{6}{13}, \quad \nu(\{2,4\}) = \frac{2}{13}, \quad \nu(\{3,4\}) = \frac{2}{13},$$

$$\nu(\{1,2,3\}) = \frac{10}{13}, \quad \nu(\{1,2,4\}) = \frac{7}{13}, \quad \nu(\{1,3,4\}) = \frac{7}{13},$$

$$\nu(\{2,3,4\}) = \frac{8}{13}, \quad \nu(\{1,2,3,4\}) = 1; \tag{4.68}$$

and it follows readily that the rational ϵ-core contains all vectors $x = (x_1, x_2, x_3, x_4) \in X$ such that

$$-\epsilon \le x_1 \le \frac{5}{13} + \epsilon, \quad -\epsilon \le x_2 \le \frac{6}{13} + \epsilon, \quad -\epsilon \le x_3 \le \frac{6}{13} + \epsilon, \tag{4.69a}$$

$$\frac{4}{13} - \epsilon \le x_1 + x_2 \le \frac{11}{13} + \epsilon, \quad \frac{4}{13} - \epsilon \le x_1 + x_3 \le \frac{11}{13} + \epsilon,$$

$$\frac{6}{13} - \epsilon \le x_2 + x_3 \le \frac{10}{13} + \epsilon, \tag{4.69b}$$

$$\frac{10}{13} - \epsilon \le x_1 + x_2 + x_3 \le 1 + \epsilon. \tag{4.69c}$$

By the method of Section 4.3, we find that

$$\epsilon_1 = -\frac{3}{26} \tag{4.70}$$

(note that $2\epsilon \ge -3/13$ is implied by (4.69c)); whence it follows from (4.69c) that

$$x_1 + x_2 + x_3 = \frac{23}{26} \tag{4.71}$$

for $x \in X^1$. Using this equality to eliminate x_3, we find after simplification (Exercise 4.11) that

$$X^1 = C^+(\epsilon_1) = \left\{ x \in X \mid \frac{3}{13} \le x_1 \le \frac{7}{26}, x_1 + x_2 \ge \frac{7}{13}, x_2 \le \frac{9}{26} \right\}. \tag{4.72}$$

Thus the least rational core is a quadrilateral, which is represented by the shaded region in Figure 4.8. We remind ourselves that this picture distorts the true

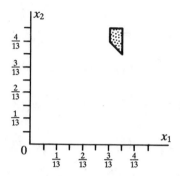

Figure 4.8 Least rational core of the antique-minding game.

quadrilateral, which, by virtue of (4.71), is imbedded in the hyperplane

$$x_4 = \frac{3}{26}. \tag{4.73}$$

By construction, for $x \in X^1$ the maximum dissatisfaction of any coalition is $-3/26$; that is, every coalition obtains at least $3/26$ more of the benefits of cooperation than it could obtain if the grand coalition had not formed. Two coalitions, namely, $\{1,2,3\}$ and $\{4\}$, obtain an excess of precisely $-3/26$, because

$$e(\{1,2,3\},x) = \frac{10}{13} - x_1 - x_2 - x_3 = -\frac{3}{26}, \qquad e(\{4\},x) = -x_4 = -\frac{3}{26} \tag{4.74}$$

for all $x \in X^1$, on using (4.22), (4.68), (4.71) and (4.73); these are the coalitions who cannot be allocated less dissatisfaction (or, if you prefer, greater satisfaction) than they receive from any imputation in the least rational core.[7] On the other hand, the excesses in X^1 of the twelve remaining coalitions still vary with x, and are strictly less than $-3/26$ at least somewhere; or, in terms of (4.61),

$$\Sigma^1 = \{\{1\}, \{2\}, \{3\}, \{1,2\}, \{1,3\}, \{1,4\}, \{2,3\}, \{2,4\}, \{3,4\},$$
$$\{1,2,4\}, \{1,3,4\}, \{2,3,4\}\}.$$

Accordingly, we exclude $\{1,2,3\}$ and $\{4\}$ from further reckoning and concentrate our attention on eliminating unfairness among the coalitions in Σ^1.

With the help of (4.22), (4.68), (4.71) and (4.73), the excesses of these coali-

---

[7] What this means in practice, of course, is that Zed has been allocated $3/26$ of the benefits of cooperation; whereas Jed, Ned and Ted have together been allocated $23/26$, but it is not yet clear how to divvy it up between them.

tions at $x \in X^1$ are readily found to be

$$e_1 = e(\{1\},x) = -x_1, \quad e_2 = e(\{2\},x) = -x_2, \quad e_3 = e(\{3\},x) = x_1 + x_2 - \frac{23}{26},$$

$$e_{12} = e(\{1,2\},x) = \frac{4}{13} - x_1 - x_2, \quad e_{13} = e(\{1,3\},x) = x_2 - \frac{15}{26},$$

$$e_{14} = e(\{1,4\},x) = \frac{3}{26} - x_1, \quad e_{23} = e(\{2,3\},x) = x_1 - \frac{11}{26},$$

$$e_{24} = e(\{2,4\},x) = \frac{1}{26} - x_2, \quad e_{34} = e(\{3,4\},x) = x_1 + x_2 - \frac{11}{13},$$

$$e_{124} = e(\{1,2,4\},x) = \frac{11}{26} - x_1 - x_2,$$

$$e_{134} = e(\{1,3,4\},x) = x_2 - \frac{6}{13},$$

$$e_{234} = e(\{2,3,4\},x) = x_1 - \frac{5}{13}. \tag{4.75}$$

It is straightforward to show that none of e_1, e_2, e_3, e_{12}, e_{13}, e_{24} or e_{34} can exceed $-3/13$ on X^1; whereas none of the remaining five excesses can be less than $-5/26$. Therefore, the maximum in definition (4.62) of ϕ_1 is effectively taken, not over the whole of Σ^1, but rather over the five coalitions $\{1,4\}$, $\{2,3\}$, $\{1,2,4\}$, $\{1,3,4\}$ and $\{2,3,4\}$; that is,

$$\phi_1(x) = \max \left(\frac{3}{26} - x_1, x_1 - \frac{11}{26}, \frac{11}{26} - x_1 - x_2, x_2 - \frac{6}{13}, x_1 - \frac{5}{13} \right), \quad x \in X^1. \tag{4.76}$$

Because ϕ_1 is now a function of two variables, its graph is three-dimensional, and we can no longer plot it in two dimensions, as we did in Figure 4.6. Instead, therefore, in Figure 4.9 we sketch its contour map; from which it is clear that the graph of ϕ_1 is shaped like an asymmetric boat or inverted roof, the lowest points of which lie on the contour $\phi_1 = -7/52$. It follows immediately that

$$\epsilon_2 = \min_{x \in X^1} \phi_1(x) = -\frac{7}{52}, \tag{4.77}$$

$$X^2 = \{x \in X \mid \phi_1(x) = \epsilon_2\} = \{x \in X \mid x_1 = \frac{1}{4}, \frac{4}{13} \leq x_2 \leq \frac{17}{52}, x_4 = \frac{3}{26}\}. \tag{4.78}$$

We can think of X^2, which has been obtained by moving inward the walls of the least rational core, as the second-order least rational core.

By construction, for $x \in X^2$ the maximum dissatisfaction of any coalition is $-7/52$. Two coalitions, namely, $\{1,4\}$ and $\{2,3,4\}$, obtain an excess of precisely $-7/52$, because $e_{14} = 0 = e_{234}$ for all $x \in X^2$ from (4.75) and (4.78). These coalitions cannot be allocated less dissatisfaction than they receive from

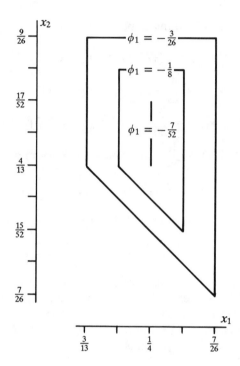

Figure 4.9   Contour map of function ϕ_1 defined over shaded region in Figure 4.8.

any imputation in X^2. On the other hand, the excesses in X^2 of the ten remaining coalitions still vary with x, and are strictly less than $-7/52$ at least somewhere; that is, if we define

$$\Sigma^2 = \{S \in \Sigma^1 \mid \text{ there exists } x \in X^2 \text{ such that } e(S,x) < \epsilon_2\}, \qquad (4.79)$$

then

$$\Sigma^2\{\{1\}, \{2\}, \{3\}, \{1,2\}, \{1,3\}, \{2,3\}, \{2,4\}, \{3,4\}, \{1,2,4\}, \{1,3,4\}\}.$$

Accordingly, we exclude $\{1,4\}$ and $\{2,3,4\}$ from further reckoning and concentrate our attention on eliminating unfairness among the coalitions in Σ^2.

By now it should be clear how we proceed. By analogy with (4.62)–(4.64), for $x \in X^2$ let

$$\phi_2(x) = \max_{S \in \Sigma^2} e(S,x) \qquad (4.80)$$

be the maximum excess at imputation x of the remaining coalitions; and let

$$\epsilon_3 = \min_{x \in X^2} \phi_2(x) \tag{4.81}$$

be its minimum. Furthermore, let X^3 consist of all imputations at which ϕ_2 achieves its minimum, i.e.,

$$X^3 = \{x \in X^2 \mid \phi_2(x) = \epsilon_3\}. \tag{4.82}$$

We can think of X^3 as the third-order least rational core. Because $x_1 = 1/4$ for $x \in X^2$, ϕ_2 can be regarded as function of x_2 alone. Moreover, because none of $e_1, e_2, e_3, e_{12}, e_{13}, e_{23}, e_{24}$ or e_{34} can exceed $-9/52$ on X^2, whereas neither of the remaining two excesses can be less than $-2/13$, the maximum in definition (4.80) of ϕ_2 is effectively taken, not over the whole of Σ^2, but only over coalitions $\{1, 2, 4\}$ and $\{1, 3, 4\}$; that is,

$$\phi_2(x) = \max\left(\frac{9}{52} - x_2, x_2 - \frac{6}{13}\right) \tag{4.83}$$

for $4/13 \le x_2 \le 17/52$. The graph of ϕ_2 is similar to Figure 4.6, and its minimum occurs where $9/52 - x_2 = x_2 - 6/13$, or $x_2 = 33/104$. Thus $\epsilon_3 = -15/104$, and

$$X^3 = \{(1/4, 33/104, 33/104, 3/26)\} \tag{4.84}$$

contains the single imputation $x^* = (1/4, 33/104, 33/104, 3/26)$. No further variation of x is possible; we have reduced unfairness as much as is possible. Thus x^* is the solution of the c-game; and Jed, Ned, Ted and Zed's fair shares of the time saved are 13/4 hours for Jed, 33/8 hours each for Ned and Ted, and 3/2 hours for Zed. Ned must still arrive at 9:00, but now leaves at 11:52:30, when Ted arrives; Ted now leaves at 1:45, when Jed arrives; and Jed now leaves at 3:30, when Zed arrives for the last turn of duty. Ned and Ted benefit most, because their advertised hours have the greatest overlap with those of the other dealers. Whether this is the conclusion that Jed, Ned, Ted and Zed would actually reach, however, is an open question. Would it be fairer to give each dealer 13/4 hours in the first instance, so that Zed can just stay at home, and transfer 7 minutes and 30 seconds of the 15 minutes that Zed doesn't need to each of Ned and Ted? Well, what do you think?

Our procedure for successively eliminating unfair imputations, until only a single imputation remains, can be generalized to apply to arbitrary n-player c-games. We construct by recursion a nested sequence

$$X = X^0 \supset X^1 \supset X^2 \ldots X^\kappa = X^* \tag{4.85}$$

of sets of imputations, a nested sequence

$$\Sigma^0 \supset \Sigma^1 \supset \Sigma^2 \ldots \Sigma^\kappa \tag{4.86}$$

of sets of coalitions, a decreasing sequence

$$\epsilon_1 < \epsilon_2 < \ldots < \epsilon_\kappa \tag{4.87}$$

of real numbers and a sequence

$$\phi = \phi_0, \phi_1, \ldots, \phi_{\kappa-1} \tag{4.88}$$

of functions such that the domain of ϕ_k is X^k. The recursion is defined for $k \geq 1$ by

$$\epsilon_k = \min_{x \in X^{k-1}} \phi_{k-1}(x), \tag{4.89a}$$

$$X^k = \{x \in X^{k-1} \,|\, \phi_{k-1}(x) = \epsilon_k\} \tag{4.89b}$$

and

$$\Sigma^k = \{S \in \Sigma^{k-1} \,|\, \text{ there exists } \; x \in X^k \; \text{ such that } \; e(S,x) < \epsilon_k\}, \tag{4.89c}$$

where $X^0 = X$, Σ^0 consists of all coalitions except $\oslash$ and N, and ϕ_k is defined by

$$\phi_k(x) = \max_{S \in \Sigma^k} e(S,x). \tag{4.90}$$

If we perform this recursion for increasing values of the positive integers, then eventually we reach a value of k for which set X^k contains a single imputation, say x^*; for a proof of this result see, for example, Wang (1988, p. 146). If we denote the final value of k by κ, then $1 \leq \kappa \leq n - 1$ (because the dimension of X^k is reduced by at least one at every step of the recursion); and if $X^\kappa = \{x^*\}$ then, according to our criterion of fairness, the imputation x^* is the fair solution of the c-game. The set $X^* = X^\kappa = \{x^*\}$ is called the nucleolus.

If $\kappa = 1$, of course, then the nucleolus coincides with least rational core, as in (4.34) and (4.56), where $n = 3$; or in (4.48a), where $n = 4$. More commonly, however, we have $\kappa > 1$, as in (4.66), where $\kappa = 2, n = 3$; or in (4.84), where $\kappa = 3, n = 4$. Technically, the task of calculating the nucleolus is an exercise in repeated linear programming, which—at least for games of moderate size—can safely be delegated to a computer. For a discussion of this and other matters related to the nucleolus see, for example, Owen (1982, pp. 244–256) or Wang (1988, pp. 137–150). Owen discusses linear programming in his Chapter 3 (pp. 34–62).

A final remark is in order. Technically, x^* is not the nucleolus; rather, it is the (only) imputation that the nucleolus X^* contains. To observe the distinction is often a nuisance, however, and we shall not hesitate to breach linguistic etiquette by referring to both x^* and X^* as the nucleolus whenever it is convenient to do so (as, for example, in Section 4.7).

TABLE 4.1 Team's best jumps (in feet).			
	J	N	T
First jump	15	20	19
Second jump	15	18	19
Third jump	15	18	18

TABLE 4.2 Prize money earned if jump counted (in dollars).			
	J	N	T
First jump	0	5	4
Second jump	0	3	4
Third jump	0	3	3

4.6   TEAM LONG-JUMPING. AN IMPROPER GAME

To encourage team spirit among schoolboys who compete as individuals, a high school has instituted a long-jumping competition for teams of two or three. The rules of the competition stipulate that each team can make up to 12 jumps, of which six count officially towards the final outcome—the best three jumps of each individual in a 2-man team, or the best two jumps of each individual in a 3-man team. Furthermore, a local business has agreed to pay a dollar per foot for each official foot jumped in excess of 15 feet. Unless—which is unlikely—nobody jumps more than 15 feet, this means that winning the competition is the same thing as maximizing dollar uptake. But the existence of prize money brings the added problem of distributing the money fairly among the team. We'll consider this as a c-game; and we will use the game to clarify the difference between what is known in the literature as the ϵ-core and what we have called the rational ϵ-core.

Let's suppose that young Jed (Player 1), young Ned (Player 2) and young Ted (Player 3) competed as a team in this year's competition. They agreed to take four jumps each, and their best three jumps are recorded (in feet) in Table 4.1; obviously, Jed had a bad day. The dollar equivalents of these jumps are recorded in Table 4.2. We see at once that Jed, Ned and Ted have earned themselves the grand sum of $0 + 0 + 5 + 3 + 4 + 4 = 16$ dollars. How should they divvy it up?

Let the benefit of cooperation, $\bar{v}(S)$, to coalition S be the prize money that the players in S would have earned if they had competed as a team. Then, of course, $\bar{v}(\{i\}) = 0, i = 1, 2, 3$, because teams of one are not allowed; and, from Table 4.2, we have

$$\bar{v}(\{1,2\}) = 11, \qquad \bar{v}(\{1,3\}) = 11, \qquad \bar{v}(\{2,3\}) = 22, \qquad \bar{v}(N) = 16.$$

Thus, from (4.16), the characteristic function is defined by

$$v(\{1,2\}) = \frac{11}{16} = v(\{1,3\}), \quad v(\{2,3\}) = \frac{11}{8} \tag{4.91}$$

and, of course, $v(\{i\}) = 0, i = 1, 2, 3, v(N) = 1$. We see at once that there is a coalition of less than all the players who could obtain more than the grand coalition. Thus, if it were possible for Ned and Ted to dissolve the grand coalition and become a 2-man team, then it would certainly be in their interests to do so. Unfortunately, however, they have already declared themselves a 3-man team. The rules of competition enforce the grand coalition.

We now digress from our long-jumping competition to introduce some more general terminology. If

$$\nu(S \cup T) \geq \nu(S) + \nu(T) \qquad (4.92)$$

for any disjoint coalitions S and T ($S \cap T = \varnothing$), then the characteristic function ν is said to be *superadditive,* and the associated c-game is said to be *proper.* If, on the other hand, there exist S and T such that (4.92) is violated, then the game is said to be *improper.* Thus all of the games we studied in Sections 4.1–4.5 were proper games, whereas the 3-player game defined by (4.91) is an improper game.

Now, whenever a game is improper, one can make a case for relaxing the condition that allocations should be nonnegative. Could not Ned and Ted demand that Jed reimburse them for the potential earnings that they have lost through joining forces with Jed? Accordingly, let the vector $x = (x_1, x_2, \ldots, x_n)$ be called a *pre-imputation* if it satisfies (4.19b), but not (4.19a); that is, if

$$x_1 + x_2 + \cdots + x_n = 1, \qquad (4.93)$$

but

$$x_i \geq 0, \qquad i = 1, 2, \ldots, n \qquad (4.94)$$

is not required. Thus pre-imputations are vectors that are group rational, but not necessarily individually rational for every player. We will denote the set of all pre-imputations by $\overline{X}$. Clearly $\overline{X} \supset X$; $\overline{X}$ is an $(n-1)$-dimensional hyperplane, which contains the simplex X.

With the concept of pre-imputation, we can define the core as

$$C(0) = \{x \in \overline{X} \mid e(S, x) \leq 0 \quad \text{for } all \text{ coalitions } S\}; \qquad (4.95)$$

because $e(\{i\}, x) \leq 0$ implies $x_i \geq 0$, this definition is equivalent to (4.25). We now define the ϵ-*core* by

$$C(\epsilon) = \{x \in \overline{X} \mid e(S, x) \leq \epsilon \quad \text{for } S \in \Sigma^0\}. \qquad (4.96)$$

Thus the rational ϵ-core is

$$C^+(\epsilon) = C(\epsilon) \cap X; \qquad (4.97)$$

and by analogy with (4.29)–(4.30), if we first define a function $\overline{\phi}$ from $\overline{X}$ to the real numbers by

$$\overline{\phi}(x) = \max_{S \in \Sigma^0} e(S, x), \qquad (4.98)$$

then we can define the ϵ-core more succinctly by

$$C(\epsilon) = \{x \in \overline{X} \mid \overline{\phi}(x) \le \epsilon\}. \tag{4.99}$$

Obviously, $C(\epsilon) \supset C^+(\epsilon)$. The contours of $\overline{\phi}$ coincide with those of ϕ on X; however, whereas contours of ϕ that meet the boundary of X must either dead-end or follow the boundary, contours of $\overline{\phi}$ may continue across. For example, in Figure 4.4 the contours $\overline{\phi} = 0$ and $\overline{\phi} = -1/21$ would be triangles with a vertex in the region above the line $x_1 + x_2 = 0$ (which lies inside $\overline{X}$ but outside X because $x_3 < 0$).

By analogy with the rational ϵ-core, there is a least value of ϵ, namely,

$$\overline{\epsilon}_1 = \min_{x \in \overline{X}} \overline{\phi}(x), \tag{4.100}$$

for which the ϵ-core exists. We refer to $C(\overline{\epsilon}_1)$ as the *least core*. Because the minimum over a larger set cannot exceed the minimum over a smaller set, a comparison of (4.100) with (4.31) makes clear that

$$\overline{\epsilon}_1 \le \epsilon_1. \tag{4.101}$$

Furthermore, if the game has a core then $\overline{\epsilon}_1 = \epsilon_1$ (and $C(\overline{\epsilon}_1) = X^1$, i.e., the least core coincides with the least rational core).

If the game is both coreless and improper, however, then the possibility[8] arises that $\overline{\epsilon}_1 < \epsilon_1$. We can illustrate this circumstance by returning now to our long-jumping game, which is both improper and coreless, because improper 3-Player c-games are always coreless (Exercise 4.13). From (4.91) and (4.99), we have

$$C(\epsilon) = \left\{ x \in \overline{X} \mid -\epsilon \le x_1 \le -\frac{3}{8} + \epsilon, \quad -\epsilon \le x_2 \le \frac{5}{16} + \epsilon, \right.$$
$$\left. \frac{11}{16} - \epsilon \le x_1 + x_2 \le 1 + \epsilon \right\}. \tag{4.102}$$

By the method of Section 4.3, we readily find that the least value of ϵ for which $C(\epsilon) \ne \oslash$ is $\overline{\epsilon}_1 = 1/4$, and that $C(1/4)$ contains only the pre-imputation $(-1/8, 9/16, 9/16)$. Thus, if the least core were a fair solution, then not only should Ned and Ted take all the prize money and divide it between themselves equally, but also Jed should pay them a dollar apiece to atone for jumping so badly.

On the other hand, the least value of ϵ for which $C^+(\epsilon) \ne \oslash$ is $\epsilon_1 = 3/8$; whence (Exercise 4.14)

$$X^1 = \left\{ x \in X \mid x_1 = 0, \quad \frac{5}{16} \le x_2 \le \frac{11}{16} \right\}, \tag{4.103}$$

---

[8]   but not the inevitability; see Exercise 4.15.

and the nucleolus is

$$X^2 = \{x^*\} = \left\{(0, \frac{1}{2}, \frac{1}{2})\right\}. \tag{4.104}$$

The fair solution is for Ned and Ted to take all the prize money and divide it equally.

Now try Exercise 4.15.

4.7 THE SHAPLEY VALUE

An alternative solution concept for cooperative games emerges when we revert from the core to the reasonable set and then try to imagine the order in which the grand coalition might actually form. From Section 4.1, if Player i is the j-th player to join the grand coalition of an n-player game, and if $T - \{i\}$ denotes the $j - 1$ players who joined prior to i, then $\nu(T) - \nu(T - \{i\})$ is a fair allocation for i. As we remarked in Section 4.1, however, we do not know the identity of T; half of all possible coalitions (including $\oslash$) contain i (Exercise 4.16), and T could be any of them. Let us denote by Π^i the set of 2^{n-1} coalitions to which Player i can belong, i.e.,

$$\Pi^i = \{S \,|\, N \supset S \quad \text{and} \quad i \in S\}; \tag{4.105}$$

for example, if $n = 4$ then

$$\Pi^1 = \{\{1\}, \{1,2\}, \{1,3\}, \{1,4\}, \{1,2,3\}, \{1,2,4\}, \{1,3,4\}, \{1,2,3,4\}\},$$
$$\Pi^2 = \{\{2\}, \{1,2\}, \{2,3\}, \{2,4\}, \{1,2,3\}, \{1,2,4\}, \{2,3,4\}, \{1,2,3,4\}\},$$
$$\tag{4.106}$$

and so on. Then all we know about T is that $T \in \Pi^i$. If we are going to reduce the reasonable set to a single fair imputation, then mustn't we know more about T than just that?

It is possible, however, that there is no more about T that can be known, at least in advance—and any solution concept, if it is going to be at all useful, must certainly be known in advance of its application. Suppose, for example, that the n players have decided to meet in the town hall at 8:00 p.m. to bargain over fair allocations, and that their order of arrival is regarded as the order in which the grand coalition formed. Then who can say what the order will be in advance? Although all will aim to be there at 8:00, some will be unexpectedly early and others unavoidably late, in ways that cannot be predicted with certainty. In other words, the order of arrival is a random variable. Therefore, if Player i is j-th to arrive, then j is a random variable, and the j-person coalition of which he becomes the last member is also a random variable. Let us denote it by Y_i. Then, as already agreed, $\nu(Y_i) - \nu(Y_i - \{i\})$ is a fair allocation for i; but because Y_i is a random variable, which can take many values, so also is $\nu(Y_i) - \nu(Y_i - \{i\})$.

TABLE 4.3 Possible orders of
formation of grand coalition of 4 players.

1234	2134	2314	2341
1243	2143	3214	2431
1324	3124	2413	3241
1342	3142	4213	3421
1423	4123	3412	4231
1432	4132	4312	4321

From all these values, how do we obtain a single number that we can regard as a fair allocation for Player i? Perhaps the best thing to do is to take the expected value, denoted by E. Then, denoting Player i's fair allocation by x_i^S, we have

$$x_i^S = E[\nu(Y_i) - \nu(Y_i - \{i\})]$$
$$= \sum_{T \in \Pi^i} (\nu(T) - \nu(T - \{i\})) \cdot \text{Prob}(Y_i = T), \qquad (4.107)$$

where the summation is taken over all coalitions containing i, and $\text{Prob}(Y_i = T)$ is the probability that the first j players to arrive are T.

If we assume that the $n\,!$ possible orders of arrival are all equally likely, then the fair imputation

$$x^S = (x_1^S, x_2^S, \ldots, x_n^S) \qquad (4.108)$$

defined by (4.107) is known as the *Shapley value*. Suppose, for example, that $n = 4$, so that the 24 possible orders of arrival are as shown in Table 4.3; and suppose that $i = 1$. Then, because $Y_1 = \{1\}$ in the first column of the table and all orders of arrival are equally likely, we have $\text{Prob}(Y_1 = \{1\}) = 6/24 = 1/4$. Similarly, because $Y_1 = \{1, 2, 3, 4\}$ in the last column of the table, we have $\text{Prob}(Y_1 = \{1, 2, 3, 4\}) = 6/24 = 1/4$, too. The first two rows of column 2 yield $\text{Prob}(Y_1 = \{1, 2\}) = 2/24 = 1/12$, whereas the middle two rows of column 3 yield $\text{Prob}(Y_1 = \{1, 2, 4\}) = 2/24 = 1/12$, also; and, continuing in this manner, we find that $\text{Prob}(Y_1 = T) = 1/12$ for all 2- and 3-player coalitions in Π^1, which is defined in this case by (4.106). Accordingly, we deduce from (4.107) that

$$x_1^S = 0 \cdot \frac{1}{4} + \left\{ \nu(\{1, 2\}) + \nu(\{1, 3\}) + \nu(\{1, 4\}) + \nu(\{1, 2, 3\}) - \nu(\{2, 3\}) \right.$$

$$\left. + \nu(\{1, 2, 4\}) - \nu(\{2, 4\}) + \nu(\{1, 3, 4\}) - \nu(\{3, 4\}) \right\} \cdot \frac{1}{12}$$

$$+ \{1 - \nu(\{2, 3, 4\})\} \cdot \frac{1}{4}, \qquad (4.109a)$$

where we have used $\nu(\varnothing) = 0$, $\nu(\{i\}) = 0$, $i = 1, 2, 3, 4$. The other three components of the Shapley value for a 4-player c-game can now be obtained

TABLE 4.4 3-player Shapley values and nucleoli.

	Shapley value, x^S	Nucleolus, x^*	Egalitarian imputation, x^E
Car pool with $d = 9$	$\frac{1}{126}(46,43,37)$	$\frac{1}{126}(50,44,32)$	$\frac{1}{126}(42,42,42)$
Car pool with $d = 1$	$\frac{1}{60}(28,22,10)$	$\frac{1}{60}(33,21,6)$	$\frac{1}{60}(20,20,20)$
Log-hauling	$\frac{1}{60}(17,20,23)$	$\frac{1}{60}(14,20,26)$	$\frac{1}{60}(20,20,20)$
Long-jumping	$\frac{1}{96}(10,43,43)$	$\frac{1}{96}(0,48,48)$	$\frac{1}{96}(32,32,32)$

from (4.109a) by cyclic permutation of the integers 1, 2, 3 and 4:

$$x_2^S = 0 \cdot \frac{1}{4} + \left\{ \nu(\{2,3\}) + \nu(\{2,4\}) + \nu(\{2,1\}) + \nu(\{2,3,4\}) - \nu(\{3,4\}) \right.$$

$$\left. + \nu(\{2,3,1\}) - \nu(\{3,1\}) + \nu(\{2,4,1\}) - \nu(\{4,1\}) \right\} \cdot \frac{1}{12}$$

$$+ \{1 - \nu(\{3,4,1\})\} \cdot \frac{1}{4}, \qquad (4.109b)$$

$$x_3^S = 0 \cdot \frac{1}{4} + \left\{ \nu(\{3,4\}) + \nu(\{3,1\}) + \nu(\{3,2\}) + \nu(\{3,4,1\}) - \nu(\{4,1\}) \right.$$

$$\left. + \nu(\{3,4,2\}) - \nu(\{4,2\}) + \nu(\{3,1,2\}) - \nu(\{1,2\}) \right\} \cdot \frac{1}{12}$$

$$+ \{1 - \nu(\{4,1,2\})\} \cdot \frac{1}{4}, \qquad (4.109c)$$

$$x_4^S = 0 \cdot \frac{1}{4} + \left\{ \nu(\{4,1\}) + \nu(\{4,2\}) + \nu(\{4,3\}) + \nu(\{4,1,2\}) - \nu(\{1,2\}) \right.$$

$$\left. + \nu(\{4,1,3\}) - \nu(\{1,3\}) + \nu(\{4,2,3\}) - \nu(\{2,3\}) \right\} \cdot \frac{1}{12}$$

$$+ \{1 - \nu(\{1,2,3\})\} \cdot \frac{1}{4}, \qquad (4.109d)$$

where, obviously, $\{2,3,1\}$ is the same as $\{1,2,3\}$, etc. Similar expressions for the Shapley allocations in a 2-player or 3-player c-game are readily found (Exercise 4.17). Note that because, from Exercise 4.19, (4.107) satisfies (4.20), the Shapley value always belongs to the reasonable set.

We are now in a position to calculate the Shapley values of all games considered so far. Shapley values for 3-player games are presented in Table 4.4, whereas those for 4-player games are presented in Table 4.5; the results are taken from Exercises 4.17–4.18. For each game, the Shapley value is compared with both the nucleolus and the egalitarian imputation

TABLE 4.5   4-player Shapley values and nucleoli.

	Shapley value, x^S	Nucleolus, x^*	Egalitarian imputation, x^E
Car pool with $d = 2$	$\frac{1}{144}(43,35,25,41)$	$\frac{1}{144}(45,33,21,45)$	$\frac{1}{144}(36,36,36,36)$
Antique-minding	$\frac{1}{312}(80,92,92,48)$	$\frac{1}{312}(78,99,99,36)$	$\frac{1}{312}(78,78,78,78)$

$$x^E = \frac{1}{n}(1,1,\ldots,1), \tag{4.110}$$

which distributes the benefits of cooperation uniformly among the players. We see at a glance that the Shapley value is, on the whole, a much more egalitarian imputation than the nucleolus; i.e., most allocations are at least as close to $1/n$ under the Shapley value as under the nucleolus. (Exceptions are provided by Player 2's allocation in the 3-person car pool with $d = 1$ and Player 1's allocation in the antique-minding game, but in each of these cases both Shapley and nucleolus allocation are close to egalitarian.) Note, in particular, that the Shapley value would pay young Jed \$1.67 for his short long jumps in Section 4.6, whereas the nucleolus wouldn't pay him anything.

Intuitively, the Shapley value is more egalitarian than the nucleolus because the nucleolus gives priority to the most dissatisfied coalitions, whereas the Shapley value grants all coalitions equal status. The nucleolus derives from core-minded thinking; whereas the Shapley value derives from reasonable-set thinking, and so it is hardly surprising that the two solutions almost never coincide (except, of course, for 2-player games—see Exercise 4.17). If the Shapley value belongs to the core (as in the car-pool games), then it does so more by accident than by design. That the core need not contain the Shapley value is immediate, because the Shapley value always exists, whereas the core does not. But even a non-empty core may not contain the Shapley value—witness the antique-minding game, where the Shapley value fails to satisfy the third inequality in (4.69b) when $\epsilon = 0$. By contrast, if the core exists then it always contains the nucleolus; and in any event, the nucleolus always belongs to the least rational core (though not necessarily the least core—witness the long-jumping game).

Although the formulae derived in Exercise 4.17 and (4.109) are adequate for our examples, an explicit expression for the Shapley value of an n-player game is easily obtained. In this regard, it is convenient to have a notation for the number of elements in a set, and so for any set A we define

$$\#(A) = \quad \text{number of elements in } A. \tag{4.111}$$

Thus, for example,

$$\#(N) = n, \quad \#(\Pi^i) = 2^{n-1}, \quad \#(\Sigma^0) = 2^n - 2, \quad \#(X^*) = 1, \quad \#(\varnothing) = 0, \tag{4.112}$$

and so on. In terms of this notation, if Player i is the j-th player to join the grand coalition, and if T denotes the first j players to join the grand coalition, then $j = \#(T)$; and $\#(T) - 1$ players have joined the grand coalition before Player i, whereas $n - j = n - \#(T)$ will join after him. Moreover, the truth of the statement that T is the coalition that Player i completes can be altered neither by a permutation of the order of the first $\#(T) - 1$ players, nor by a permutation of the order of the last $n - \#(T)$ players. There are $(\#(T) - 1)!$ permutations of the first kind, and $(n - \#(T))!$ permutations of the second kind. Accordingly, the number of orders in which the players can join the grand coalition in such a way that Player i completes coalition T is $(\#(T) - 1)! \cdot 1 \cdot (n - \#(T))!$ But there are precisely $n!$ orders of any kind in which the players can join the grand coalition; whence, if all orders are equally likely, we have

$$\text{Prob}(Y_i = T) = \frac{(\#(T) - 1)!\,(n - \#(T))!}{n!}. \tag{4.113}$$

Thus, from (4.107), Player i's allocation under the Shapley value is

$$x_i^S = \frac{1}{n!} \sum_{T \in \Pi^i} (\#(T) - 1)!\,(n - \#(T))!\,(\nu(T) - \nu(T - \{i\})), \tag{4.114}$$

where Π^i is defined by (4.105). Despite the ease with which we obtained this result, however, the Shapley value of an n-player game is not in general an easy vector to calculate, because each component involves a summation over 2^{n-1} coalitions.

Which is the fairer imputation—the nucleolus or the Shapley value? Well, what do you think?

4.8 SIMPLE GAMES. THE SHAPLEY-SHUBIK POWER INDEX

You may recall that 0 and 1 were the only values taken by the normalized characteristic function, ν, defined by (4.52). C-games with this property are said to be *simple*. In other words, a c-game is simple if either $\nu(S) = 0$ or $\nu(S) = 1$ for every coalition S (not just $\oslash$ and N).

Simple games arise most readily in the context of voting. Suppose, for example, that the Mathematics Department in a liberal arts college is recruiting for a new professor. Prospective faculty are interviewed one at a time, beginning with the candidate whose credentials on paper look most impressive. Immediately after each interview, the existing faculty meet to vote on the candidate; and if the vote is sufficiently favorable, then the candidate is offered a position—and no more candidates are interviewed unless, and until, he turns it down.

Now, in this department there has always been tension between pure and applied mathematicians, with a temptation for one group to exploit the other in the conflict over hiring. To guard against this temptation, it is enshrined in the department's constitution that a candidate is nominated if, and only if, he secures the vote of at least 50% of both the pure and the applied mathematicians on the existing faculty. Thus every new professor, whether pure or applied, has at least some measure of broad support throughout the existing faculty.

In this recruitment process, the purpose of cooperation among the faculty is to ensure that a candidate is hired. Every coalition of faculty is either strong enough to ensure the recruitment of its particular candidate, in which case it reaps the entire benefit of cooperation; or too weak to ensure that its candidate is hired, in which case it reaps no benefit at all. We can therefore partition the set of all coalitions into the set of winning coalitions—denoted by W—and the set of losing coalitions, which comprises all others. It is then natural to define the characteristic function, ν, by

$$\nu(S) = \begin{cases} 0 & \text{if } S \notin W \\ 1 & \text{if } S \in W. \end{cases} \tag{4.115}$$

Thus the recruitment process yields a simple game. More generally, the characteristic function of any simple game has the form (4.115), where W is the set of coalitions to which ν assigns the value 1.

The Shapley value of a simple game can be interpreted as an index of power. To see this, let us denote by P^i the set of coalitions in which Player i's vote is crucial for victory; i.e., the set of winning coalitions that would become losing coalitions if Player i were removed. In symbols:

$$P^i = \{S \mid S \in \Pi^i, \quad S \in W, \quad S - \{i\} \notin W\}. \tag{4.116}$$

Now, if $S \in W$ and $S - \{i\} \in W$, then $\nu(S) = 1 = \nu(S - \{i\})$; whereas if $S \notin W$ and $S - \{i\} \notin W$, then $\nu(S) = 0 = \nu(S - \{i\})$. Thus $\nu(S) - \nu(S - \{i\}) = 0$ unless $S \in W$ and $S - \{i\} \notin W$, or $S \in P^i$; in which case, $\nu(S) - \nu(S - \{i\}) = 1 - 0 = 1$. It now follows immediately from (4.107) that

$$x_i^S = \sum_{T \in P^i} \text{Prob}(Y_i = T), \tag{4.117}$$

where Y_i is the coalition that Player i was last to join. The right-hand side of (4.117) is the probability that Player i's vote is crucial (to some coalition), and it is therefore a measure of Player i's voting power. In particular, if all possible orders of coalition formation are equally likely, then from (4.113) we have

$$x_i^S = \frac{1}{n!} \sum_{T \in P^i} (\#(T) - 1)! \, (n - \#(T))! \tag{4.118}$$

We refer to (4.118) as the Shapley-Shubik power index.

Suppose, for example, that currently there are five faculty: three pure mathematicians—Players 1 to 3, say—and two applied (Players 4 and 5). Then at least two pure mathematicians and one applied mathematician must vote for a candidate to secure his nomination, so that the set of winning coalitions is

$$W = \Big\{ \{1,2,4\}, \{1,2,5\}, \{1,3,4\}, \{1,3,5\}, \{2,3,4\}, \{2,3,5\}, \{1,2,3,4\},$$

$$\{1,2,3,5\}, \{1,2,4,5\}, \{1,3,4,5\}, \{2,3,4,5\}, N \Big\}, \tag{4.119}$$

where $N = \{1,2,3,4,5\}$. From (4.116) and (4.119), we have

$$P^1 = \big\{ \{1,2,4\}, \{1,2,5\}, \{1,3,4\}, \{1,3,5\}, \{1,2,4,5\}, \{1,3,4,5\} \big\},$$
$$P^4 = \big\{ \{1,2,4\}, \{1,3,4\}, \{2,3,4\}, \{1,2,3,4\} \big\}, \tag{4.120}$$

and similarly for P^2, P^3 and P^5; see Exercise 4.21. It now follows from (4.118) and (4.120) that the Shapley-Shubik power index is

$$x^S = \left(\frac{7}{30}, \frac{7}{30}, \frac{7}{30}, \frac{3}{20}, \frac{3}{20} \right); \tag{4.121}$$

a pure mathematician has 7/30 of the voting power, whereas an applied mathematician has only 3/20. Collectively, applied mathematicians are 40% of the faculty but have only 30% of the voting power. Of course, this seems unfair; and so we had better hope—for their sake—that an applied mathematician is hired. Or had we? See Exercise 4.22. Then try Exercises 4.23–4.24.

4.9   COMMENTARY

In Chapter 4 we have introduced characteristic functions (Section 4.1) and a variety of c-game solution concepts; specifically, imputations and the reasonable set (Section 4.1), excess, the core, rational ϵ-core and least rational core (Section 4.2), the nucleolus (Section 4.5), superadditivity, proper c-games, pre-imputations and the ϵ-core (Section 4.6) and the Shapley value (Section 4.7). We have applied these ideas to a number of bargaining problems, e.g., sharing the costs of a car pool among three (Sections 4.1–4.2) or four (Section 4.3) individuals, and sharing duties in an antique dealership (Section 4.5); and we have illustrated that realistic c-games can be either coreless (Section 4.4) or improper (4.6). For all of these games we have compared the nucleolus and Shapley value with the egalitarian imputation (Section 4.7). For a comparison of the nucleolus and Shapley value in the assessment of airport landing fees, see Owen (1982, Section XI.4).

    In Section 4.8 we have adapted the Shapley value for use as an index of power, and we have applied it to power sharing in an academic department. This Shapley-Shubik index is not the only index of power, however, and a popular alternative is the Banzhaf-Coleman index; see Exercise 4.25 and Owen (1982,

Chapter X), where both indices are applied to voting in U.S. presidential elections.

EXERCISES 4

4.1 Show from (4.20) that the reasonable set for Section 4.1's car pool with $d = 9$ is the partially speckled hexagon in Figure 4.3. Show that for the car pool with $d = 1$ the reasonable set is the partially speckled hexagon in Figure 4.5.

4.2 Find the rational ϵ-core of the 3-person car pool with $d = 1$.

4.3 (i)   Find the least rational core for the 3-person car pool when $d = 9$; i.e., deduce (4.34) from (4.33).

(ii)   Find the least rational core for the 3-person car pool when $d = 6$.

4.4 Find the least rational core for the 4-person car pool when $d = 1$.

4.5 Find the least rational core for the 4-person car pool when $d = 8$.

4.6 Find the least rational core for the 4-person car pool when $d = 18$.

4.7 (i)   For a 2-player c-game, verify that X is a 1-dimensional line segment imbedded in 2-dimensional space. Sketch a 1-dimensional representation of X, and verify that $C^+(0) = X$ (thus $\epsilon_0 = 0$). What is the characteristic function? What is the least rational core?

(ii)   What is the least rational core for the game defined by (4.52)?

4.8 Calculate the rational ϵ-core of the log-hauling game; i.e., verify (4.55). Find the least rational core.

4.9 Show that a 3-person c-game is coreless if

$$v(\{1,2\}) + v(\{1,3\}) + v(\{2,3\}) > 2.$$

Verify that this condition is satisfied by the log-hauling game of Section 4.4.

4.10 Jed, Ned and Ted are antique dealers who conduct their businesses in separate but adjoining rooms of a common premises. Jed's advertised hours are from 12:00 noon until 4:00 p.m., Ned's hours are from 9:00 a.m. until 3:00 p.m. and Ted's from 1:00 p.m. until 5:00 p.m. Because the dealers have other jobs and the store is never so busy that one individual could not take care of everyone's customers, it is in the dealers' interests to pool their time in minding the store; there is no need for two people between noon and 1:00 p.m. or between 3:00 p.m. and 4:00 p.m, or for three people between 1:00 p.m. and 3:00 p.m. Thus Jed can arrive later than noon or leave earlier than 4:00 p.m., Ted can arrive later than 1:00 p.m. and Ned can leave earlier than 3:00 p.m. But how much later or earlier? What is a fair allocation of store-minding duty for each of the dealers?

4.11 Verify (4.68)–(4.73) and (4.75).

4.12 Consider the 4-player c-game whose characteristic function is defined by

$$v(S) = \frac{1}{2} \quad \text{if} \quad \#(S) = 3,$$

$$v(S) = \frac{1}{2} \quad \text{if} \quad \#(S) = 2, \quad \text{except} \quad v(\{1,3\}) = \frac{1}{4}, \quad v(\{2,4\}) = 0;$$

and, of course, $v(\oslash) = 0$, $v(N) = 1$ and $v(\{i\}) = 0$ for $i \in N$, where $N = \{1, 2, 3, 4\}$. Show that the least rational core is the line segment

$$X^1 = \left\{ x \mid x = \frac{1}{8}(1 + 3t, \ 3 - 3t, \ 1 + 3t, \ 3 - 3t), \quad 0 \le t \le 1 \right\},$$

but that its mid-point $(5/16, 3/16, 5/16, 3/16)$ is not the nucleolus.[9]

4.13 Show that every improper 3-player c-game is coreless.

4.14 Verify (4.103)–(4.104).

4.15 How should young Jed, young Ned and young Ted have split the proceeds from the long-jump competition described in Section 4.6 if their jumps (in feet) had been as follows?

	J	N	T
First jump	18	20	19
Second jump	16	18	19
Third jump	15	18	18

4.16 Show that, in any n-player c-game, each Player belongs to precisely 2^{n-1} coalitions.

4.17 (i)   Find the Shapley value of an arbitrary 2-player c-game.

(ii)   Find the Shapley value of an arbitrary 3-player c-game.

(iii)   Hence verify Table 4.4

4.18 (i)   Verify (4.109)

(ii)   Hence verify Table 4.5.

4.19 Prove that (4.107) satisfies (4.20).

4.20 A characteristic function game is said to be *symmetric* if every coalition's bargaining strength depends only on the number of players in it; i.e., if there exists some function f from the real numbers to the real numbers such that $v(T) = f(\#(T))$ for all coalitions T. Prove that if a symmetric game has a core, then its core must contain the egalitarian imputation x^E defined by (4.110).

4.21 (i)   Verify (4.120), and obtain the corresponding expressions for P^2, P^3 and P^5.

(ii)   Verify (4.121).

4.22 In Section 4.8's example of a mathematics department, there are currently three pure and two applied mathematicians. Which would increase an applied mathematician's voting power more (in terms of hiring the seventh member of the faculty)—hiring an applied mathematician or hiring a pure mathematician? Elucidate.

---

[9]   This exercise is from Maschler, Peleg and Shubik (1979, p. 335).

4.23 In any simple game, Player i is a *dummy* if $P^i = \oslash$ and a *dictator* if $P^i = \Pi^i$.

    (i)   Can there be more than one dummy? Either prove that this is impossible, or produce an example of a simple game with more than one dummy.

    (ii)   Prove that there cannot be more than one dictator. Produce an example of a game with a dictator.

4.24 Nassau County in New York State is run by a board of six supervisors. When this board votes on an issue, each supervisor casts—either for or against the motion—a number of votes that until December, 1937 was roughly proportional to the size of his electoral district. At that time, votes were allotted to each district—at roughly one per 10,000 of population—according to the second column of the table below (Grofman and Scarrow, 1979, pp. 178–179); and because the supervisors had a total of 29 votes among them, 15 votes were required in favor to carry a motion by simple majority. In January, 1938, however (without any change in the population), the numbers of votes allotted to two of the districts were reduced according to the third column of the table, thus reducing the total number of votes from 29 to 25. Nevertheless, the number of votes required to carry a motion was not reduced to 13; it remained instead at 15.

In terms of game theory—why?

District	Number of votes in December 1937	Number of votes in January 1938
Glen Cove	1	1
Hempstead #1	9	7
Hempstead #2	9	7
Long Beach	1	1
North Hempstead	6	6
Oyster Bay	3	3

Hint: See the previous exercise.

4.25 An alternative to the Shapley-Shubik power index for a simple game is the Banzhaf-Coleman index, i.e, the imputation $x^B = (x_1^B, x_2^B, \ldots, x_n^B)$ defined by

$$x_i^B = \frac{\#(P^i)}{\#(P^1) + \#(P^2) + \cdots + \#(P^n)}, \qquad 1 \le i \le n,$$

where $\#$ is defined by (4.111) and P^i by (4.116).

    (i)   Why is it reasonable to interpret x^B as an index of power?

    (ii)   In Section 4.8's Mathematics Department, does an applied mathematician have more or less power according to the Banzhaf-Coleman index than according to the Shapley-Shubik index?

    (iii)   Which do you consider more suitable as an index of power, x^S or x^B?

5

The Prisoner's Dilemma & the Rationality of Cooperation

To team—or not to team? That is the question. Chapters 3 and 4 have already shown us that circumstances abound in which players do better by cooperating than by competing. Indeed if ν denotes a normalized characteristic function, then Player i has an incentive to cooperate with coalition $S-\{i\}$ whenever $\nu(S) > 0$. But an incentive to cooperate does not imply cooperation, for we have also seen in Section 3.4 that if one of two players is committed to cooperation, then it may be rational for the other to cheat and play noncooperatively. Then how, in such circumstances, is cooperation enforced?

To reduce this question to its barest essentials, we return in this Chapter to the symmetric, 2-player, noncooperative game that we introduced in Exercise 1.25, and which has come to be known as the "prisoner's dilemma."[1] The prisoner's dilemma has two pure strategies C (for Cooperate) and D (for Defect),

---

[1]   This game descends from Merrill Flood, Melvin Dresher and A. W. Tucker; see Straffin (1980).

TABLE 5.1 Payoff matrix for the classic version of the prisoner's dilemma.

	REMAIN SILENT	IMPLICATE
REMAIN SILENT	Short	Long
IMPLICATE	Very short	Medium

and payoff matrix

$$\begin{bmatrix} R & S \\ T & P \end{bmatrix}, \tag{5.1}$$

where

$$T > R > P > S; \tag{5.2a}$$

thus R is the payoff to a C-strategist against a C-strategist, S the payoff to a C-strategist against a D-strategist, and so on. We are already familiar with this game from the exercises. We discovered in Exercise 1.25 that DD is the only Nash-equilibrium strategy combination (pure or mixed); in Exercise 2.7 that D is a strong ESS; and in Exercise 3.10 that CC is the Nash bargaining solution. We can consolidate these findings by saying that, because $T > R$ and $P > S$, D is the unique best reply to both C and D; in other words, D is a dominant strategy. Thus, by symmetry, it is rational for each player to select strategy D, whence each obtains payoff P. If each were to cooperate by selecting C, however, then each would obtain a higher payoff, namely, R. We have discovered the paradox of the prisoner's dilemma: although mutual cooperation would yield a higher reward, mutual defection is rational (but only because there exists no mechanism for enforcing cooperation).

To see why this game is called the prisoner's dilemma, imagine that two prisoners in solitary confinement are suspected of some heinous crime—for which, however, there is no hard evidence. A confession is therefore needed, and the police attempt to persuade each prisoner to implicate the other. Each prisoner is told that her sentence will depend on whether she remains silent or implicates the other prisoner, according to the payoff matrix in Table 5.1. Let us suppose that long, medium, short and very short sentences are, respectively, d years, c years, b years and a years, so that $d > c > b > a$. Then because the prisoners would like to spend as little time in jail as possible, we have $R = -b$, $S = -d$, $T = -a$ and $P = -c$, so that (5.2a) is satisfied. Although the prisoners would both prefer a short sentence, they will settle for a medium sentence, because neither can be sure that the other will cooperate: if one player were to remain silent, in the hope that the other would also remain silent, then the second player could cheat—by implicating the first player—and thus obtain the shortest sentence of all. Therefore, unable to guarantee the other's silence, each player will implicate the other.

In this chapter, the prisoner's dilemma and related games will enable us to investigate rationales for cooperation. For the sake of simplicity, we will consider only games restricted to pure strategies. We begin with some concrete examples of the prisoner's dilemma. We then study ways of escape from its paradox.

5.1   CROSSROADS WITH SLOW DRIVERS: A PRISONER'S DILEMMA OF SORTS

An example of a game satisfying (5.2a) is Crossroads with slow drivers, with Wait (W) as the cooperative strategy and Go (G) as the defecting strategy. From Chapter 1, Player 1's payoff matrix for the symmetric version of Crossroads is

$$\begin{bmatrix} -\epsilon - \tau/2 & -\tau \\ 0 & -\delta - \tau/2 \end{bmatrix},$$

where τ is a driver's transit time and, from (1.1), $\delta > \epsilon > 0$. (This matrix differs from Table 1.1 because W is now the first pure strategy, and G the second.) Comparing with (5.1), we have $R = -\epsilon - \tau/2, S = -\tau, T = 0, P = -\delta - \tau/2$; and if the drivers are so slow that $\tau > 2\delta$, then (5.2a) is satisfied. We note in passing that the Hawk-Dove game is also a prisoner's dilemma (with Dove as the cooperative strategy) when the reproductive value of a territory exceeds the reproductive cost of injury from contesting it.

Because $-\epsilon - \tau/2 < -\tau/2$, however, the average of the payoffs from strategy combinations WG and GW exceeds the payoff from WW; accordingly, slow drivers can extricate themselves from their dilemma by alternating between W and G in repeated plays of the game. More generally, this escape from the prisoner's dilemma is available whenever $R < (S+T)/2$. Although—as observed by May (1987)—such alternation would still require cooperation, it is customarily excluded from consideration by requiring that payoffs also satisfy

$$R > \frac{S+T}{2}; \tag{5.2b}$$

see, for example, Axelrod (1984, p. 10). There is a sense, perhaps, in which games that satisfy (5.2a) but not (5.2b) are more susceptible to cooperation—at the very least, the rationale for cooperation is more transparent. Henceforward we will consider only prisoner's dilemmas that satisfy all of (5.2).[2] A well known example, used by Axelrod (1984) for a computer tournament, involves the payoffs

---

[2]   In defining the prisoner's dilemma, some authors require in addition to (5.2) that $2P < S + T$; see, for example, Pruitt (1967), Boyd and Richerson (1988) and Rasmusen (1989). The additional requirement is satisfied by two of our principal examples (Sections 5.2, 5.3), but not necessarily by the third (Section 5.9).

$$R = 3, \quad S = 0, \quad T = 5, \quad P = 1, \tag{5.3}$$

and from time to time we shall use these payoffs for illustration. Note, however, that they are purely arbitrary.

5.2   A LABORATORY ANALOGUE OF THE PRISONER'S DILEMMA

We can obtain the prisoner's dilemma with fewest parameters if we set $S = 0$ and $T = P + R$ in (5.1). Then the game is defined by the matrix

$$\begin{bmatrix} R & 0 \\ R+P & P \end{bmatrix}, \quad R > P > 0, \tag{5.4}$$

and (5.2) is clearly satisfied.

The matrix (5.4) suggests an experiment in which the prisoner's dilemma could be played repeatedly by laboratory animals. The apparatus for this experiment consists of a partitioned cage, each half of which contains a food chute, a decision lever with spring attachment, and an "exhaust" column for rejected food items. In Figure 5.1, XY represents the partition, which is transparent. The food chutes, which are themselves partitioned (along FK), slope gradually downward from EG or HL to the top of the partition XY. One side of each chute (extending from EF or KL) supplies food items of value R, and the other side (extending from FG or HK) supplies food items of value P, where $P < R$. The sides of the chutes slope slightly upward from the line FK—just enough to ensure that items of food, having rolled down the chute, come to rest against the partition (see the plan view in Figure 1, where food items are represented by dotted spheres). The lowest segment of the partition that divides a chute in half is also the top of a lever, which in its neutral position prevents either food item from falling into the exhaust column beneath; see the side view in Figure 1, where the level AB is presumed beyond an animal's reach from the floor of the cage. By sliding one of the levers to the left or right (or operating some other mechanism to the same effect), an animal in either half of the cage can push one of the food items over the side of the chute. The other item will fall into the exhaust column and through the floor of the cage (and the animal will be unable to intercept it). If the animal pushes the lever to the left, then it chooses strategy D: the item of value P falls into its own half of the cage (and the item of value R is lost). If it pushes the lever to the right, however, then it chooses strategy C: the item of value R slides onto the cross-hatched area in Figure 1, which slopes downward from EH or GL and toward XY. Thus the item falls into the other animal's half of the cage (and the item of value P is lost).

For each play of the game, a pair of food items is supplied simultaneously to each half of the cage. Each animal has two choices. It can either Defect, in which case it retains the item of value P; or it can Cooperate, in which case

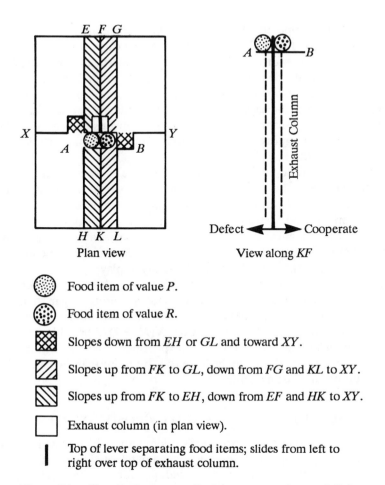

E F G

A ⊙⊙ B

X ── Y

A   B

Exhaust Column

Defect ◄──► Cooperate

H K L

Plan view   View along *KF*

Food item of value *P*.

Food item of value *R*.

Slopes down from *EH* or *GL* and toward *XY*.

Slopes up from *FK* to *GL*, down from *FG* and *KL* to *XY*.

Slopes up from *FK* to *EH*, down from *EF* and *HK* to *XY*.

Exhaust column (in plan view).

Top of lever separating food items; slides from left to right over top of exhaust column.

Figure 5.1   Sketch of apparatus for laboratory analogue of (5.4).

it gives the item of value R to the other animal. Thus the payoff to each for mutual cooperation is R, whereas the payoff to each for mutual defection is P; and if one animal defects while the other cooperates, then the former's payoff is $P + R$ and the latter's zero. In other words, the game has payoff matrix (5.3). Of course, if an animal's daily appetite is a, and if the game is played n times per day, then it is necessary to ensure that $a \geq nR$, whence $a/n > P > 0$.

The suggested apparatus should not be overly difficult to construct. Obviously, one must prevent the animals from climbing up the partition and obtaining food without using the levers. But this could be achieved, even for large mammals, by modifying the apparatus so that all food items must pass through a sufficiently long pipe attached at A (or the corresponding point in the other half of the cage) before falling to the floor of the cage. To ensure that neither animal is rewarded before the other, it would be necessary to cap the food pipes with trap doors that opened only when the second animal had made its choice. It would also be necessary to make the exhaust columns opaque on any side facing the other half of the cage; then, even if the animals operated their levers at different times, no information about the first mover's choice would be transferred to the second mover in the meantime, and the animals' choices could be regarded as simultaneous.[3]

The animals could be trained to play the game via two preliminary manœuvres. During one of these manœuvres, an animal would play solitaire in a cage whose partition had been removed. Thus payoffs would be either P or R, because the animal could retrieve items of value R from the other half of the cage. During the other manœuvre, an animal would play solitaire with the partition restored. Thus the payoffs would be either 0 or P. After some combination of these manœuvres, the animals should be ready to play.

Even two trained animals would enable one to observe a sequence of plays between fixed opponents, and the results should be interesting in their own right. Nevertheless, one would probably wish to train several animals, say $N + 1$, where $N > 1$—not only to collect data from the $N(N + 1)/2$ possible pairwise interactions, but also to observe animals in the prisoner's dilemma against randomly chosen opponents (and one might have to train more than two animals merely as an insurance against mortality).[4]

5.3 A GAME OF FORAGING AMONG OVIPOSITION SITES

For a further example of the prisoner's dilemma in which (5.2) is satisfied, let the players be a pair of insects foraging over a patch of N oviposition sites. They forage randomly, and their searches are independent, so that all sites are equally likely to be visited next. Each site has the potential to support one or two eggs, and each insect begins to forage with a plentiful supply (N eggs or more). If

---

[3] Even with this precaution, there remains the possibility that an animal will fail to push either lever. To allow for this, let us add a third strategy E (for eschew). Then payoff matrix (5.4) is replaced by

$$\begin{bmatrix} R & 0 & 0 \\ P + R & P & P \\ R & 0 & 0 \end{bmatrix}.$$

Clearly, D is still the dominant strategy and C the best cooperative strategy; and so this possibility does not detract from the value of the experiment (although it complicates the mathematical description of it).

[4] For further discussion of this experiment, see Section 5.10.

one egg is laid at a site, then the probability that it will survive to maturity is r_1. If two eggs are laid, then the corresponding survival probability for each is r_2 (and if three or more were laid, then the survival probability for each would be zero). Thus the expected number of offspring from a site is r_1 or $2r_2$, according to whether one or two eggs are laid, and we will assume that $r_1 > 2r_2$. Let us define the ratio

$$\delta = \frac{r_1}{r_2}. \tag{5.5}$$

Then $\delta > 2$.

We assume that the insects arrive at the patch simultaneously, and we measure time discretely from the moment of their arrival. Let the duration of the game be n units of (discrete) time, or periods. In each period, let λ be the probability that an insect survives and remains on the patch, hence $1 - \lambda$ the probability that it leaves the patch or dies; and if an insect has survived on the patch, let ϵ be the probability that it finds a site, and $1 - \epsilon$ the probability that it finds no site (hence zero the probability that it finds more than one site). We will assume that an insect oviposits only during periods it survives on the patch, and that it never oviposits more than once per visit to a site. Henceforward, we will use survival to mean surviving and remaining on the patch.

In each period, if it finds a site where less than two eggs have been laid, then an insect can behave either cooperatively or noncooperatively. A cooperative insect will oviposit only if a site is empty, but a noncooperative insect will lay a second egg at sites where an egg has been laid by the other insect; we assume that insects recognize their eggs. The rationality behind such noncooperation is provided by the inequality $r_1 > 2r_2$: a second egg at the other insect's site yields a payoff of r_2, which is positive, whereas a second egg at the insect's own site yields a payoff of $2r_2 - r_1$, which is negative. If an insect behaves cooperatively during every period, then we shall say that the insect plays strategy C; whereas, if the insect behaves noncooperatively during every period, then we shall say that the insect plays strategy D. No other strategies for oviposition will be considered. (In particular, as stated at the outset, we do not consider mixed strategies.)

For the sake of simplicity, we now further assume that $n = 1$, so that the length of the game is a single period. The corresponding "tree" of events is shown upside down in Figure 5.2, with the "root" of the tree on top. Each branch of this tree corresponds to a *conditional* event, i.e., an event that can happen only if the preceding (conditional) event has happened; and the number on the branch is the corresponding *conditional* probability, i.e., the probability that the event happens, given that the event corresponding to the previous branch has already happened. Each path through the tree from the root to a "leaf" represents a sequence of conditional events; and the number in a rectangle at the end of this path is the corresponding payoff to Player 1. To obtain the probability of this payoff, we simply multiply together all conditional probabilities along the path.

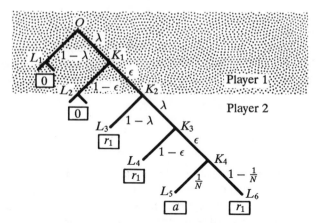

Figure 5.2   The event tree for the single-period foraging game, showing payoffs to Player 1.

Note that branches in the shaded region represent events that can happen to Player 1, whereas the remaining branches represent events in the life of Player 2.

Let us now begin at the root. The first right-hand branch, from O to K_1, corresponds to the event that Player 1 survives the period—which happens with probability λ. The next right-hand branch, from the vertex at K_1 to the vertex at K_2, corresponds to the event that Player 1 locates a site—conditional, of course, upon survival. Conditional upon surviving and locating a site, Player 1 is assured of a non-zero payoff; however, the size of that payoff depends on Player 2. The left-hand branch from the vertex at K_2 to the leaf at L_3 corresponds to the event that Player 2 does not survive the period; the payoff to Player 1 is then r_1. The right-hand branch from the vertex at K_2 to the vertex at K_3 plus the left-hand branch from K_3 to L_4 represent the event that Player 2 survives the period but fails to find a site (conditional, of course, upon Player 1 surviving and locating a site); in which case, the payoff to Player 1 is still r_1. Continuing in this manner, the right-hand path from K_3 through K_4 to the leaf at L_6 corresponds to the event that Player 2 locates one of the $N - 1$ sites that Player 1 did not locate—with (conditional) probability $(N - 1)/N$, because all sites are equally likely to be found. Again, the payoff to Player 1 is r_1. If both players locate the same site, however—which corresponds to the path from O to L_5, then the payoff to Player 1 depends upon the players' strategies. Let us denote it by $a(u_1, v_1)$, where u_1 is Player 1's strategy, and v_2 is Player 2's. Finally, the left-hand branches from O and K_1 represent the events that Player 1 either does not survive, or survives without finding a site; in either case, the payoff is zero. (Note that, strictly, the tree in Figure 5.2 is incomplete; L_1 and L_2 are vertices, not leaves, and to complete the tree we would have to append at each vertex the unshaded part of the tree. Because the payoff to Player 1 would still be zero, however, there is nothing to be gained from doing so.)

We can now compute the expected value of Player 1's payoff in terms of a. All we need do is to multiply each payoff by the product of all conditional probabilities on branches leading to that payoff, then add. Thus Player 1's reward is

$$0 \cdot (1-\lambda) + 0 \cdot \lambda(1-\epsilon) + r_1 \cdot \lambda\epsilon(1-\lambda) + r_1 \cdot \lambda^2\epsilon(1-\epsilon) + a \cdot \frac{\lambda^2\epsilon^2}{N} + r_1 \cdot \lambda^2\epsilon^2 \left(1 - \frac{1}{N}\right)$$

$$= \epsilon\lambda\left(\left(1 - \frac{\epsilon\lambda}{N}\right) r_1 + \frac{\epsilon\lambda a}{N}\right). \tag{5.6}$$

If our insects locate the same site, and if both are C-strategists—that is, if $u_1 = C = v_1$—then the first to arrive will oviposit, whereas the second will not; in other words, the first to arrive will obtain r_1, whereas the second to arrive will obtain zero. Let us assume that, if they do locate the same site, then they are equally likely to locate it first. Then Player 1's (conditional) expected payoff is

$$a(C, C) = \frac{1}{2}r_1 + \frac{1}{2} \cdot 0 = \frac{r_1}{2}. \tag{5.7a}$$

If both are D-strategists—that is, if $u_1 = D = v_1$—then both will oviposit, regardless of who is first to arrive, and each will obtain payoff r_2. Thus

$$a(D, D) = r_2. \tag{5.7b}$$

If, on the other hand, Player 1 is a C-strategist but Player 2 a D-strategist, then Player 1 will oviposit only if she is the first to arrive; in which case, she will obtain only r_2, because Player 2 will oviposit behind her. Thus

$$a(C, D) = \frac{1}{2}r_2 + \frac{1}{2} \cdot 0 = \frac{r_2}{2}. \tag{5.7c}$$

Finally, if Player 1 is a D-strategist but Player 2 is a C-strategist, then Player 1 will oviposit even if Player 2 arrives first, in which case Player 1 will obtain r_2; whereas if Player 1 arrives first, then Player 2 will fail to oviposit, and so Player 1's payoff will be r_1. Accordingly,

$$a(D, C) = \frac{1}{2}r_1 + \frac{1}{2}r_2 = \frac{1}{2}(r_1 + r_2). \tag{5.7d}$$

Substitution from (5.7) into (5.6) now yields the payoff matrix

$$\begin{bmatrix} R & S \\ T & P \end{bmatrix} = \epsilon\lambda \begin{bmatrix} \frac{\epsilon\lambda}{N} \cdot \frac{r_1}{2} + \left(1 - \frac{\epsilon\lambda}{N}\right) r_1 & \frac{\epsilon\lambda}{N} \cdot \frac{r_2}{2} + \left(1 - \frac{\epsilon\lambda}{N}\right) r_1 \\ \frac{\epsilon\lambda}{N} \cdot \frac{r_1 + r_2}{2} + \left(1 - \frac{\epsilon\lambda}{N}\right) r_1 & \frac{\epsilon\lambda}{N} \cdot r_2 + \left(1 - \frac{\epsilon\lambda}{N}\right) r_1 \end{bmatrix}. \tag{5.8}$$

Because $r_1 > 2r_2\,(\delta > 2)$, we have $T > R > P > S$ and $2R > S + T$, so that (5.2) is satisfied. In other words, the game is a prisoner's dilemma.

Now might be a good time to attempt Exercise 5.24.

5.4   TIT FOR TAT: A RECIPROCATIVE STRATEGY

Having seen two examples of the prisoner's dilemma in which (5.2) is satisfied, we now investigate possible escapes from its paradox. An important idea in this regard is that of *reciprocity:* one good turn deserves another; and one bad turn deserves another, too. To be more precise, reciprocity means that one good turn *now* deserves another *later;* and similarly for bad turns. Thus reciprocity is an inherently dynamic concept; it is impossible to reciprocate if the game is played only once, and we shall therefore assume that it is played repeatedly. Indeed it is convenient to define a brand new game, of which a single play consists of all the plays of the prisoner's dilemma that an animal—whether human as in Section 5.1, bird or mammal as in Section 5.2, or insect as in Section 5.3—makes within some specified interval of time. We call this brand new game the *iterated prisoner's dilemma,* or *IPD*; and whenever a prisoner's dilemma is imbedded in an iterated prisoner's dilemma, we shall refer to each play of the prisoner's dilemma as a *move* of the *IPD*.

Of course, an animal that cooperates on the first play of a prisoner's dilemma—i.e., on the first move of an *IPD*—might well cooperate at all subsequent times. But whereas its strategy in the prisoner's dilemma would be C, as defined above, its strategy in the *IPD* would be

$$ALLC = (C, C, C, C, \dots, C), \tag{5.9}$$

for "at all times cooperate." More generally, in the iterated prisoner's dilemma, pure strategy u—and we consider only pure strategies—consists of a sequence $u_1, u_2, \dots, u_n$ of prisoner's-dilemma strategies, where prisoner's dilemma strategy u_k is used on move k of the *IPD* and n is the number of moves; or, if we regard this sequence as a vector, then

$$u = (u_1, u_2, \dots, u_n). \tag{5.10}$$

Although C and D are the only values that u_k can take, there would be 2^n values that u could take even if strategies had to be unconditional; (5.9) is one such value, and

$$ALLD = (D, D, D, D, \dots, D), \tag{5.11}$$

for "at all times defect," is another. But *IPD* strategies need not be unconditional: they can also be contingent upon opponents' strategies—a prerequisite, of course, for reciprocity. The paragon of such a strategy is tit for tat, or *TFT*, which cooperates on the first move and subsequently plays whatever prisoner's-dilemma strategy an opponent used on the previous move. Thus, if the prisoner's-dilemma strategies adopted by a player's opponent are denoted by $v_1, v_2, \ldots$, then

$$TFT = (C, v_1, v_2, \ldots, v_{n-1}) \tag{5.12}$$

—if, that is, n is finite. We shall now suppose, however, that n may be infinite (though with vanishingly small probability).

Let the number of moves in an *IPD* be denoted by the (integer-valued) random variable M, so that $\text{Prob}(M \geq 1) = 1$. Conditional upon there being a k-th move in the *IPD*, let $\phi(u_k, v_k)$ be that move's payoff to prisoner's-dilemma strategy u_k against prisoner's-dilemma strategy v_k; thus, from (5.1), $\phi(C, C) = R$, $\phi(C, D) = S$, $\phi(D, C) = T$ and $\phi(D, D) = P$. Then the actual payoff to prisoner's-dilemma strategy u_k against prisoner's-dilemma strategy v_k from move k of the *IPD* is the random variable

$$F_k(u_k, v_k) = \begin{cases} \phi(u_k, v_k) & \text{if } M \geq k \\ 0 & \text{if } M < k; \end{cases} \tag{5.13}$$

and the reward from move k of the game is

$$\begin{aligned} E[F_k(u_k, v_k)] &= \phi(u_k, v_k) \cdot \text{Prob}(M \geq k) + 0 \cdot \text{Prob}(M < k) \\ &= \phi(u_k, v_k) \, \text{Prob}(M \geq k), \end{aligned} \tag{5.14}$$

where E denotes expected value. Thus, if $f(u, v)$ is the reward to strategy u against strategy v from (all moves of) the *IPD*, then

$$f(u, v) = \sum_{k=1}^{\infty} E\{F_k(u_k, v_k)\} = \sum_{k=1}^{\infty} \phi(u_k, v_k) \, \text{Prob}(M \geq k). \tag{5.15}$$

Let us now suppose that there are only three (pure) strategies, namely, *ALLC*, *ALLD* and *TFT*, where *ALLC* is strategy 1, *ALLD* is strategy 2 and *TFT* is strategy 3. Then a 3×3 payoff matrix A for the *IPD* can be computed directly from (5.15), with $a_{12} = f(ALLC, ALLD)$, $a_{23} = f(ALLD, TFT)$, and so on. For example,

$$\begin{aligned} a_{23} &= \phi(D, C)\text{Prob}(M \geq 1) + \sum_{k=2}^{\infty} \phi(D, D)\text{Prob}(M \geq k) \\ &= T + P \sum_{k=2}^{\infty} \text{Prob}(M \geq k). \end{aligned} \tag{5.16}$$

But (Exercise 1)

$$E[M] = \sum_{k=1}^{\infty} k \cdot \text{Prob}(M = k) \equiv \sum_{k=1}^{\infty} \text{Prob}(M \geq k) \tag{5.17}$$

(assuming, of course, that both series converge); whence, if we define

$$\mu = E[M], \tag{5.18}$$

so that $\mu \geq 1$, then

$$\sum_{k=2}^{\infty} \text{Prob}(M \geq k) = \mu - 1. \tag{5.19}$$

Thus, from (5.16), $a_{23} = T + P(\mu - 1)$. Similarly, $a_{32} = S + P(\mu - 1)$. Furthermore, it is clear that the expected payoff to *ALLC* against *ALLD* is just $\phi(C, D)$ times the expected number of moves, or $a_{12} = S\mu$; and that $a_{11} = a_{13} = a_{31} = a_{33}$, because *TFT* always cooperates with *ALLC*. Thus the payoff matrix is

$$A = \begin{bmatrix} R\mu & S\mu & R\mu \\ T\mu & P\mu & T + P(\mu - 1) \\ R\mu & S + P(\mu - 1) & R\mu \end{bmatrix}. \tag{5.20}$$

We see at once that each entry of the third row is at least as great as the corresponding entry of the first row and in once case strictly greater, provided only that $\mu > 1$ (for which reason, strategy 1 is said to be *weakly dominated* by strategy 3). Let us therefore remove strategy 1 from the game (although see Exercise 5.26), and consider instead the *IPD* with only two (pure) strategies, *ALLD* and *TFT*, with *ALLD* re-defined as strategy 1 and *TFT* as strategy 2. The payoff matrix for this reduced *IPD* is

$$A = \begin{bmatrix} P\mu & T + P(\mu - 1) \\ S + P(\mu - 1) & R\mu \end{bmatrix}. \tag{5.21}$$

Let us define

$$\mu_c = \frac{T - P}{R - P}. \tag{5.22}$$

If $\mu < \mu_c$, then each entry of the first row in (5.21) exceeds the corresponding entry of the second row, so that *ALLD* is a dominant strategy, and hence also a strong ESS (Exercise 2.21). If $\mu > \mu_c$, however, then both $a_{11} > a_{21}$ and $a_{22} > a_{12}$; whence, from (2.50), both *ALLD* and *TFT* are evolutionarily stable strategies. Thus initial conditions will determine which strategy emerges as the winning strategy in a large population of animals, some of whom adopt *ALLD*, the remainder of whom adopt *TFT*. According to the dynamics of Section 2.6, for example, *TFT* will emerge as victorious only if (on substituting from (5.21) into (2.57)) its initial frequency exceeds the critical value

$$\gamma = \frac{P - S}{P - S + (R - P)(\mu - \mu_c)}. \tag{5.23}$$

The greater the amount by which μ exceeds μ_c, the easier it is to satisfy this condition. Thus maintenance of cooperation via reciprocity—specifically, via *TFT*—requires two things: first, that the average number of interactions be sufficiently high, or (which is essentially the same thing) that the probability of further interaction be sufficiently high; and second, that the initial proportion of *TFT*-strategists be sufficiently large.

Until now, we have allowed M to be any (integer-valued) random variable with $\mu > 1$. Further progress is difficult, however, unless we specify the distribution of M. Accordingly, we will assume henceforward that there is constant probability w of further interaction, which implies (Exercise 5.2) that M has the geometric distribution defined by

$$\text{Prob}(M \geq k) = w^{k-1}, \qquad k \geq 1. \tag{5.24}$$

Then

$$\mu = \frac{1}{1 - w}, \tag{5.25}$$

so that our condition for *TFT* to be evolutionarily stable, namely, $\mu > \mu_c$, becomes

$$w > \frac{T - R}{T - P}, \tag{5.26}$$

on using (5.22).

We mentioned at the end of Section 5.1 that Axelrod (1984) used the payoff matrix defined by (5.3) for a computer tournament. The game that was played in the second round of this tournament—which had 63 contestants—was the iterated prisoner's dilemma described above.[5] Axelrod chose w so that the median number of moves in a game would be 200; in other words, so that $\text{Prob}(M \leq 200) = 0.5$. But $\text{Prob}(M \leq 200) = 1 - \text{Prob}(M \geq 201) = 1 - w^{200}$, from (5.26). Thus Axelrod's value of w is determined by $1 - w^{200} = 0.5$, or

$$w = (0.5)^{0.005} = 0.99654. \tag{5.27}$$

We will refer to the *IPD* defined by (5.3) and (5.27) as Axelrod's prototype.

5.5   OTHER RECIPROCATIVE STRATEGIES

Tit for tat is a *nice, forgiving* and *provocable* strategy based on reciprocity. It is nice, because it always begins by cooperating. It is forgiving, because if an

---

[5]   The strategies were *RNDM*, defined in Exercise 5.10, *TFT*, submitted by Professor Anatol Rapoport, and 61 other strategies submitted by contestants in six countries and from a variety of academic disciplines. For full details, see Axelrod (1984, pp. 40–54). In the first round of the tournament, which had fewer contestants, the number of moves was fixed at 200. Again, see Axelrod (1984, pp. 30–40) for details.

opponent—after numerous defections—suddenly begins to cooperate, then *TFT* will cooperate on the following move. And *TFT* is provocable, because it always responds to a defection with a defection. By contrast, *ALLD* is a *nasty* strategy, that is, a strategy that always defects on the first move. For that matter, *ALLD* always defects, so it is the meanest strategy imaginable.

TFT is not, however, the only example of a nice, forgiving and provocable strategy based on reciprocity. A more forgiving nice strategy is *TF2T*, or tit for two tats, which always cooperates on the first *two* moves, but thereafter plays *TFT*; in other words,

$$TF2T = (C, C, v_2, v_3, \ldots), \tag{5.28}$$

where v denotes the other player's strategy. In a sense, *TF2T* is one degree more forgiving than *TFT*. A homogeneous *TFT* population is indistinguishable from a homogeneous *TF2T* population—or indeed any mixture of the two strategies—because both populations always cooperate; but the strategies are distinguishable in the presence of any nasty strategies, because *TF2T* will forgive an initial defection, whereas *TFT* will punish it on the second move. In particular, if *TFT* were to play against $STCO = (D, C, C, \ldots)$, for "slow to cooperate," then mutual cooperation would be established only at the third move; whereas if *TF2T* were to play against *STCO*, then mutual cooperation would be established at the second move. The question therefore arises: is *TFT* too mean? You might like to answer this question yourself; see Exercise 5.3.

In a sense, *STCO* is the least exploitative of all the nasty strategies, and *ALLD* is the most exploitative. In between lies *STFT*, for "suspicious tit for tat," which always defects on the first move, but thereafter plays *TFT*; in other words,

$$STFT = (D, v_1, v_2, \ldots). \tag{5.29}$$

A homogeneous *ALLD* population is indistinguishable from a homogeneous *STFT* population (or any mixture of the two strategies), because both populations always defect; but the strategies are distinguishable in the presence of any nice strategies, because *STFT* will reciprocate an initial cooperation, whereas *ALLD* will exploit it. To see how *TFT* fares against these nasty strategies, let us compute the payoff matrix for the *IPD* with *ALLD* (strategy 1), *TFT* (strategy 2) and *STFT* (strategy 3). Of course, a_{11}, a_{12}, a_{21} and a_{22} are still defined by (5.21); moreover, because (5.11) and (5.29) imply that *STFT* and *ALLD* always suffer mutual defection, we have $a_{13} = a_{31} = a_{33} = P\mu$. If, on the other hand, $u = TFT$ and $v = STFT$, then from (5.12) and (5.29) we have $\phi(u_1, v_1) = \phi(C, D) = S$, $\phi(u_2, v_2) = \phi(D, C) = T$, $\phi(u_3, v_3) = \phi(C, D) = S$, $\phi(u_4, v_4) = \phi(D, C) = T$, and so on; in other words,

$$\phi(u_{2j-1}, v_{2j-1}) = S, \qquad \phi(u_{2j}, v_{2j}) = T, \qquad j = 1, 2, 3, \ldots, \tag{5.30}$$

with *TFT* and *STFT* trapped in an endless war of reprisal. From (5.15), (5.24) and (5.30), it therefore follows that

$$a_{23} = f(TFT, STFT) = \sum_{k=1}^{\infty} \phi(u_k, v_k) w^{k-1}$$

$$= \sum_{j=1}^{\infty} S w^{2j-2} + \sum_{j=1}^{\infty} T w^{2j-1} = (S + Tw) \sum_{j=1}^{\infty} (w^2)^{j-1}$$

$$= \frac{S + wT}{1 - w^2},$$

$$(5.31)$$

on setting $\beta = w^2$ in the standard formula

$$\sum_{j=1}^{\infty} \beta^{j-1} = \frac{1}{1 - \beta}, \qquad 0 \le \beta < 1, \tag{5.32}$$

for the sum of a geometric series. Similarly (Exercise 5.4), $a_{32} = (T + wS)/(1 - w^2)$. Thus the payoff matrix is

$$A = \begin{bmatrix} P\mu & T + P(\mu - 1) & P\mu \\ S + P(\mu - 1) & R\mu & \dfrac{\mu(S + wT)}{1 + w} \\ P\mu & \dfrac{\mu(T + wS)}{1 + w} & P\mu \end{bmatrix}, \tag{5.33}$$

where μ is defined by (5.25). Applying (2.50), we discover that now neither *ALLD* nor *STFT* is evolutionarily stable. *ALLD* is collectively stable, because $a_{11} \ge a_{j1}$ for $j = 2, 3$; but it is not evolutionarily stable, because neither $a_{11} > a_{31}$ nor $a_{13} > a_{33}$ is satisfied. *STFT* is collectively stable if $a_{33} \ge a_{23}$, or

$$w \le \frac{P - S}{T - P}; \tag{5.34}$$

but even then it is not evolutionarily stable, because neither $a_{33} > a_{13}$ nor $a_{31} > a_{11}$. On the other hand, (5.26) implies $a_{22} > a_{12}$; and if also $a_{22} > a_{32}$, that is, if $w > (T - R)/(R - S)$, then *TFT* is evolutionarily stable. In other words, *TFT* is the sole *ESS* of this *IPD* if

$$w > \max \left(\frac{T - R}{T - P}, \frac{T - R}{R - S} \right). \tag{5.35}$$

When (5.35) is satisfied, a *TFT* population can be invaded by neither a small army of *STFT*-strategists nor a small army of *ALLD*-strategists—nor any combi-

nation of the two, because *TFT* is a strong *ESS* (of the game defined by (5.33)).[6]
Of course, (5.35) does not imply that *TFT* can invade an *ALLD* population, because *ALLD* is collectively stable (and evolutionarily stable in the absence of *STFT*). But if (5.34) is violated, i.e., if $w > (P - S)/(T - P)$, then *STFT* has no such resistance to *TFT*. In particular, if

$$S + T \geq P + R, \tag{5.36}$$

then

$$w > \frac{T - R}{R - S} \tag{5.37}$$

implies (5.35), which in turn implies $w > (P - S)/(T - P)$; so that, not only is a *TFT* population immune to invasion by *STFT* (in the *IPD* defined by (5.33)), but also a single *TFT*-strategist is enough to conquer an entire *STFT* population. Note that (5.36) is satisfied with strict inequality by Axelrod's prototype, and with equality by both the laboratory game of Section 5.2 and the foraging game of Section 5.3. Nevertheless, not every prisoner's dilemma satisfies (5.36); see Section 5.9 for an exception.

We have seen that if the probability of further interaction is sufficiently high, specifically, if (5.35) is satisfied, then *TFT* is uninvadable by the pair of exploitative strategies, *STFT* and *ALLD*. But could a more forgiving strategy do just as well? The obvious way to answer this question is to compute the payoff matrix for the *IPD* with *ALLD* (strategy 1), *STFT* (strategy 2) and *TF2T* (strategy 3). Because *STFT* and *ALLD* always suffer mutual defection, we now have $a_{11} = a_{12} = a_{21} = a_{22} = P\mu$; and because *TF2T* always cooperates with itself, we have $a_{33} = R\mu$. From (5.11) and (5.28), if $u = ALLD$ and $v = TF2T$, then $\phi(u_1, v_1) = \phi(D, C) = T$, $\phi(u_2, v_2) = \phi(D, C) = T$ and $\phi(u_k, v_k) = \phi(D, D) = P$ for $k \geq 3$. Thus

$$a_{13} = f(ALLD, TF2T) = \sum_{k=1}^{\infty} \phi(u_k, v_k) \cdot w^{k-1} = T + wT + \sum_{k=3}^{\infty} P \cdot w^{k-1}$$

$$= T + wT + w^2 P \sum_{j=1}^{\infty} w^{j-1} = T(1 + w) + w^2 P\mu, \tag{5.38}$$

on using (5.15), a change of summation index ($j = k - 2$) and (5.32) with $\beta = w$ (μ is defined by (5.25)). Continuing in this manner, we find (Exercise 5.4) that the payoff matrix is

---

[6]   Axelrod (1984) has proved that *TFT* is collectively stable (but not evolutionarily stable) against any deviant strategy (not just *ALLD* or *STFT*) when *w* is greater than or equal to the right-hand side of (5.35).

$$A = \begin{bmatrix} P\mu & P\mu & T(1+w) + w^2 P\mu \\ P\mu & P\mu & T + Rw\mu \\ S(1+w) + w^2 P\mu & S + Rw\mu & R\mu \end{bmatrix}. \tag{5.39}$$

We see at once that $a_{33} - a_{23} = R - T < 0$, so that $TF2T$ is invadable by $STFT$; whereas TFT is not invadable. Even if $STFT$ were absent, we see from (5.39) that $TF2T$ can withstand $ALLD$ only if $R\mu > T(1 + w) + w^2 P\mu$ or

$$w > \sqrt{\frac{T-R}{T-P}}; \tag{5.40}$$

whereas (5.26) implies that TFT can withstand $ALLD$ if only $w > (T-R)/(T-P)$, which is more readily satisfied. In Axelrod's prototype, for example, this means that TFT, but not $TF2T$, can withstand $ALLD$ whenever $0.5 < w < 0.7071$. The conclusion is clear: $TF2T$ is too forgiving to persist as an orthodox strategy if infiltrated by $STFT$, and less resistant to invasion (in the sense of requiring higher w) than TFT when infiltrated by $ALLD$.

Although $STFT$ can invade $TF2T$, it does not necessarily eliminate it. To see this, let us model a population's long-term dynamics in terms of strategies according to (2.65), so that if $x_k(n)$ is the proportion adopting strategy k in generation n, then

$$x_1(n) + x_2(n) + x_3(n) = 1, \tag{5.41}$$

and proportions evolve according to

$$\overline{W}(n)\{x_1(n+1) - x_1(n)\}$$
$$= x_1(n)\{x_2(n)\{W_1(n) - W_2(n)\} + x_3(n)\{W_1(n) - W_3(n)\}\}$$

$$\overline{W}(n)\{x_2(n+1) - x_2(n)\}$$
$$= x_2(n)\{x_1(n)\{W_2(n) - W_1(n)\} + x_3(n)\{W_2(n) - W_3(n)\}\}$$

$$\overline{W}(n)\{x_3(n+1) - x_3(n)\}$$
$$= x_3(n)\{x_1(n)\{W_3(n) - W_1(n)\} + x_2(n)\{W_3(n) - W_2(n)\}\}, \tag{5.42}$$

where

$$W_k(n) = a_{k1}x_1(n) + a_{k2}x_2(n) + a_{k3}x_3(n), \quad 1 \le k \le 3 \tag{5.43}$$

is the reward to strategy k in generation n and

$$\overline{W}(n) = x_1(n)W_1(n) + x_2(n)W_2(n) + x_3(n)W_3(n) \tag{5.44}$$

is the average reward to the entire population; clearly $\overline{W}(n) > 0$. In view of (5.41), we can determine how the population evolves by following the point with coordinates $(x_1(n), x_2(n))$ in the triangle

$$0 \le x_1 \le 1, \quad 0 \le x_2 \le 1, \quad 0 \le x_1 + x_2 \le 1. \tag{5.45}$$

As in Chapter 4, where (x_1, x_2, x_3) was an imputation, the upper boundary $x_1 + x_2 = 1$ of triangle (5.45) corresponds to $x_3 = 0$ and x_3 increases toward the southwest, with $x_3 = 1$ at the point $(0, 0)$.

On using (5.39) and (5.41), we find after routine algebra that

$$W_1 - W_2 = \mu w x_3 \{T - R - w(T - P)\}$$

$$W_1 - W_3 = \mu\{x_1(1 - w^2)(P - S) + x_2(P - S - (R - S)w)$$

$$\qquad + x_3(T - R - w^2(T - P))\} \tag{5.46}$$

$$W_2 - W_3 = \mu\{x_1(1 - w^2)(P - S)$$

$$\qquad + x_2(P - S - (R - S)w) + x_3(T - R)(1 - w)\}.$$

For the sake of simplicity, let us now choose Axelrod's payoffs (5.3). Then, on substituting from (5.46) and using (5.41), we can rewrite (5.42) as

$$\overline{W}(n)\{x_k(n + 1) - x_k(n)\} = \phi_k(x_1(n), x_2(n)), \quad k = 1, 2, 3, \tag{5.47}$$

where

$$\phi_1(x_1, x_2) = \mu x_1(1 - x_1 - x_2)\{a + cx_1 - dx_2\}$$

$$\phi_2(x_1, x_2) = \mu x_2(1 - x_1 - x_2)\{b + cx_1 - dx_2\} \tag{5.48}$$

$$\phi_3(x_1, x_2) = -\mu(1 - x_1 - x_2)\{(x_1 + x_2)(cx_1 - dx_2) + ax_1 + bx_2\},$$

and

$$a = 2(1 - 2w^2), \quad b = 2(1 - w), \quad c = 3w^2 - 1, \quad d = 1 + w, \tag{5.49}$$

again after routine algebra. Let us at least assume that *TF2T* can withstand *ALLD*. Then, from (5.40), $w > 1/\sqrt{2}$ and $a < 0 < c, d > b > 0$.

It is convenient here to define parallel lines L_1, L_2 by

$$L_1 : cx_1 - dx_2 + a = 0, \quad L_2 : cx_1 - dx_2 + b = 0. \tag{5.50}$$

These lines are sketched in Figure 5.3, together with both branches of the hyperbola H defined by

$$H : (cx_1 - dx_2)(x_1 + x_2) + ax_1 + bx_2 = 0. \tag{5.51}$$

This hyperbola has foci in the shaded region of Figure 5.3, where $\phi_3 < 0$; whereas, in the unshaded region, $\phi_3 > 0$ (Exercise 5.5). Because ϕ_1 is negative to the left of L_1 and positive to the right of L_1, from (5.47)–(5.48) we have $x_1(n + 1) < x_1(n)$ when $(x_1(n), x_2(n))$ lies to the left of L_1, but $x_1(n + 1) > x_1(n)$ when $(x_1(n), x_2(n))$ lies to the right of L_1. Similarly, $x_2(n + 1) < x_2(n)$ when $(x_1(n), x_2(n))$ lies above L_2, whereas $x_2(n + 1) > x_2(n)$ when $(x_1(n), x_2(n))$ lies below L_2; and $x_3(n + 1) < x_3(n)$ or $x_3(n + 1) > x_3(n)$ according to whether

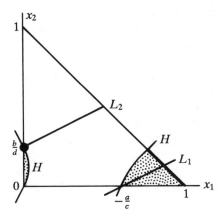

Figure 5.3 Equilibrium points in the triangle (5.45) for the *IPD* with strategies *ALLD* (frequency x_1), *STFT* (frequency x_2), and *TF2T* (frequency $1 - x_1 - x_2$).

$(x_1(n), x_2(n))$ lies in the shaded or unshaded part of the triangle (5.45). Therefore, if $(x_1(0), x_2(0))$ lies in the interior of triangle (5.45) and either to the left of H or between its two branches, then $(x_1(n), x_2(n))$ converges to $(0, b/d)$ as $n \to \infty$; whereas, if $(x_1(0), x_2(0))$ lies sufficiently far to the right of H, then $(x_1(n), x_2(n))$ converges to the line $x_1 + x_2 = 1$ as $n \to \infty$.

Now, (ξ_1, ξ_2) is a population *equilibrium point* if $(x_1(n_0), x_2(n_0)) = (\xi_1, \xi_2)$ implies $(x_1(n), x_2(n)) = (\xi_1, \xi_2)$ for all $n \geq n_0$; whence, from (5.47), (ξ_1, ξ_2) is an equilibrium point if, and only if, $\phi_1(\xi_1, \xi_2) = 0 = \phi_2(\xi_1, \xi_2)$. Thus $(0, b/d)$, where H meets L_2 on the x_2-axis, is an equilibrium point (marked by a dot in Figure 5.3). There is also an equilibrium point, namely, $(-a/c, 0)$ on the x_1-axis. All other equilibrium points lie on the line $x_1 + x_2 = 1$. Indeed every point on the line segment that joins $(0,1)$ to $(1,0)$ is an equilibrium point. But those between $(0,1)$ and $((d - b)/(d + c - b + a), (a + c)/(d + c - b + a))$, where H intersects $x_1 + x_2 = 1$, are *unstable*, because the slightest increase in x_3 from 0 will displace $(x_1(n), x_2(n))$ into the unshaded region, where it begins a relentless march towards $(0, b/d)$. Similarly, $(-a/c, 0)$ is unstable, because the slightest leftward displacement of $(x_1(0), x_2(0))$ will again send $(x_1(n), x_2(n))$ to $(b/d, 0)$, and the slightest rightward displacement will send it towards the line $x_1 + x_2 = 1$. But $(b/d, 0)$ is a *locally stable* equilibrium point, because it attracts $(x_1(n), x_2(n))$ from any point $(x_1(0), x_2(0))$ in its vicinity—indeed, from any point to the left of H or between its two branches. By contrast, equilibria on $x_1 + x_2 = 1$ between $((d - b)/(d + c - b + a), (a + c)/(d + c - b + a))$ and $(1,0)$ are only *metastable*, because a slight displacement of $(x_1(0), x_2(0))$ from (ξ_1, ξ_2) will neither return $(x_1(n), x_2(n))$ to (ξ_1, ξ_2), nor send it far away; rather, $(x_1(n), x_2(n))$ will shift to a neighbouring equilibrium on the line $x_1 + x_2 = 1$. All of these statements are readily verified by considering the signs of ϕ_1, ϕ_2 and ϕ_3 in the various regions of the triangle (5.45). We can now confirm that, even if *STFT* invades *TF2T*, it does not necessarily eliminate it. Observe that, in Figure 5.3, (0,0) corresponds to a homogeneous *TF2T* population, (1,0) to a homogeneous *ALLD* population and (0,1) to a homogeneous *STFT* population. Infiltration of a *TF2T* population by *STFT* or *ALLD* corresponds to displacing $(x_1(0), x_2(0))$ slightly from the origin, which will send $(x_1(n), x_2(n))$ to $(0, b/d)$ as $n \to \infty$. Thus *TF2T* is not eliminated. Rather, *ALLD* is eliminated, the proportion of *STFT* increases to b/d, and the proportion of *TF2T* decreases from 1 to $1 - b/d = (3w - 1)/(1 + w)$. It can be shown more generally that, provided $w > (P - S)/(R - S)$, the final composition of the population will be a mixture of *STFT* and *TF2T* in which the proportion of *TF2T* is

$$x_3(\infty) = 1 - x_2(\infty) = \frac{w(R - S) - (P - S)}{(1 - w)(T - R) + w(R - S) - (P - S)}; \qquad (5.52)$$

see Exercise 5.6.

Let us now restore *TFT*. In (5.33) it was strategy 2; whereas *ALLD* was strategy 1, and *STFT* was strategy 3. In (5.39), where *TFT* was absent, we promoted *STFT* to strategy 2 and introduced *TF2T* as strategy 3. With all four strategies together, it is convenient to demote *ALLD* from 1 to 4 and relabel as follows:

$$
\begin{aligned}
TFT: &\quad \text{strategy 1} \\
TF2T: &\quad \text{strategy 2} \\
STFT: &\quad \text{strategy 3} \\
ALLD: &\quad \text{strategy 4.}
\end{aligned}
\qquad (5.53)
$$

The advantage is that nice and nasty strategies are now adjacent, and from Exercise 5.7 the payoff matrix is

$$
A = \begin{bmatrix}
R\mu & R\mu & \dfrac{\mu(S + wT)}{1 + w} & S + P(\mu - 1) \\
R\mu & R\mu & S + Rw\mu & S(1 + w) + w^2 P\mu \\
\dfrac{\mu(T + wS)}{1 + w} & T + Rw\mu & P\mu & P\mu \\
T + P(\mu - 1) & T(1 + w) + w^2 P\mu & P\mu & P\mu
\end{bmatrix},
\qquad (5.54)
$$

with μ as usual defined by (5.25). On applying (2.50), we see that *ALLD* is collectively stable (for any w), and that *TFT* is collectively stable if (5.35) is satisfied. But neither strategy is evolutionarily stable: *ALLD* is incapable of eliminating the other nasty strategy, namely, *STFT*; and *TFT* is incapable of eliminating the other nice strategy, namely, *TF2T*.

Indeed no strategy—that is, no pure strategy, because we have expressly forbidden mixed strategies—can resist invasion by an arbitrary mixture of infiltrators, even if w is sufficiently large.[7] Broadly speaking, the reason for this is that with any collectively stable strategy we can associate a second strategy that, although quite distinct, is distinguishable only in the presence of a third strategy; and if the second strategy does better than the first against the third, then the frequency of the second strategy can increase. To see this, let us first consider the *IPD* with strategies *TFT*, *TF2T* and *STFT*, whose payoff matrix is

$$A = \begin{bmatrix} R\mu & R\mu & \dfrac{\mu(S + wT)}{1 + w} \\[2ex] R\mu & R\mu & S + Rw\mu \\[2ex] \dfrac{\mu(T + wS)}{1 + w} & T + Rw\mu & P\mu \end{bmatrix}, \tag{5.55}$$

obtained from (5.54) by deleting the final row and column; and let us assume that (5.35) is satisfied. Then *TFT* is collectively stable, and $w > (T - R)/(R - S)$ implies $a_{23} > a_{13}$, so that *TF2T* is a second strategy, distinct from *TFT*, that does better against a third strategy, namely, *STFT* (without which *TF2T* would be indistinguishable from *TFT*). The long-term dynamics can again be described by (5.47); but because the strategies are different now, in place of (5.48)–(5.49) we have

$$\phi_1(x_1, x_2) = \mu x_1 (1 - x_1 - x_2)\{a - cx_1 - dx_2\}$$
$$\phi_2(x_1, x_2) = \mu x_2 (1 - x_1 - x_2)\{b - cx_1 - dx_2\} \tag{5.56}$$
$$\phi_3(x_1, x_2) = \mu(1 - x_1 - x_2)\{(x_1 + x_2)(cx_1 + dx_2) - ax_1 - bx_2\},$$

where

$$a = \frac{(T - P)w - (R - S)}{1 + w}, \qquad b = w(R - S) - (P - S),$$
$$c = S + T - P - R, \qquad d = c + (2R - S - T)w \tag{5.57}$$

and (5.35) implies $d > 0, d > b > a > c$ (Exercise 5.8).

We can again deduce the long-term dynamics by following the point with coordinates (x_1, x_2) in the triangle (5.45). Let us first suppose that (5.36) is satisfied, i.e., $S + T \geq P + R$. Then $d > b > a > c$, so that in Figure 5.4(a) we have $\phi_1 > 0$ below L_1 and $\phi_2 > 0$ below L_2, where the parallel lines L_1 and L_2 are re-defined by

---

[7] A formal proof is given by Boyd and Lorberbaum (1987), who show that no (pure) strategy in the *IPD* can resist invasion if

$$w > \min \left(\frac{T - R}{T - P}, \frac{P - S}{R - S} \right),$$

hence if $w > 1/3$ in Axelrod's prototype.

$$L_1 : cx_1 + dx_2 = a, \qquad L_2 : cx_1 + dx_2 = b. \tag{5.58}$$

We also have $\phi_3 > 0$ above the upper branch of the hyperbola H, now redefined by

$$H : (x_1 + x_2)(cx_1 + dx_2) = ax_1 + bx_2; \tag{5.59}$$

H intersects L_2 at the point $(0, b/d)$ but lies entirely above L_1. (The lower branch of H passes through the origin, but otherwise lies outside the triangle.)

The point $(0, b/d)$, where $x_3 = (d - b)/d > 0$, is again the only locally stable equilibrium. On $x_1 + x_2 = 1$ there exists, however, a whole line segment of metastable equilibria—and (x_1, x_2) may be attracted to one of these, rather than to $(0, b/d)$. To see this, let us first suppose that $(x_1(0), x_2(0))$ lies in the smaller, hatched triangle with a vertex at $(1, 0)$. Then because $\phi_1 > 0$, $\phi_2 > 0$, $\phi_3 < 0$, (5.47) implies that the point $(x_1(n), x_2(n))$ will always move rightwards, upwards and toward the line $x_1 + x_2 = 1$. Thus $x_3(\infty) = 0$, and $x_1(\infty) + x_2(\infty) = 1$; furthermore, $x_2(\infty) > x_2(0)$, so that $TF2T$ invades. On the other hand, $STFT$ is eliminated; and $x_1(\infty) > x_1(0)$, so that the frequency of TFT is higher than initially. Indeed because L_1 intersects the line $x_1 + x_2 = 1$ where $x_1 = (d - a)/(d - c)$, we see that TFT is bound to increase in frequency whenever

$$x_1(0) > \frac{(T - R)(1 - w) + (2R - S - T)w^2}{(2R - S - T)w(1 + w)}. \tag{5.60}$$

(For Axelrod's prototype, this condition reduces to $x_1(0) > 0.5026$.)

If $(x_1(0), x_2(0))$ lies in the unshaded region of Figure 5.4(a), then $(x_1(n), x_2(n))$ may converge either to the line $x_1 + x_2 = 1$ or to the point $(0, b/d)$. If, however, $(x_1(0), x_2(0))$ lies in the shaded region of Figure 5.4(a), then convergence to $(0, b/d)$ and elimination of TFT are assured.

A similar analysis applies to the case where $P + R > S + T$. Then (Exercise 5.9)

$$\frac{P - S}{T - P} > \frac{P - S}{R - S} > \frac{T - R}{T - P} > \frac{T - R}{R - S}, \tag{5.61}$$

so that (5.35) implies $w > (T - R)/(T - P)$. Nevertheless, w can be either larger or smaller than each of $(P - S)/(T - P)$, $(P - S)/(R - S)$ and $(P + R - S - T)/(2R - S - T)$; and the third of these, though smaller than $(P - S)/(R - S)$, can be either larger or smaller than $(T - R)/(T - P)$. So various cases are possible, and Figure 5.4 shows two: In Figure 5.4(b), where $(0, b/d)$ is the only locally stable equilibrium, $w > (P - S)/(T - P)$; whereas in Figure 5.4(c), where $(0, 0)$ is the only locally stable equilibrium, $(P - S)/(R - S) > w > (P + R - S - T)/(2R - S - T)$. The smaller the value of w, the larger the shaded region in which (x_1, x_2) is guaranteed to be attracted to $x_1 = 0$. Nevertheless, the hatched region in Figure 5.4, where (5.60) is satisfied and TFT is bound to increase in frequency, is

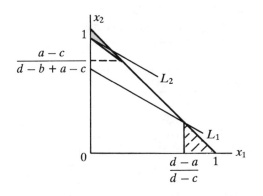

(a) $S + T \geq P + R$

$$w > \frac{T - R}{R - S}$$

$$d > b > a > c > 0$$

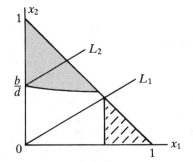

(b) $P + R > S + T$

$$w > \frac{P - S}{T - P}$$

$$d > b > a > 0 > c$$

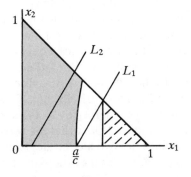

(c) $P + R > S + T$

$$\frac{P - S}{R - S} > w > \frac{P + R - S - T}{2R - S - T}$$

$$d > 0 > b > a > c$$

Figure 5.4　Domains of attraction in the triangle (5.45) for the *IPD* with strategies *TFT* (frequency x_1), *TF2T* (frequency x_2), and *STFT* (frequency $1 - x_1 - x_2$). In the hatched region, (x_1, x_2) is attracted to the line $x_1 + x_2 = 1$. In the shaded region, (x_1, x_2) is attracted to $(0, b/d)$ in Figures 5.4(a) and 5.4(b) but to $(0, 0)$ in Figure 5.4(c).

TABLE 5.2 Numerical solution of (2.65) with *TFT* as strategy 1, *TF2T* as strategy 2, *STFT* as strategy 3 and *ALLD* as strategy 4. Initially, the proportion of *TFT* is 7/10, and the other strategies are equally represented.

n	$x_1(n)$	$x_2(n)$	$x_3(n)$	$x_4(n)$
0	0.700	0.100	0.100	0.100
1	0.791	0.119	0.064	0.026
2	0.827	0.129	0.038	0.006
3	0.843	0.134	0.022	0.001
4	0.851	0.137	0.012	0.000
5	0.855	0.138	0.007	0.000
6	0.857	0.139	0.004	0.000
7	0.858	0.140	0.002	0.000
8	0.859	0.140	0.001	0.000
9	0.859	0.140	0.001	0.000
10	0.859	0.140	0.000	0.000
11	0.860	0.140	0.000	0.000

still finite; and if the whole population were using *TFT* just before infiltration by *STFT* and *TF2T* at time $n = 0$, then $(x_1(0), x_2(0))$ would have to lie close to $(1, 0)$ and hence within the hatched region. Of course, a fresh infiltration of *STFT* would displace (x_1, x_2) from the line $x_1 + x_2 = 1$, slightly toward the southwest. The population would subsequently evolve to a new metastable equilibrium, still on the line $x_1 + x_2 = 1$ but nearer to $(0, 1)$. In the course of time, repeated infiltrations by *STFT* could nudge (x_1, x_2) all the way along the line $x_1 + x_2 = 1$, slowly decreasing the fraction of *TFT*; so that (x_1, x_2) would eventually enter the shaded region, to be attracted by $x_1 = 0$. At that stage, *TFT* would have been eliminated (and also *TF2T* in Figure 5.4(c)). But whether this would actually happen is far beyond the scope of our dynamic model, namely, (5.47).

The dynamics are more difficult, both to analyze and to visualize, when *ALLD* is present also. But it is easy to solve (2.65) numerically, and Table 5.2 shows a sample calculation for Axelrod's prototype when $x_1(0) = 0.7$ and the other three strategies are equally represented initially. Notice that the two nasty strategies are summarily dispatched; and because the two nice strategies are incapable of eliminating one another, the final composition of the population is 86% *TFT* and 14% *TF2T*.

Two remarks are now in order. First, as we have said before, insofar as no (pure) strategy can resist invasion by every conceivable combination of deviant strategies, the iterated prisoner's dilemma has no uninvadable strategy. But this does not mean that *TFT* cannot persist as an orthodox *IPD* strategy, for the simple reason that strategies capable of displacing it may be either absent or too rare. As we have remarked already in Section 2.7, whether a strategy is evolutionarily stable will always depend upon the scope of the strategy set. By suitably enlarging it, most of the strategies that have ever been claimed as *ESS*s for one game or another could almost certainly be destabilized. For example, if in Crossroads we allowed a third strategy, Z, which stands for "instantly convert your car into a motorcycle, so that you can proceed at once regardless of what the other motorist does, and zoom," then clearly Z would be a dominant strategy, and would replace Section 2.3's *ESS* as the solution of the game. But not every motorist drives Jane Bond's car.[8] Likewise, *STFT* might not emerge as a deviant strategy sufficiently often to sustain the process for eliminating *TFT* that we described in the last paragraph but one.

Second, impressive empirical support for the persistence of *TFT* as an orthodox strategy has been marshalled by Axelrod (1984, pp. 48–52), who conducted a simulation of the iterated prisoner's dilemma in a population of computer programs submitted to his tournament. Initially, all programs were represented; subsequently, Axelrod allowed the composition of the population to evolve, essentially according to the dynamics of Section 2.6, and found that the frequency of *TFT* was always higher than that of any other strategy and increased steadily. (Indeed *TFT* was easily the most successful strategy in the computer tournament itself, although this was a round-robin tournament, in which every strategy played every other strategy once).

In the light of these remarks, we should interpret (5.35) as a *necessary* condition for *TFT* to be uninvadable. If this condition is satisfied, then *TFT may* persist as an orthodox strategy, simply because a mixture of deviant strategies that could invade it may not be represented. If (5.35) is not satisfied, however, then there is little hope that *TFT* will persist, because deviant strategies that can eliminate it are so simple as virtually to be guaranteed to arise.

Nevertheless, there are circumstances in which (5.35) is inappropriate even as a necessary condition, because—as we shall demonstrate in Section 5.7—it is based on two tacit assumptions, namely, that the population is very large, and that opponents, though randomly selected at the beginning of the game, are retained for its duration. But the population may not be large, and opponents may be drawn at random throughout the game—which would happen, for example, if Section 5.2's laboratory game were played repeatedly by randomly chosen pairs of trained animals. Let us therefore relax both assumptions.

5.6   MATHEMATICAL MODEL OF DYNAMIC VERSUS STATIC INTERACTION

Given *TFT*'s success in Axelrod's computer tournament and the remarks at the end of the previous section, we would like to obtain some theoretical insights into the resilience of this strategy in a finite population. In this section, we shall

---

8   Jane Bond is female Agent 007.

consider two different modes of interaction: first, a mode in which players select their opponents at random, but retain them for the duration of the game; and second, a mode in which opponents are drawn randomly from the population throughout the game.

Consider therefore a population of $N + 1$ individuals, of whom N_k play strategy k in the *IPD*. Thus, with m strategies, we have

$$N_1 + N_2 + \cdots + N_m = N + 1. \tag{5.62}$$

Because opponents are not necessarily fixed, it no longer makes sense to construct a payoff matrix for the entire game; instead, we construct a payoff matrix for each move, and use it to derive expressions for the expected payoffs to the various strategies against all possible opponents. Let $\phi(k)$ denote this $m \times m$ matrix, i.e., for $1 \leq j, l \leq m$, let $\phi_{jl}(k)$ be a j-strategist's payoff from interaction k if the interaction is with an l-strategist; and, for $j = 1, 2, \ldots, m$, let W_j denote a j-strategist's reward from the game. Then, in place of (5.14), the reward from move k of the game—conditional upon encountering an l-strategist—is

$$\phi_{jl}(k) \cdot \text{Prob}(M \geq k), \tag{5.63}$$

where M as usual is the number of interactions.

In the case where opponents are drawn at random throughout, let π_{jl} denote the probability that a j-strategist's next interaction is with an l-strategist (assumed the same on every move). Then the (unconditional) reward from move k of the game is

$$\sum_{l=1}^{m} \pi_{jl} \phi_{jl}(k) \cdot \text{Prob}(M \geq k), \tag{5.64}$$

because the opponent uses strategy l at move k with probability π_{jl}; and the reward from the entire game is

$$W_j = \sum_{k=1}^{\infty} \left(\sum_{l=1}^{m} \pi_{jl} \phi_{jl}(k) \right) \text{Prob}(M \geq k), \qquad 1 \leq j \leq m. \tag{5.65a}$$

On the other hand, in the case where players interact with fixed opponents, for some value of l a j-strategist's opponent is known to be an l-strategist from the first move onwards; whence (5.63) implies that the reward from the entire game, assessed at the first move, is

$$\sum_{k=1}^{\infty} \phi_{jl}(k) \cdot \text{Prob}(M \geq k), \qquad 1 \leq j \leq m, \qquad 1 \leq l \leq m.$$

Before the first move the identity of l is unknown, however; and so to obtain the reward we must average this expression over the distribution of possible opponents, which yields

$$W_j = \sum_{l=1}^{m} \left(\sum_{k=1}^{\infty} \phi_{jl}(k) \cdot \text{Prob}(M \geq k) \right), \qquad 1 \leq j \leq m. \qquad (5.65b)$$

Clearly, the same expression for W_j results in either case.

Let us now define

$$x_j = \frac{N_j}{N}, \qquad 1 \leq j \leq m \qquad (5.66)$$

and

$$\alpha = \frac{1}{N}, \qquad (5.67)$$

so that (5.62) implies

$$x_1 + x_2 + \cdots + x_m = 1 + \alpha. \qquad (5.68)$$

Then, because the probability that a j-strategist interacts with an l-strategist is N_l/N if $l \neq j$ but $(N_j - 1)/N$ if $l = j$, the probabilities of interaction are defined by

$$\pi_{jl} = x_l - \alpha \delta_{jl}, \qquad 1 \leq j, l \leq m, \qquad (5.69)$$

where we define $\delta_{jl} = 0$ if $j \neq l$ but $\delta_{jj} = 1$; and, on using (5.26), we have

$$W_j = \sum_{k=1}^{\infty} w^{k-1} \left(\sum_{l=1}^{m} (x_l - \alpha \delta_{jl}) \phi_{jl}(k) \right), \qquad 1 \leq j \leq m. \qquad (5.70)$$

Further progress requires an explicit expression for the $m \times m$ matrix $\phi(k)$. Let us therefore choose $m = 4$ in (5.70) and define the strategies as in (5.53). Then, because *TFT* or *TF2T* always cooperate with one another, the payoff to *TFT* or *TF2T* against *TFT* or *TF2T* at interaction k is independent of k:

$$\phi_{11}(k) = \phi_{12}(k) = \phi_{21}(k) = \phi_{22}(k) = R, \qquad 1 \leq k < \infty. \qquad (5.71a)$$

Similarly, because *STFT* or *ALLD* always defect against one another, we have

$$\phi_{33}(k) = \phi_{34}(k) = \phi_{43}(k) = \phi_{44}(k) = P, \qquad 1 \leq k < \infty. \qquad (5.71b)$$

For all other values of j and l, however, $\phi_{jl}(k)$ depends on k.

Let σ_k denote the probability that an individual's opponent at encounter k has been encountered before, let γ_k denote the probability that the opponent has previously been encountered more than once, and let ϵ_k denote the probability that the opponent has previously been encountered an even number of times (hence $1 - \epsilon_k$ the probability that the opponent has been encountered an odd number of times). Then, because *TFT* cooperates with *STFT* on odd-numbered encounters (whereas the opponent defects) but defects against *STFT* on even-numbered encounters (when the opponent cooperates), we have

$$\phi_{13}(k) = \epsilon_k S + (1 - \epsilon_k)T, \qquad 1 \le k < \infty; \qquad (5.72a)$$

and similarly,

$$\phi_{31}(k) = \epsilon_k T + (1 - \epsilon_k)S, \qquad 1 \le k < \infty. \qquad (5.72b)$$

Because *TFT* cooperates with *ALLD* on a first encounter but thereafter defects, we have

$$\phi_{14}(k) = \sigma_k P + (1 - \sigma_k)S, \qquad 1 \le k < \infty; \qquad (5.72c)$$

and similarly,

$$\phi_{23}(k) = \sigma_k R + (1 - \sigma_k)S, \qquad 1 \le k < \infty; \qquad (5.72d)$$
$$\phi_{32}(k) = \sigma_k R + (1 - \sigma_k)T, \qquad 1 \le k < \infty; \qquad (5.72e)$$
$$\phi_{41}(k) = \sigma_k P + (1 - \sigma_k)T, \qquad 1 \le k < \infty. \qquad (5.72f)$$

Again, because *TF2T* cooperates against *ALLD* on a first or second encounter, but thereafter defects, we have

$$\phi_{24}(k) = \gamma_k P + (1 - \gamma_k)S, \qquad 1 \le k < \infty; \qquad (5.72g)$$

and similarly,

$$\phi_{42}(k) = \gamma_k P + (1 - \gamma_k)T, \qquad 1 \le k < \infty. \qquad (5.72h)$$

The matrix $\phi(k)$ has now been defined; and, from (5.68)–(5.72), we obtain the following expressions for $W_1, \dots, W_4$:

$$W_1 = \sum_{k=1}^{\infty} w^{k-1}\{(x_1 - \alpha + x_2)R + x_3(\epsilon_k S + (1 - \epsilon_k)T)$$
$$+ x_4(\sigma_k P + (1 - \sigma_k)S)\} \qquad (5.73a)$$

$$W_2 = \sum_{k=1}^{\infty} w^{k-1}\{(x_1 + x_2 - \alpha)R + x_3(\sigma_k R + (1 - \sigma_k)S)$$
$$+ x_4(\gamma_k P + (1 - \gamma_k)S)\} \qquad (5.73b)$$

$$W_3 = \sum_{k=1}^{\infty} w^{k-1}\{x_1(\epsilon_k T + (1 - \epsilon_k)S) + x_2(\sigma_k R + (1 - \sigma_k)T)$$
$$+ (x_3 - \alpha + x_4)P\} \qquad (5.73c)$$

$$W_4 = \sum_{k=1}^{\infty} w^{k-1}\{x_1(\sigma_k P + (1 - \sigma_k)T) + x_2(\gamma_k P + (1 - \gamma_k)T)$$
$$+ (x_3 + x_4 - \alpha)P\}. \qquad (5.73d)$$

If players interact with the same opponent throughout the game then, clearly,

$$\sigma_1 = 0; \quad \sigma_k = 1, \quad k \geq 2$$
$$\gamma_1 = 0, \quad \gamma_2 = 0; \quad \gamma_k = 1, \quad k \geq 3 \tag{5.74}$$
$$\epsilon_k = \frac{1}{2}\left(1 - (-1)^k\right), \quad k \geq 1.$$

We shall say in this case that the interaction is *static*. In the case of static interaction, explicit expressions for $W_1, \ldots, W_4$ follow readily from (5.72)–(5.74). On using (5.32) and the related formula

$$\sum_{k=1}^{\infty} k\beta^{k-1} = \frac{1}{(1-\beta)^2}, \quad 0 \leq \beta < 1, \tag{5.75}$$

for summing the derivative of the geometric series, we obtain (Exercise 5.11):

$$W_1 = \mu(x_1 + x_2 - \alpha)R + \frac{\mu x_3(S + Tw)}{1 + w} + x_4(S + \mu wP) \tag{5.76a}$$

$$W_2 = \mu(x_1 + x_2 - \alpha)R + x_3(S + \mu wR) + x_4(S(1 + w) + \mu w^2 P) \tag{5.76b}$$

$$W_3 = \frac{\mu x_1(T + Sw)}{1 + w} + x_2(T + \mu wR) + \mu(x_3 + x_4 - \alpha)P \tag{5.76c}$$

$$W_4 = x_1(T + \mu Pw) + x_2(T(1 + w) + \mu w^2 P) + \mu(x_3 + x_4 - \alpha)P, \tag{5.76d}$$

where μ is defined by (5.25). Note that the difference in payoffs between the two nice strategies, *TFT* and *TF2T*, is

$$W_1 - W_2 = \frac{\mu x_3 w(T - R - w(R - S))}{1 + w} + x_4 w(P - S), \tag{5.77}$$

which vanishes if $x_3 = 0 = x_4$. Because the coefficient of x_4 is positive when $x_4 \neq 0$, *TFT* always does better than *TF2T* against *ALLD*; similarly, *TF2T* does better than *TFT* against *STFT* when $w > (T - R)/(R - S)$, because the coefficient of x_3 is then negative.

If, on the other hand, opponents are drawn at random throughout the game, then we shall say that the interaction is *dynamic*. Because $\alpha = 1/N$ is the probability per interaction of meeting any specific opponent, the probability that the opponent at interaction k has not been encountered during the previous $k - 1$ interactions is

$$\sigma_k = 1 - (1 - \alpha)^{k-1}, \quad k \geq 1. \tag{5.78a}$$

Similarly, the probability that the opponent has been encountered precisely once, during the previous $k - 1$ interactions, is $(k - 1)\alpha(1 - \alpha)^{k-1}$; whence

$$\gamma_k = 1 - (1 - \alpha)^{k-1} - (k - 1)\alpha(1 - \alpha)^{k-1}. \tag{5.78b}$$

Because zero is an even number, $\epsilon_1 = 1$. Moreover, the number of previous encounters with an opponent is even at interaction k if either it was even at interaction $k-1$ and the opponent was then different, or it was odd at interaction $k - 1$ and the opponent was then the same. Thus

$$\epsilon_1 = 1$$
$$\epsilon_k = (1 - \alpha)\epsilon_{k-1} + \alpha(1 - \epsilon_{k-1}), \qquad k \geq 2.$$

The solution of this difference equation (Exercise 5.11) is

$$\epsilon_k = \frac{1}{2}\left(1 + (1 - 2\alpha)^{k-1}\right), \qquad k \geq 1. \tag{5.78c}$$

Explicit expressions for $W_1, \ldots, W_4$ follow readily from (5.72), (5.73) and (5.78). On using (5.32) and (5.75), we obtain

$$W_1 = \mu R(x_1 + x_2 - \alpha) + \frac{x_3}{2}\left(\mu(S + T)\right.$$
$$\left. + \lambda_2(S - T)\right) + x_4\left(\mu P + \lambda_1(S - P)\right) \tag{5.79a}$$

$$W_2 = \mu R(1 - x_4) + \lambda_1 x_3(S - R) + x_4\left(\mu P - \frac{\lambda_1^2(P - S)}{\lambda_2}\right) \tag{5.79b}$$

$$W_3 = \frac{x_1}{2}\left(\mu(S + T) + \lambda_2(T - S)\right)$$
$$+ x_2\left(\mu R + \lambda_1(T - R)\right) + \mu(x_3 + x_4 - \alpha)P \tag{5.79c}$$

$$W_4 = x_1\left(\mu P + \lambda_1(T - P)\right)$$
$$+ x_2\left(\mu P + \frac{\lambda_1^2(T - P)}{\lambda_2}\right) + \mu(x_3 + x_4 - \alpha)P, \tag{5.79d}$$

where we have defined

$$\lambda_1 = \frac{1}{1 - w + \alpha w}, \qquad \lambda_2 = \frac{1}{1 - w + 2\alpha w} \tag{5.80}$$

(so that $\mu > \lambda_1 > \lambda_2$). Note that if either (2.60) or (2.65) with $m = 4$ is used for long-term dynamics, then either (2.58) or (2.63) must be replaced by (5.79) under dynamic interaction (and by (5.73) under static interaction).

We will apply this model in the following two sections. First, however, you should attempt Exercise 5.12.

5.7   STABILITY OF A NICE POPULATION
UNDER STATIC INTERACTION

In this section, we consider the stability of a nice population under static interaction. Given our remarks at the end of Section 5.5, our goal will be to seek necessary conditions for population stability; and if a strategy is to be stable against all possible deviation, then it must at least be stable against pure infiltration by a single nasty player.

We begin by considering the stability of *TFT* against *ALLD*. Thus $N_2 = N_3 = 0$ (hence $x_2 = 0 = x_3$), and (5.76) implies

$$\begin{aligned} W_1 &= \mu(x_1 - \alpha)R + x_4(S + \mu wP), \\ W_4 &= x_1(T + \mu wP) + \mu(x_4 - \alpha)P. \end{aligned} \tag{5.81}$$

For a *TFT* population to be stable against pure infiltration by *ALLD*, it must at least be true that W_1 exceeds W_4 when $N_1 = N$ and $N_4 = 1$. Accordingly, we set $x_1 = 1$ and $x_4 = \alpha$ in (5.81) to obtain

$$W_1 - W_4 = \mu(R - P) - (T - P) - \alpha\{\mu(R - P) + P - S\}. \tag{5.82}$$

Straightforward algebraic manipulation now shows that this expression is positive when

$$R - P + (1 - w)(P - S) + N\{T - R - w(T - P)\} < 0, \tag{5.83}$$

which requires both

$$w > \frac{T - R}{T - P} \tag{5.84}$$

(for a negative coefficient of N in (5.83)) and

$$N > \frac{R - P + (1 - w)(P - S)}{w(T - P) - (T - R)}. \tag{5.85}$$

Next we consider the stability of *TFT* against *STFT*. Now $N_2 = 0 = N_4$ (hence $x_2 = 0 = x_4$), and (5.76) implies that

$$\begin{aligned} W_1 &= \mu(x_1 - \alpha)R + \lambda_0\mu x_3(S + wT) \\ W_3 &= \lambda_0\mu x_1(T + wS) + \mu(x_3 - \alpha)P, \end{aligned} \tag{5.86}$$

where

$$\lambda_0 = \frac{1}{1 + w}. \tag{5.87}$$

It follows from (5.86) that

$$W_1 - W_3 = \mu\{R + \alpha P - \lambda_0(1 + \alpha)(T + wS) + (S + T - P - R)x_3\}. \tag{5.88}$$

For a *TFT* population to be stable against pure infiltration by *STFT*, it must at least be true that W_1 exceeds W_3 when $N_1 = N$ and $N_3 = 1$. Accordingly, we set $x_1 = 1$ and $x_3 = \alpha$ in (5.88). Then

$$W_1 - W_3 = \lambda_0\mu\{w(R - S) - (T - R) - \alpha((1 - w)(T - R) + 2R - S - T)\} \tag{5.89}$$

is positive when both

$$w > \frac{T - R}{R - S} \tag{5.90}$$

and

$$N > \frac{(1 - w)(T - R) + 2R - S - T}{w(R - S) - (T - R)}. \tag{5.91}$$

For sufficiently large N, (5.84), (5.85), (5.90) and (5.91) reduce to (5.35). Thus the analysis of Section 5.4 corresponds to static interaction in a large population.

A similar analysis can be applied to the other nice strategy, $TF2T$. For $TF2T$ to be stable against pure infiltration by $ALLD$, we require (Exercise 5.14)

$$w > \sqrt{\frac{T - R}{T - P}} \tag{5.92a}$$

and

$$N > \frac{R - P + (1 - w^2)(P - S)}{w^2(T - P) - (T - R)}, \tag{5.92b}$$

which agrees with (5.40) when N is sufficiently large. But no value of w is large enough to make $TF2T$ stable against $STFT$. To see this, we set $x_1 = 0 = x_4$ in (5.76), obtaining

$$\begin{aligned} W_2 &= \mu(x_2 - \alpha)R + x_3(S + \mu wR) \\ W_3 &= x_2(T + \mu wR) + \mu(x_3 - \alpha)P. \end{aligned} \tag{5.93}$$

For $x_2 = 1$ and $x_3 = \alpha$, (5.93) implies

$$W_2 - W_3 = R - T - \alpha(R - S), \tag{5.94}$$

which is always negative. Thus the frequency of $STFT$ will always increase; $TF2T$ is too nice a strategy to resist invasion. On the other hand, $TF2T$ need not be eliminated. For $x_2 = \alpha$ and $x_3 = 1$, (5.93) implies

$$W_2 - W_3 = \mu(R - P) - (R - S) - \alpha\{T - R + \mu(R - P)\}, \tag{5.95}$$

which is positive if

$$w > \frac{P - S}{R - S} \tag{5.96}$$

and

$$N > \frac{(1 - w)(T - R) + R - P}{w(R - S) - (P - S)}. \tag{5.97}$$

Assuming that (5.96) and (5.97) are both satisfied, let us define

$$x_{es} = \frac{\{w(R - S) - (P - S)\}N - (1 - w)(R - S)}{\{(1 - w)(T - R) + w(R - S) - (P - S)\}N}. \tag{5.98}$$

Then, because $x_2 + x_3 = 1 + \alpha$, we find that $W_2 - W_3$ is negative if $x_2 > x_{es}$ but positive if $x_2 < x_{es}$, so that the population will reach equilibrium at a mixture of *TF2T* and *STFT* in which the proportion of *TF2T* is $x_{es}/(1 + \alpha)$. In the limit as $N \to \infty$, of course, (5.98) tends to the equilibrium frequency (5.52).

If $R - S > T - P$, then there is a range of values of w, specifically, $(T - R)/(T - P) < w < \sqrt{(T - R)/(T - P)}$, for which *TFT* is stable against pure infiltration by *STFT* or *ALLD*, whereas *TF2T* is not. Of course, $T - P$ may exceed $R - S$; but if also $2(R - S)^2 > (T - R)(T + R - S - P)$, then there is still a range, $(T - R)/(R - S) < w < \sqrt{2(T - R)/(T + R - S - P)}$, for which *TFT* is stable against pure infiltration, whereas *TF2T* is not. These conditions are satisfied, for example, by Axelrod's prototype.

Of course, we more or less knew all this in Section 5.5, and it could be argued that our finite-N analysis has done little more than recover the results of that section. Things are very different, however, when opponents are drawn at random throughout the game—or, as we have chosen to say, when the interaction is dynamic.

5.8   STABILITY OF A NICE POPULATION UNDER DYNAMIC INTERACTION

We now consider the stability of a nice population under dynamic interaction. Some mathematical preliminaries will facilitate analysis, both here and in Exercises 5.19–5.20. Accordingly, let us define quadratic polynomials ϕ_1, ϕ_2, ϕ_3 (which have nothing to do with the matrix ϕ in Section 5.6) and $\Delta_1, \Delta_2, \Delta_3$ by

$$\phi_j(N) = (1 - w)(T - R)N^2$$
$$+(R - S - wa_j)N + w(a_j - R + S), \qquad j = 1, 2, 3, \qquad (5.99)$$

$$\Delta_j(w) = (R - S - wa_j)^2$$
$$-4w(1 - w)(T - R)(a_j - R + S), \qquad j = 1, 2, 3, \qquad (5.100)$$

where

$$a_1 = 2R - P - S, \quad a_2 = 3R - 2S - T, \quad a_3 = \frac{5R - 3S - T - P}{2}, \quad (5.101)$$

so that (5.2) implies

$$a_j > R - S, \qquad j = 1, 2, 3. \qquad (5.102)$$

Then because

$$\Delta_j(0) > 0, \qquad \Delta_j((R - S)/a_j) < 0, \qquad \Delta(1) > 0,$$

the smaller root of the quadratic equation $\Delta_j(w) = 0$ satisfies $0 < w < (R - S)/a_j$, and the larger root satisfies $(R - S)/a_j < w < 1$. Let ξ_j denote the larger root; i.e., define

$$\xi_j = \frac{2(a_j - R + S)\sqrt{(T-R)(T-S)} + a_j(R-S) + 2(T-R)(a_j - R + S)}{a_j^2 + 4(T-R)(a_j - R + S)},$$

$$j = 1, 2, 3. \tag{5.103}$$

Then, whenever $\xi_j < w < 1$, we have $\Delta_j(w) > 0$; and so the equation $\phi_j(N) = 0$ has two real roots, both of which are positive by (5.102). Let the greater of these roots be denoted by $N_j(w)$. Then, for $j = 1, 2, 3$, we have established that $\phi_j(N) < 0$ if

$$\xi_j < w < 1 \tag{5.104}$$

and

$$\frac{w(a_j - R + S)}{(1 - w)(T - R)N_j(w)} < N < N_j(w), \tag{5.105}$$

where

$$N_j(w) = \frac{wa_j - R + S + \sqrt{\Delta_j(w)}}{2(1 - w)(T - R)}, \qquad j = 1, 2, 3, \tag{5.106}$$

is the larger root of $\phi_j(N) = 0$. (The lower bound in (5.105) is the smaller root.) After these preliminaries we can now proceed.

First, we consider the stability of *TFT* against pure infiltration by *ALLD*. Thus $N_2 = 0 = N_3$, and (5.79) implies

$$W_1 = \mu(x_1 - \alpha)R + x_4(\mu P - \lambda_1(P - S))$$
$$W_4 = x_1\{\mu P + \lambda_1(T - P)\} + \mu(x_4 - \alpha)P. \tag{5.107}$$

Proceeding as in Section 3, we require for stability that $W_1 > W_4$ when $N_1 = N$ and $N_4 = 1$. On setting $x_1 = 1$ and $x_4 = \alpha$ in (5.107), this condition reduces (Exercise 5.16) to

$$\phi_1(N) < 0. \tag{5.108}$$

Thus necessary conditions for the stability of *TFT* are

$$w > \xi_1 \tag{5.109a}$$

$$\frac{w(R - P)}{(1 - w)(T - R)N_1(w)} < N < N_1(w), \tag{5.109b}$$

where ξ_1 is defined by (5.103) and N_1 by (5.106). For example, in Axelrod's prototype we have $\xi_1 = 0.869$ and $N_1(w) = 285.5$; the lower bound on N in (5.109b) is then $N > 1.009$, and satisfied if only $N \geq 2$. Thus a necessary condition is $N + 1 \leq 3 \leq 286$.

Generally, the lower bound in (5.105) is trivially satisfied by $N \geq 2$ unless w is very close to ξ_j; in which case, the range of values admitted by (5.105) is too small to be of interest. For example, with Axelrod's payoffs (5.3) but $w = 0.87$, (5.109b) requires $2.38 < N < 2.81$, which is not satisfied by any integer value of N. Thus our interest lies principally in the upper bound, N_j.

Next we consider the stability of *TFT* against pure infiltration by *STFT*. Thus $x_2 = 0 = x_4$, and (5.79) implies

$$W_1 = \mu R(x_1 - \alpha) + \frac{1}{2}x_3\{\mu(T + S) - \lambda_2(T - S)\}$$

$$W_3 = \frac{1}{2}x_1\{\mu(T + S) + \lambda_2(T - S)\} + \mu(x_3 - \alpha)P. \tag{5.110}$$

We require for stability that $W_1 > W_3$ when $N_1 = N$ and $N_3 = 1$; in other words, that

$$W_1 - W_3 = \mu\{R + \alpha P - (1 + \alpha)(T - \lambda_2\alpha w(T - S)) + x_3(S + T - P - R)\} \tag{5.111}$$

is positive when $x_1 = 1$ and $x_3 = \alpha$. The resulting necessary condition is found (Exercise 5.16) to be

$$\phi_2(N) < 0. \tag{5.112}$$

Thus *TFT* is stable against pure infiltration by *STFT* if

$$\frac{w(2R - S - T)}{(1 - w)(T - R)N_2(w)} < N < N_2(w), \tag{5.113}$$

where ξ_2 is defined by (5.103) and N_2 by (5.106). For example, in Axelrod's prototype we have $\xi_2 = 0.930$ and $N_2(w) = 141.5$. The lower bound on N in (5.113b) is then $N > 1.018$, and so resistance to *STFT* requires $N + 1 \leq 3 \leq 142$.

A similar analysis applies to the other nice strategy, *TF2T*. In a population of *TF2T* and *ALLD*, we have $N_1 = 0 = N_3$ and

$$W_2 = \mu(x_2 - \alpha)R + x_4\left\{\mu P - \frac{\lambda_1^2(P - S)}{\lambda_2}\right\}$$

$$W_4 = x_2\left\{\mu P + \frac{\lambda_1^2(T - P)}{\lambda_2}\right\} + \mu(x_4 - \alpha)P. \tag{5.114}$$

For stability, we require $W_2 > W_4$ when $x_2 = 1$ and $x_4 = \alpha$ or

$$(1 - w)^2(T - R)N^3 + (1 - w)\{2(T - R)w + (1 - w)(R - S)\}N^2$$
$$+ w\{2(1 - w)(R - S) - w(R - P)\}N + w^2(R - P) < 0, \tag{5.115}$$

which requires in particular that $w > 2(R - S)/\{3R - 2S - P\}$, because the coefficient of N in (5.115) must be negative. As we would expect, (5.115) is more difficult to satisfy than (5.108); for example, in Axelrod's prototype it requires $3 \le N + 1 \le 16$.

If *TF2T* is still the orthodox strategy but *STFT* the deviant strategy, so that $N_1 = 0 = N_4$, then (5.79) implies

$$W_2 = \mu R - \lambda_1 x_3 (R - S)$$
$$W_3 = x_2 \{\mu R + \lambda_1 (T - R)\} + \mu (x_3 - \alpha) P; \tag{5.116}$$

and $x_2 = 1, x_3 = \alpha$ yields

$$W_2 - W_3 = -\lambda_1 \{T - R + \alpha(R - S)\}, \tag{5.117}$$

which is negative. Thus *STFT* increases in number: regardless of whether interaction is static or dynamic, *TF2T* is too nice a strategy to resist invasion by *STFT*. On the other hand, *TF2T* need not be eliminated. For $x_2 = \alpha$ and $x_3 = 1$, (5.116) implies

$$W_2 - W_3 = \lambda_0(R - P) - \lambda_1(R - S) - \alpha\{\lambda_0(R - P) + \lambda_1(T - R)\}, \tag{5.118}$$

which is positive if $\psi(N)$ defined by

$$\psi(N) = (1 - w)(P - S)N^2 + \{T - P - w(T + R - 2P)\}N + w(R - P) \tag{5.119}$$

is negative (requiring in particular that $w > (T - P)/(T + R - 2P)$). Routine manipulations (Exercise 5.17) now establish that $\psi(N) < 0$ whenever

$$w > \xi_4 \quad \text{and} \quad \frac{w(R - P)}{(1 - w)(P - S)N_4(w)} < N < N_4(w), \tag{5.120}$$

where

$$\xi_4 = \frac{(T - P)(T + R - 2P) + 2(R - P)(P - S) + 2(R - P)\sqrt{(P - S)(T - S)}}{(T + R - 2P)^2 + 4(P - S)(R - P)} \tag{5.121}$$

satisfies $(T - P)/(T + R - 2P) < \xi_4 < 1$ and $N_4(w)$ is the larger root of $\psi(N) = 0$ (whose existence is guaranteed by $w > \xi_4$). Assuming that (5.120) is satisfied—in Axelrod's prototype, for example, this requires $3 \le N + 1 \le 571$—let us define

$$x_{ed} = \frac{w(2R - P - S) - R + S - N(1 - w)(P - S)}{w(R - P) + N(1 - w)(S + T - P - R)}. \tag{5.122}$$

Then, because $x_2 + x_3 = 1 + \alpha$, we find that $W_2 - W_3$ is negative if $x_2 > x_{ed}$ but positive if $x_2 < x_{ed}$, so that the population will reach equilibrium at a mixture of *TF2T* and *STFT* (in which the proportion of *TF2T* is $x_{ed}/(1 + \alpha)$).

Three conclusions can be drawn from this analysis. First, we have shown that *TFT* cannot be stable under dynamic interaction unless

$$w > \max(\xi_1, \xi_2) \tag{5.123a}$$

and

$$N < \min\{N_1(w), N_2(w)\}, \tag{5.123b}$$

where ξ_1, ξ_2 and N_1, N_2 are defined by (5.103) and 5.106). But routine algebra (Exercise 5.18) shows that (5.2) implies $\xi_1 > (T - R)/(T - P)$ and $\xi_2 > (T - R)/(R - S)$. Thus (5.123) requires a higher discount parameter than (5.35): the probability of further encounters must be higher under dynamic interaction than under static interaction for *TFT* to be a stable orthodox strategy. Second, we see that (5.108), (5.112) and (5.115) are all false as $N \rightarrow \infty$. Thus, when interaction is dynamic, reciprocity cannot maintain cooperation if the population is too large, essentially because nasty strategies can then profit from too many first encounters and too few second or higher encounters—in other words, too few opportunities for punishment. And third, *TF2T* is again too forgiving to be a stable orthodox strategy, although it can coexist with *STFT* if the population is small enough.

Finally, we note if $S = 0$ and $T = P + R$ (as in Section 5.2), then $\xi_1 = \xi_2$, $N_1 = N_2$ and (5.123) simplifies considerably; see Exercise 5.23. Then try Exercise 5.21.

5.9   COOPERATION AGAINST A COMMON ENEMY

We have seen that it is possible to *sustain* cooperation via reciprocity in the iterated prisoner's dilemma—provided, of course, that a player's probability of further interaction is high enough. But how is cooperation *initiated*? Recall that in the simplest *IPD* we considered, namely, the game in which *ALLD* and *TFT* are the only strategies, both strategies are evolutionarily stable if $\mu > \mu_c$, where μ_c is defined by (5.22); and that *TFT* will become the orthodox strategy only if $x_2(0)$, the initial fraction of *TFT*-strategists in the game with matrix (5.21), exceeds the value γ defined by (5.23). But what if $x_2(0) < \gamma$? How is cooperation initiated then? One possibility is that sometimes the game with payoff matrix (5.1) is a prisoner's dilemma, and sometimes C is a dominant strategy, according to whether the environment in which the game is played is lenient or harsh. If so, then cooperation could be initiated by selfish behavior during a harsh phase, and sustained throughout a lenient phase by reciprocity. Then, as it were, the environment would play the role of a common enemy—which is surely the ultimate enforcer of cooperation. How many times have you heard it said that the only way ever to accomplish wholesale cooperation among humans would be to invite aliens from outer space to invade our planet?

To illustrate the effect of a common enemy, we turn to another kind of game—wild animals—for a further example of the prisoner's dilemma. Suppose that an army of rangers in jeeps is employed to protect an endangered species. These rangers patrol at random, and are advised to confront poachers—who are quite ruthless—only in pairs, the accepted custom being that any poacher is intercepted by the nearest two rangers. Let us suppose that a poacher has been spotted, and that the nearest two rangers have been identified (because, say, the rangers are all in radio contact). If one of these rangers confronts the poacher, then we shall say that the ranger selects strategy C, the cooperative strategy; whereas, if the ranger desists from confronting the poacher, then we shall say that she selects strategy D, the defector's strategy. The poacher, however, will not be granted the status of a player; rather, she is the rangers' common enemy. This does not mean that poachers have no strategic possibilities; but because our interest is the behavior of the rangers, we disregard the poachers' strategies (and instead incorporate their behavior into the parameters of our model, namely, ϵ, q and Q defined below).

There are two kinds of encounter between ranger and poacher, deliberate or accidental. The first arises when the ranger elects to confront the poacher; in which case, an encounter between ranger and poacher is certain. The second arises when the ranger desists from confrontation, but is nevertheless unlucky enough to find herself on the poacher's path; in which case, we suppose that an encounter between ranger and poacher occurs with probability $\epsilon(< 1)$, regardless of whether the other ranger cooperates or defects (think of a defector as stationary, and a cooperator or poacher as always moving). When a poacher encounters a ranger, let the probability that the poacher inflicts injury on the ranger be Q or q, according to whether the ranger is isolated or reinforced by her colleague; and assume that if a poacher encounters a defecting ranger accidentally, then the encounter will be isolated only if the other ranger is also defecting (because if she is cooperating, then her jeep will be right on the poacher's heels when the poacher meets the other ranger). Then, if the payoff to a ranger is the probability of avoiding injury, the interaction between rangers has payoff matrix

$$A = \begin{bmatrix} R & S \\ T & P \end{bmatrix} = \begin{bmatrix} 1-q & 1-Q \\ 1-\epsilon q & 1-\epsilon Q \end{bmatrix}; \tag{5.124}$$

and it is straightforward to show (Exercise 5.22) that the game with this matrix is a prisoner's dilemma whenever

$$q < \epsilon Q \tag{5.125}$$

(implying in particular that $Q > q$). Note that if there are $N + 1$ rangers, then the iterated game is an example of the *IPD* we analyzed in the previous section. Note also that (5.124)–(5.125) imply $P + R > S + T$, so that (5.36) is violated.

Now, in constructing our payoff matrix, we have assumed that the only difference between cooperating and defecting lies in the probability of accidental discovery by a poacher—the rows of (5.124) would be identical if ϵ were equal to 1. We are therefore assuming that, conditional upon an encounter, a lone ranger who attacks a poacher has no advantage over a lone ranger who is suprised by a poacher on the run. If there is any truth at all to the old adage that

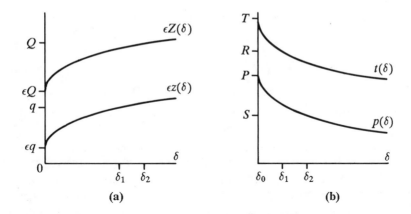

Figure 5.5   Variation with δ of defector's payoffs in games against a common enemy.

attack is the best form of defence, then this assumption is false; rather, if the probability of injury while confronting alone is Q, then the probability of injury while defecting alone should be, not Q, but Z, where $Z > Q$. Similarly, if the probability of injury while confronting in pairs is q, then the probability of injury to a defector whose opponent is cooperating should be, not q, but z, where $z > q$—partly because the defector does not have the advantage of attack, but also because the cooperator may not be so hot on the heels of the poacher as to guarantee effective reinforcement (especially if she is mad at her colleague for defecting). We also expect $Z > z$. To allow (5.124) as a special case of the analysis that follows, however, we will weaken the inequalities $Z > Q, z > q$ to $Z \geq Q, z \geq q$. Furthermore, we will assume that poachers are becoming more and more ruthless as time goes by in inflicting injuries on rangers they surprise, so that, if $\delta \geq 0$ is a measure of ruthlessness, then z and Z are increasing functions of δ. Let $\delta = 0$ correspond to (5.124). Then the payoff matrix for the game at ruthlessness δ becomes

$$A(\delta) = \begin{bmatrix} R & S \\ T(\delta) & P(\delta) \end{bmatrix} = \begin{bmatrix} 1-q & 1-Q \\ 1-\epsilon z(\delta) & 1-\epsilon Z(\delta) \end{bmatrix}, \qquad (5.126)$$

where

$$z(0) = q, \qquad Z(0) = Q \qquad (5.127)$$

and

$$z(\delta) < Z(\delta), \quad z'(\delta) > 0, \quad Z'(\delta) > 0, \quad 0 < \delta < \infty. \qquad (5.128)$$

Clearly, confrontation is the only rational strategy if poachers are infinitely ruthless against defectors. Therefore C must be dominant as $\delta \rightarrow \infty$ or

$$\epsilon z(\infty) > q, \qquad \epsilon Z(\infty) > Q. \tag{5.129}$$

Together, (5.127)–(5.129) imply the existence of unique δ_1 and δ_2 such that

$$\epsilon z(\delta_1) = q, \qquad \epsilon Z(\delta_2) = Q. \tag{5.130}$$

It need not be true that $\delta_1 < \delta_2$. Nevertheless, we shall assume this; see Figure 5.5(a).

It is clear from inspection of (5.124) that the rangers' game at ruthlessness δ is a prisoner's dilemma only if $0 \le \delta < \delta_1$. For $\delta_1 < \delta < \delta_2$, we have $R > T(\delta)$ and $S < P(\delta)$, so that both C and D are evolutionarily stable, and the final composition of the ranger population is determined by the initial fraction of cooperators; if most of the rangers are cooperating initially, then all will be cooperating eventually, and vice versa. For $\delta_2 < \delta < \infty$, however, we have $R > T(\delta)$ and $S > P(\delta)$, so that C is a dominant strategy; what is best for the group is then also best for the individual. In summary, if the poachers are sufficiently ruthless (but not infinitely ruthless) then cooperation is the only rational strategy; whereas if the poachers are not ruthless enough, then the rangers remain locked in a prisoner's dilemma.

If we think of the poachers as a harsh environment for the rangers, then what we have shown is that cooperation can emerge under adverse conditions purely as a response to changes in environmental parameters, and without any need for reciprocity. More generally, we can conceive of games with payoff matrix

$$A(\delta) = \begin{bmatrix} R & S \\ t(\delta) & p(\delta) \end{bmatrix} \tag{5.131a}$$

satisfying

$$t(\delta_0) = T > R > \frac{S+T}{2}, \quad p(\delta_0) = P > S, \quad R > S, \tag{5.131b}$$

$$R > p(\delta), \qquad t(\delta) > p(\delta), \qquad p'(\delta) < 0,$$
$$t'(\delta) < 0, \qquad 0 \le \delta_0 < \delta < \infty \tag{5.131c}$$

and

$$t(\infty) < R, \qquad p(\infty) < S, \tag{5.131d}$$

so that there exist unique δ_1 and δ_2 satisfying

$$t(\delta_1) = R, \qquad p(\delta_2) = S; \tag{5.131e}$$

Figure 5.5b is drawn for the case where $\delta_1 < \delta_2$. Here δ is a parameter that measures adversity; and δ_0 is a base value, at which adversity is so slight that the players are still locked in a prisoner's dilemma. Obviously, the ranger game is a special case of (5.131), in which $R = 1 - q$, $S = 1 - Q$, $t(\delta) = 1 - \epsilon z(\delta)$,

$p(\delta) = 1 - \epsilon Z(\delta)$ and $\delta_0 = 0$; but other such games can be constructed. Indeed it can be shown that if the interaction between insects in Section 5.3 is extended to n periods, and if the insects are unable to recognize their eggs, and if half the number of sites exceeds the probability per period of finding a site times the average number of periods an insect survives on the patch—a perfectly natural assumption if we wish sites to be abundant when the insects start to forage—then the foraging game in the limit as $n \to \infty$ is essentially an example of (5.131), with δ equal to the ratio of survival probabilities defined by (5.5) and

$$\frac{5}{2} = \delta_0 < \delta_1 < \delta_2 < \frac{11}{4}; \tag{5.132}$$

see Mesterton-Gibbons (1991, Section 3) for details. What this means is that a very modest increase in environmental adversity—here a decrease in the ratio of the survival probability of a paired egg to that of a solitary egg from $2/5 = 0.4$ to $4/11 = 0.36$—can be all it takes to convert a game in which only defection is individually rational ($\delta < \delta_1$) to a game in which only cooperation is individually rational ($\delta > \delta_2$).

5.10   COMMENTARY

In Chapter 5, we have defined the prisoner's dilemma and produced three new examples; namely, Section 5.2's laboratory game, Section 5.3's foraging game, and the ranger game of Section 5.9. In Sections 5.4 and 5.5, we defined the iterated prisoner's dilemma; we analyzed it as a game restricted to pure strategies, and we showed how the reciprocative strategy *TFT* could maintain cooperation. In Section 5.6, we constructed a model of the *IPD* in a finite population; and in the next two sections we used this model to develop necessary conditions for *TFT* to be stable under both static (Section 5.7) and dynamic (Section 5.8) modes of interaction. Finally, in Section 5.9, we demonstrated that cooperation can emerge, without reciprocity, as an individually rational response to environmental adversity.

Although the experiment of Section 5.2—which has not yet been performed, but appears attractive in the extent to which laboratory animals can be made aware of their dilemma—was designed with small mammals in mind, it is readily adapted to other animals, because it reduces in essence to a choice for each animal of giving either P to itself or $R(> P)$ to the other. Indeed equivalent experiments have been performed with human subjects by Evans and Crumbaugh (1966) and Pruitt (1967), who replaced the payoffs P and R by sums of money. Other experiments with human subjects have instead used the matrix (5.1); Rapoport and Chammah (1965) took $S + T = 0$, and other experiments are cited in the reviews by Trivers (1971) and Colman (1982, Chapter 7). By and large, these experiments underscore the difficulties of achieving mutual cooperation (even when the prisoner's dilemma is iterated). Sustained mutual defection was a characteristic outcome; moreover, even when subjects did cooperate, it was impossible to confirm or deny reciprocity—*ALLC* versus *ALLC*, *TFT* versus *TFT*, and *TFT* versus *ALLC* all generate the same cooperative outcome in a repeated binary interaction.

Prisoner's-dilemma experiments with humans date from the fifties and sixties (although they continue to be performed—witness Friedland (1990)). By comparison, experiments with other animals began quite recently. An experiment with rats was performed by Flood *et al.* (1983), who replaced P and R in Section 5.2 by delays to reinforcement (by food); and an experiment with starlings has been performed by Dr. J. C. Reboreda (private communication). Both experiments have reaffirmed the difficulties of achieving cooperation. Evidence of reciprocity has been found by Milinski (1987) in an experiment with sticklebacks and by Dugatkin (1988) in an experiment with guppies, but their results are controversial; see Lazarus and Metcalfe (1990), Masters and Waite (1990), Milinski (1990a, b) and Reboreda and Kacelnik (1990). We should emphasize, moreover, that these experiments mimic circumstances in which cooperation has been observed in the wild, having evolved by natural selection; assuming cooperation, the experiment asks *how* cooperation is maintained. By contrast, the experiment suggested in Section 5.2 asks *whether* there is cooperation (but if so, then it also asks how). In the first case, cooperation is—as it were—learned by natural selection; in the second case, cooperation—if it arises—is learned by the organism's own (as opposed to its ancestors') experience. For a discussion of learning rules in the context of evolutionary stability, see Harley (1987) and references therein; see also Maynard Smith (1982, Chapter 5). For a more general discussion of models of learning, see Kacelnik and Krebs (1985), Mangel (1990b), and references therein.

Recommended literature on the evolution of cooperation and the prisoner's dilemma includes Axelrod and Hamilton (1981), Axelrod (1984), Becker (1986), Dawkins (1989, Chapters 10 and 12), May (1981, 1987), Maynard Smith (1982, Chapter 13) and Trivers (1971 and 1985, Chapter 15). Literature published prior to 1988 is cited by Axelrod and Dion (1988), and typically involves games restricted to pure strategies; see, for example, Feldman and Thomas (1987), who consider an *IPD* in which different players have different probabilities of further interaction. More recent work on the prisoner's dilemma typically considers mixed strategies, which we in this chapter have not discussed; see, for example, Borštnik *et al.* (1990), Nowak and Sigmund (1989, 1990) and Nowak (1990). Nevertheless, our neglect of mixed strategies in Sections 5.6–5.8 is to some extent bolstered by Vickery's (1987, 1988) contention that only pure strategies can be evolutionarily stable in a finite population.

In our analysis of the effects of dynamic interaction on the *IPD* in a finite population, we assumed throughout that interactions were binary; but it is possible instead to assume that each interaction is between one individual and the remainder of the population. The rationality of cooperation has been studied in this context by Schelling (1978) and Boyd and Richerson (1988). Boyd and Richerson's principal conclusion, that conditions allowing the evolution of reciprocal cooperation become extremely restrictive as group size increases, parallels our finding in Section 5.8 that *TFT* is stable only if the population does not exceed a certain critical size. For a more recent example of this approach, see Dugatkin (1990).

Inequality (5.36)—which ensures that, if *TFT* is stable against *STFT*, then also a single *TFT*-strategist can invade an *STFT* population—is rarely discussed, though Nowak (1990, p. 109) has described circumstances in which cooperation cannot be maintained if this inequality is violated (and if there is no probability that the game will end). Nevertheless, numerical illustrations are typically chosen to satisfy it; for example, with equality in Shubik (1970), Boyd (1989, p. 52) and Clark (1990, p. 154), and with strict inequality in Axelrod (1984) and Lima (1990). Whereas in Sections 5.4–5.8 we assumed that an *IPD* could last forever (though with vanishingly small probability), Lima considers the possibility that the *IPD* must terminate after a finite number of moves. He shows that selfish behavior on early moves can endanger one's opponent to such an extent that she may not survive until later moves—even to be defected against—and if the payoff from playing alone is even lower than the payoff from mutual defection, then mutual cooperation on earlier moves can be rational. There is no reciprocity here; rather, Lima's escape from the prisoner's dilemma resembles a game against a common enemy in which the common enemy is solitude.

Indeed one cannot escape from the prisoner's dilemma without somehow enriching the original game. In Sections 5.4–5.8 we iterated the game, making the duration of the iterated game a random variable; and in Section 5.9 we allowed payoffs to vary with an environmental parameter; whereas Lima (1989) introduced elements of both. By contrast, Robson (1990) enriches the game by enlarging the strategy set to let players signal one another, in a way that "seems to render the evolution of cooperation ultimately inevitable." We can tune most readily into Robson's wavelength by considering the following analogy. Let an *IPD* in an infinite population be restricted to three pure strategies, *NTFT*, *TF2T* and *STFT*, where *NTFT* (for no-nonsense *TFT*) plays *TFT* except against *TF2T*, when it plays *STFT*. We could imagine that hard-nosed *TFT*-strategists are so weary of soft-hearted *TF2T*-strategists, who weaken the stability of an otherwise excellent orthodox strategy, that they have learned to punish them for being so forgiving. It is not difficult to show that the payoff matrix for this *IPD* is (5.55) with $a_{12} = T + Rw\mu$ and $a_{21} = S + Rw\mu$ in place of $a_{12} = R\mu = a_{21}$, so that *NTFT* is the only *ESS*. But how could *NTFT* recognize its opponent as *TF2T*? How could *TF2T* (unintentionally) signal this information to *TFT*? More generally, if signals have a role to play in enforcing cooperation, then how do they work? Only explicit modelling of the dynamics of information transfer can answer such questions. Note, moreover, that transforming *TFT* into *NTFT* by means of a signal is merely a special case of transforming a collectively stable strategy into a uniquely best reply to itself by means of some enrichment of the game; for a further example, see Boyd (1989).

EXERCISES 5

5.1 Establish (5.17).

5.2 (i) Show that if there is constant probability w of further interaction in the iterated prisoner's dilemma, then the number of moves has distribution (5.24).

(ii) Verify (5.25).

5.3 Under the conditions of Section 5.4

(i) Show that $TF2T$ can be invaded by $STCO$, whereas TFT cannot be invaded by $STCO$ if (5.37) is satisfied.

(ii) Determine the final composition of the population when $STCO$ invades $TF2T$.

5.4 Verify (5.33) and (5.39).

5.5 Verify that H defined by (5.51) is a hyperbola, and that ϕ_3 is negative in the shaded region of Figure 5.3.

5.6 Verify (5.52).

5.7 Verify (5.54).

5.8 Verify (5.56)–(5.57) and that (5.35) implies $d > 0, d > b > a > c$.

5.9 Verify that $P + R > S + T$ implies (i) (5.61) and (ii)

$$\frac{P - S}{R - S} > \frac{P + R - S - T}{2R - S - T}.$$

5.10 A player who cooperates or defects with equal probability in the IPD is said to use strategy $RNDM$. Extend the IPD of Section 5.5 to five strategies, with $RNDM$ as strategy 5 (in other words, define the fifth row and column of the 5×5 move-k payoff matrix $\phi(k)$).

5.11 (i) Obtain (5.76).

(ii) Obtain (5.78c).

5.12 With regard to the iterated prisoner's dilemma, we showed in Section 5.4 that $TF2T$ does better than TFT against $STFT$ whenever $w > (T - P)/(R - S)$, assuming of course that no other strategies are present; see the remarks after (5.55). But $TF2T$'s first two payoffs against $STFT$ are S and R, whereas TFT's first two payoffs are S and T. Thus, because $S + wT > S + wR$, $TF2T$'s advantage over TFT (against $STFT$) does not emerge until the third encounter.

Under dynamic interaction, however, we would expect third encounters with the same individual to be rather infrequent. Does this mean that $TF2T$ loses this advantage over TFT when opponents are drawn at random throughout the game? Why or why not? *Hint*: use (5.79).

5.13 A player who cooperates or defects with equal probability in the IPD is said to use strategy $RNDM$. Show that, under static interaction, TFT is stable against $RNDM$

for sufficiently large N if (5.35) is satisfied.

5.14 Obtain (5.92).

5.15 A player who cooperates or defects with equal probability in the *IPD* is said to use strategy *RNDM*. Find necessary conditions for *TF2T* to be stable against infiltration by *RNDM* under static interaction.

5.16 Verify (5.108) and (5.112).

5.17 Verify that (5.120) implies $\psi(N) < 0$, where ψ is defined by (5.119).

5.18 Show that (5.2) implies $\xi_1 > (T - R)/(T - P)$ and $\xi_2 > (T - R)/(R - S)$, where ξ_1 and ξ_2 are defined by (5.103).

5.19 Let *TFT* be the orthodox strategy and *RNDM*, defined in Exercise 5.10, the only deviant strategy in an iterated prisoner's dilemma. With *RNDM* as strategy 5 (and $N_2 = N_3 = N_4 = 0$), find expressions for the expected payoffs W_1 and W_5 under dynamic interaction. Hence find conditions for *TFT* to be stable against *RNDM* when opponents are drawn at random.

5.20 Let *TF2T* (strategy 2) be the orthodox strategy and *RNDM*, defined in Exercise 5.10, the only deviant strategy in an iterated prisoner's dilemma. With *RNDM* as strategy 5 (and $N_1 = N_3 = N_4 = 0$), find expressions for the expected payoffs W_2 and W_5 under dynamic interaction. Hence find conditions for *TF2T* to be stable against *RNDM* when opponents are drawn at random.

5.21 The entire analysis of Section 5.8 is predicated on perfect recognition and recall; that is, we assume that players always recognize opponents they have met before, and always remember whether they cooperated or defected. Show that if recognition were absent, then dynamic interaction would make *TFT* unstable at all values of w and N, because *ALLD* would always invade.

5.22 Verify that, subject to (5.125), (5.124) satisfies (5.2).

5.23 How could Section 5.2's experiment be used to test the theory developed in Section 5.8? Discuss constraints on the parameters.

5.24 According to Pruitt (1967), a prisoner's dilemma is *decomposable* if choosing C can be made equivalent to keeping payoff σ_c for oneself and giving ω_c to the other player, and if choosing D can be made equivalent to keeping payoff σ_d for oneself and giving ω_d to the other player.

    (i)   Show that this requires $\sigma_c + \omega_d = S$, and find three other equations that $\sigma_c, \sigma_d, \omega_c$ and ω_d must satisfy.

    (ii)   What condition must T, R, P and S satisfy, if the prisoner's dilemma is decomposable?

    (iii)   If the game is decomposable, is its decomposition unique?

    (iv)   Is the laboratory game of Section 5.2 decomposable?

    (v)   Is the foraging game of Section 5.2 decomposable?

    (vi)   Is the ranger game of Section 5.9 decomposable?

5.25 **(i)**   A further example of a decomposable prisoner's dilemma is provided by Dawkins (1989, pp. 184–186), who considers a population of animals that are unable to remove parasites from certain parts of their bodies. In an encounter between two such animals, a cooperator grooms the other animal, thereby improving its ability to survive and reproduce; whereas a defector refuses to groom the other animal (but allows itself to be groomed by it). Let b be the benefit (in terms of reproductive success) of being groomed and c the cost (in the same units) of grooming another animal. Write down the payoff matrix for an interaction between two animals, together with a condition that makes it a prisoner's dilemma.

(ii)   Under dynamic interaction (Section 5.8), Dawkins considers an *IPD* with the following three (pure) strategies:

1. Grudger: Always groom a stranger, but never groom an animal that has defected against you (even once) in the past.

2. Cheat: Never groom anyone (but allow yourself to be groomed).

3. Sucker: Always groom anyone (regardless of previous behavior).

To which three strategies in Section 5.8 do Grudger, Cheat and Sucker correspond?

(iii) Obtain necessary conditions for Grudger to be uninvadable.

(iv)   Show that, provided these conditions are satisfied, Grudger will eliminate both Cheat and Sucker if

$$N_1 > \frac{N(1 - w)(Nc + b)}{w(b - c)} + 1$$

initially, where w is the probability of further interaction and there are N_1 Grudgers in a population of $N + 1$ animals. (Necessary conditions (iii) ensure that the right-hand side of this inequality does not exceed the population size.)

5.26   Consider the *IPD* in which *TFT* is subject to mixed infiltration by *ALLC* and *ALLD*. Show that *TFT*—though not an *ESS* of the game with matrix (5.20)— will nevertheless increase in frequency under static interaction if both (5.84) and (5.85) are satisfied, provided only that its initial frequency be sufficiently large. Repeat your analysis for dynamic interaction and obtain the corresponding result.

6

Appraisal

Our short introduction to game-theoretic modelling is almost over, but before concluding we pause to ask: How valuable are games? To answer this question we must first reflect on the purpose of mathematical models.

Crudely, we can classify models of natural or social phenomena as either *descriptive* or *prescriptive,* or as some combination of the two. A descriptive model is an attempt to say what things or animals *do* do, in the active sense of the verb. A celebrated example of a purely descriptive model is Newton's model of gravitation, which says that what planets do is to obey the inverse-square law

$$F = \frac{GMm}{r^2},\tag{6.1}$$

where G is the gravitational constant, M the mass of the sun, m the mass of a planet, r the distance between their centers of mass and F their mutual force of attraction. By contrast, a prescriptive model is an attempt to say what decision makers *should* do, in the modal sense of the verb. An example of a purely prescriptive model is the simple, "lot-size" inventory model, which says that if a dealer sells quantity Q of some product per year, and if he must pay a set-up cost c_1 to order a batch (of any size), and if he must pay storage cost c_2 per unit stock per year, and if demand for the product is uniform, and if he wishes to minimize costs, then he should order the product in batches of size

$$u^* = \sqrt{\frac{2c_1Q}{c_2}}, \tag{6.2}$$

because u^* is the value of u that minimizes the total annual cost,

$$c_1 \cdot \frac{Q}{u} + c_2 \cdot \frac{u}{2}. \tag{6.3}$$

Nevertheless, this model is purely prescriptive only because we have been careful to qualify its prediction by so many ifs. In particular, if we neglect the cost-minimization condition, then the model becomes at least partly descriptive—because if we still insist that the dealer should order u^*, then we tacitly assume that what dealers do is to minimize costs of ordering. More generally, whenever we use an optimization model to say what a decision maker should do, we tacitly assume at the very least that he is trying to maximize the thing we have called his reward; and often we assume much more. Thus every prescriptive model has at least some descriptive elements. The converse, however, is false—witness Newton's model of gravitation, which has no prescriptive elements.

Where do games lie on this spectrum of description and prescription? Insofar as games are optimization models, it appears that their purpose is prescriptive. Four Ways tells us how drivers should behave at a 4-way junction, Store Wars tells us how managers should set their prices, and so on. If we were to observe decision makers following the recommendations of these or any other models, then our immediate reply to the question—why do these people behave in this way?—would be: Because this is the behavior that optimizes their rewards. Now, humans and other animals have interacted strategically for many thousands of years. Over the course of time, they have evolved behavior to deal with such interactions; and it is reasonable to suppose that, by a process of trial and error, the behavior they exhibit *in familiar situations* is already the behavior that optimizes their rewards. If so, then there is no more prescribing for a model to do. But what if the observed behavior is exceedingly curious? Shouldn't we then wonder: Why is this behavior optimal? In other words: What game are the players playing? In such circumstances, the purpose of games is purely descriptive.

To take a concrete example, we saw in Section 2.8 that the spider *O. civitas* can behave most oddly when disturbed from its lair. A disturbed spider may enter the lair of another spider. But the homeowner, far from shooing the intruder out, will scurry off to bump another spider from its lair; and that spider will scurry off to bump yet another spider from its lair; and so on, often until most of the spiders in a colony have been displaced from their homes. But the spider *O. civitas* has frequented rocks for countless generations, and it must surely be familiar with getting disturbed; in which case, we would expect its strategy to be evolutionarily stable. But what is the game for which its strategy is an *ESS*? Concerning this question, in Sections 2.7–2.8 we built a model of owner-intruder interactions. We postulated a reward and a strategy set, and we found a parameter regime with a unique *ESS* that resembles the spider's observed behavior. Thus the model suggests an answer to our question; and because we assumed that spider behavior is optimal, our model is wholly descriptive.

A further illustration of the use of games as descriptive models emerges from Section 4.7. At the end of that Section we posed the question: Which is the fairer imputation in a *c*-game—the nucleolus or the Shapley value? One approach to answering this question would be first to assume that decision makers who even bother to form the grand coalition must be fair-minded people; and second to collect some data on how, for example, various car pools—while blissfully ignorant of game theory—have in practice divided the benefits of their cooperations. Then we could regard as fairer the imputation that was closer on balance to the observed division of benefits. Our use of models would again be descriptive.

Now, in a given instance, the purpose of a game is always either descriptive or prescriptive. Nevertheless, in different instances, the same model can be used for different purposes. For example, Four Ways can also be used as a descriptive model. In Exercise 2.1's interpretation of this game, τ is the junction transit time, and δ and $\epsilon(< \delta)$ are the time penalties for selfishness and altruism, respectively. Different values of these parameters correspond to different traffic conditions: $\delta < \tau/2$ to light traffic, in which the line of cars at a junction is short; and $\delta > \tau/2$ to heavy traffic, in which the line of cars at a junction is long, and the time penalty for selfishness severe. The model's primary prediction is that G (selfishness) is optimal if $\delta < \tau/2$; whereas a mixture of G, W (altruism) and C (impatient altruism) is optimal if $\delta > \tau/2$. If we are prepared to assume that drivers who arrive simultaneously at a 4-way junction from opposite directions already behave so as to minimize delay, then the model predicts that they behave more selfishly when traffic is light than when traffic is heavy. Do they? I suspect that, if anything, the opposite is true—but, either way, our use of Four Ways would be descriptive.

Although a model may have different purposes in different instances, it is only when its purpose has been declared that we can begin to assess the model's value. In this regard, it is widely accepted that the ultimate test of a descriptive model is its ability to predict observable data. As every student of calculus knows,

Newton's model of gravitation predicts that planets have elliptical orbits; and because this prediction agrees so well with observations, we accept that (6.1) is—for all practical purposes—correct. Nevertheless, the model would have been valuable even if it had predicted some other kind of orbit, because it would have told Newton that (6.1) was wrong; and perhaps he would have found something else to replace it.

There is a world of difference, however, between the older science of astronomy and the newer natural and social sciences. One of those differences is that relevant data in the newer sciences are often inaccurately known. Therefore, if a model is going to make useful predictions, then it is at least desirable and often essential that the model should be *robust*, i.e., insensitive to small changes in parameter values. For example, estimates of the parameters δ and τ in Four Ways may be subject to considerable error. Nevertheless, the model's primary prediction depends—as we have just seen—only on the sign of $\delta - \tau/2$, and that may be known with some degree of confidence.

To further illustrate this property of robustness: We saw in Sections 2.7–2.8 that the *ESS* of Owners and Intruders is insensitive to the values of the parameters K, ϵ, λ and σ. If the strategy *DH* were an *ESS* only for special values of these parameters, then our interpretation of *O. civitas* behavior would carry no weight at all, because there would be no reason to suppose that K, ϵ, λ and σ actually take those special values. Because the model is robust, however, our interpretation requires only that ϵ and $1 - \lambda$ be small, and $1 - \sigma$ not too small; and that K be neither too small nor too large. Even if we cannot estimate these parameters accurately, we may have reason to believe that these constraints are satisfied.

Though the *ultimate* test of a descriptive model may be its ability to predict observable data, a model can be valuable even if it fails to do so. A discrepancy between model and data is merely the precursor of better models and increased understanding of the phenomenon we are trying to capture; and if there hadn't been a discrepancy, then we might never even have seen the need for improving the model. For example, the experiment described in Section 5.2 may provide at least a partial test of the model developed in Section 5.8; see Exercise 5.23. If, however, the model is found wanting in this respect, then it doesn't mean that the model was worthless; on the contrary, the discrepancy will indicate that certain effects ignored by the model are too important to be excluded—and the experiment may suggest which effects they are, so that a better model can be constructed.

We now consider prescriptive models—for which, however, there appears to be no widely accepted criterion of worth, although flexibility is at least an important factor. Prescriptive models are flexible if they are easily altered to suit a specific instance. Thus, for example, the car pool games are flexible, because their cost functions are readily adapted to different locations; and Four Ways is flexible, because its solution is known for arbitrary values of δ, ϵ and τ. Flexibility makes models applicable to qualitatively similar but quantitatively different interactions (car pools are much the same wherever you go, but their cost functions differ numerically).

Indeed it is desirable to build prescriptive models with sufficient flexibility that two decision makers who agree over what to optimize, but disagree over parameter values, can both use the same model to derive an optimal decision. For example, two dealers who believe in minimizing ordering costs (6.3)—but who disagree over values of the parameters Q, c_1 and c_2—can both use the lot-size inventory model to determine their optimal batch size, u^*, because subjective estimates of Q, c_1 and c_2 can be inserted into (6.2) to produce subjective values of u^*. There is absolutely no need for the first dealer to know anything about the second dealer's perceptions of Q, c_1 and c_2, or vice versa. Except in Section 1.7, however, we have had to assume throughout this book that players' rewards and decision sets are common knowledge—and relaxing this assumption makes game-theoretic analysis considerably more difficult.

Here two remarks are in order. First, the assumption of common knowledge may simply be quite reasonable. Then games are valuable as descriptive models if they make robust predictions, and games are valuable as prescriptive models if they are flexible enough to be widely applicable. Second, there is a large and growing literature in which the assumption of common knowledge is relaxed. This literature distinguishes between *incomplete* information, i.e., partial knowledge of a conflict's structure; and *imperfect* information, i.e., partial knowledge of a conflict's history. To illustrate the first type of partial information, recall that in Store Wars Nan and San had a common perception of the maximum amount they could charge for their product. Thus Nan's price, p_1, and San's price, p_2, had a common upper bound, namely, αc. If Nan and San had different perceptions, however, then the constraints $p_1 \le \alpha c, p_2 \le \alpha c$ would have to be replaced by $p_1 \le \alpha_1 c, p_2 \le \alpha_2 c$, where $\alpha_1 \ne \alpha_2$; and there would be no reason to suppose that Nan knew α_2 and San knew α_1. Thus information would be incomplete. To illustrate the second type of partial information, consider once more the iterated prisoner's dilemma in a finite population. If the players interacted at random, and if a player met a particular opponent for the first time on the first move and for the second time on the third move, then he would have no idea what his opponent did on the second move—even though, by the third move, it would be part of the conflict's history (and very useful to know), and even though he had complete knowledge of the conflict's structure (random interaction, same payoff matrix for everyone, etc.). Thus information would be imperfect.

Clearly, you cannot possibly know a conflict's history if you don't even know its structure, although you can know its structure without knowing its history. Thus incomplete information is always imperfect, although imperfect information can still be complete. Indeed technically all our games have had complete but imperfect information, because history is defined to include the present, and so simultaneity of action implies imperfect information.

As a practical matter, if there are things we don't know, then—regardless of whether our ignorance is an imperfection or an incompleteness—we either exclude them from our models, or include them as parameters; or else we call them random variables and assign them distributions. The characteristic feature of the literature on games of incomplete information—which generalizes Chapter 1's concept of Nash equilibrium to so-called Bayesian Nash equilibrium—is that these distributions are allowed to be subjective for any player, and to be updated as new information is acquired. Thus games of incomplete information possess more flexibility than games of complete information. But this is an introductory text, and we cannot cover everything. Instead we refer to the literature; see, for example, Phlips (1988) and Rasmusen (1989).

Von Neumann and Morgenstern's treatise on game theory is now almost half a century old. Yet despite much scholarly activity in recent years, difficulties surround almost every solution concept for any kind of game. How does one distinguish among Nash equilibria of noncooperative games? How does one distinguish among the nucleolus, the Shapley value and the egalitarian imputation as the solution of a c-game? It is possible, of course, that different answers apply in different circumstances. Nevertheless, answers remain to be found, in large measure because game theory is still insufficiently dynamic—if we knew the algorithm by which players converged on a fair division of the benefits of cooperation, or if we knew the algorithm by which players converged on a Nash equilibrium, then we would also know which solution they arrived at. Perhaps in the future we will have a general theory of strategic behavior that explicitly models the dynamics of information transfer, whose significance we saw in Section 5.10. Such a theory would allow individuals both to receive and to transmit information—i.e., *learn* and *signal*—throughout their interaction, to do so either honestly or deceitfully, and to modify behavior in response to new information (whether real or imagined). But animal behavior is extremely complicated, and valuable progress toward such a theory can still be made—especially in the short term—not by seeking a general dynamic, but rather by building a greater variety of explicitly dynamical models of specific conflicts in which behavior has been observed.[1]

In conclusion: There is trouble with games, to be sure. But where there is trouble, there is also opportunity, and games are ripe for new ideas and applications. In other words, games are an attractive topic for research, and I hope that this book has helped to entice you toward them.

---

[1]   A rich source of such data is electoral behavior, yet game-theoretical modelling of strategic voting is still in its infancy; see, for example, Brams and Fishburn (1983, pp. 139–141).

Solutions
to Selected Exercises

CHAPTER 1

1.1 The Hawk-Dove game is equivalent to the symmetric version of Crossroads with $\epsilon = 0$.

1.3 Note that the equilibrium is strong, as defined in Section 1.6.

1.5 Let $f_1 = Ju_1 + Ku_2$. Then region C in Figure 1.6 corresponds to $J < 0, K < 0$; region B to $J < 0, K > 0$ to the right of the line segment joining (α, β) and $((\sigma + 1)/2, 0)$, to $J = 0, K > 0$ on the line, and to $K > J > 0$ to the left of it; and region A to $J > K > 0$ below the line joining (α, β) and $(0, 1 - \theta)$, to $J > 0, K = 0$ on the line, and to $J > 0, K < 0$ above it. Similarly, the seven rows of Table 1.8 correspond, respectively, to $J > 0, K < 0$ or $J > K > 0$; $J < 0, K > 0$ or $K > J > 0$; $J < 0$, $K < 0; J = 0, K < 0; J < 0, K = 0; J = K > 0$; and $J = K = 0$.

1.7 g is defined by $g(s) = G'(s), 0 < s < 20$.

1.8 To obtain, for example, (1.59c), note from (1.57) that if $(u, v) \in D_C$ then

$$\frac{\partial f_1}{\partial u} = \frac{c}{25}\{(u - v + 6)(v - 3u + 6) + 70\}, \quad \frac{\partial f_1}{\partial u^2} = \frac{2c}{25}\{2(v - 6) - 3u\};$$

whence f_1 has a maximum for $\max(0, v - 6) \le u \le v - 1$ at

$$u = \frac{1}{3}\left(2(v - 6) + \sqrt{(v - 6)^2 + 210}\right),$$

provided this number (which clearly exceeds $\max(0, v - 6)$) is less than or equal to $v - 1$, or $v \ge 11/2$. Otherwise the maximum is at $u = v - 1$.

1.9 To obtain, for example, (1.62c), note that because $(u, v) \in D_C$ implies

$$\frac{\partial f_2}{\partial v} = \frac{c}{75}\left((3v - 2u - 12)^2 - (u + 6)^2 + 90\right) \ge 0$$

if $(u + 6)^2 \le 90$, the maximum of f_2 on D_C is at $v = u + 6$ if $u \le 3(\sqrt{10} - 2)$. If $u > 3(\sqrt{10} - 2)$, however, then f_2^C has a local minimum for $u + 1 \le v \le u + 6$ at

$v = v_{up}(u)$, where

$$v_{up}(u) = \frac{1}{3}\left(2(u + 6) + \sqrt{(u + 6)^2 - 90}\right);$$

and it will have a local maximum for $u + 1 \leq v \leq u + 6$ at $v = v_{down}(u)$, where

$$v_{down}(u) = \frac{1}{3}\left(2(u + 6) - \sqrt{(u + 6)^2 - 90}\right),$$

provided $v_{down}(u) \geq u + 1$, or $u \leq 9/2$. But this local maximum is not the maximum for $3(\sqrt{10} - 2) \leq u \leq 9/2$, because straightforward (if somewhat tedious) calculations show that

$$f_2^C(u, u + 6) - f_2^C\left(u, v_{down}(u)\right) \geq 0, \quad \text{if} \quad 3(\sqrt{10} - 2) \leq u \leq 4,$$
$$f_2^C(u, 10) - f_2^C\left(u, v_{down}(u)\right) \geq 0, \quad \text{if} \quad 4 \leq u \leq 9/2.$$

For $9/2 < u \leq 9$, the maximum (for $u + 1 \leq v \leq 10$) must be either at $v = u + 1$ or at $v = 10$; and

$$f_2^C(u, u + 1) - f_2^C(u, 10) = \frac{c}{5}(9 - 2u)(u - 9) \geq 0$$

shows that it is at $v = u + 1$.

1.11   As we move further to the left along the interval $3(\sqrt{10} - 2) \leq u \leq 9/2$, the points $(u, v_{up}(u))$ and $(u, v_{down}(u))$ defined in the solution to Exercise 1.9 move closer and closer together, until they coalesce at the point $(3(\sqrt{10} - 2), 2\sqrt{10})$. Thus R_2 in Figure 1.12 is defined by:

$v = u + 6$ $\qquad\qquad\qquad\qquad$ if $\quad 0 \leq u \leq 2(\sqrt{10} - 3)$
$v = 2\sqrt{10}$ $\qquad\qquad\qquad\qquad$ if $\quad 2(\sqrt{10} - 3) \leq u \leq 3(\sqrt{10} - 2)$
$v = \frac{1}{3}\left\{2(u + 6) - \sqrt{(u + 6)^2 - 90}\right\}$ if $\quad 3(\sqrt{10} - 2) \leq u \leq 9/2$
$v = u + 1$ $\qquad\qquad\qquad\qquad$ if $\quad 9/2 \leq u \leq 4\sqrt{10} - 13/2$
$v = 2\sqrt{10}$ $\qquad\qquad\qquad\qquad$ if $\quad 4\sqrt{10} - 13/2 \leq u \leq 2\sqrt{10}.$

1.16   For Player 1 (Nan), from (1.74) we have

$$f_1(u^*, v^*, z^*) - f(u, v^*, z^*) = 16ac\pi(u - 1/6)^2 \geq 0,$$

and similarly for the other players.

1.19   (i)   When $\tau_1 > 2\delta$, $\tau_2 > 2\delta$ we have $(\tilde{u}, \tilde{v}) = (1, 1) = (u^*, v^*)$.

   (ii)   When $\tau_1 < 2\epsilon$, $\tau_2 < 2\epsilon$ we have

$$(\tilde{u}, \tilde{v}) = \frac{1}{\delta + \epsilon}(\epsilon - \tau_2/2, \epsilon - \tau_1/2),$$

which lies neither in R_1 nor in R_2.

   (iii)   For $\tau_1 < 2\epsilon$, $\tau_2 < 2\epsilon$, straightforward calculation now shows that

$$f_1(\tilde{u}, \tilde{v}) = -(\delta + \tau_2/2)\theta_2, \qquad f_2(\tilde{u}, \tilde{v}) = -(\delta + \tau_1/2)\theta_1,$$

where θ_1 and θ_2 are defined by (1.26); and these are Nash-equilibrium rewards, from Table 1.5.

1.20 Because $v \geq 0, z \geq 0, v + z$ is minimized with respect to (v, z) by $v = 0 = z$. Thus $m_1(u) = 8ac\pi u(1/3 - 2u)$, and similarly for m_2, m_3. We deduce that the unique max-min strategies for the three players are

$$\bar{u} = \frac{1}{12}, \quad \tilde{v} = \frac{1}{16}, \quad \tilde{w} = \frac{5}{48}.$$

1.21 The unique Nash equilibrium is $(u^*, v^*, z^*) = \left(\frac{17}{120}, \frac{7}{40}, \frac{11}{60}\right)$.

1.24 **(i)** I's payoff matrix is now

	H	D	B
H	$\frac{1}{2}(\rho - C)$	ρ	$\frac{1}{4}(3\rho - C)$
D	0	$\frac{\rho}{2}$	$\frac{\rho}{4}$
B	$\frac{1}{4}(\rho - C)$	$\frac{3\rho}{4}$	$\frac{\rho}{2}$

and II's matrix the transpose thereof. Let strategies u and v be defined as in Section 1.4. Then $B = (0, 0)$, and the payoff to each player when both select B is $f_1(0, 0, 0, 0) = \rho/2$. If Player 1 now unilaterally adopts a *different* strategy $u \neq (0, 0)$, then her payoff against B is

$$f_1(u_1, u_2, 0, 0) = u_1 \cdot \frac{1}{4}(3\rho - C) + u_2 \cdot \frac{\rho}{4} + (1 - u_1 - u_2) \cdot \frac{\rho}{2};$$

and because either u_1 or u_2 must be positive, we have

$$f_1(0, 0, 0, 0) - f_1(u_1, u_2, 0, 0) = \frac{1}{4}\{(C - \rho)u_1 + \rho u_2\} > 0$$

if $\rho < C$ (essentially because $\rho/2$ is the largest element in column 3 of I's payoff matrix). Similarly for Player 2 (again because $\rho/2$ is the largest element in row 3 of II's payoff matrix.) Thus B is a strong Nash-equilibrium strategy.

(ii) It is perhaps unlikely that both owner and intruder would share the same values of ρ and C, and perhaps even less likely that they would have equal chances of victory if both were to select either H or D (as we have assumed in Tables 1.3 and 1.4).

1.25 $f_1(u, v) = -u\{(P - S)(1 - v) + (T - R)v\} + Tv + P(1 - v)$, which is maximized by $u = 0$. Similarly for f_2. Thus the only Nash equilibrium is $(0, 0)$.

1.26 Make prices dimensionless by defining

$$u = \frac{p_1}{4cL}, \quad v = \frac{p_2}{4cL}. \tag{a}$$

Also, define dimensionless parameters μ and σ by

$$\mu = \frac{b - a}{2L}, \quad \sigma = \frac{b + a}{2L}; \tag{b}$$

note that $0 < \mu < \sigma < 1, \mu + \sigma < 1$. Now $|p_1 - p_2| \leq 2c(b - a)$ becomes $|u - v| \leq \mu$, so that the decision set is

$$D = \{(u, v) | \max(0, v - \mu) \leq u \leq v + \mu, \max(0, u - \mu) \leq v \leq u + \mu\}.$$

Let the residential coordinate of the next customer be the random variable X. Then the next customer will buy from the first store if $X < a$ or $a < X < b$ and

$$p_1 + 2c(X - a) < p_2 + 2c(b - X); \tag{c}$$

i.e., if

$$0 < X < \frac{p_2 - p_1}{4c} + \frac{1}{2}(a + b). \tag{d}$$

Because X is distributed uniformly between $x = 0$ and $x = L$, the probability of the above event is $(p_2 - p_1)/4cL + (a + b)/2L$; whence, by reasoning similar to that which led to (1.51), the first player's reward is $p_1((p_2 - p_1)/4cL + (a + b)/2L)$. Thus

$$f_1(u, v) = 4cLu(v - u + \sigma).$$

Similarly,

$$f_2(u, v) = 4cLv(u - v - \sigma + 1).$$

In calculating R_1, let us first suppose that $0 \le v \le \mu$. Then $\max(0, v - \mu) = 0$, and f_1 has its maximum on $0 \le u \le v + \mu$ where $u = (v + \sigma)/2$ if $(v + \sigma)/2 \le v + \mu$, but where $u = v + \mu$ if $(v + \sigma)/2 > v + \mu$; in other words, where

$$u = \begin{cases} v + \mu & \text{if } v < \sigma - 2\mu \\ \frac{1}{2}(v + \sigma) & \text{if } v \ge \sigma - 2\mu. \end{cases} \tag{e}$$

The boundary segment $u = v + \mu$ is irrelevant if $\mu < \sigma < 2\mu$; whereas the interior segment $u = (v + \sigma)/2$ is irrelevant if $3\mu < \sigma < 1$. Similarly, for $\mu < v < \infty$, we have $\max(0, v - \mu) = v - \mu$; and f_1 has its maximum on $v - \mu \le u \le v + \mu$ where

$$u = \begin{cases} v + \mu & \text{if } v < \sigma - 2\mu \\ \frac{1}{2}(v + \sigma) & \text{if } \sigma - 2\mu \le v \le \sigma + 2\mu \\ v - \mu & \text{if } v > \sigma + 2\mu. \end{cases} \tag{f}$$

The lower boundary segment $u = v + \mu$ is irrelevant if $\sigma < 3\mu$. Combining our results for $0 \le v \le \mu$ with those for $\mu < v < \infty$, we find that R_1 is defined by

$$u = \begin{cases} \frac{1}{2}(v + \sigma), & 0 \le v \le \sigma + 2\mu \\ v - \mu, & \sigma + 2\mu < v < \infty \end{cases} \tag{g}$$

if $\sigma < 2\mu(b > 3a)$ and by (f) if $\sigma > 2\mu(b < 3a)$.

Similar arguments can be used to calculate R_2. Indeed it is hardly necessary to repeat the analysis, because the symmetry between f_1 and f_2 enables us to deduce the results from (f) and (g) by swapping u with v, and σ with $1 - \sigma$. Thus R_2 is defined by

$$v = \begin{cases} \frac{1}{2}(u + 1 - \sigma), & 0 \le u \le 1 - \sigma + 2\mu \\ u - \mu, & 1 - \sigma + 2\mu < u < \infty \end{cases} \tag{h}$$

if $1 - \sigma < 2\mu(3b - a > 2L)$, but by

$$v = \begin{cases} u + \mu, & 0 \le u \le 1 - \sigma - 2\mu \\ \frac{1}{2}(u + 1 - \sigma), & 1 - \sigma - 2\mu < u \le 1 - \sigma + 2\mu \\ u - \mu, & 1 - \sigma + 2\mu < u < \infty \end{cases} \tag{i}$$

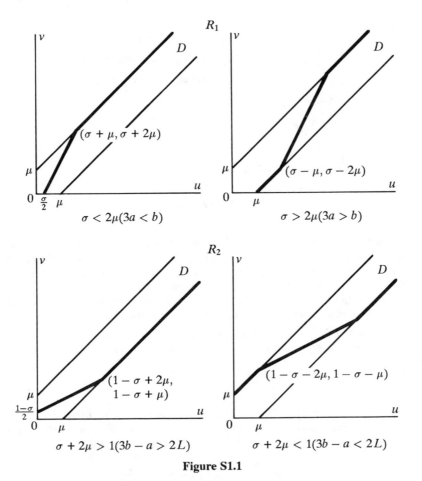

Figure S1.1

if $1 - \sigma > 2\mu(3b - a < 2L)$. The rational reaction sets are sketched in Figure S1.1.

To find all Nash equilibria, we must calculate $R_1 \cap R_2$ in all possible cases. Suppose, to begin with, that $\sigma < 2\mu$. Then, by inspection of Figure S1.1, R_1 meets R_2 in a single point if $\sigma + 2\mu > 1$; or if $\sigma + 2\mu < 1$, but $(\sigma + \mu, \sigma + 2\mu)$ lies above $(1 - \sigma - 2\mu, 1 - \sigma - \mu)$ on the line $v = u + \mu$, that is, if $2\sigma + 3\mu > 1$. The point of intersection, the Nash equilibrium, is then

$$(u^*, v^*) = \frac{1}{3}(\sigma + 1, 2 - \sigma). \tag{j}$$

If $\sigma < 2\mu$ and $\sigma + 2\mu < 1$ but $2\sigma + 3\mu < 1$, however, then $R_1 \cap R_2$ is the line segment joining $(\sigma + \mu, \sigma + 2\mu)$ to $(1 - \sigma - 2\mu, 1 - \sigma - \mu)$.

Now suppose that $\sigma > 2\mu$. If also $2\sigma + 3\mu < 1$, then $R_1 \cap R_2$ is still the line segment joining $(\sigma + \mu, \sigma + 2\mu)$ to $(1 - \sigma - 2\mu, 1 - \sigma - \mu)$. If $2\sigma + 3\mu > 1$ and the point

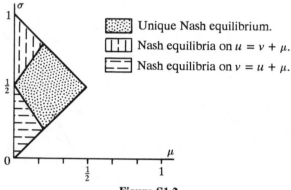

Figure S1.2

$(1 - \sigma + 2\mu, 1 - \sigma + \mu)$ lies above the point $(\sigma - \mu, \sigma - 2\mu)$ on the line $u = v + \mu$, i.e., if $1 - 3\mu < 2\sigma < 1 + 3\mu$, then (j) is again the unique Nash equilibrium. If the point $(1 - \sigma + 2\mu, 1 - \sigma + \mu)$ lies below the point $(\sigma - \mu, \sigma - 2\mu)$, however, i.e., if $2\sigma > 1 + 3\mu$, then $R_1 \cap R_2$ is the line segment joining $(1 - \sigma + 2\mu, 1 - \sigma + \mu)$ to $(\sigma - \mu, \sigma - 2\mu)$. Combining these results, we find that the region in the $\mu - \sigma$ plane for which there exists a unique Nash equilibrium is the speckled region in Figure S1.2.

Because $a = L(\sigma - \mu)$, $b = L(\sigma + \mu)$, the triangle $\mu \geq 0$, $\sigma \geq \mu$, $\sigma + \mu \leq 1$ in the $\mu - \sigma$ plane is mapped to the triangle $0 \leq a \leq b \leq L$ in the $a - b$ plane by the matrix

$$\begin{bmatrix} -L & L \\ L & L \end{bmatrix},$$

as shown in Figure S1.3. The speckled region, corresponding to store locations for which there is a unique Nash equilibrium, contains points in the $a - b$ plane at which $b + 2L \geq 5a$ and $5b \geq a + 2L$; or, which is the same thing, points at which

$$b - a \geq 4 \max\left(a - \frac{L}{2}, \frac{L}{2} - b\right). \tag{k}$$

We see, in particular, that there is a unique Nash equilibrium if the stores are located on opposite sides of $x = L/2$, but a multiplicity of solutions if both are located near $x = 0$ or $x = L$.

1.27 (i) I's payoff matrix is now

	H	D	R
H	$(\rho - C)/2$	ρ	$(\rho - C)/2$
D	0	$\rho/2$	$\rho(1 - \lambda)/2$
R	$(\rho - C)/2$	$\rho(1 + \lambda)/2$	$\rho/2$

and II's matrix the transpose thereof. To show that R is a strong Nash- equilibrium strategy, see the solution to Exercise 1.24.

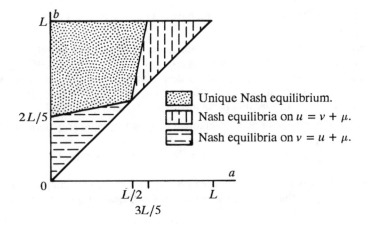

Figure S1.3

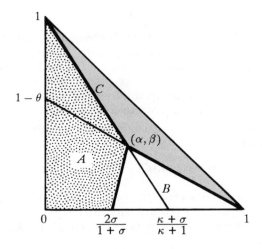

Figure S1.4

(ii)   No. (See, for example, Exercise 2.8.)

1.29   Figure 1.6 is replaced by Figure S1.4, where

$$\kappa = \frac{\mu}{\delta};$$

and α, β and θ are defined, not by (1.41)–(1.42) but by

$$\alpha = \frac{(\sigma + \gamma)(\sigma + \kappa)}{\kappa + (\kappa + 1)\gamma + \sigma^2}, \quad \beta = \frac{(1 - \sigma)(\kappa - \sigma)}{\kappa + (\kappa + 1)\gamma + \sigma^2}, \quad \theta = \frac{\sigma + \gamma}{\kappa + \gamma};$$

and σ and γ are defined by (1.32) and (1.41). With σ and β redefined as above, Tables 1.8–1.10 are unchanged. In (i) we have $\sigma = 1/3$, $\kappa = 4/3$, $\gamma = 2/3$ and

$(\alpha, \beta) = (5/9, 2/9)$; whereas in (ii) we have $\sigma = 1/4$, $\kappa = 3/4$, $\gamma = 1/2$ and $(\alpha, \beta) = (4/9, 2/9)$.

1.30 To show that $(1,0)$ is a strong Nash-equilibrium strategy combination, we must show that $f_1(1, 0) > f_1(u, 0)$ for all u such that $0 \le u < 1$, *and* that $f_2(1, 0) > f_2(1, v)$ for all v such that $0 < v \le 1$. Likewise, to show that $(0,1)$ is strong, we must show that $f_1(0, 1) > f_1(u, 1)$ for all u such that $0 < u \le 1$, *and* that $f_2(0, 1) > f_2(0, v)$ for all v such that $0 \le v < 1$. Verifying these inequalites is routine algebra.

1.31 It reduces the speckled region in Figure S1.2 to the curvilinear quadrilateral

$$\frac{1}{9} \max(5 - 5\sigma - \sigma^2, -1 + 7\sigma - \sigma^2) \le \mu \le \min(\sigma, 1 - \sigma),$$

requiring in particular that $\mu \ge 1/4$ or $b - a \ge L/2$. Thus a unique Nash equilibrium exists only if the stores are located sufficiently near to opposite ends of the line segment $0 \le x \le L$.

CHAPTER 2

2.1 Note that a large value of δ is especially likely when there is more than one car in both northbound and southbound lanes at the junction, because then another vehicle is likely to have captured the space into which, if *GG* has been selected, one of the players must reverse before a path can be cleared. Thus $\delta > \tau/2$ is likely to hold at busy junctions, and we can interpret the inequality as saying that the junction is slow, rather than that the drivers are fast; and vice versa.

2.2 (i) Because (u^*, u^*) is a Nash-equilibrium strategy combination if $(u^*, u^*) \in R_1 \cap R_2$, we must show that

$$f_1(u^*, u^*) = \max_u f_1(u, u^*), \qquad f_2(u^*, u^*) = \max_v f_2(u^*, v),$$

where $f_2(v, u) = f_1(u, v) = f(u, v)$, as in (2.22). These two conditions are equivalent to $f_1(u^*, u^*) \ge f_1(u, u^*)$ for all u and $f_2(u^*, u^*) \ge f_2(u^*, v)$ for all v, both of which are equivalent to $f(u^*, u^*) \ge f(v, u^*)$ for all v. But this is implied by (2.29).

    (ii) No (unless $u^* = v^*$). Consider, for example, the strategy combinations $(1,0)$ and $(0,1)$ in Section 2.3's symmetric version of Crossroads.

2.5 See Mesterton-Gibbons (1990, pp. 13–14).

2.7 The only Nash equilibrium, $(0,0)$, is also an *ESS*.

2.8 We already know from Exercise 1.27 that R is a strong Nash-equilibrium strategy; hence R is a strong *ESS*. To show that $(1/2, 1/2)$ is an *ESS*, proceed as at the end of Section 2.3 (for Four Ways).

2.10

$$f(u^*, v) - f(u, v) = C^2 \sigma_f \frac{(1 - 2v)^2}{2v} > 0 \quad \text{if} \quad v \ne 1/2.$$

2.11 Trajectories that begin on the boundary of Δ where $p_1 p_2 = 0$ must remain in that boundary and converge to $(0,0)$ as $t \rightarrow \infty$.

2.14   Define

$$y(t) = 1 - \sum_{k=1}^{m} x_k(t).$$

Then $y(0) = 1$, by (2.60); and, on using (2.59), we have

$$\frac{dy}{dt} = -\sum_{k=1}^{m} \frac{dx_k}{dt} = -\kappa \sum_{k=1}^{m} x_k W_k + \kappa \overline{W} \sum_{k=1}^{m} x_k = -\kappa \overline{W} \left(1 - \sum_{k=1}^{m} x_k\right) = -\kappa \overline{W} y.$$

The solution of this differential equation subject to $y(0) = 0$ is $y(t) = 0$, or (2.61).

2.15   Suppose, for example, that $\epsilon = 0.1$, $\lambda = 0.9$, $\sigma = 0.7$ and $x(0) = (0, 0, 1, 0) = y(0)$. Then $a_{ij} = \epsilon = 0.1$, $1 \leq i, j \leq 4$, for $K = 1$, and the payoff matrices for $K = 2, \ldots, 7$ are

$K = 2$:

0.1782	0.1840	0.1842	0.1900
0.1779	0.1837	0.1779	0.1837
0.1779	0.1840	0.1839	0.1900
0.1776	0.1837	0.1776	0.1837

$K = 3$:

0.2403	0.2551	0.2555	0.2710
0.2397	0.2548	0.2396	0.2548
0.2400	0.2551	0.2553	0.2710
0.2395	0.2548	0.2394	0.2548

$K = 4$:

0.2902	0.3157	0.3161	0.3439
0.2896	0.3161	0.2893	0.3161
0.2906	0.3157	0.3168	0.3439
0.2901	0.3161	0.2897	0.3161

$K = 5$:

0.3308	0.3675	0.3676	0.4095
0.3306	0.3693	0.3297	0.3693
0.3326	0.3675	0.3703	0.4095
0.3324	0.3693	0.3314	0.3693

$K = 6$:

0.3641	0.4120	0.4116	0.4686
0.3648	0.4161	0.3629	0.4161
0.3680	0.4120	0.4173	0.4686
0.3686	0.4161	0.3667	0.4161

$K = 7$:

0.3917	0.4505	0.4491	0.5217
0.3938	0.4575	0.3905	0.4575
0.3984	0.4505	0.4589	0.5217
0.4002	0.4575	0.3969	0.4575

You can see that DH is the unique *ESS* for $K = 4, \ldots, 7$, and you can readily confirm that *DH* remains the unique *ESS* for all higher values of K; except in the limit as $K \rightarrow \infty$, when $a_{33} \rightarrow 1$ and $a_{4j} \rightarrow 1$ for all $1 \leq j \leq 4$ (because there are more sites than animals, an inveterate Dove is guaranteed to find a site eventually).

2.16   Let $A(K)$ denote the payoff matrix when the conflict lasts for K units of time. Then the payoff matrix should be replaced by its expected value

$$E[A] = \sum_{k=1}^{\infty} A(k) \cdot \text{Prob}(K = k).$$

Suppose, for example, that in every time unit there is constant probability w that the conflict will last for another unit of time; i.e., $\text{Prob}(K \geq k) = w^{k-1}$, $k \geq 1$. Then $\text{Prob}(K = k) = \text{Prob}(K \geq k) - \text{Prob}(K \geq k + 1) = (1 - w)w^{k-1}$; and

$$E[A] = (1 - w) \sum_{k=1}^{\infty} w^{k-1} A(k).$$

For $\epsilon = 0.1$, $\lambda = 0.9$, $\sigma = 0.7$ and $x(0) = (0, 0, 1, 0) = y(0)$, it is clear from the previous exercise that DH will be the unique ESS provided only that w is sufficiently large, and similarly for other values of ϵ, σ and λ.

2.17   See Section 2.8.

2.18   With $q(y_3)$ defined by (2.82) we have

$$H_1(x,y) = x_1 \left(1 - q(y_3)v_2 \left(1 - \frac{1}{2}(1 - \lambda)u_1 \right) \right)$$
$$+ \alpha x_3 \left(1 - \sigma(1 - u_2)(y_1 + y_2) - \frac{1}{2}\sigma(1 + \lambda)u_2 v_1 y_1 \right)$$
$$H_2(x,y) = \frac{1}{2}\lambda \left(u_1 v_2 x_1 q(y_3) + \epsilon \sigma u_2 v_1 x_3 y_1 \right) + x_2 \left(1 - v_2 q(y_3) \right)$$
$$H_3(x,y) = (1 - u_1)v_2 x_1 q(y_3) + x_3 \{ 1 - \epsilon + \epsilon \sigma (1 - u_2)(y_1 + y_2) \}$$
$$H_4(x,y) = q(y_3)v_2 \left(x_2 + \frac{1}{2}u_1 x_1 \right) + \frac{1}{2}\epsilon \sigma u_2 v_1 x_3 y_1 + x_4$$

and

$$H_k(x,y) = H_{k-4}(y,y)$$

for $k = 5, \dots, 8$.

2.19   Increasing ϵ favors DH; increasing σ favors HH.

2.20   Suppose, for example, that $\epsilon = 0.1$, $\lambda = 0.9$ and $\sigma = 0.7$. Then Table 2.3 is unchanged (to four significant figures); whereas Table 2.2 is replaced by

0.620	0.704	0.683	0.794	0.591	0.686	0.663	0.794	0.503	0.623	0.598	0.794
0.593	0.671	0.573	0.671	0.578	0.671	0.556	0.671	0.529	0.671	0.499	0.671
0.602	0.704	0.671	0.794	0.588	0.686	0.671	0.794	0.543	0.623	0.671	0.794
0.570	0.671	0.541	0.671	0.570	0.671	0.541	0.671	0.570	0.671	0.541	0.671

$$\lambda = 0 \qquad\qquad \lambda = 0.2 \qquad\qquad \lambda = 0.9$$

You can see that the difference is negligible.

2.21   (ii)   Let k be a strong ESS, and let i be any infiltrator. Then

$$W_k - W_i = (a_{kk} - a_{ik})x_k + \sum_{\substack{j=1 \\ j \neq k}}^{m}(a_{kj} - a_{ij})x_j.$$

Because x_j is small for every $j \neq k$, and because $a_{kk} > a_{ik}$ and x_k is approximately 1, the last $m - 1$ terms on the right-hand side can be neglected. Thus $W_k > W_i$ for any $i \neq k$; whence either (2.60) or (2.65) implies $x_k(\infty) = 1$.

2.22   (iii)   To 2 significant figures, $\alpha_c = 0.72$. Note that if $\alpha_c - \alpha$ is a small positive number then x_3 decreases at first, but ultimately rises rapidly to 1.

(iv)   The use of (2.65) with (2.63) and (2.92), though suggestive, is not strictly valid because a_{ij} in (2.92) is the payoff to an i-strategist against a homogeneous population of j-strategists; in a heterogeneous population, the strategy of an opponent would not be fixed. An analogous problem and its resolution are discussed in Section 5.6.

CHAPTER 3

3.2 (i)   We have $\partial\psi/\partial c = -5f_1 + 5f_2 + 20c - 8$, whence

$$c = \frac{1}{4}(f_1 - f_2) + \frac{2}{5}.$$

Now substitute into (3.7) and simplify.

(ii)   The small curvilinear triangles would correspond to $v > 1$ and $v < 0$, respectively, under the mapping f defined by (3.4).

3.3 (ii)   From Figure 3.1, $(-8/5, -12/5)$ lies on $f(L(3/5))$; whence from (3.6) with $c = 3/5$ we have $v = 1/5$. Thus $(-8/5, -12/5)$ is the reward from strategy combination $(u, v) = (3/5, 1/5)$. Similarly, $(-12/5, -8/5)$ is the reward from strategy combination $(u, v) = (1/5, 3/5)$.

3.8 (i)   This follows readily from (3.47) and $\bar{x}_1 \geq 0, \bar{x}_2 \geq 0$.

(ii)   From (3.48), we have $\bar{d}(u, v) = g_1(u)g_2(v)$, where g_1 increases from a negative value at $u = 0$ to a positive maximum at $u = \alpha_1$ and then decreases again to a negative value at $u = 1$; and similarly for g_2. Thus the maximum of $\bar{d}$ over the unshaded region in Figure E3.1 must occur either at $(1,0)$, or at $(0,1)$; or at (α_1, α_2). Straightforward calculation shows that

$$(\delta + \epsilon)^2 \bar{d}(1, 0) = \left(\delta - \frac{\tau_1}{2}\right)\left(\delta + \frac{\tau_2}{2}\right)\left(\epsilon - \frac{\tau_1}{2}\right)\left(\epsilon + \frac{\tau_2}{2}\right)$$

$$(\delta + \epsilon)^2 \bar{d}(0, 1) = \left(\delta - \frac{\tau_2}{2}\right)\left(\delta + \frac{\tau_1}{2}\right)\left(\epsilon - \frac{\tau_2}{2}\right)\left(\epsilon + \frac{\tau_1}{2}\right)$$

and

$$(\delta + \epsilon)^2 \bar{d}(\alpha_1, \alpha_2) = \left(\frac{\tau_1 + \tau_2}{4}\right)^4;$$

and the Nash bargaining solution can be identified simply by comparing these three magnitudes.

(iii)   No. If $\tau_1 = \tau_2 = \tau$ in Crossroads between fast drivers, then (α, α) is the unique Nash bargaining solution whenever

$$\frac{\delta\epsilon}{\sqrt{\delta^2 + \epsilon^2}} < \frac{\tau}{2} < \epsilon,$$

where $\alpha_1 = \alpha_2 = \alpha$.

3.10 (i)   By the method of Section 3.1, you can show that $\overline{F}$ is a quadrilateral with vertices at $(P, P), (S, T), (R, R)$ and (T, S); these points correspond, respectively, to $(0,0), (1,0), (1,1)$ and $(0,1)$ in D. (Hence $\overline{F}$ is symmetric about $f_1 = f_2$.) By the method of Section 1.7, the max-min reward vector is (P, P). Thus P and P_G both consist of the pair of line segments joining $(1, 1)$ to $(1, 0)$ and $(0, 1)$, and P^* is the subset joining $(1, a)$ to $(a, 1)$, where $a = (P - S)/(R - S)$.

(ii)   The Nash bargaining solution is at $(1,1)$ in D, corresponding to (R,R) in $\overline{F}$. By symmetry, and in view of (i), it is sufficient to show that $\overline{d} = (f_1 - P)(f_2 - P)$ takes its maximum on the line segment from (R,R) to (T,S) at (R,R), which is readily established by using the equation of the line segment to write $\overline{d}$ as a function of either f_1 or f_2 alone.

3.11   First show that the triangle $\overline{F}$ contains $(\tilde{f}_1, \tilde{f}_2)$. Then the area $(f_1 - \tilde{f}_1)(f_2 - \tilde{f}_2)$ of the rectangle whose diagonal joins (f_1, f_2) to $(\tilde{f}_1, \tilde{f}_2)$ is maximized with one corner on the line segment (3.55), whose equation can be used to write the area as a function of either f_1 or f_2 alone. The Nash bargaining reward vector is thus found to be

$$f = -\frac{1}{2}[\tau_2, \tau_1] + \frac{(\tau_1 - \tau_2)(\tau_1\tau_2 - 4\delta\epsilon)}{8\tau_1\tau_2(\delta + \epsilon)}[\tau_2, -\tau_1];$$

and the corresponding correlated strategy is

$$\hat{\omega} = (0, -f_2/\tau_1, -f_1/\tau_2, 0).$$

Note that $f_1 = f_2$ when the game is symmetric (but there is *no* interpersonal comparison of utilities).

CHAPTER 4

4.2   See (4.58).

4.3   (ii) $\epsilon_1 = -8/45$ and $C^+(\epsilon_1) = \{(19/45, 16/45, 2/9)\}$.

4.4 $X^1 = C^+(-1/9) = \{(1/3, 2/9, 1/9, 1/3)\}$.

4.6 $\epsilon_1 = -7/80$ and $C^+(\epsilon_1) = \{(21/80, 59/240, 11/48, 21/80)\}$.

4.7   (i) X can be represented as the interval $[0, 1]$ of the x_1-axis, with x_1 increasing to the right and $x_2(= 1 - x_1)$ to the left; although it is really that part of the line $x_1 + x_2 = 1$ which extends from the point $(1, 0)$ to the point $(0, 1)$. The characteristic function is defined by $v(\{1\}) = 0 = v(\{2\})$, $v(\{1, 2\}) = 1$. $C^+(\epsilon)$ is defined by $-x_1 \leq \epsilon, -x_2 \leq \epsilon, x_1 + x_2 = 1$ or $-\epsilon \leq x_1 \leq 1 + \epsilon$, which requires $\epsilon \geq -1/2$; but there are no other restrictions on ϵ. Thus $\epsilon_1 = -1/2$, $X^1 = \{(1/2, 1/2)\}$.

(ii) $x \in C^+(\epsilon)$ requires x_1, x_2 and $x_1 + x_2$ to lie between $-\epsilon$ and $1 + \epsilon$; whence $\epsilon_1 = -1/3, X^1 = \{(1/3, 1/3, 1/3)\}$.

4.10   Let Jed be Player 1, Ned Player 2 and Ted Player 3; and let the benefit of cooperation be the time saved in hours. Then $\overline{v}(\{1\}) = 0, \overline{v}(\{2\}) = 0, \overline{v}(\{3\}) = 0, \overline{v}(\{1, 2\}) = 3, \overline{v}(\{1, 3\}) = 3, \overline{v}(\{2, 3\}) = 2$ and $\overline{v}(\{1, 2, 3\}) = 6$. The core is a pentagon (and coincides with the reasonable set). The least rational core is

$$X^1 = C^+(-2/9) = \{(4/9, 5/18, 5/18)\}.$$

Thus fair shares of the time saved are 8/3 hours for Jed and 5/3 hours each for Ned and Ted. Jed should arrive at 1:20 p.m. and leave at 2:40 p.m., Ned should leave at 1:20 p.m. and Ted should arrive at 2:40 p.m.; Jed benefits most because his advertised hours have the greatest overlap with those of the other dealers.

4.12 $\epsilon_1 = 0$, and the nucleolus is $(1/4, 1/4, 1/4, 1/4)$.

4.13   A 3-player game is improper if and only if $v(S) > 1$, where S is one of the 2-player coalitions. Suppose $S = \{a, b\}$, and let $N = \{a, b, c\}$. Then, if the game has a core, there must exist at least one x such that we require $x_a + x_b \geq v(S) > 1, x_c \geq 0$; but this is impossible, because $x_a + x_b + x_c = 1$.

4.14   To calculate X^1, replace $x_1 \geq -\epsilon, x_2 \geq -\epsilon$ and $x_1 + x_2 \leq 1 + \epsilon$ in (4.102) by, respectively, $x_1 \geq 0, x_2 \geq 0$ and $x_1 + x_2 \leq 1$ (equivalent to replacing $x \in \overline{X}$ by $x \in X$), then use the method of Section 4.3. Because $e(\{2, 3\}, x) = 3/8$ on X^1, we have

$$\Sigma^1 = \{\{1\}, \{2\}, \{3\}, \{1, 2\}, \{1, 3\}\}.$$

Moreover, because $e(\{2\}, x) = -x_2$ and $e(\{3\}, x) = x_2 - 1$ are never greater than $-5/16$ on X^1, whereas the other three excesses are nonnegative, for $x \in X^1$ we have

$$\phi_1(x) = \max\left(0, \frac{11}{16} - x_2, x_2 - \frac{5}{16}\right),$$

which takes its minimum ϵ_2 where $x_2 = 1/2$.

4.15   Prize money (in dollars) would have been earned as follows if the jumps had all counted:

	J	N	T
First jump	3	5	4
Second jump	1	3	4
Third jump	0	3	3

The official proceeds are \$20. Thus the characteristic function is

$$v(\{1, 2\}) = \frac{3}{4}, \qquad v(\{1, 3\}) = \frac{3}{4}, \qquad v(\{2, 3\}) = \frac{11}{10}$$

and

$$C(\epsilon) = \{x \in \overline{X} \mid -\epsilon \leq x_1 \leq -\frac{1}{10} + \epsilon, -\epsilon \leq x_2 \leq \frac{1}{4} + \epsilon, \frac{3}{4} - \epsilon \leq x_1 + x_2 \leq 1 + \epsilon\}.$$

By the method of Section 4.3, the least value of ϵ for which the inequalities are consistent is $\overline{\epsilon}_1 = 1/5$, which is also the value of ϵ_1; and then $x_1 = 1/10, x_2 = 9/20$. Thus the least core, rational least core and nucleolus all coincide; they contain the single imputation $x^* = (1/10, 9/20, 9/20)$. Jed gets \$2, Ned and Ted \$9 each.

4.17   **(i)**   The Shapley value (and the nucleolus) for a 2-player game coincides with (4.110).

(ii)   The Shapley value for a 3-player c-game is the imputation whose transpose is

$$\left(x^s\right)^T = \frac{1}{6}\begin{bmatrix} v(\{1, 2\}) \\ v(\{2, 3\}) \\ v(\{3, 1\}) \end{bmatrix} + \frac{1}{6}\begin{bmatrix} v(\{1, 3\}) \\ v(\{2, 1\}) \\ v(\{3, 2\}) \end{bmatrix} + \frac{1}{3}\begin{bmatrix} 1 \\ 1 \\ 1 \end{bmatrix} - \frac{1}{3}\begin{bmatrix} v(\{2, 3\}) \\ v(\{3, 1\}) \\ v(\{1, 2\}) \end{bmatrix}.$$

(iii) Hence, for example, the Shapley value for the 3-person car pool is

$$x^S = \frac{1}{6(3+2d)}(10+4d, 7+4d, 1+4d).$$

4.19 *Hint*: don't forget that

$$\sum_{T \in \Pi^i} \text{Prob}(Y_i = T) = 1.$$

4.22 Hiring a pure mathematician. If an applied mathematician were hired, then the Shapley-Shubik index would give each professor one sixth of the power—as is obvious intuitively, because there would then be an equal number of pure and applied mathematicians. If a pure mathematician were hired, however, then the Shapley-Shubik index would give each of the two applied mathematicians a fifth of the power and each of the four pure mathematicians only 3/20 of the power.

4.23 (i) Suppose, for example, that nation E has committed an outrage, and that nations A, B, C and D are contemplating a military blockade. Suppose that these four nations have, respectively, 50,000, 300,000, 400,000 and 200,000 troops, and that 700,000 troops are needed to enforce the blockade. Then, in terms of enforcing the blockade, a coalition of nations is winning if it has more than 700,000 troops, and otherwise losing; in which case, nations A and D are dummies.

(ii) If Player i is a dictator, then $\{i,j\}$ is winning but $\{j\}$ is losing for any $j \neq i$; hence Player j cannot be a dictator. For the illustration, raise one nation's army in (i) to 700,000 troops.

4.24 Before the change, Glen Cove, Long Beach and Oyster Bay were all dummies.

4.25 (i) For a discussion of points relevant to (i) and (iii) see, for example, Brams (1975, Chapter 5).

(ii) From (4.120) we deduce that $x^B = (3/13, 3/13, 3/13, 2/13, 2/13)$ whence slightly more power is attributed to an applied mathematician (however, to two decimal places the indices agree). Broadly speaking, although it is common for x^S and x^B to agree qualitatively, it is unusual for them to agree quantitatively; and it is not unusual for them to assign power in radically different ways—see, for example, Brams (1975, p. 193).

CHAPTER 5

5.1 Define

$$S(n) = \sum_{k=1}^{n} \text{Prob}(k \leq M \leq n) = \sum_{k=1}^{n} \sum_{j=k}^{j=n} \text{Prob}(M = j).$$

Then $S(1) = \text{Prob}(M = 1)$; and for all $n \geq 2$,

$$S(n) = \sum_{k=1}^{n-1}\sum_{j=k}^{j=n} \text{Prob}(M = j) + \text{Prob}(M = n)$$

$$= \sum_{k=1}^{n-1}\left(\sum_{j=k}^{j=n-1} \text{Prob}(M = j) + \text{Prob}(M = n)\right) + \text{Prob}(M = n)$$

$$= \sum_{k=1}^{n-1}\sum_{j=k}^{j=n-1} \text{Prob}(M = j) + (n - 1) \cdot \text{Prob}(M = n) + \text{Prob}(M = n)$$

$$= S(n - 1) + n \cdot \text{Prob}(M = n).$$

Therefore

$$\sum_{n=1}^{N} n \cdot \text{Prob}(M = n) = \text{Prob}(M = 1) + \sum_{n=2}^{N} n \cdot \text{Prob}(M = n)$$

$$= \qquad S(1) \quad + \sum_{n=2}^{N}\{S(n) - S(n - 1)\} = S(N).$$

Now let $N \rightarrow \infty$.

5.2 **(i)** For all $k = 1, 2, \ldots$, we have $\text{Prob}(M \geq k + 1 \mid M \geq k) = w$ (where $\text{Prob}(U \mid V)$ denotes the conditional probability of U, given V). Also, $\text{Prob}(M \geq k + 1) = \text{Prob}(M \geq k + 1 \mid M \geq k) \cdot \text{Prob}(M \geq k) = w\text{Prob}(M \geq k)$; and clearly $\text{Prob}(M \geq 1) = 1$. Therefore, if we define $\xi_k = \text{Prob}(M \geq k)$, then we must solve the difference equation $\xi_{k+1} = w\xi_k$, $k \geq 1$, with initial condition $\xi_1 = 1$. The result is (5.24).

(ii) Because $\text{Prob}(M \geq k) = w^{k-1}$ and the probability of no further interaction is $1 - w$, we have $\text{Prob}(M = k) = w^{k-1}(1 - w)$. Therefore

$$\mu = E[M] = (1 - w)\sum_{k=1}^{\infty} kw^{k-1} = \frac{1}{1 - w},$$

on using (5.75).

5.3 **(i)** $f(TF2T, TF2T) = R\mu < T + wR\mu = f(STCO, TF2T)$; whereas $f(TFT, TFT) = R\mu > T + wS + w^2R\mu = f(STCO, TFT)$ if (5.37) is satisfied.

(ii) If $STCO$ is strategy 1 and $TF2T$ strategy 2, then

$$W_1 = x_1(P + wR\mu) + x_2(T + wR\mu), \quad W_2 = x_1(S + wR\mu) + x_2R\mu$$

so that $W_1 - W_2 = (P - S)x_1 + (T - R)x_2 > 0$ for all x_1, x_2. Hence all $STCO$. The average expected payoff to the population is thereby reduced from R to $P + wR\mu$.

5.5 H is a conic section with positive discriminant $(c + d)^2$, hence a hyperbola. The left-hand branch of this hyperbola passes through $(0, 0)$ and $(0, b/d)$; the right-hand branch passes through $(-a/c, 0)$ and meets the line $x_1 + x_2 = 1$ where $x_1 = (d - b)/(d + c - b + a)$ and $x_2 = (a + c)/(d + c - b + a)$. The sign of the quantity

$$(cx_1 - dx_2)(x_1 + x_2) + ax_1 + bx_2$$

is either negative in the shaded region and positive in the unshaded region, or vice versa. To determine which, simply evaluate the quantity at a single point (not on the hyperbola), e.g., $(1, 0)$, where the quantity takes the positive value

$$c + a = 1 - w^2.$$

For further details see a calculus text.

5.6 See Section 5.6.

5.9 (i) Use the identity $(P - S)(T - P) - (R - S)(T - R) \equiv (R - P)(P + R - S - T)$.

5.10 The payoff to $ALLD$ against $RNDM$ is T or P with equal probability, whereas the payoff to $RNDM$ against $ALLD$ is equally likely to be S or P; and the payoff to $RNDM$ against $RNDM$ is equally likely to be any of the four payoffs R, S, T or P. Thus

$$\phi_{45}(k) = \frac{1}{2}(T + P), \qquad \phi_{54}(k) = \frac{1}{2}(S + P), \qquad \phi_{55}(k) = Q,$$

where

$$Q = \frac{1}{4}(R + S + T + P).$$

From arguments similar to those employed in Section 5.5, we also obtain

$$\phi_{15}(k) = Q\sigma_k + \frac{1}{2}(R + S)(1 - \sigma_k), \qquad \phi_{51}(k) = Q\sigma_k + \frac{1}{2}(R + T)(1 - \sigma_k),$$

$$\phi_{25}(k) = Q\gamma_k + \frac{1}{2}(R + S)(1 - \gamma_k), \qquad \phi_{52}(k) = Q\gamma_k + \frac{1}{2}(R + T)(1 - \gamma_k),$$

$$\phi_{35}(k) = Q\sigma_k + \frac{1}{2}(T + P)(1 - \sigma_k), \qquad \phi_{53}(k) = Q\sigma_k + \frac{1}{2}(S + P)(1 - \sigma_k),$$

for $1 \leq k < \infty$.

5.11 (i) Observe that the difference equation has an equilibrium (independent of k) solution $\epsilon_k = 1/2, k \geq 1$; which, however, does not satisfy the starting condition $\epsilon_1 = 1$. Therefore, define the perturbation $\eta_k = \epsilon_k - 1/2$, and obtain for it both a difference equation and a starting condition. You should now find it easy to obtain η_k (and hence $\epsilon_k = \eta_k + 1/2$).

5.12 The frequency of third encounters with the same individual depends on N. From (5.79) with $x_4 = 0$ we have

$$W_1 - W_2 = \frac{1}{2} \alpha\lambda_1 wx_3 \{\lambda_2(T - S) - \mu(2R - S - T)\},$$

which is negative whenever

$$N < \frac{(2R - S - T)w}{(1 - w)(T - R)}.$$

In the case of Axelrod's prototype, this condition requires $N + 1 \leq 145$, which would have to be satisfied if *TFT* were stable against *STFT*—see the remarks following (5.113).

5.13 From (5.70), with $m = 5$ and $x_2 = x_3 = x_4 = 0$, (5.71), (5.74) and Exercise 5.10 we have

$$W_1 = \mu(x_1 - \alpha)R + \frac{1}{2}x_5(R + S + 2\mu wQ)$$

$$W_5 = \frac{1}{2}x_1(R + T + 2\mu wQ) + \mu(x_5 - \alpha)Q,$$

where $x_5 = N_5/N$ and Q is defined above. In the usual way, we require $W_1 > W_5$ when $N_1 = N$ and $N_5 = 1$. On setting $x_1 = 1$ and $x_5 = \alpha$, we obtain

$$W_1 - W_5 = \frac{1}{4}\mu\{w(T + R - P - S) - 2(T - R) - \alpha((1 - w)(T + P - R - S) + 3R - S - T - P)\},$$

which is positive when both

$$w > \frac{2(T - R)}{T + R - P - S} \tag{a}$$

and

$$N > \frac{(1 - w)(T + R - P - S) + 3R - S - T - P}{w(T + R - P - S) - 2(T - R)}.$$

Now, if $S + T \geq P + R$, then $(T - R)/(R - S) \geq 2(T - R)/(T + R - P - S) \geq (T - R)/(T - P)$; whereas if $S + T < P + R$, then $(T - R)/(R - S) < 2(T - R)/(T + R - P - S) < (T - R)/(T - P)$. Thus, for sufficiently large N, (a) is implied by (5.35).

5.14 In a population of *TF2T* and *ALLD*, we have $N_1 = 0 = N_3$, and (5.76) implies

$$W_2 = \mu(x_2 - \alpha)R + x_4\{S(1 + w) + \mu w^2 P\}$$
$$W_4 = x_2\{T(1 + w) + \mu w^2 P\} + \mu(x_4 - \alpha)P.$$

For *TF2T* to be stable, we require $W_2 > W_4$ when $N_2 = N$ and $N_4 = 1$; whence, on setting $x_2 = 1$ and $x_4 = \alpha$, we find that $W_2 - W_4 > 0$ implies (5.92).

5.15 In a population of *TF2T* and *RNDM*, we have $N_1 = N_3 = N_4 = 0$ and

$$W_2 = \mu(x_2 - \alpha)R + \frac{1}{2}x_5\{(1 + w)(R + S) + 2\mu w^2 Q\}$$

$$W_5 = \frac{1}{2}x_2\{(1 + w)(T + R) + 2\mu w^2 Q\} + \mu(x_5 - \alpha)Q.$$

Now $W_2 > W_5$ when $x_2 = 1$ and $x_5 = \alpha$ if

$$w > \sqrt{\frac{2(T - R)}{T + R - S - P}}$$

and

$$N > \frac{2R - S - T + (1 - w^2)(T - S) + w^2(R - P)}{w^2(T + R - P - S) - 2(T - R)}.$$

Note that, because *TF2T* is nicer than *TFT*, greater probability of further interaction is required than in Exercise 5.13.

5.18 We have $\xi_1 - (T-R)/(T-P) =$

$$\frac{(R-P)\{K + 2(T-P)\sqrt{(T-R)(T-S)} + 2(T-R)(2R-P-T)\}}{(T-P)\{(2R-P-S)^2 + 4(T-R)(R-P)\}}.$$

where $K = (2R-P-S)(2R-S-T)$. But Axelrod's inequalities imply $T-S > T-R$, whence

$$\sqrt{(T-R)(T-S)} > T-R.$$

Therefore

$$\xi_1 - \frac{T-R}{T-P} > \frac{(R-P)\{(2R-P-S)(2R-S-T) + 4(T-R)(R-P)\}}{(T-P)\{(2R-P-S)^2 + 4(T-R)(R-P)\}} > 0,$$

and similarly for ξ_2.

5.19 With $RNDM$ as strategy 5 (and $N_2 = N_3 = N_4 = 0$), we have

$$W_1 - W_5 = \mu(R-Q) - \frac{1}{2}\lambda_1(1+\alpha)\{R + T - 2Q\} + \frac{1}{2}x_5\{2\mu(Q-R) + \lambda_1(R-P)\},$$

where $x_5 = N_5/N$ and Q is defined in the solution to Exercise 5.10. Proceeding in the usual way, we require for stability that $W_1 - W_5 > 0$ when $x_1 = 1$ and $x_5 = \alpha$; and this condition readily reduces to $\phi_3(N) < 0$, where ϕ_3 is defined by (5.99) and (5.101) with $j = 3$. Thus TFT is stable against infiltration by $RNDM$ if $w > \xi_3$ and $w(3R - S - T - P)/\{2(1-w)(T-R)N_3(w)\} < N < N_3(w)$, where ξ_3 is defined by (5.101) and (5.103), and N_3 by (5.101) and (5.106). For example, in Axelrod's prototype we have $\xi_3 = 0.899$ and $N_3(w) = 213.5$; and the lower bound on N in (5.105) is then $N > 1.012$. Thus the population is stable against $RNDM$ if $N + 1 \leq 3 \leq 214$.

5.20 The rewards are

$$W_2 = \mu(x_2 - \alpha)R + x_5\left\{\mu Q - \frac{\lambda_1^2(2Q-R-S)}{2\lambda_2}\right\}$$

$$W_5 = x_2\left\{\mu Q - \frac{\lambda_1^2(2Q-R-T)}{2\lambda_2}\right\} + (x_5 - \alpha)\mu Q.$$

For stability, we require $W_2 > W_5$ when $x_2 = 1$ and $x_5 = \alpha$ or

$$2(1-w)^2(T-R)N^3 + 2(1-w)\{2w(T-R) + (1-w)(R-S)\}N^2$$
$$+ 4w\{(1-w)(R-S) - w(R-Q)\}N + 4w^2(R-Q) < 0,$$

where Q is defined in the solution to Exercise 5.10; which requires in particular that $w > 4(R-S)/\{7R - 5S - T - P\}$, because the coefficient of N in the inequality must be negative. For Axelrod's prototype we require $3 \leq N + 1 \leq 91$.

5.21 Consider a population of $N + 1$ indistinguishable individuals, of whom N_1 play TFT and $N_4 = N - N_1 + 1$ play $ALLD$ in an IPD where opponents are drawn at random. Then (5.70) still yields correct expressions, W_1 and W_4, for the rewards from the game to TFT and $ALLD$; but ϕ_{11}, ϕ_{14} and ϕ_{41} in (5.71)–(5.72) must now be modified for absence of recognition. Let θ_k denote the probability that a TFT-strategist cooperates during its k-th interaction. Then $\theta_1 = 1$, because TFT is a nice strategy;

and

$$\theta_k = \left(\frac{N_1 - 1}{N}\right)^{k-1} = (x_1 - \alpha)^{k-1}$$

for $k \geq 2$, because interaction is random, the probability of meeting another *TFT*-strategist is still $x_1 - \alpha$, and absence of recognition implies that *TFT* will cooperate on move k only if on its previous move it has encountered a *TFT*-strategist that cooperated (i.e., because $\theta_k = (x_1 - \alpha)\theta_{k-1}$). Thus, because $1 - \theta_k$ is the probability that a *TFT*-strategist will defect on interaction k, we have

$$\phi_{11}(k) = \theta_k\{R\theta_k + S(1 - \theta_k)\} + (1 - \theta_k)\{T\theta_k + P(1 - \theta_k)\}$$
$$= (P + R - S - T)\theta_k^2 + (S + T - 2P)\theta_k + P.$$

Similarly,

$$\phi_{14}(k) = S\theta_k + P(1 - \theta_k), \qquad \phi_{41}(k) = T\theta_k + P(1 - \theta_k), \qquad \phi_{44}(k) = P.$$

On substituting into (5.70), with $m = 4$ and $x_2 = 0 = x_3$, and on using (5.32) and (5.68), we readily obtain

$$W_4 = \mu P + \frac{(x_1 - \alpha)(T - P)}{1 - w(x_1 - \alpha)}$$

and

$$W_1 = W_4 - \frac{P - S}{1 - w(x_1 - \alpha)} - \frac{(x_1 - \alpha)(S + T - P - R)}{1 - w(x_1 - \alpha)^2}.$$

It follows that $W_4 > W_1$ (immediately in the case where (5.36) is satisfied and after a little algebra where $P + R > S + T$).

5.22   Note that, if $q < \epsilon Q$, then

$$2R - S - T > \frac{q}{\epsilon} + \epsilon q - 2q = \frac{q}{\epsilon}(1 - \epsilon)^2 > 0.$$

5.23   With $S = 0$ and $T = P + R$, (5.123) becomes $w > \xi(q)$ and $N < \overline{N}(q, w)$, where we define $q = P/R(< 1)$,

$$\xi(q) = \frac{q + 2(1 - q)\{1 + q + \sqrt{q(1 + q)}\}}{4 - 3q^2}$$

and

$$\overline{N}(q, w) = \frac{(2 - q)w + \sqrt{(4 - 3q^2)w^2 - 2(2 - 2q^2 + q)w + 1} - 1}{2(1 - w)q}.$$

As q increases from 0 to 1, ξ increases monotonically from $\xi(0) = 1/2$ to $\xi(1) = 1$.

In a laboratory, N could not be too large; and it would be impractical to vary w, because each new value of w would require the animals to be retrained. On the other hand, it should be possible to alter q quite readily. Thus the sign of $w - \xi(q)$ should be controlled as a function of q, not w. Suppose, for example, that we choose $w = 4/5$. Then $w - \xi(q) = 0.8 - \xi(q)$ is positive if $q < 0.294$ (to three significant figures) and negative if $q > 0.294$. Thus we could test the model of Section 5.8 by choosing two values of q, one larger than 0.294 but the other smaller than 0.294, and imbedding the experiment of Section 5.2 in an iterated prisoner's dilemma among $N+1$ animals who interact at random. Suppose, for example, that we choose $q = 1/2$ and $q = 1/4$. Then, with w held fixed at 4/5, (5.105) and (5.123) predict that TFT is unstable against $ALLD$ when $q = 1/2$ for any value of N, but stable against $ALLD$ when $q = 1/4$ if $2 < N < 6$. Because this inequality is satisfied if $4 \leq N + 1 \leq 6$, we could test the theory with four to six animals.

5.24 **(ii)** $P + R = S + T$.

(iii) No. The equations in (i) are satisfied by infinitely many values of σ_c, σ_d, ω_c and ω_d.

5.25 **(i)** The payoff matrix is (5.1) with $R = b - c$, $S = -c$, $T = b$ and $P = 0$; $b > c$ ensures that (5.2) is satisfied.

(ii) Cheat $= ALLD$ and Sucker $= ALLC$ by definition. Grudger is not by definition the same as TFT because Grudger, though nice, is completely unforgiving; nevertheless, Grudger $= TFT$ in this particular IPD because $ALLC$ and $ALLD$ are the only other strategies.

(iii) From (5.109), necessary conditions for Grudger to be uninvadable are

$$w > \frac{2(b - c)\{c + \sqrt{c(b + c)}\} + b(2b - c)}{4b^2 - 3c^2}$$

and

$$N < \frac{w(2b - c) - b + \sqrt{[w(2b - c) - b]^2 - 4wc(1 - w)(b - c)}}{2c(1 - w)}.$$

(iv) In (5.47) we have

$$\phi_1(x_1, x_2) = x_1 x_2 \{(\mu - \lambda_1)(b - c)x_1 - \mu\alpha(b - c) - \lambda_1(1 + \alpha)c\}$$

where μ, x_1, x_2, α and λ are defined by (5.25), (5.66), (5.67) and (5.80). Note that the coefficient of x_2 in the squiggly bracket is in the first instance $(S + T - P - R)\mu$, but vanishes because the prisoner's dilemma is decomposable. Thus a sufficient condition for Grudger to eliminate both Cheat and Sucker is that $\phi_1 > 0$ when $x_2 > 0$, or

$$x_1 > \frac{\mu\alpha(b - c) + \lambda_1(1 + \alpha)c}{(\mu - \lambda_1)(b - c)},$$

which after some rearrangement is the desired condition.

References

Axelrod, R. (1984). The Evolution of Cooperation. Basic Books, New York.

Axelrod, R. and D. Dion (1988). The Further Evolution of Cooperation. *Science* **242,** 1385–1390.

Becker, L. C. (1986). Reciprocity. Routledge & Kegan Paul, London, U.K.

Böhm-Bawerk, E. von (1959). Capital and Interest, Volume II (translated from German, original 1889). Libertarian Press, South Holland, Illinois.

Borel, E. (1953). On Games That Involve Chance and the Skill of the Players (translated from French, original 1924). *Econometrica* **21,** 101–115.

Borštnik, B., D. Pumpernik, I. L. Hofacker, & G. L. Hofacker (1990). An ESS-Analysis for Ensembles of Prisoner's Dilemma's Strategies. *Journal of Theoretical Biology* **142,** 189–200.

Boyd, R. (1989). Mistakes Allow Evolutionary Stability in the Repeated Prisoner's Dilemma Game. *Journal of Theoretical Biology* **136,** 47–56.

Boyd, R. & J. P. Lorberbaum (1987). No Pure Strategy is Evolutionarily Stable in the Repeated Prisoner's Dilemma Game. *Nature* **327,** 58–59.

Boyd, R. & P. J. Richerson (1988). The Evolution of Reciprocity in Sizable Groups. *Journal of Theoretical Biology* **132,** 337–356.

Brams, S. J. (1975). Game Theory and Politics. Macmillan, New York.

Brams, S. J. & P. C. Fishburn (1983). Approval Voting. Birkhäuser, Boston.

Brams, S. J., A. Schotter & G. Schwödiauer (editors) (1979). Applied Game Theory. Physica-Verlag, Vienna.

Burgess, J. W. (1976). Social Spiders. *Scientific American* **234,** No. 3, 100–106.

Cannings, C. & G. T. Vickers (1988). Patterns of ESS's II. *Journal of Theoretical Biology* **132,** 409–420.

Charnov, E. L. (1982). The Theory of Sex Allocation. Princeton University Press, Princeton, New Jersey.

Clark, C. W. (1990). Mathematical Bioeconomics: The Optimal Management of Renewable Resources, 2nd edition. John Wiley, New York.

Clark, C. W. & R. C. Ydenberg (1990). The Risks of Parenthood II. Parent-Offspring Conflict. *Evolutionary Ecology* **4**, 312–325.

Clutton-Brock, T. H. & P. H. Harvey (editors) (1978). Readings in Sociobiology. W. H. Freeman, San Francisco.

Colman, A. M. (1982). Game Theory and Experimental Games. Pergamon Press, Oxford.

Cournot, A. A. (1897). Researches into the Mathematical Principles of the Theory of Wealth (translated from French, original 1838). Macmillan, New York.

Crawford, V. P. (1990). Nash Equilibrium and Evolutionary Stability in Large- and Finite-Population "Playing the Field" Models. *Journal of Theoretical Biology* **145**, 83–94.

Cressman, R. (1990). Strong Stability and Density-Dependent Evolutionarily Stable Strategies. *Journal of Theoretical Biology* **145**, 319–330.

Dawkins, R. (1989). The Selfish Gene, 2nd edition. Oxford University Press, Oxford, U.K.

Devaney, R. L. (1989). An Introduction to Chaotic Dynamical Systems, 2nd edition. Addison-Wesley, Menlo Park, California.

Devaney, R. L. (1990). Chaos, Fractals and Dynamics. Addison-Wesley, Menlo Park, California.

Devaney, R. L. & L. Keen (editors) (1989). Chaos and Fractals: The Mathematics Behind the Computer Graphics. American Mathematical Society, Providence, Rhode Island.

Dugatkin, L. A. (1988). Do Guppies Play Tit-for-Tat During Predator Inspection Visits? *Behavioral Ecology and Sociobiology* **23**, 395–399.

Dugatkin, L. A. (1990). N-person Games and the Evolution of Co-operation: A Model Based on Predator Inspection in Fish. *Journal of Theoretical Biology* **142**, 123–135.

Edgeworth, F. Y. (1881). Mathematical Psychics. Kegan Paul, London.

Evans, G. W. & C. M. Crumbaugh (1966). Effects of Prisoner's Dilemma Format on Cooperative Behavior. *Journal of Personality and Social Psychology* **3**, 486–488.

Feldman, M. W. & E. A. C. Thomas (1987). Behavior-Dependent Contests for Repeated Plays of the Prisoner's Dilemma II: Dynamical Aspects of the Evolution of Cooperation. *Journal of Theoretical Biology* **128**, 297–315.

Fisher, R. A. (1930). The Genetical Theory of Natural Selection. Oxford University Press, Oxford, U.K.

Flood, M., K. Lendenmann & A. Rapoport (1983). 2 × 2 Games Played by Rats: Different Delays of Reinforcement as Payoffs. *Behavioral Science* **28**, 65–78.

Friedland, N. (1990). Attribution of Control as a Determinant of Cooperation in Exchange Interactions. *Journal of Applied Social Psychology* **20**, 303–320.

Grofman, B. and H. Scarrow (1979). Iannucci and Its Aftermath: The Application of the Banzhaf Index to Weighted Voting in the State of New York. In Brams *et al.* (1979), pp. 168–183.

Harley, C. B. (1987). Learning Rules, Optimal Behaviour, and Evolutionary Stability. *Journal of Theoretical Biology* **127**, 377–379.

Harsanyi, J. C. (1967). Games with Incomplete Information Played by "Bayesian" Players. Part I: The Basic Model. *Management Science* **14**, 159–182.

Harsanyi, J. C. (1968a). Games with Incomplete Information Played by "Bayesian" Players. Part II: Bayesian Equilibrium Points. *Management Science* **14**, 320–334.

Harsanyi, J. C. (1968b). Games with Incomplete Information Played by "Bayesian" Players. Part III: The Basic Probability Distribution of the Game. *Management Science* **14**, 486–502.

Harsanyi, J. C. (1975). The Tracing Procedure: A Bayesian Approach to Defining a Solution for n-Person Games. *International Journal of Game Theory* **4**, 61–94.

Harsanyi, J. C., and R. Selten (1988). A General Theory of Equilibrium Selection in Games. MIT Press, Cambridge, Massachusetts.

Hines, W. G. S. (1987). Evolutionarily Stable Strategies: A Review of Basic Theory. *Theoretical Population Biology* **31**, 195–272.

Hofbauer, J., and K. Sigmund (1988). The Theory of Evolution and Dynamical Systems. Cambridge University Press, Cambridge, U.K.

Houston, A. I. & J. M. McNamara (1987). Singing to Attract a Mate: A Stochastic Dynamic Game. *Journal of Theoretical Biology* **129**, 57–68.

Houston, A. I. & J. M. McNamara (1988). Fighting for Food: A Dynamic Version of the Hawk-Dove Game. *Evolutionary Ecology* **2**, 51–64.

Jeter, M. (1986). Mathematical Programming. Marcel Dekker, New York.

Kacelnik, A. & J. R. Krebs (1985). Learning to Exploit Patchily Distributed Food. In Sibly and Smith (1985), pp. 189–205.

Kaitala, V., K. Lindström & E. Ranta (1989). Foraging, Vigilance and Risk of Predation in Birds—a Dynamic Game Study of ESS. *Journal of Theoretical Biology* **138**, 329–345.

Kalai, E., and D. Samet (1984). Persistent Equilibria in Strategic Games. *International Journal of Game Theory* **13**, 129–144.

Lazarus, J. & N. B. Metcalfe (1990) Tit-for-Tat Cooperation in Sticklebacks: A Critique of Milinski. *Animal Behaviour* **39**, 987–988.

Lessard, S. (1990). Evolutionary Stability: One Concept, Several Meanings. *Theoretical Population Biology* **37**, 159–170.

Lima, S. L. (1989). Iterated Prisoner's Dilemma: An Approach to Evolutionarily Stable Cooperation. *American Naturalist* **134**, 828–834.

Luce, R. D. and H. Raiffa (1957). Games and Decisions. John Wiley, New York.

Luenberger, D. (1984). Linear and Nonlinear Programming, 2nd edition. Addison-Wesley, Reading, Massachusetts.

Mangasarian, O.L. (1969). Nonlinear Programming. McGraw-Hill, New York.

Mangel, M. (1990a). A Dynamic Habitat Selection Game. *Mathematical Biosciences* **100**, 241–248.

Mangel, M. (1990b). Dynamic Information in Uncertain and Changing Worlds. *Journal of Theoretical Biology* **146,** 317–332.

Mangel, M. & C. W. Clark. (1988). Dynamic Modeling in Behavioral Ecology. Princeton University Press, Princeton, New Jersey.

Maschler, M., B. Peleg and L. S. Shapley (1979). Geometric Properties of the Kernel, Nucleolus and Related Solution Concepts. *Mathematics of Operations Research* **4,** 303–338.

Masters, W. & T. Waite (1990). Tit-for-Tat During Predator Inspection or Shoaling? *Animal Behaviour* **39,** 603–604.

May, R. M. (1981). The Evolution of Cooperation. *Nature* **292,** 291–292.

May, R. M. (1987). More Evolution of Cooperation. *Nature* **327,** 15–17.

Maynard Smith, J. (1982). Evolution and the Theory of Games. Cambridge University Press, Cambridge, U.K.

Maynard Smith, J. (1988). Can a Mixed Strategy be Stable in a Finite Population? *Journal of Theoretical Biology* **130,** 247–251.

Maynard Smith, J. & G. R. Price (1973). The Logic of Animal Conflict. *Nature* **246,** 15–18.

McNamara, J. M. and A. I. Houston (1989). State-Dependent Contests for Food. *Journal of Theoretical Biology* **137,** 457–479.

Mesterton-Gibbons, M. (1989). A Concrete Approach to Mathematical Modelling. Addison-Wesley, Redwood City, California.

Mesterton-Gibbons, M. (1990). A Game-Theoretic Analysis of a Motorist's Dilemma. *Mathematical and Computer Modelling* **13,** No. 2, 9–14.

Mesterton-Gibbons, M. (1991). An Escape from 'the Prisoner's Dilemma.' *Journal of Mathematical Biology* **29,** 251–269.

Milinski, M. (1987). Tit-for-Tat in Sticklebacks and the Evolution of Cooperation. *Nature* **325,** 433–435.

Milinski, M. (1990a) No Alternative to Tit-for-Tat Cooperation in Sticklebacks. *Animal Behaviour* **39,** 989–991.

Milinski, M. (1990b). On Cooperation in Sticklebacks. *Animal Behaviour* **40,** 1190–1191.

Myerson, R. B. (1978). Refinements of the Nash Equilibrium Concept. *International Journal of Game Theory* **7,** 73–80.

Nash, J. F. (1950). The Bargaining Problem. *Econometrica* **18,** 155–162.

Nash, J. F. (1951). Non-cooperative games. *Annals of Mathematics* **54,** 286–295.

Nowak, M. (1990). Stochastic Strategies in the Prisoner's Dilemma. *Journal of Theoretical Biology* **38,** 93–112.

Nowak, M. & K. Sigmund (1989). Game-Dynamical Aspects of the Prisoner's Dilemma. *Applied Mathematics and Computation* **30,** 191–213.

Nowak, M. & K. Sigmund (1990). The Evolution of Stochastic Strategies in the Prisoner's Dilemma. *Acta Applicandæ Mathematicæ* **20,** 247–265.

Owen, G. (1982). Game Theory, 2nd edition. Academic Press, New York.

Phlips, L. (1988).The Economics of Imperfect Information. Cambridge University Press, Cambridge, U.K.

Pruitt, D. G. (1967). Reward Structure and Cooperation: The Decomposed Prisoner's Dilemma Game. *Journal of Personality and Social Psychology* **7**, 21–27.

Rapoport, A. & A. M. Chammah (1965). Prisoner's Dilemma: A Study in Conflict and Cooperation. University of Michigan Press, Ann Arbor, Michigan.

Rasmusen, E. (1989). Games and Information. Basil Blackwell, Oxford, U.K.

Reboreda, J. C. & A. Kacelnik (1990). On cooperation, Tit-for-Tat, and Mirrors. *Animal Behaviour*, **40**, 1188–1189.

Robson, A. I. (1990). Efficiency in Evolutionary Games: Darwin, Nash and the Secret Handshake. *Journal of Theoretical Biology* **144**, 379–396.

Schaffer, M. E. (1988) Evolutionarily Stable Strategies for a Finite Population and a Variable Contest Size. *Journal of Theoretical Biology* **132**, 469–478.

Schelling, T. C. (1978) Micromotives and Macrobehavior. Norton, New York.

Schmeidler, D. (1969) The Nucleolus of a Characteristic Function Game. *SIAM Journal of Applied Mathematics* **17**, 1163–1170.

Selten, R. (1975). Reexamination of the Perfectness Concept for Equilibrium Points in Extensive Games. *International Journal of Game Theory* **4**, 25–55. Reprinted in Selten (1988), pp. 1–31.

Selten, R. (1988). Models of Strategic Rationality. Kluwer, Dordrecht.

Shubik, M. (1970). Game Theory, Behavior and the Paradox of the Prisoner's Dilemma: Three Solutions. *Journal of Conflict Resolution* **14**, 181–193.

Shubik, M. (1982). Game Theory in the Social Sciences. MIT Press, Cambridge, Massachusetts.

Shubik, M. (1984). A Game-Theoretic Approach to Political Economy (Volume 2 of Game Theory in the Social Sciences). MIT Press, Cambridge, Massachusetts.

Sibly, R. M. & R. H. Smith (editors) (1985). Behavioural Ecology. Blackwell Scientific Publications, Oxford, U.K.

Straffin, P. D. (1980). The Prisoner's Dilemma. *UMAP Journal* **1**, No. 1, 101–103.

Taylor, P. & L. Jonker (1978). Evolutionarily Stable Strategies and Game Dynamics. *Mathematical Biosciences* **40**, 145–156.

Trivers, R. (1971). The Evolution of Reciprocal Altruism. *Quarterly Review of Biology* **46**, 35–57. Reprinted in Clutton-Brock and Harvey (1978), pp. 189–226.

Trivers, R. (1985). Social Evolution. Benjamin/Cummings, Menlo Park, California.

van Damme, E. E. C. (1987). Stability and Perfection of Nash Equilibria. Springer-Verlag, Berlin, Germany.

Vickers, G. T. & C. Cannings (1988). Patterns of ESS's I. *Journal of Theoretical Biology* **132**, 387–408.

Vickery, W. L. (1987) How to Cheat Against a Simple Mixed Strategy ESS. *Journal of Theoretical Biology* **127**, 133–139.

Vickery, W. L. (1988) Reply to Maynard Smith. *Journal of Theoretical Biology* **132**, 375–378.

Vincent, T. L. & J. S. Brown (1988). The Evolution of ESS Theory. *Annual Review of Ecology and Systematics* **19**, 423–43.

Vincent, T. L., and W. J. Grantham (1981). Optimality in Parametric Systems. John Wiley, New York.

von Neumann, J., and O. Morgenstern (1953). Theory of Games and Economic Behavior, 3rd edition. Princeton University Press, Princeton, New Jersey.

Wang, J. (1988). The Theory of Games. Oxford University Press, Oxford, U.K.

Wiggins, S. (1990). Introduction to Applied Nonlinear Dynamical Systems and Chaos. Springer-Verlag, New York.

Zeuthen, F. (1930). Problems of Monopoly and Economic Welfare. G. Routledge, London, U.K.

Index